State-Building as Lawfare

State-Building as Lawfare explores the use of state and non-state legal systems by both politicians and ordinary people in postwar Chechnya. The book addresses two interrelated puzzles: why do local rulers tolerate and even promote non-state legal systems at the expense of state law, and why do some members of repressed ethnic minorities choose to resolve their everyday disputes using state legal systems instead of non-state alternatives? The book documents how the rulers of Chechnya promote and reinvent customary law and Sharia in order to borrow legitimacy from tradition and religion, increase autonomy from the metropole, and accommodate communal authorities and former rebels. At the same time, the book shows how prolonged armed conflict disrupted the traditional social hierarchies and pushed some Chechen women to use state law, spurring state formation from below.

EGOR LAZAREV is an Assistant Professor of Political Science at Yale University and a Scholar at the Harvard Academy for International and Area Studies.

Cambridge Studies in Comparative Politics

General Editor
Kathleen Thelen *Massachusetts Institute of Technology*

Associate Editors
Catherine Boone   *London School of Economics*
Thad Dunning   *University of California, Berkeley*
Anna Grzymala-Busse   *Stanford University*
Torben Iversen   *Harvard University*
Stathis Kalyvas   *University of Oxford*
Melanie Manion   *Duke University*
Susan Stokes   *Yale University*
Tariq Thachil   *University of Pennsylvania*
Erik Wibbels   *Duke University*

Series Founder
Peter Lange *Duke University*

Other Books in the Series

Christopher Adolph, *Bankers, Bureaucrats, and Central Bank Politics: The Myth of Neutrality*

Michael Albertus, *Autocracy and Redistribution: The Politics of Land Reform*

Michael Albertus, *Property without Rights: Origins and Consequences of the Property Rights Gap*

Santiago Anria, *When Movements Become Parties: The Bolivian MAS in Comparative Perspective*

Ben W. Ansell, *From the Ballot to the Blackboard: The Redistributive Political Economy of Education*

Ben W. Ansell and Johannes Lindvall, *Inward Conquest: The Political Origins of Modern Public Services*

Ben W. Ansell and David J. Samuels, *Inequality and Democratization: An Elite-Competition Approach*

Ana Arjona, *Rebelocracy: Social Order in the Colombian Civil War*

Leonardo R. Arriola, *Multi-Ethnic Coalitions in Africa: Business Financing of Opposition Election Campaigns*

(continued after index)

State-Building as Lawfare

Custom, Sharia, and State Law in Postwar Chechnya

EGOR LAZAREV

Yale University

CAMBRIDGE
UNIVERSITY PRESS

Shaftesbury Road, Cambridge CB2 8EA, United Kingdom

One Liberty Plaza, 20th Floor, New York, NY 10006, USA

477 Williamstown Road, Port Melbourne, VIC 3207, Australia

314–321, 3rd Floor, Plot 3, Splendor Forum, Jasola District Centre,
New Delhi – 110025, India

103 Penang Road, #05–06/07, Visioncrest Commercial, Singapore 238467

Cambridge University Press is part of Cambridge University Press & Assessment,
a department of the University of Cambridge.

We share the University's mission to contribute to society through the pursuit of
education, learning and research at the highest international levels of excellence.

www.cambridge.org
Information on this title: www.cambridge.org/9781009245951

DOI: 10.1017/9781009245913

First published 2023

A catalogue record for this publication is available from the British Library.

*A Cataloging-in-Publication data record for this book is available from the Library of
Congress*

ISBN 978-1-009-24595-1 Hardback

To Satsita Israilova

Contents

Contents

Figures and Tables

Figures

Tables

Acknowledgments

This book became possible thanks to the incredible support I received from many people whom I met in Chechnya and elsewhere in the North Caucasus. Here I can only name scholars and public figures who encouraged me to use their real names, but I am deeply grateful to every single person who participated in the survey, agreed to an interview, allowed me to become part of their life, shared their stories with me, and introduced me to their families and friends.

I dedicate this book to Satsita Israilova, Director of the National Library of the Chechen Republic. During the many months that I stayed with Satsita, every evening we ended up drinking strong tea and talking. Satsita not only provided me with a sense of home on my field trips to Chechnya and tirelessly guided me through the complex matters of custom, family relations, Chechen history, and civilian experiences during the wars but also became a dear friend. The depth of our conversations cannot be fully reflected in this book.

My thanks also go to Khamzat Asabaev. A lawyer and entrepreneur who works at the top global level, Khamzat cares deeply about what is happening in his home region. While some people expressed doubts that an outsider like me could ever understand the complexities of Chechen customary law and Sharia as it is practiced in the region, Khamzat always supported my academic explorations.

I am indebted to Chechen social scientists who shared with me their wisdom on the region's history and contemporary sociopolitical developments. First and foremost, I want to thank Professor Lida Kurbanova, whose guidance in matters of gender and family relations was crucial for my understandings in this domain. Lida and her family and Professor

Lema Turpalov helped me a great deal with organizing the survey, and I would like to acknowledge the excellent work of my team of survey interviewers. The study also benefited from exchanges with political scientists Abbaz Osmaev and Marat Ilyasov on post-conflict political developments and with historian Mairbek Vatchagaev on the turbulent period of the 1990s and from advice from the late Chechen ethnographer Said-Magomed Khasiev, whose knowledge of the intricacies of customary law was truly unparalleled.

The book grew out of a dissertation defended at Columbia University. Tim Frye chaired my committee and has been a wonderful advisor. Even though elders and imams are perhaps not the type of political actors Tim is used to dealing with, our shared interest in how individuals and groups maintain social order led to many productive discussions. Tim read countless drafts of research and grant proposals, articles, job market presentations, the dissertation, and finally the book manuscript and always offered valuable and helpful feedback. My other professors at Columbia – Daniel Corstange, Don Green, Kimuli Kasara, Vicky Murillo, Tonya Putnam, and Jack Snyder – and my graduate school comrades – Ashraf Ahmed, Clava Brodsky, Jerome Doyon, Anselm Hager, Jorge Mangonnet, Tamar Mitts, Kunaal Sharma, Gosha Syunyaev, David Szakonyi, Adam Valen Levinson, and Colleen Wood – gave me advice and support at different points in this project.

The inspiration for this research came from Georgi Derluguian's book *Bourdieu's Secret Admirer in the Caucasus.* After I finished reading the book overnight, I emailed the author out of the blue, which led to a mentorship and friendship I cherish. Conversations with Georgi taught me how to do fieldwork in both insightful and ethical ways and how to link ethnographic observations to big theoretical questions. From my very first trip to the Caucasus in 2010, Georgi has always been reading my field diaries. He also taught me to choose good boots for walking around mountainous villages.

In my early steps in academia, I was privileged to learn from Vladimir Gel'man; as an undergrad, I took his class on the methodology of social sciences at the European University at St. Petersburg. This class taught me the nuts and bolts of the social sciences and fundamentally shaped my way of thinking. Most importantly, Vladimir taught me how to ask meaningful research questions. Since then, Vladimir has read all drafts of my writing, including the manuscript of this book, and he always provides great suggestions about how to sharpen an argument.

I owe a great intellectual debt to Sally Engle Merry. My study benefited a lot from the class on legal anthropology I took with her at NYU, when I was only starting to dive into the world of legal pluralism. Over the years, Sally has read several versions of this work (despite the presence of regression tables inside the text) and has always found intriguing angles that she pushed me to explore. I am happy to have known Sally. Her scholarship remains an inspiration.

I largely wrote this book during my time at the Harvard Academy for International and Area Studies. The Academy hosted a book workshop where Melani Cammett, Erica Chenoweth, Fotini Christia, Tim Colton, Tamir Moustafa, and Roger Petersen generously gave the entire manuscript their detailed critical reading. Their suggestions helped me to seriously revise the text and, I believe, made the book much better.

Over the years, numerous colleagues have commented on presentations of my research and various iterations of this manuscript. I am especially grateful to Ana Arjona, Laia Balcells, Kristin Bakke, Lisa Blaydes, Jane Burbank, Jesse Driscoll, Matthew Evangelista, Eugene Finkel, Amaney Jamal, Jordan Gans-Morse, Scott Gehlbach, Kevan Harris, Kathryn Hendley, Yoshiko Herrera, Timur Kuran, Alex Kustov, Zoe Marks, Kimberly Marten, Terry Martin, Mark Massoud, Vera Mironova, Peter Rutland, Cyrus Samii, Konstantin Sonin, and Josh Tucker. Boris Sokolov read more versions of this text than anybody else did and always pushed me to formulate a big picture story about the state and social order. Anton Sobolev deserves a special thanks for helping to scrape the unique datasets of several hundred thousand hearings in the Justice-of-the-Peace Courts and make beautiful figures for the book.

I was lucky to begin my professional academic career at the Department of Political Science at the University of Toronto. There, I met a wonderful group of colleagues, some of whom would become close friends. I am especially thankful to Filiz Kahraman, who provided detailed comments on how to better connect my study with law and society scholarship, and to Diana Fu, who gave advice on writing ethnography. My writing benefited from my critical engagement with a fantastic group of scholars with interests in the post-Soviet world – Adam Casey, Seva Gunitsky, Alexis Lerner, Matthew Light, Ed Schatz, Peter and Susan Solomon, and Lucan Way.

I finished writing the book after I joined the Department of Political Science at Yale. This was not my first time at Yale – previously I was a pre-doc fellow at the Order, Conflict, and Violence program, where my research was enriched by conversations with Stathis Kalyvas, Jay Lyall,

Juan Masullo, Virginia Oliveros, Mara Revkin, and Anastasia Shesterinina. My colleagues working on related topics of traditional authorities, state-building, gender, and conflict – Kate Baldwin, Sarah Khan, Isabela Mares, Dan Mattingly, Liz Nugent, Steven Wilkinson, and Libby Wood – have read various versions of the manuscript and shared their insights. The reading group on post-socialism run by Doug Rogers and the Political Violence and Its Legacies workshop have been great forums of ideas. Chetana Sabnis, Grace Lan, and Catherine Zou deserve special thanks for carefully reading the manuscript in its penultimate form and for helping me improve it.

In Russia, I have received great advice on the organization of the survey work from Sergey Khaikin, a Moscow-based sociologist, who conducted public opinion polls in Chechnya during the course of the war. I have also learned much from my colleagues in the study of the Caucasus – Irina Starodubrovskaya, Konstantin Kazenin, and Evgeny Varshaver. Their studies of legal pluralism in Dagestan, which were conducted in parallel with my study in Chechnya, informed my understanding of the region and formed a comparative perspective for my study. I have presented my project and subsequently some of the results of my study at the Institute for the Rule of Law at the European University at St. Petersburg, and I am very thankful to the colleagues there for their serious treatment of this work from a socio-legal perspective.

At Cambridge University Press, I am thankful to my editor Rachel Blaifeder, Robert Judkins, Shaheer Husanne, and the two anonymous reviewers, who provided kind and thorough feedback that greatly improved the book. I am also thankful to Kathleen Thelen and the series reviewer for accepting my book into the *Studies in Comparative Politics*. Thank you to Zach Reyna and Alexei Stephenson, who edited the manuscript at different stages and made it readable, Bill Nelson, who produced the maps, and Sergey Lobachev, who made the index.

I am very grateful to Chechen artist Asya Umarova for allowing me to use her artwork "Goodbye, Grandma" for the cover of the book. This artwork represents an episode from *tezet*, a three-day Chechen wake, when relatives, friends, neighbors, and colleagues come to the house to pay respects. It captures the moving boundary between the private and the public, which is one of the central themes of this book.

An earlier version of Chapter 8 appeared as an article: "Laws in conflict: Legacies of war, gender, and legal pluralism in Chechnya." *World Politics* 71, no. 4 (2019): 667–709. I thank the editors and anonymous reviewers at the journal for their incisive comments. I use these materials with permission from Cambridge University Press.

The Harriman Institute at Columbia University provided funding for the field trips to the region and the Frederick W. Hilles Publication Fund at the MacMillan Center at Yale supported work towards the publication of the manuscript.

Finally, I want to thank my family. My mother Tatiana, my aunt Galina, and my brother Alexei had to worry during my long trips to Chechnya. They were always supportive of my studies and made my short visits back home the most rewarding time. My life partner Renata Mustafina read many versions of this manuscript. She also inspires me to be a more thoughtful scholar with her own example.

FIGURE 0.1 Map of the region

Introduction

Turpal-Ali, a young man, and Deshi, a young woman from one of the villages in Chechnya, were in love and wanted to get married.[1] But Deshi's parents were strongly against their marriage. The issue was that Turpal-Ali and Deshi were distant relatives and according to Chechen customary law, known as *adat*, a bride and a groom cannot be related within seven generations. Turpal-Ali then decided to arrange a bride-kidnapping, a practice also justified by references to custom. Turpal-Ali and his friends kidnapped Deshi from the street and brought her to his family home, hoping that this act would change her parents' decision. Families of women kidnapped this way often force them to stay and get married to avoid potential rumors and ultimately protect family honor. However, Deshi's parents remained firm. They took their daughter back. Then they appealed for religious arbitration – a Sharia trial – against Turpal-Ali. Unlike adat, Sharia sees bride-kidnapping as a gross transgression. Deshi was apparently complicit in the kidnapping, but she denied it during the Sharia arbitration. A local qadi, an Islamic judge, heard the case and ruled that Turpal-Ali should be punished with flogging, forty strokes. According to custom, any corporal punishment is a serious offense against one's honor and Turpal-Ali's family became very angry at Deshi and her family.

---

[1] I use pseudonyms throughout the book, except when I write about or quote public figures – state officials, high-level religious leaders, and academics, who wanted to be named and did not express any politically sensitive opinions. For Chechen and Russian words, I use a simplified Library of Congress transliteration standard, except for names that have appeared prominently in Western publications.

Some time later, the elders of the village were drinking vodka at the river bank. Alcohol is effectively banned in Chechnya, but some Chechens who belong to the older "Soviet" generation still manage to get liquor. During this gathering, Musa, Turpal-Ali's family patriarch, publicly offended Deshi's honor by calling her a slut. In response, Said, Deshi's family patriarch, punched Musa in the face. When Musa came home, he told his three sons that he had been beaten by Said. The sons took baseball bats and knives and went to Said's house to avenge the offense. Despite the fact that Said was much older than the attackers, he was able to fight back. In fact, he was a master of wrestling, and during the fight he took a knife away from one of Musa's sons and killed him with it. The murder trial that I attended in a district court judged Said according to Russian state law. In parallel, the two families were negotiating to avoid blood revenge, another major customary institution, in response to the murder of Musa's son. The fact that Said killed the man in an act of self-defense mattered little. According to adat, blood must be avenged with blood. As a part of the informal resolution between the two feuding sides, Said's family was banished from the village. The details of the events that led to the murder and the negotiations regarding blood revenge were not heard in the courtroom – I learned them in the corridors of the court.

This anecdote illustrates the state of legal pluralism in contemporary Chechnya. Even though there is only one de jure legal system – Russian statutory law – there are also powerful parallel systems of de facto law: one based on customary law (adat) and another based on Islamic law (Sharia). Individuals have to navigate the complex interrelationships between these legal systems and sometimes have to choose which forum to bring their disputes to.

The presence of multiple alternative legal systems also has a tremendous political significance. References to adat and Sharia have become commonplace in media reports on Chechnya. For example, after the large-scale insurgent attack on Chechnya's capital Grozny on December 4, 2014, the Head of the Chechen Republic Ramzan Kadyrov proclaimed through his Instagram account that relatives of people who killed police officers would be expelled from the region "without the right to return, and their houses will be razed to the ground." A few days later, unidentified militias burned the houses of the alleged terrorists' families. The government referred to the principle of collective punishment, which is one of the core principles of the Chechen customary law, but which violates Russian state law. Magomed Daudov, the Speaker of the Chechen Parliament and Kadyrov's closest associate, went even further.

Once he called for Sharia arbitration against a politician from the neighboring Republic of Ingushetia. Another time, he announced blood revenge against a popular anti-government blogger. Both Kadyrov and Daudov are high-level Russian state officials in charge of implementing Russian state law. Yet they publicly appealed to non-state legal systems rooted in tradition and religion. On the institutional level, the government of Chechnya semi-formally introduced qadi courts (a Sharia forum) and councils of elders (a customary forum) all across the region, even though these institutions are not compatible with Russian law.

THE PUZZLES

The persistence and power of non-state legal systems in Chechnya should not be surprising, especially given the long history of resistance to Russian rule and state repression in the region. In the post-Soviet period, resistance and repression culminated in two bloody wars (1994–1996 and 1999–2009).[2] In the mid-1990s, Chechnya was a de facto independent state where Sharia law was implemented. During the wars, many Chechens mobilized to fight the Russian army. In turn, the Russian army used brutal violence against the population. Thus, the long history of the conflict can potentially explain why many Chechens reject state-sponsored justice and turn to religious and customary authorities to solve their disputes.

But not all Chechens reject state law. Consider the case of Seda, a woman who lived in Grozny, the capital of Chechnya. Seda was kicked out of her home by her husband and his relatives when she was seven months pregnant. She returned to her parents' home, where she gave birth to a girl. A few months later, the relatives of her former husband arrived at her parents' house and demanded that she return "their child." According to Chechen customary law, children belong to their paternal family. Seda's male relatives agreed with the reasoning of her former husband's family and gave the baby away. Despite social pressure to

---

[2] The periodization of the Second Chechen War is complicated. The Russian government never recognized it as a war and framed it as a counterterrorist operation. It started in 1999. By summer 2000, the Russian army had taken over all the major cities and declared that the military operation was over. However, the guerilla war and counterinsurgency raged on for another 6–7 years. The Russian government lifted the counterterrorist operation status in Chechnya in 2009, which is the official end of the conflict. People in Chechnya also have different views on when the war ended.

accept her fate, Seda filed a lawsuit in a state court. The court ruled in her favor and returned Seda's daughter to her.

Seda's behavior is not an anomaly. From 2009, when the Second Chechen War officially ended, to 2016, when I finished my field research, Russian state courts in Chechnya, which were literally reestablished on the war's ruins, heard more than half a million cases.[3] The vast majority of them – around 70 percent – were civil disputes. Given that Russian state law was considered the "law of the enemy" during the war, and that reliance on it can be penalized by family and community ostracism, the fact that state law is nevertheless utilized in dispute resolution in postwar Chechnya is striking. No less striking is that the government of the Chechen Republic, which is formally in charge of implementing state law, openly promotes customary law and Sharia, as the anecdotes above indicate. In this book, I address these two interrelated puzzles. First, I study government policies towards non-state legal systems – the legal politics of state-building from above. Second, I explore the individual legal preferences and behavior that constitute state-building from below.

THE ARGUMENT

This book argues that state-building can be productively explored through the lens of lawfare – the use of state and non-state legal systems to achieve political, social, or economic goals.[4] I employ the notion of lawfare to capture the agency of politicians and lay individuals within the structural conditions of legal pluralism, a situation when state law co-exists with non-state legal systems. I contend that legal pluralism is not just an artifact of a weak state or underdevelopment. Nor is it simply a reflection of a ruler's ideology or an aspect of local culture. Politicians

---

[3] To be precise, from 2009 to 2016 the courts heard 522,476 cases. Civil disputes constituted 69 percent of all cases. The Justice-of-the-Peace Courts heard 68 percent of the cases, and the courts of general jurisdiction remaining 32 percent. Calculated by the author based on government statistics from the Judicial Department of the Chechen Republic (*Upravlenie Sudebnogo Departamenta v Chechenskoy Respublike*).

[4] In using the term "lawfare," I build on the conceptual framework proposed by Mark Massoud. See Massoud, Mark Fathi. *Law's fragile state: Colonial, authoritarian, and humanitarian legacies in Sudan.* Cambridge University Press, 2013. The anthropological understanding of lawfare adopted in this book is different from its understanding in security studies as the use of law as a weapon of war. For the latter perspective see, for example, Dunlap Jr., Charles J. "Lawfare today: A perspective." *Yale Journal of International Affairs* (2008): 146–154, and Kittrie, Orde *Lawfare: Law as a weapon of war.* Oxford University Press, 2016.

sometimes suppress non-state legal systems and often ignore them, but in other political configurations they strategically promote legal pluralism. Individuals sometimes attach strong normative commitments to justice systems based on tradition and religion, but in other situations strategically "shop" between state and non-state forums. Top-down legal politics and individual legal beliefs and behaviors together shape the particular form of state-building.

The keys to the puzzles of state-building lawfare in places like Chechnya – i.e., conflict-ridden peripheries where the local population is culturally distinct from the core group of the state – are found in the political and social cleavages that exist within these regions. The major political cleavage that arises is from conditions of nested sovereignty – empires in the past and federalism now. Almost all of the peripheries of postcolonial states are characterized by acute problem of fragmented social control. Aceh in Indonesia, Mindanao in the Philippines, each of the seven ethnic states in Myanmar, Kashmir in India, the Kurdish regions of Turkey, Syria, and Iraq, the Anglophone regions of Cameroon, the Tuareg regions in Mali, the Mexican state of Chiapas, and many other "rogue" peripheries illustrate this point. Communities living in these peripheries have their own systems of justice that are often rooted in tradition and religion. Under the conditions of nested sovereignty, both central and peripheral rulers in these peripheries may pursue their own state-building projects and lawfare based on manipulation of the plural systems of justice.

The central societal cleavage of state-building lawfare is gender. Family life, and in particular the regulation of female sexuality is a major arena for struggles over social control. Questions about who can marry and/or divorce whom as well as how; who inherits property; and notions of honor and shame are crucial for national, ethnic, and religious boundary-making. Consequently, the state and social forces expend special effort to control these spheres. Deshi's and Seda's stories exemplify the critical role that gender plays in peripheral state-building lawfare.

Both political and societal cleavages that drive state-building lawfare in the periphery are actualized and intensified by armed conflict. The canonical theoretical approach associated with Charles Tilly links state-building to external warfare.[5] The account presented in this book changes the focus to internal conflict, in particular the separatist armed struggle that

---

[5] Tilly, Charles. *Coercion, capital, and European states,* AD 990–1992. Oxford: Blackwell, 1990.

fractures nested sovereignty and leads to competitive state-building. Studying the interrelationship between warfare and lawfare has an important analytical advantage. Legal pluralism is deeply embedded in history and culture. Conflict serves as a shock that destabilizes societies and presents an opportunity to explore the micro-foundations of individual behavior and government policies under legal pluralism. In this book, I understand conflict as a process: the radical rupture of "normal" social life as a result of experiences of violence that leave profound social and political legacies.

Conflict and political violence accompanied state-building lawfare throughout Chechen history. Legal pluralism developed in Chechnya in the nineteenth century as a result of Russian colonization and anticolonial armed struggle. I argue that when the metropole's grip on the periphery is firm, legal politics is dictated by center's ideology and state capacity. The Russian Empire institutionalized legal pluralism in Chechnya in the nineteenth century as a part of its divide-and-rule strategy and as a response to low state capacity and the orientalist vision of the local society. The Soviet authorities, driven by their high-modernist ideology of legal centralism and relying on soaring state capacity, attempted to eradicate custom and Sharia in Chechnya. However, the project ultimately failed because of Stalin's forced deportation of the entire Chechen nation to Central Asia in 1944. This brute use of state violence strengthened Chechen national identity and alienated Chechens from state law. Yet when the metropole's power falters as a result of political crisis or conflict, local rulers turn legal pluralism into an arena for lawfare aimed at ensuring their political survival.

The book documents how in postwar Chechnya the regional government headed by Kremlin-imposed ruler Ramzan Kadyrov promotes customary law and Sharia to facilitate local political control. First, this policy allows the local ruler to borrow legitimacy from tradition and religion, which both have great appeal among the Chechen population and especially among men. Second, it increases the autonomy of the regional authorities from Moscow, the metropole. Third, it follows the rationale of coalition-building: the local government incorporates the traditional authorities and ideological supporters of non-state legal systems into its coalition.

The decade-long separatist armed conflict transformed the nature of coalition-formation through the militarization of authority. The war brought men who used to carry guns into government offices. Even though many of them now wear suits rather than uniforms, their governance practices differ fundamentally from those of the ideal type of Weberian bureaucrat. These rebels-turned-bureaucrats are strong ideological supporters of custom and Sharia. Promotion of non-state legal systems in postwar Chechnya can be interpreted as a concession to this powerful constituency.

At the same time, the conflict paradoxically created demand for state law from below. I document how the experiences of state violence during the First Chechen War led to an alienation from the Russian state among the local population. However, everything changed during the Second War. Collective state violence during the Second War led to deep structural transformations. It ruined traditional hierarchies and spurred the penetration of state law into Chechen family and community life. What was distinct about the Second War? It was more brutal, longer in time, and involved massive inter-Chechen violence. The effects of these conflict-induced structural transformations overshadowed the strengthening of ethnic and religious identities in response to state violence.

The Second Chechen War was a blow to all hierarchies – whether generational, clan, or class, but especially in gender relations. As a result, after the war, a sizable share of Chechen women started using the Russian state legal system, a system that, in contrast to customary law and Sharia, at least formally acknowledges gender equality. State law is corrupt, inefficient, slow, and its use is associated with community and family ostracism. Yet, many Chechen women prefer to use state law.

My study suggests that the disruption of gender hierarchies can be attributed to several interrelated mechanisms. Perhaps the most significant cultural change was that the conflict forced women to enter the public sphere. Women became the representatives of their families and communities and as such interacted with military and civilian administrations. Even women who remained traditionalists at heart had to learn the bureaucratic practices of the Russian state. At the same time, conflict gave rise to militarized masculinity and neotraditionalism among Chechen men. This divergence was multiplied by changes in bargaining power within families due to wartime transformations of gender positions in the labor market. Simply put, the war left many men unemployed and many women became the breadwinners in their families. Furthermore, the effect of the disruption of gender hierarchies was exacerbated by the more general process of community disintegration. Extended families and communities became substantially less powerful as a result of the killings of influential leaders, mass migration, and intracommunal feuds.

This change diminished the ability of the extended family and community to apply social pressure against women who used state courts. Finally, after the war, many of the NGOs created during wartime refocused on gender problems and served as support structures for women's legal mobilization.

This book shows that women's legal mobilization in Chechnya faced a strong backlash from the Chechen regional government. The most notorious manifestations of the neotraditionalist policies of the Chechen government have been the semiformal introduction of polygamy, support for the practice of honor killings, and the imposition of a restrictive women's dress code. Furthermore, the men in charge of state law actively disrupt its functioning. For instance, law enforcement agencies often do not enforce child custody decisions in favor of mothers who, like Seda, won their cases in court. This backlash can be interpreted as an attempt to build a political order on the re-traditionalization of social order.

Thus, this book reverses the classic story of state-building. In contrast to the dominant narrative, in which the government attempts to penetrate a strong society, and the society resists these attempts, this book shows how local agents of the government can undermine state justice systems by promoting non-state institutions, and how some segments of the population can voluntarily use formal state law that might seem foreign to them. The book shows that legal pluralism is an inherently political phenomenon, an arena of contestation between individuals, social groups, and political actors.

SIGNIFICANCE OF THE STUDY

This book is about Chechnya, a tiny region approximately the size of Connecticut or Northern Ireland. However, its role in post-Soviet Russian politics has been inversely proportional to its size. For instance, Vladimir Putin's rise to power from relative obscurity has often been attributed to his initiation of the Second Chechen War. Speculations about Chechnya abound in Russian and Western media, but academic studies on the ground have been rare. This book provides an account that incorporates both the notorious Chechen warlords and ordinary Chechens, with a particular focus on their everyday life, disputes, worldviews, and narratives about history. The book deals with the politicized and controversial issues of Sharia law, armed conflict, and gender relations. It de-exoticizes these phenomena by relating them to state-building under legal pluralism.

The issue of legal pluralism is relevant well beyond Chechnya. In his grand account of the formation of Western law, historian Harold Berman observed that "the coexistence and competition within the same community of diverse jurisdictions and diverse legal systems" was "perhaps the most distinctive characteristic of the Western legal tradition."[6] Some degree of legal pluralism is present in all contemporary societies. Even in places with a strong rule of law, formal state laws coexist and interact with alternative dispute resolution forums, adjudication among religious minorities, university codes of honor, and internal corporate statutes.

Legal pluralism is particularly pervasive, however, in postcolonial societies and so-called fragile or weak states, where formal state institutions compete for jurisdiction with powerful legal systems that are rooted in religion and tradition. According to some scholarly estimates, as many as sixty-one countries explicitly recognize some form of traditional governance and customary law.[7] In many other countries and regions, non-state legal systems operate without being formally recognized. For example, in Afghanistan after the U.S. invasion, the formal state legal system coexisted with Taliban courts, which operated according to Sharia, as well as with arbitration through a myriad of customary organizations.[8] In sub-Saharan Africa, many countries grant substantial de jure powers to customary leaders or informally guarantee these chiefs nonintervention in their jurisdiction.[9] Recently, there has been a resurgence of traditional governance in Latin America.[10] Quite often,

---

[6] Berman, Harold J. *Law and revolution, the formation of the western legal tradition.* Harvard University Press, 1983: 9.

[7] Holzinger, Katharina, Roos Haer, Axel Bayer, Daniela M. Behr, and Clara Neupert-Wentz. "The constitutionalization of indigenous group rights, traditional political institutions, and customary law." *Comparative Political Studies* 52, no. 12 (2019): 1775–1809.

[8] Giustozzi, Antonio and Adam Baczko. "The politics of the Taliban's shadow judiciary, 2003–2013." *Central Asian Affairs* 1, no. 2 (2014): 199–224; Murtazashvili, Jennifer. *Informal order and the state in Afghanistan.* Cambridge University Press, 2016; Swenson, Geoffrey. "Why US efforts to promote the rule of law in Afghanistan failed." *International Security* 42, no. 1 (2017): 114–151.

[9] Baldwin, Kate. *The paradox of traditional leaders in democratic Africa.* Cambridge University Press, 2016; Boone, Catherine. *Property and political order in Africa: Land rights and the structure of politics.* Cambridge University Press, 2014. Mamdani, Mahmood. *Citizen and subject: Contemporary Africa and the legacy of late colonialism.* Princeton University Press, 1996; Ubink, Janine. *Traditional authorities in Africa: Resurgence in an era of democratisation.* Leiden University Press, 2008.

[10] Carter, Christopher. *States of extraction: The emergence and effects of indigenous autonomy in the Americas.* PhD Dissertation, University of California, Berkeley, 2020; Díaz-Cayeros, Alberto, Beatriz Magaloni, and Alexander Ruiz-Euler.

legal systems based on tradition and religion are promoted at the subnational level. For example, some provinces in Indonesia, Malaysia, Nigeria, and Pakistan have recently adopted Sharia regulations, and states in Mexico have recognized traditional governance. These places are characterized by nested sovereignty – a political arrangement that allows for local rulers' political autonomy and thus approximates the imperial setup of indirect rule, which was a fertile ground for legal pluralism in the past.

Legal pluralism is a fascinating phenomenon in itself: how does a society function when there are multiple alternative rules of the game? Political theorists and legal scholars have long been writing about its normative implications for sovereignty, secularism, understanding of law and violence, legitimacy, minority rights, etc. – the list goes on.[11] This book looks at legal pluralism to rethink state-building.

State-building, understood as the institutionalization of the long-term domination of state organizations and personnel in society, has three major dimensions: coercive, extractive, and regulatory, or to put it simply, violence, taxes, and justice. Academic literature focuses primarily on the coercive and extractive dimensions. In this book, I shift attention to the regulatory dimension, that is, the use of state law vis-à-vis alternative forms of social control.[12] The issue of social control is essential because its

"Traditional governance, citizen engagement, and local public goods: Evidence from Mexico." *World Development* 53 (2014): 80–93; Van Cott, Donna Lee. "A political analysis of legal pluralism in Bolivia and Colombia." *Journal of Latin American Studies* 32, no. 1 (2000): 207–234. Yashar, Deborah. *Contesting citizenship in Latin America: The rise of indigenous movements and the postliberal challenge.* Cambridge University Press, 2005.

[11] Benhabib, Seyla. *The claims of culture: Equality and diversity in the global era.* Princeton University Press, 2002; Cohen, Jean, and Cecile Laborde, *Religion, secularism, and constitutional democracy.* Columbia University Press, 2016; Cover, Robert. *Narrative, violence, and the law: The essays of Robert Cover.* University of Michigan Press, 1992; Tamanaha, Brian. *Legal pluralism explained: History, theory, consequences.* New York: Oxford University Press, 2021.

[12] I build on Joel Migdal's approach to state-building. Migdal, Joel. *Strong societies and weak states: State-society relations and state capabilities in the Third World.* Princeton University Press, 1988; *State in society: Studying how states and societies transform and constitute one another.* Cambridge University Press, 2001. Among the recent contributions to understanding of state-building through the lenses of law, see Boucoyannis, Deborah. *Kings as judges: Power, justice, and the origins of Parliaments.* Cambridge University Press, 2021; Fabbe, Kristin. *Disciples of the state?: Religion and state-building in the former Ottoman world.* Cambridge University Press, 2019, and Franco-Vivanco, Edgar. "Justice as checks and balances: Indigenous claims in the courts of colonial Mexico." *World Politics* 73, no. 4 (2021): 712–773.

distribution reflects the relationship among the state, religion, and tradition as competing sources of authority.

This book disaggregates the state by acknowledging the presence of multiple sources of social control and multiple layers of political authority where actors have different interests in the pace and scope of implementation of state-building. It questions the perspective that state rulers always seek to monopolize social control and attempt to suppress alternative non-state legal institutions. That view is based on the idealized Westphalian picture of sovereignty. The reality of state-building is often quite different. Scholars have highlighted that there is a variety of state-building forms, from centralized rational-legal states to the loose conglomerates of local notables, chiefs, and religious elites, and even local bandits and warlords.[13] Often there is also drastic variation in state penetration within countries. As a result, in many states, legitimate use of force and lawmaking and enforcement have never been fully monopolized and social control has remained fragmented. In this light, promotion of non-state legal systems should be considered not an anomaly, but a viable strategy of state-building, especially if we recognize that the main aim for state-building is often the political survival of those who are in charge of the state.

I show how legal pluralism might directly strengthen local rulers in situations of nested sovereignty. For them, the promotion of non-state legal systems can be a viable strategy for establishing authoritarian enclaves by ensuring autonomy from the center, incorporating communal elites, and legitimizing their rule. Thus, this book opens a new perspective on the politicization of law and the judicialization of politics, especially in authoritarian contexts.[14] My study also shows that rulers turn to law not

---

[13] Barkey, Karen. *Bandits and bureaucrats*. Cornell University Press, 1994; Boone, Catherine. *Property and political order in Africa: Land rights and the structure of politics*. Cambridge University Press, 2014; Driscoll, Jesse. *Warlords and coalition politics in post-Soviet states*. Cambridge University Press, 2015; Reno, William. 1999. *Warlord politics and African states*. Lynne Rienner Publishers, 1999; Marten, Kimberly. *Warlords: Strong-arm brokers in weak states*. Cornell University Press, 2012; Staniland, Paul. "States, insurgents, and wartime political orders." *Perspectives on Politics* 10, no. 2 (2012).

[14] For a review, see Moustafa, Tamir. "Law and courts in authoritarian regimes." *Annual Review of Law and Social Science* 10 (2014): 281–299. See also Gallagher, Mary. *Authoritarian legality in China: Law, workers, and the state*. Cambridge University Press, 2017; Popova, Maria. *Politicized justice in emerging democracies: a study of courts in Russia and Ukraine*. Cambridge University Press, 2012; Shen-Bayh, Fiona. *Undue process: Persecution and punishment in autocratic courts*. Cambridge University Press, 2022; Stern, Rachel. *Environmental litigation in China: A study in political ambivalence*.

only to prosecute potential political challengers, build appealing legal conditions to attract investment, and strengthen discipline within the bureaucracy. They also care about such mundane cases as divorce, car accidents, or small debt, because the ways these cases are resolved affect the ruler's legitimacy and their coalitions of support. Even petty disputes affect high politics.

By looking at state-building from below, this book reformulates the classic question of "Why people obey the law" into the issue of "Which law people obey." Most studies of state-building have treated it as a top-down, government-driven process. However, state-building can also occur from the bottom-up. It is expressed in the choices of state institutions over non-state ones. For centuries, many people actively sought to avoid the state – James Scott described this phenomenon as "the art of not being governed."[15] Social scientists have also shown that individuals are able to govern themselves without intervention from the state; examples include the diamond market of New York City; the cattle industry in Shasta County, California; medieval long-distance Jewish traders; fishermen in Alanya, Turkey; brokers in the trading markets of early post-Soviet Moscow; and many more.[16] When individuals are unable to govern themselves and do not trust the state, they often turn for justice to mafias, gangs, warlords, or vigilantes.[17] In many situations, informal non-state institutions compete with the state; however, despite recognition of the importance of this competition between institutions, there has

Cambridge University Press, 2013. Wang, Yuhua. *Tying the autocrat's hands: The rise of the rule of law in China.* Cambridge University Press, 2015.

[15] Scott, James C. *The art of not being governed: An anarchist history of upland Southeast Asia.* Yale University Press, 2009.

[16] Bernstein, Lisa. "Opting out of the legal system: Extralegal contractual relations in the diamond industry." *The Journal of Legal Studies* 21, no. 1 (1992): 115–157; Ellickson, Robert. *Order without law: How neighbors settle disputes.* Harvard University Press, 1991; Greif, Avner. *Institutions and the path to the modern economy: Lessons from medieval trade.* Cambridge University Press, 2006; Ostrom, Elinor. *Governing the commons.* Cambridge University Press, 1990; Frye, Timothy. *Brokers and bureaucrats: Building market institutions in Russia.* University of Michigan Press, 2000.

[17] Gambetta, Diego. *The Sicilian mafia: The business of private protection.* Harvard University Press, 1993; Skarbek, David. *The social order of the underworld: How prison gangs govern the American penal system.* Oxford University Press, 2014; Smith, Nicholas Rush. *Contradictions of democracy: Vigilantism and rights in post-apartheid South Africa.* Oxford University Press, 2019; Volkov, Vadim. *Violent entrepreneurs: The use of force in the making of Russian capitalism.* Cornell University Press, 2002.

been little systematic research on individuals' preferences for the state versus its alternatives.[18]

A legal pluralism framework highlights the crucial role of gender in state-building. Scholarship on state-building has focused primarily on class cleavage. However, gender conflicts also order state–society relations. For instance, Gregory Massell has shown that in the absence of class conflict, the Bolshevik state in Central Asia provoked gender conflict in order to penetrate its dense society.[19] In fact, gender is especially likely to become the central cleavage of state-building under legal pluralism. Customary law as a cornerstone of clan-based governance is often explicitly discriminatory toward women. Although religious law, and Sharia in particular, can promote women's rights under certain circumstances, secular laws in the twenty-first century generally provide more protections for women against discrimination, at least on paper.[20] As a result, issues related to control of sexuality, honor, and shame become an important arena of boundary-making between the state and society.

The book also contributes to the exploration of state-building and the rule of law in the aftermath of violent conflict. Evidence from Colombia to Sudan and from Guatemala to Iraq, demonstrates that violent conflict increases the need for dispute resolution and also exacerbates the complexity of the presence of multiple legal systems by politicizing the authorities in charge of the competing legal systems.[21] Recent studies have

[18] Among rare exceptions, Belge and Blaydes explored the choices between state and non-state dispute resolution in Cairo and Istanbul, and Gans-Morse and Wang explored the choices between state and non-state institutions in post-Soviet Russia and China, respectively. See Belge, Ceren, and Lisa Blaydes. "Social capital and dispute resolution in informal areas of Cairo and Istanbul." *Studies in Comparative International Development* 49, no. 4 (2014): 448–476; Gans-Morse, Jordan. *Property rights in post-Soviet Russia.* Cambridge University Press, 2017. Wang, *Tying the autocrat's hands.*

[19] Massell, Gregory. *The surrogate proletariat: Moslem women and revolutionary strategies in Soviet Central Asia, 1919–1929.* Princeton University Press Princeton, 1974. Subsequent studies presented a more complex picture of Soviet gender policies in Central Asia that cast doubt on the surrogate proletariat thesis. See Northrop, Douglas. *Veiled empire: Gender and power in Stalinist Central Asia.* Cornell University Press, 2004; Kamp, Marianne. *The new woman in Uzbekistan: Islam, modernity, and unveiling under communism.* University of Washington Press, 2006.

[20] Charrad, Mounira. *States and women's rights: The making of postcolonial Tunisia, Algeria, and Morocco.* University of California Press, 2001; Sezgin, Yüksel. *Human Rights under state-enforced religious family laws in Israel, Egypt and India.* Cambridge University Press, 2013.

[21] Arjona, Ana. *Rebelocracy.* Cambridge University Press, 2016; Bateson, Regina. *Order and violence in postwar Guatemala.* PhD dissertation. Yale University, 2013; Blair, Robert. *Peacekeeping, policing, and the rule of law after civil war.* Cambridge

shown as well that the dismissal and misunderstanding of non-state legal systems in conflict-ridden environments can lead to narrow-minded rule of law policymaking that is bound to fail.[22] Some studies argue that state recognition and promotion of non-state authorities helps to maintain peace, while others paint non-state legal authorities as potential spoilers of state-building projects.[23] Given that the establishment of the rule of law is a primary concern in post-conflict settings, this line of research is urgent in terms of both theoretical and policy implications.

I do not claim that the prevalence of state law over informal dispute resolution systems is a normatively desirable outcome. In the end, even in advanced post-industrial democratic societies, people settle the majority of their disputes through informal mechanisms rather than courts.[24] Legal anthropology and sociolegal studies have consistently shown that taking a dispute to court is very much the exception in all societies – it is the nuclear option.[25] Another consideration is that state and non-state authorities are not always strict alternatives, but often complements.[26]

University Press, 2021; Cheng, Christine. *Extralegal groups in post-conflict Liberia: How trade makes the state.* Oxford University Press, 2018; Ginsburg, Tom. "Rebel Use of Law and Courts." *Annual Review of Law and Social Science* 15 (2019): 495–507; Isser, Deborah. *Customary justice and the rule of law in war-torn societies.* US Institute of Peace Press, 2011; Lake, Milli. "Building the rule of war: Postconflict institutions and the micro-dynamics of conflict in Eastern DR Congo." *International Organization* 71, no. 2 (2017): 281–315; Revkin, Mara. "The legal foundations of the Islamic State." *The Brookings Project on US Relations with the Islamic World* 23 (2016).
[22] Lubkemann, Stephen, Deborah Isser, and Peter Chapman. "Neither state nor custom – just naked power: The consequences of ideals-oriented rule of law policy-making in Liberia." *The Journal of Legal Pluralism and Unofficial Law* 43, no. 63 (2011): 73–109; Swenson, "Why US efforts to promote the rule of law in Afghanistan failed."
[23] Mustasilta, Katariina. "Including chiefs, maintaining peace? Examining the effects of state–traditional governance interaction on civil peace in sub-Saharan Africa." *Journal of Peace Research* 56, no. 2 (2019), 203–219; Menkhaus, Ken. "Governance without government in Somalia: Spoilers, state building, and the politics of coping." *International Security* 31, no. 3 (2006): 74–106.
[24] Ellickson, *Order without law*; Macaulay, Stewart. "Non-contractual relations in business: A preliminary study." *American Sociological Review* 28 (1963): 55–67.
[25] Felstiner, William, Richard Abel, and Austin Sarat. "The emergence and transformation of disputes: Naming, blaming, claiming..." *Law and Society Review* 15, no. 3 (1980): 631–654; Nader, Laura, and Harry F. Todd. *The disputing process: Law in ten societies.* Columbia University Press, 1978.
[26] Baldwin, *The paradox of traditional leaders in democratic Africa*; Murtazashvili, *Informal order and the state in Afghanistan*; Tsai, Lily. *Accountability without democracy: Solidary groups and public goods provision in rural China.* Cambridge University Press, 2007; Van der Windt, Peter, Macartan Humphreys, Lily Medina, Jeffrey F. Timmons, and Maarten Voors. "Citizen attitudes toward traditional and state

However, where non-state legal systems directly contradict or challenge state law, their relative prevalence is a crucial indicator of the particular path toward state-building that is being pursued.

EVIDENCE

No book about legal matters can skip a discussion of evidence. My analysis explores the case of postwar Chechnya and places it in historical and comparative perspectives. The historical analysis traces transformations in state-building and legal pluralism in Chechnya under different reincarnations of nested sovereignty: imperial polity, high-modernist Soviet state, and post-Soviet federation. This comparison allows me to explore the impact of different configurations of state capacity and ideology, and different forms of state violence. The comparison of the legacies of two post-Soviet wars which were separated by just a few years highlights the drastically different social and political effects of the two conflicts. The recent history of these conflicts allows me to reconstruct state-building efforts by talking to people who experienced this period, rather than simply relying on historical sources, which tend to better preserve the perspective of the rulers and the elites.

My comparative analysis contrasts state-building lawfare in Chechnya with the neighboring Muslim-majority regions of Russia, namely, Ingushetia and Dagestan.[27] Ingushetia is almost an ideal comparison point for the post-Soviet political developments in Chechnya. The Ingush people live under the same constellation of legal systems as Chechnya's population: Russian state law, Sharia, and custom. Like the Chechens, the Ingush people belong to the Vainakh ethnic group; they share customs and social structure. Until 1992, Checheno-Ingushetia was a single federal unit within the USSR and subsequently Russia, but in 1992 they separated: Chechnya proclaimed independence from Russia while Ingushetia remained within the Russian Federation. As a result, Ingushetia was not directly affected by the Chechen wars. Thus, Ingushetia can provide insight into how the interrelationship between state and non-state legal systems pans out in the absence of armed

authorities: Substitutes or complements?" *Comparative Political Studies* 52, no. 12 (2019): 1810–1840.

[27] On the substantive, theoretical, and methodological benefits on subnational research, see Giraudy, Agustina, Eduardo Moncada, and Richard Snyder, eds. *Inside countries: Subnational research in comparative politics.* Cambridge University Press, 2019.

conflict. Dagestan is Chechnya's neighbor to the east. It is a gem for comparative political research because it exhibits high levels of ethnolinguistic diversity. Dagestan has a distinguished Islamic legal tradition. It shares with Chechnya a history of resistance to Russian colonization, Soviet rule, and of post-Soviet turbulence. Unlike Chechnya, however, Dagestan did not experience large-scale armed conflict and has a highly fragmented and competitive political field. Within Chechnya, I also leverage variation in legal beliefs and behavior across communities and individuals. This allows me to explore state-building lawfare at several levels of analysis: macro, meso, and micro.

The fieldwork for this study consisted of seven research trips to Chechnya that took place in 2014–2016 and lasted for approximately seven months, as well as additional trips to the neighboring regions and trips to interview Chechen diasporas in Europe. I was mostly based in Grozny, the capital of Chechnya, but also extensively travelled to other towns and villages. The locations were selected to represent different geographic regions and to capture the variation in experiences of collective violence.

Throughout my fieldwork, I conducted semi-structured interviews, informal conversations, and observations. In particular, I rely on interviews with seventy-eight key interlocutors. I interviewed authorities in charge of all three alternative legal systems: judges, prosecutors and police officers (Russian state law), imams and qadis (Sharia), and elders (adat). I also interviewed state officials, lawyers, members of NGOs, as well as Chechen intelligentsia – university professors, ethnographers, historians, and journalists. In addition to individual interviews, I organized group discussions, including discussions with the councils of elders in two locations. During the interviews with legal authorities, I asked my respondents about the most common disputes, how these disputes were usually resolved (actual practices), and how they believed the disputes should be resolved (normative beliefs). Another set of interviews was primarily focused on conflict experiences. I interviewed former politicians and former fighters; present-day government officials; local members of different NGOs, who helped displaced Chechens in Ingushetia and victimized families in Chechnya throughout the Second War and counterinsurgency campaign; and local academics and journalists, who covered the conflict. The interviewees represented different political sides during the war, different regions, and different wartime roles. Through these interviews, I aimed to reconstruct the history of individual and community victimization, wartime governance, and politics.

In addition to the interviews, another principal method of the study was observation. Most importantly, I attended several hearings at the state federal court in one of the Chechen towns that allowed me to observe cases like the trial of Said. I also observed several Sharia arbitrations conducted by district qadis. Other observations were of the behavior of government officials, the work of the NGOs, classes at local universities, academic conferences, prayers at mosques, weddings, funerals, and even conversations in cafés.

Based on these qualitative materials, I identified the most common disputes in Chechnya, traced their resolution practices, and reconstructed justifications for choices between alternative systems. This analysis allowed me to form a rich descriptive account of legal pluralism in Chechnya. To further investigate legal beliefs and behaviors, I relied on the quantitative analysis of original surveys and data of court cases in postwar Chechnya.

To analyze preferences for state law versus alternative legal systems based on religion and custom, I conducted a survey of Chechnya's population. No major Russian or international polling firms work in Chechnya. Lev Gudkov, the head of Levada Center, the most authoritative survey research firm in Russia even said in an interview:

We do not conduct surveys in Chechnya, because it is meaningless ... The levels of fear and terror makes it meaningless ... Survey research in Chechnya is like survey research under Stalin: you'll get only positive responses.[28]

Originally, I was also skeptical about the possibility of survey research in Chechnya, but a successful pilot survey proved me wrong. One of the key features of the survey was the use of local enumerators. My consultations with local researchers suggested that many people in Chechnya would not talk to outsiders. Therefore, I hired and trained a team of interviewers who were either students at local universities or junior research fellows at the Chechen branch of the Academy of Sciences. Employing local enumerators helped me to obtain a high response rate as well as trust from the respondents.[29] Another principal feature of my survey was that it was grounded in my immersive qualitative research. The main survey questions aimed to reveal preferences for alternative

---

[28] Polovinko, Vyacheslav. "Idet sistematicheskaya rabota po podderzhaniyu straha" [There is a systematic work to maintain fear]. *Novaya Gazeta*, July 3, 2019.

[29] 81.4 percent of selected households agreed to take part in the study (N = 1,213). See details of survey sampling and implementation in Lazarev, Egor. "Laws in conflict: Legacies of war, gender, and legal pluralism in Chechnya." *World Politics* 71, no. 4 (2019): 667–709.

legal systems and were based on a set of vignettes – scenarios of disputes – uncovered in my interviews and observations.

In addition to the attitudinal survey data, I also collected behavioral data from state courts. The North Caucasus is infamous for the difficulty of accessing any administrative data and for the poor quality of data that is found. Even the actual population of the Chechen Republic is unclear. Officially, it is 1.4 million people, but my conversations with local officials usually converged at a number around one million. Perhaps the most telling example of the unreliability of administrative data from Chechnya is found in an article that shows how the fabrication of official statistics led to a remote mountainous Chechen district, Sharoy, being declared the wealthiest territory in all of Russia.[30] However, quite miraculously, I was able to obtain official reports on the number of cases heard in the Justice-of-the-Peace Courts in Chechnya from 2011 to 2014 and assemble a massive record of court hearings in these courts from the government webpages. Analysis of these different types of data and data from different sources allows me to draw a rich picture of social reality in Chechnya and triangulate the evidence.

The empirical focus on Chechnya, no doubt a unique place, imposes scope conditions for this study. Chechnya is not an independent country, but a part of the Russian Federation. I do not attempt to explore the influence of the Chechen conflict on state–society relations in the rest of Russia.[31] Russia is a federation and federalism creates a formal framework for indirect rule by allowing regional governments to implement their own politics of state-building to some degree. Thus, federalism or more broadly, nested sovereignty, is a key scope condition. Nontrivial also is that Chechnya was a part of the Soviet Union, a system of government that has had lasting social and political legacies.[32] To sum

---

[30] Zhegulev, Ilya. "The Virtual Reality of Chechen Recordkeeping." *Meduza*, May 9, 2016.

[31] For such analysis see Baev, Pavel. "Instrumentalizing counterterrorism for regime consolidation in Putin's Russia." *Studies in Conflict & Terrorism* 27, no. 4 (2004): 337–352; Lieven, Anatol. *Chechnya: Tombstone of Russian power.* Yale University Press, 1998; Malashenko, Aleksei, and Dmitry Trenin. *Vremia Yuga: Rossiia v Chechne, Chechnia v Rossii [The time of the South: Russia in Chechnya, Chechnya in Russia].* Moscow: Gendalf, 2002; Oushakine, Serguei. *The Patriotism of despair: Nation, war, and loss in Russia.* Cornell University Press. Ithaca, 2009; Sakwa, Richard, ed. *Chechnya: From past to future.* Anthem Press, 2005.

[32] Beissinger, Mark, and Stephen Kotkin, eds. *Historical legacies of communism in Russia and Eastern Europe.* Cambridge University Press, 2014; Heathershaw, John, and Edward Schatz, eds. *Paradox of power: The logics of state weakness in Eurasia.* University of Pittsburgh Press, 2017; Pop-Eleches, Grigore, and Joshua A. Tucker. *Communism's shadow: Historical legacies and contemporary political attitudes.* Princeton University Press, 2017.

up, Chechnya is a postcolonial, post-conflict, post-Soviet society that is a part of a federation. Imposing all these scope conditions simultaneously leaves us with a rather narrow focus. Instead, I use each of these conditions as analytical bridges to other cases. I hope that this deep analysis of the Chechen case enables better understanding of other manifestations of indirect rule, peripheral state-building, federalism, post-Soviet, postcolonial, and post-conflict political developments, both historical and contemporary.

ORGANIZATION OF THE BOOK

The rest of the book is organized in three parts. Part I includes two chapters very different from each other – on theory and ethnography. Chapter 1 introduces the theoretical framework of state-building as law-fare. The chapter starts by outlining the building blocks of state-building at the periphery: legal pluralism, nested sovereignty, gender cleavage, and armed conflict. The rest of the chapter is divided between the reasoning about political order – government policies towards legal pluralism, and about social order – individual choices among different legal systems that, in aggregate, amount to state-building from below. Chapter 2 presents ethnographic narratives on my immersion in Chechen social life, my reflections on the role of positionality and subjectivity in shaping the research, the ethics of the study, and grounded perspectives on the key elements of the story: legal pluralism, conflict, and the foundations of social and political orders in Chechnya.

Part II analyzes the politics of legal pluralism. Chapter 3 provides a historical analysis of state-building in Chechnya through the lens of legal pluralism. There, I give an account of the formation and development of legal pluralism under the Russian imperial administration and the Soviet rule. The chapter shows that the politics of the imperial and Soviet authorities toward legal pluralism can be explained by state capacity and ideology. Chapter 4 covers the post-Soviet period of de facto independent Chechen statehood and the armed conflict in the 1990s. The chapter shows that when peripheral authorities acquire room to maneuver vis-à-vis the metropole, their policies toward legal pluralism are dictated by the struggles for political survival. Chapter 5 further develops the political logic of legal pluralism promotion by investigating the political order established by Ramzan Kadyrov in postwar Chechnya. The chapter documents the widespread instrumental use of non-state legal systems. It then shows that Ramzan Kadyrov promoted non-state legal systems in order to win legitimacy, increase his autonomy from the federal center, and build a coalition of support from non-state authorities and former rebels.

Chapters 6–8, which constitute Part III, explore legal politics from below. Chapter 6 is a descriptive account of legal pluralism in contemporary Chechnya. I describe the actors in charge of dispute resolution, the most common disputes, their forms of resolution, and the legal consciousness of the population. I then explore the factors that drive individual preferences for alternative legal systems and spatial variations in legal behavior. Chapter 7 presents an analysis of the legacies of conflict in legal preferences and behavior at the individual, community, and societal levels. The analysis shows that while collective violence during the First War led to alienation from the Russian state among the Chechen population, the Second War led to community fragmentation and the demand for state law. Chapter 8 explores the legacy of the wartime disruption of gender hierarchies and women's mobilization through state law. It presents a general picture of gender relations in Chechnya and its evolution over time. Special attention is paid to the role of women during the conflict. The analysis shows that conflict, and in particular the Second War, created conditions for women to mobilize state law to advance their interests. The chapter also brings attention to the backlash against war-induced transformations of gender roles and women's legal mobilization.

The Conclusion situates the politics of legal pluralism in a comparative perspective by contrasting Chechnya with other Russian regions and other contexts of postcolonial and post-conflict political development. I also discuss the implications of this study for our understanding of legal pluralism as an instrument of domination and of law as the "weapon of the weak," as well as reflect on the implications of my findings for post-Soviet Russian politics.

PART I

THEORY AND ETHNOGRAPHY

I

State-Building as Lawfare

The View from Above and from Below

How does the state manage to impose the rules that regulate everyday life? The answer to this question, first broached by Joel Migdal, defines state-building through the distribution of social control. Following this view, social control is the main resource or "currency" for which the state and different social forces compete.[1] Even in "strong states" like the United States, social control is contested. For example, diamond trade in New York City is largely regulated through the Orthodox Jewish community's emphasis on Scripture and the enforcement of collective reputation.[2] Furthermore, the Brooklyn Hasidic community has its own rabbinic court system, which even handles criminal allegations.[3] There are also various Christian religious groups in the United States that have obtained enormous power through arbitration clauses. The *New York Times* reported:

For generations, religious tribunals have been used in the United States to settle family disputes and spiritual debates. But through arbitration, religion is being used to sort out secular problems like claims of financial fraud and wrongful death. Customers who buy bamboo floors from Higuera Hardwoods in Washington State must take any dispute before a Christian arbitrator, according to the company's website. Carolina Cabin Rentals, which rents high-end vacation properties in the Blue Ridge Mountains of North Carolina, tells its customers that disputes may be resolved according to biblical principles.[4]

---

[1] Migdal, *Strong societies and weak states*; *State in society*.
[2] Bernstein, "Opting out of the legal system."
[3] Aviv, Rachel. "The outcast." *New Yorker*. November 3, 2014.
[4] Corkery, Michael, and Jessica Silver-Greenberg. "In religious arbitration, scripture is the rule of law." *New York Times*. November 2, 2015.

In states that face "strong societies" based on ethnic, religious, familial, and other group solidarities, social control is fragmented, and numerous systems of justice can operate simultaneously. Under these conditions, state-building takes the form of lawfare: the pragmatic use of different, potentially conflicting legal forums by politicians and individuals. In this chapter, I will outline a theoretical guide for studying peripheral state-building through the lens of lawfare.

First, I discuss the building blocks of peripheral state formation: legal pluralism, nested sovereignty, gender cleavage, and armed conflict. Legal pluralism is about fragmented social control. State–society struggles for social control are complicated because both state and society are internally divided. The concept of nested sovereignty highlights how the state is divided in both imperial and federal settings. Society, too, is fragmented among many lines. The most influential theories of state formation emphasize class divisions and elite factions. Instead, I focus our attention on gender as the central societal cleavage of state formation. Armed conflict disrupts preexisting political and social orders, sharpens the gender divide, and intensifies the struggle for social control. Building on this foundation, the second part of the chapter theorizes state-building lawfare from above. In particular, I outline when and why central and peripheral authorities promote non-state legal systems, as well as how conflict changes the political logic of legal pluralism promotion. The third part of the chapter is about state-building lawfare from below – focusing on individual choices between state and non-state legal systems. It also speculates about how conflict transforms the driving forces behind these choices – in identities and social norms – as well as resources, interests, and hierarchies, with a special focus on gender relations.

The proposed theoretical framework is tailored to state peripheries, but this can be seen as an advantage rather than a limitation, because focusing on remote peripheries allows us to travel back in time and see how the modern state penetrates de facto stateless societies and identify the local conditions that promote or impede this process. The context of armed conflict is crucial here because it brings to life the Hobbesian state of nature. Legal pluralism further approximates the state of nature with its multiple systems of competing rule-making authority – state, religion, community, and family that all operate in parallel at the same time.[5]

---

[5] Here I build on Mampilly, who wrote: "Though this is not commonly understood, Hobbes believed that the state of nature was not just the absence of government, but *the state of plural governance*, a situation he considered inherently unstable and in need of

This layout is, of course, imperfect because of changes in the international system and in the very meaning of the state over time, but it can nevertheless be theoretically fruitful as it allows us to see state-building both from above and from below, and highlights the parts of the story that often cannot be found in the classic accounts of state-building, such as seemingly petty family disputes. I will argue that these petty disputes have implications for understanding large political processes.

STATE-BUILDING BLOCKS IN THE PERIPHERY

Legal Pluralism

The concept of legal pluralism was introduced in the 1970s and quickly became one of the central notions in legal anthropology and socio-legal studies.[6] At the same time, the concept has become a subject of emotionally loaded, heated debates. For example, legal scholar Brian Tamanaha wrote an influential critical article titled "The folly of the 'social scientific' concept of legal pluralism." On the other side, anthropologist Franz von Benda-Beckmann published an article "Who is afraid of legal pluralism?"[7]

The fundamental issue at stake in this debate is the definition of "law." What is law? Can non-state systems of private ordering be considered law? The origin of the debate can be traced to one of the classics of anthropology, Bronislaw Malinowski's *Crime and custom in savage society*, where he investigated how "primitive societies" maintained order without European law. Malinowski concluded that law among the Trobriand of Melanesia was not to be found in "central authority, codes, courts, and constables," but rather in social relations or regularized conduct and patterns of behavior. In the same spirit, anthropologist Leopold Pospisil concluded that "every functioning subgroup in the

transcendence." See Mampilly, Zachariah Cherian. *Rebel rulers: insurgent governance and civilian life during war.* Cornell University Press, 2012: 36.

[6] Galanter, Marc. "Justice in many rooms: courts, private ordering, and indigenous law." *Journal of Legal Pluralism and Unofficial Law* 13, no. 19 (1981): 1–47; Griffiths, John. "What is legal pluralism?" *Journal of Legal Pluralism and Unofficial Law* 18, no. 24 (1986): 1–55; Hooker, Michael. *Legal pluralism: An introduction to colonial and neo-colonial laws.* Oxford University Press, 1975; Merry, Sally Engle. "Legal pluralism." *Law and Society Review* 22 (1988): 869–896; Tamanaha, "Legal pluralism explained."

[7] Tamanaha, Brian. "The folly of the social scientific concept of legal pluralism." *Journal of Law and Society* 20 (1993): 192; von Benda-Beckmann, Franz. "Who's afraid of legal pluralism?" *Journal of Legal Pluralism and Unofficial Law* 34, no. 47 (2002): 37–82.

society has its own legal system," and Laura Nader and Harry Todd
stated in their book on disputes: "Not all law takes place in courts."[8] The
problem with this approach to law, however, is that it is so broad that it
often makes it indistinguishable from social norms.

I follow the realist approach that defines law through enforcement.
Max Weber, the founder of this tradition, wrote that "an order will be
called law if it is externally guaranteed by the probability that coercion
(physical or psychological), to bring about conformity or avenge violation, will be applied by a staff of people holding themselves specially
ready for that purpose."[9] Legal anthropologist E. Adamson Hoebel
extended this definition to capture non-state legal systems. He wrote:
"A social norm is legal if its neglect or infraction is regularly met, in
threat or in fact, by the application of physical force by an individual or
group possessing the socially recognized privilege of so acting."[10]
Hoebel's definition delinks custom from culture by emphasizing the role
of authority and sanctions in the functioning of non-state legal systems.[11]
Following this tradition, I understand both state and non-state systems of
justice, based on custom and religion, as *legal systems* insofar as they
include sets of procedural and substantive rules, institutions, and personnel for inducing or enforcing compliance with their rules. Customary and
religious legal systems, though, have a distinct nature, and there are
important caveats to be made to this claim.

The scholarship in law and society studies shows that in many
instances what is labeled "customary law" is not customary or traditional, but instead the product of colonial encounters and imagination.[12]
For example, Francis Snyder has shown how French colonizers created
"customary law" in Senegal to advance their economic interests through
their own ideology of land ownership. Mahmood Mamdani has argued

---

[8] Malinowski, Bronislaw. *Crime and custom in savage society*. Transaction Publishers,
    1926; Pospisil, *Anthropology of law*, 1974; Nader and Todd, *The disputing process*.
[9] Weber, Max. *On law in economy and society*. Simon and Schuster, 1954: 5.
[10] Hoebel, E. Adamson. *The law of primitive man: A study in comparative legal dynamics*.
    Harvard University Press, 1954: 28.
[11] Belge, Ceren. *Whose law? Clans, honor killings and state-minority relations in Turkey
    and Israel*. PhD diss., University of Washington, 2008: 158.
[12] Chanock, Martin. *Law, custom, and social order: The colonial experience in Malawi and
    Zambia*. Cambridge University Press, 1985; Mamdani, *Citizen and subject*; Moore, Sally
    Falk. *Social facts and fabrications. "Customary" law on Kilimanjaro, 1880–1980*. CUP
    Archive, 1986; Snyder, Francis. "Colonialism and legal form: The creation of 'customary
    law' in Senegal." *Journal of Legal Pluralism and Unofficial Law* 13, no. 19 (1981):
    49–90.

that the colonial powers' appropriation and transformation of customary law strengthened local elites – chiefs, who dramatically increased their despotic power. More generally, the codification and selective interpretations of customary law by colonial powers and their local intermediaries fundamentally changed the nature of indigenous dispute resolution. Consequently, customary law, as we know it in its contemporary manifestation, should be considered as a historically specific product of colonialism. Thus, one has to be careful when talking about the "customary" in customary law. However, this does not mean that customary law must be rejected as a legal system altogether. Substantive norms of customary law are often based on the principles of agnatic kinship. Most importantly, customary law assumes that the subject of law is the family or clan, rather than the individual. Perhaps the best known example of customary law is the Pashtun tribal code *Pashtunwali*. Customary law, though, is not necessarily tied to lineage groups and can be organized territorially.[13] Authorities in charge of customary dispute resolution are usually lineage or community elders and chiefs of different names. Enforcement in customary law is based on social pressure, withdrawal of social status, ostracism, and direct violence, for example through blood feuds.

Similarly, there is the issue of whether religious arbitration can be recognized as *legal* in the full sense of the term. We saw that this is often the case with religious arbitration in the United States, in the beginning of the chapter. Religious organizations in postcolonial situations usually have even larger regulatory power through a combination of elaborated norms, specialized authorities, and enforcement. This is especially pronounced in the case of Islam. Muslims around the world view Sharia as a "total discourse,"[14] that is, the most encompassing regulations of all spheres of life, including the legal sphere. As Mounira Charrad states, "Being a Muslim entails accepting a system of jurisprudence."[15] Sharia is based on the *Koran* and *Sunna* – the sayings and deeds of the Prophet Muhammad. Historical and anthropological research has shown that Sharia is not just a set of rules, but also a set of social practices, institutions, and personnel.[16] Islamic law has been characterized as a broad

---

[13] Murtazashvili, *Informal order and the state in Afghanistan*.

[14] Messick, Brinkley. *The calligraphic state: Textual domination and history in a Muslim society*. University of California Press, 1996: 2.

[15] Charrad, *States and women's rights*, 29.

[16] Bowen, John Richard. *Islam, law, and equality in Indonesia: An anthropology of public reasoning*. Cambridge University Press, 2003; Hallaq, Wael. *The impossible state: Islam, politics, and modernity's moral predicament*. Columbia University Press, 2014; Hefner,

cultural system, which determines ideas about truth, rights, and specialized personhood.[17] Matthew Erie in his study of the interrelationship
between state law and Sharia in China argues that locals perceive Sharia
as law and, therefore, that it should be considered law. One of his
interlocutors put it very sharply: "We consider it law. If we fail to abide
by what the Qur'an says in this life, then we will be punished in the
afterlife .... If you don't think these are law, then you don't understand
Islam."[18]

After going through these murky conceptual issues of legal pluralism,
the next challenge is to decide how to study it. Many theoretical accounts
of legal pluralism across disciplines focus on the description of the complex relationships between state and non-state legal systems. For example,
there is a lasting theoretical distinction between weak and strong legal
pluralism.[19] The former occurs when the state regulates or even incorporates non-state legal systems, and the latter when state and non-state legal
systems operate in parallel independently from each other. However, any
society under legal pluralism is characterized by the profound mutual
influence of state law and non-state legal systems. Anthropologist Sally
Falk Moore highlighted these interdependencies with the concept of the
semi-autonomous social field.[20] To reflect these interdependencies,
I assume that state and non-state legal *systems* jointly constitute legal
order.

In political science, Gretchen Helmke and Steven Levitsky conceptual-
ize legal pluralism in their typology of the interactions between formal

Robert W., ed. *Shari'a politics: Islamic law and society in the modern world*. Indiana
University Press, 2011; Hussin, Iza. *The politics of Islamic law: Local elites, colonial
authority, and the making of the Muslim state*. University of Chicago Press, 2016;
Massoud, Mark Fathi. *Shari'a, Inshallah: Finding God in Somali legal politics*.
Cambridge University Press, 2021; Messick, Brinkley. *Shari'a scripts: A historical anthropology*. Columbia University Press, 2017. There is a distinction between Sharia as the
divine path or God-given justice and *fiqh* (lit. "understanding") of Islamic jurisprudence
as applied by jurists.

[17] Rosen, Lawrence. *The anthropology of justice: Law as culture in Islamic society*.
Cambridge University Press, 1989.

[18] Erie, Matthew S. *China and Islam: The prophet, the party, and law*. Cambridge
University Press, 2016: 16.

[19] Griffiths, "What is legal pluralism?"

[20] Moore wrote that semi-autonomous fields "can generate rules and customs and symbols
internally, but that it is also vulnerable to rules and decisions and other forces emanating
from the larger world by which it is surrounded." See Moore, Sally Falk. "Law and social
change: the semi-autonomous social field as an appropriate subject of study." *Law and
Society Review* 7, no. 4 (1973): 720.

and informal institutions. They distinguish four patterns of interactions: complementary, accommodating, competing, and substitutive. The authors put legal pluralism in the box of competing interactions, since state and non-state legal systems embody qualitatively different principles and procedures and, as a result, "adherence to custom law at times required a violation of state law (and vice versa)."[21] Another typology, developed by Geoffrey Swenson, distinguishes between combative, competitive, cooperative, and complementary paradigms of legal pluralism.[22] These approaches provide good descriptive frameworks, but leave little space for analyzing the motivations of actors who have to navigate state and non-state legal systems: politicians, government officials, communal elites, families, and individuals. Without attending to the actors, we cannot fully understand where state and non-state institutions come from, how they are sustained, and why they change.

To capture the agency dimension of legal pluralism, I borrow Mark Massoud's concept of *legal politics*. Massoud defines legal politics as "the use and promotion of legal tools, practices, arrangements, and resources to achieve political, social, or economic objectives."[23] Legal politics can be both top-down – carried out by state rulers and other elites – and bottom-up or associated with individual uses of a legal system to advance one's interests and rights. Taken together, legal politics from above and from below are a rough equivalent of the anthropological notion of *lawfare* as the use of law to achieve political ends.[24] I apply the concept of lawfare to the conditions of legal pluralism. I thus focus on the use of both state and non-state legal systems, especially in situations of jurisdictional conflicts between them. Related to this is the historical notion of *jurisdictional politics*, understood as "conflicts over the preservation, creation, nature, and extent of different legal forums and authorities."[25] In this book, I use the concepts of lawfare, legal politics, and jurisdictional politics interchangeably to study and explain how political actors and lay individuals navigate legal pluralism. Legal pluralism is about the

---

[21] Helmke, Gretchen, and Steven Levitsky. "Informal institutions and comparative politics: A research agenda." *Perspectives on Politics* 2, no. 4 (2004): 729.

[22] Swenson, Geoffrey. "Legal pluralism in theory and practice." *International Studies Review* 20, no. 3 (2018): 438–462.

[23] Massoud, *Law's fragile state*, 24.

[24] Comaroff, Jean, and John L. Comaroff, eds. *Law and disorder in the postcolony*. University of Chicago Press, 2008.

[25] Benton, Lauren. *Law and colonial cultures: Legal regimes in world history, 1400–1900*. Cambridge University Press, 2002: 10.

fragmented nature of social control — the horizontal division of power between the state and non-state social forces. Next, I consider the vertical divisions within the state itself.

Nested Sovereignty

State-building understood through the lens of social control – as the capacity to penetrate society – relies on the classic Weberian notion of the state as "a monopoly of authoritative binding rule-making, backed up by a monopoly of the means of physical violence."[26] One of Weber's key requirements for the modern state is separation of public law from private law, that is, non-state legal systems. Even though this approach is canonical, it can be productively criticized for relying on an overly simplified idea of the state. For instance, historian Paul Halliday wrote, "For all legal pluralism's sharp critique of state centrism, that critique was made possible only by accepting the hoariest conception of the state: the so-called Westphalian model of internally coherent, territorially defined states."[27] This model of exclusive state control over political decisions made on state territory has always been more of an ideal or myth than reality.

Migdal too has criticized the view of the state as if it were "a coherent, integrated, and goal-oriented body."[28] This view, Migdal stresses, is about the *image* of the state. State practices are very different from this image and may even directly contradict it. In practice, various parts or fragments of the state might ally with societal groups outside the state to advance their political and economic interests. This distorts the neat distinction between the private and public spheres. It also leads to the paradoxical situation in which the state is an internally contradictory entity, parts of which can work in contrary directions and support conflicting forms of social control, which thus seem to undermine state sovereignty. Anna Grzymala-Busse and Pauline Jones argued that this perspective is true for the post-communist state, which is neither centralized nor coherent, and characterized by multiple centers of authority-

---

[26] Mann, Michael. "The autonomous power of the state: Its origins, mechanisms and results." *European Journal of Sociology* 25, no. 2 (1984): 188.

[27] Halliday, Paul. "Laws' histories." In *Legal pluralism and empires.* New York University Press, 2013: 259–278.

[28] Migdal, *State in society*, 12.

building. In addition, the boundary between state and society is often blurred.[29]

In this book, state sovereignty is envisioned as nested. I focus on the territorial organization of the state – whether in the guise of empire and colonialism as in the past, or in the guise of federalism as in the present. While it is true that even unitary states are internally fragmented, the formalization of this nested sovereignty in empire and federalism crystallizes state fragmentation.

The classic form of nested sovereignty is empire. Nowadays empires have been replaced by nation-states, but throughout history, empires have been the dominant form of political organization and occupied the central place in political imagination. Historically, legal pluralism was often the product of empires. Lauren Benton and Richard Ross have noted that empires "invariably relied on layered legal arrangements within composite polities."[30] This is not surprising given that the very concept of empire assumes that different peoples within the polity will be governed differently. In other words, managing diversity was a major governing principle of empire. Furthermore, law as "the cutting edge of colonialism" was a key tool for organizing this difference and maintaining social, religious, ethnic, and racial boundaries in imperial projects.[31]

Empires were legally plural both in their core regions, which were considered "homeland" (for example, provinces in France, confessional assemblies in the Ottoman Empire, corporations in England and the Netherlands), and in their overseas colonies.[32] Historical sociologist Karen Barkey writes that "Empires were forced to deal with this plurality because of the manner in which they expanded, incorporating and accommodating local cultures at different times and under different circumstances in a piecemeal way."[33] As an example, she explores how the Ottoman Empire ruled religious minorities through the *millet* system – community self-governance that included religious courts for Christian and Jewish subjects of the sultan.

---

[29] Grzymala-Busse, Anna, and Pauline Jones Luong. "Reconceptualizing the state: Lessons from post-communism." *Politics and Society* 30, no. 4 (2002): 529–554.

[30] Benton, Lauren, and Richard J. Ross, eds. *Legal pluralism and empires, 1500–1850.* New York University Press, 2013: 1.

[31] Chanock, *Law, custom, and social order*, 4.

[32] Burbank, Jane, and Frederick Cooper. "Rules of law, politics of empire." In Benton and Ross, *Legal pluralism and empires*, 281.

[33] Barkey, Karen. "Aspects of legal pluralism in the Ottoman Empire." In Benton and Ross, *Legal pluralism and empires*, 83.

Jane Burbank and Frederic Cooper, other leading historians of empire, have highlighted that "In legal matters, as in military and economic ones, the most critical challenge for empires was securing the effective and loyal service from intermediaries."[34] They have shown that imperial intermediaries could take on different guises: a governor, a general, a tax collector, as well as a tribal representative, a cleric, a colonial official, a local notable, a judge – indeed, of anyone in charge of actual day-to-day governance. Empires always had multiple legal arenas: courts, advisory councils, religious institutions, imperial commissions, regional administrations, etc. In all of these venues, intermediaries were caught in contradictory positions that required them "simultaneously to maintain their own community's law and to yield to the law of the imperial power."[35]

In empires, local authorities sometimes sought "to broaden jurisdictional claims of the colonizers in order to push for cultural inclusiveness" and sometimes defended and reinvented "traditional authorities" as a way to increase their own autonomy by "creating special status" regimes.[36] Preserving cultural and legal differences made the intermediaries' work indispensable to the metropole and local population, and so re-entrenched their authority. This fluid and complex nature of imperial legal orders further gave local leaders room to maneuver *vis-à-vis* the metropole, other local elites, and the population in general. Thus, local political elites were key players in the formation of legal pluralism. For example, Iza Hussin documents how local elites in India, Egypt, and Malaysia negotiated the scope, content, and application of laws with the British colonial authorities. Hussin clearly shows that the autonomy these local elites negotiated over the matters of family life, religion, and culture, became the major source of their power.[37]

Even after empires left the world stage in the mid-twentieth century, nation-state has not simply become the only form of political organization. Federalism is another major contemporary political alternative. A federation can be defined as "a layered form of sovereignty in which some powers rest in separate political units while others are located at the center."[38] The most prominent theories of federalism link it to the historical experience of the United States and highlight its contractual nature.

---

[34] Burbank and Cooper, "Rules of law, politics of empire," 282.
[35] Barkey, "Aspects of legal pluralism in the Ottoman Empire," 101.
[36] Benton, *Law and colonial cultures*, 9.   [37] Hussin, *The politics of Islamic law*.
[38] Burbank, Jane, and Frederick Cooper. *Empires in world history: Power and the politics of difference.* Princeton University Press, 2010: 10.

However, the majority of the world's population today live in federal polities that emerged as a result of post-imperial transformations and devolutions (e.g., India, Pakistan, Brazil, South Africa, Russia, Malaysia). This fact allows historian Alexander Semyonov to argue that federal political arrangements are "a direct consequence of imperial diversity" and that they "often reveal the same challenges of ethno-territorial nationalism, uneven development, and *de facto* layered citizenships."[39] Thus, the link between legal pluralism and federalism is no less theoretically relevant than the role of legal pluralism in empires. In both arrangements, local rulers – intermediaries between the metropole, the federal center, communal elites, and the rest of the population – are cemented as the key actors of the politics of legal pluralism. This reiterates the wisdom that "all state formation is in essence local."[40]

Gender Cleavage

State-building lawfare is especially contested in the domain of family law. This calls for a gendered perspective on state-building. I rely on the definition developed by Mala Htun and Lauren Weldon: "Gender is not just an attribute of individual identity or a type of performance but a collection of institutions: a set of rules, norms, and practices, widely held and somewhat predictable – though not uncontested – that constructs what it means to be or to belong to a particular sex group."[41] Contestations over these rules, norms, and practices constitute the key cleavage of state-building lawfare.

The state was a latecomer to the regulation of family life. Htun and Weldon described this process in the following way:

Historically, family law consisted of rules, norms, and decisions over kinship and reproduction that were interpreted and administered by traditional rulers including chiefs, heads of clans, and religious officials. The decision to impose central power over family law, or to delegate its administration to traditional and religious authorities, marked a crucial juncture in the state building process.[42]

---

[39] Semyonov, Alexander. "The ambiguity of federalism as a postimperial political vision: editorial introduction." *Ab Imperio*, no. 3 (2018): 30.

[40] Taylor, Brian. *State building in Putin's Russia: Policing and coercion after communism.* Cambridge University Press, 2011: 23.

[41] Htun, Mala, and S. Laurel Weldon. *The logics of gender justice: State action on women's rights around the world.* Cambridge University Press, 2018: 4 This section heavily relies on Htun and Weldon's systematic review of family law across the world.

[42] Ibid.: 124.

State rulers indeed chose different trajectories of state-building in the domain of family law. For example, Mounira Charrad has shown how the leadership of postcolonial Morocco adopted a conservative version of Islamic family law to appease the patriarchal interests of the rural tribal elites, while central leaders in Tunisia, who were relatively autonomous from kin groupings, introduced secularized egalitarian family law to further undermine tribal authorities.[43]

Jurisdictional conflicts over family life have large distributional consequences. The dominant interpretations of customary law are often explicitly discriminatory toward women.[44] For instance, in Morocco under the 1900 version of some customary codes, Berber women had no inheritance rights, no property rights, no right to consent, no minimum marriageable age, and no right for divorce. Similarly, according to Kabyle customary law, which was applied among the Berbers of Algeria until the national Family Code was enacted in 1984, women had no rights to inheritance, no property rights, and practically no custody rights over their children.[45]

It is widely believed that Islamic law also puts women in a disadvantaged position. Originally Sharia brought a major improvement in women's status over the customary practices prevalent in pre-Islamic Arabia. For instance, women obtained a right for a fixed share of inheritance and were allowed to own and manage property, including the dower. Historical and anthropological research has also shown that Islamic law gives women agency to protect their rights: women often successfully mobilize Islamic legal notions to improve their living conditions.[46] At the same time, gender inequality remains an integral part of Islamic family law, especially when it is appropriated and enforced by the state.[47] As Charrad shows, "Islamic family law places women in

---

[43] Charrad, *State and women's rights.*

[44] Hudson, Valerie M., Donna Lee Bowen, and P.L. Nielsen. "Clan governance and state stability: The relationship between female subordination and political order." *American Political Science Review* 109, no. 03 (2015): 535–555.

[45] Charrad, *State and Women's Rights*: 47; Wyrtzen, Jonathan. *Making Morocco: Colonial intervention and the politics of identity.* Cornell University Press, 2016: 223.

[46] Ahmed, Leila. 1992. *Women and gender in Islam: Historical roots of a modern debate.* Yale University Press; Hirsch, Susan. *Pronouncing and persevering: Gender and the discourses of disputing in an African Islamic court.* University of Chicago Press, 1998; Mahmood, Saba. *Politics of piety: The Islamic revival and the feminist subject.* Princeton University Press, 2005; Mir-Hosseini, Ziba. *Marriage on trial: A study of Islamic family law.* IB Tauris, 1993; Osanloo, Arzoo. *The politics of women's rights in Iran.* Princeton University Press, 2009.

[47] Sezgin, *Human rights under state-enforced religious family laws in Israel, Egypt and India.*

subordinate status by giving power over women to men as husbands and male kin."[48] Women are required to obey their husbands, care for children, and do housekeeping. Men have the right to control their wives' behavior, such as when and how they go out in public. Women receive half of the amount of inheritance of male shares. Polygamy is an obvious factor of gender inequality, too. Men also enjoy far greater rights to divorce and are the legal guardians of their children. In some places, state codifications of Islamic law reformed these provisions toward greater equality, but according to Htun and Weldon's analysis, Muslim women's legal disadvantages persist.[49]

Western civil and common law systems also have been explicitly discriminatory toward women for the greater part of history. The Napoleonic Code adopted in many countries stated that the wife owes obedience to her husband. A husband had control over the property and activities of his wife. Most Catholic countries in Europe and Latin America did not permit divorce until the mid- to late-twentieth century.[50] Western statutory codes started to move toward gender equality in the late nineteenth century. However, the changes were incremental and slow, and in some places, for instance, Switzerland, were not completed until the late twentieth century.[51]

Colonialism brought Western statutory law overseas and imposed it onto indigenous legal systems. As a result, the link between family and gender and state-building has been profoundly shaped by colonialism. Colonial powers codified diverse and fluid indigenous practices of family law, thereby also inventing the traditions and forging the communities that this law was applied to. What was codified were often conservative versions of the kinship rules. For example, Iza Hussin documented how local matriarchal laws in some parts of colonial Malaysia were replaced by more patriarchal customs by the British.[52] In addition, colonialism endowed traditional leaders with the authority to apply these conservative rules. And precisely because colonialism made traditional leaders impotent in all other domains, these traditional rulers fell with even more gusto on the policing of gender and family relations, which had become indispensable for their preservation as local elites.

---

[48] Charrad, *State and women's rights*: 28.
[49] Htun and Weldon, *The logics of gender justice*: 273–285.
[50] Htun, Mala. *Sex and the state: Abortion, divorce, and the family under Latin American dictatorships and democracies*. Cambridge University Press, 2003.
[51] Htun and Weldon, *The logics of gender justice*.
[52] Hussin, *The politics of Islamic law*.

According to Htun and Weldon, the experience of communism had the opposite effect to that of colonialism. Guided by ideological doctrine, communist governments "sought to reduce religious power and expand women's rights. They replaced conservative family laws with egalitarian models, which endured for the most part into the postcommunist era."[53] For example, Vietnam's *Marriage and Family Law* of 1959 banned forced marriages, child marriages, and polygamy as well as introduced equality between men and women in rights, obligations, property, and parenting. Communist transformations of family law aimed to destroy the power of traditional and religious elites, as well as to ensure women's participation in the labor force.

The struggles for social control in family matters have always been especially politicized in the peripheries where the population is culturally distinct. For example, Jonathan Wyrtzen documents how French colonial authorities in Morocco used discrepancies in women's status in customary and Islamic legal systems to reify an ethnic division between Berbers and Arabs.[54] Moreover, local communal authorities have a lot at stake in these classification struggles. Ceren Belge shows that the power of the clans in the Kurdish periphery of Turkey and the Palestinian periphery of Israel rests on "certain family practices, such as early, arranged, endogamous and polygamous marriages, the withholding of inheritance rights from women, and under certain conditions, the murder of female members that harm the family reputation."[55] Thus, communal authorities and extended families, along with women often organized in groups or involved in movements, are the crucial actors of gendered state-building lawfare.

Both the gender cleavage (key societal divide) and the nested sovereignty (key political divide) are actualized in response to the armed conflict. Thus, conflict is the last building block we need to have for a theory of state-building lawfare.

Order, Conflict, and Violence

Internal armed conflict might seem like the exact opposite of state-building, understood as bringing social and political order. Yet, conflict and order are not just opposites, but also interrelated phenomena. Dan Slater has explained the divergence in state-building forms in Southeast Asia drawing on the legacies of contentious politics, including internal

---

[53] Htun and Weldon, *The logics of gender justice*: 123.
[54] Wyrtzen, *Making Morocco*: 222.   [55] Belge, *Whose law?*: 22.

armed conflict.[56] Douglass North and his coauthors similarly claim that social order arises from elite efforts to curb violence.[57] These studies have challenged the consensus that internal conflicts are the "wrong kind of wars" for state-building in contrast to external warfare, which has long been theorized as a major driver of state formation, at least in Europe.

Furthermore, order exists amidst conflict. Ana Arjona has highlighted that despite the fact that conflict is associated with chaos, order is often established and maintained at the community level through "social contracts" between rebels and civilians.[58] Relatedly, Zachariah Mampilly writes that rebels acting as a counterstate can produce social and political orders by constructing effective governance structures.[59] Both authors distinguish dispute resolution systems as a key strategic element in rebel social order. Developing this line of reasoning, Paul Staniland argues that the absence of the monopoly on violence does not mean "disorder" or "incomplete state-building," but instead represents "its own distinctive form of order."[60] Order established during conflicts naturally leaves some mark even after the conflict. For example, Regina Bateson shows how experiences of violence during armed conflict affected postwar social order in the practices of dealing with crime in Guatemala.[61]

I focus on the social and political legacies of separatist conflict. Separatist armed conflict is a culmination of the struggle for local autonomy between the center and the periphery. Separatism fractures sovereignty and politicizes the issue of law and more generally, the system of governance emerging in the periphery. The legacies of separatist conflict actualize in the behavior of government officials, social organizations, and individuals during contestations for social control. It is important to note though that conflict is not just about violence. It is a complex phenomenon that embodies many components and takes many different forms, including mobilization, recruitment, military organization, territorial control, etc. In order to make conflict legible for further analysis, I rely on Elisabeth Wood's framework of the social processes of conflict. Wood defines the social processes of conflict as "the transformation of

---

[56] Slater, Dan. *Ordering power: Contentious politics and authoritarian leviathans in Southeast Asia.* Cambridge University Press, 2010.

[57] North, Douglass, John Joseph Wallis, and Barry Weingast. *Violence and social orders: A conceptual framework for interpreting recorded human history.* Cambridge University Press, 2009.

[58] Arjona, *Rebelocracy.*   [59] Mampilly, *Rebel Rulers.*

[60] Staniland, "States, insurgents, and wartime political orders."

[61] Bateson, *Order and Violence in postwar Guatemala.*

social actors, structures, norms, and practices, that happen as a result of civil war violence."[62]

Conflict manifests differently at the different levels of aggregation of social life. Often the society-wide master cleavage, including the separatist conflict that contests sovereignty, is not meaningful at the local level, where vendettas and political competition might dominate the nature of violence in particular communities.[63] Similarly, the social and political processes of civil war differ at the different levels of aggregation. At the individual and community levels, the most pronounced social processes of war are triggered by violence against civilians. Although there are many forms of violence and many actors who perpetrate it, I concentrate primarily on collective violence perpetrated by the state. Collective violence is a form of targeting civilians based on group identity (e.g., ethnicity X) or community (e.g., village Y).[64] Collective violence is especially likely to leave lasting social legacies for individuals and communities. For example, historian Max Bergholz highlights how the collective violence in Bosnia during World War II was "a generative force in transforming the identities, relations, and lives of the many."[65] The secessionist nature of conflict makes it more likely that the state will employ collective violence based on an ascriptive identity that lay behind separatism rather than individual political allegiance and behavior.[66]

The legacies of violence are conditioned by local political and social contexts. The social context of violence is determined first and foremost by the characteristics of communities. Community is a key level of analysis in the study of political violence because the state victimizes communities with its collective violence and the communities often serve as the organizational knots of resistance. Victimization at the community level is not merely an aggregation of individual victimizations because it affects

---

[62] Wood, Elisabeth Jean. "The social processes of civil war: The wartime transformation of social networks." *Annual Review of Political Science* 11 (2008): 540.

[63] Kalyvas, Stathis. *The logic of violence in civil war.* Cambridge University Press, 2006; Balcells, Laia. *Rivalry and Revenge.* Cambridge University Press, 2017.

[64] Gutiérrez-Sanín, Francisco, and Elisabeth Jean Wood. "What should we mean by 'pattern of political violence'? Repertoire, targeting, frequency, and technique." *Perspectives on Politics* 15, no. 1 (2017): 20–41; Steele, Abbey. *Democracy and Displacement in Colombia's Civil War.* Cornell University Press, 2017.

[65] Bergholz, Max. *Violence as a generative force: Identity, nationalism, and memory in a Balkan community.* Cornell University Press, 2016: 6.

[66] Mampilly, *Rebel rulers.*

not only individuals, but also the relations between them: social networks, roles, hierarchies, and authority structures.[67]

The macro-perspective on separatist conflict is about who won the war – the center or the periphery – and no less importantly, how the war ended. International relations scholars have shown that the form of war termination determines the postwar distribution of power resources.[68] The major distinction drawn in this scholarship is between decisive military victory and negotiated settlement or stalemate. This multilevel conceptualization of conflict allows me to encompass the transformations of both political and social orders that lay the foundation for peripheral state-building. Let me start with political order.

POLITICAL ORDER: LEGAL POLITICS FROM ABOVE

Usually, political order is understood as stability – the absence of coups, civil wars, and upheavals. Yet as I mentioned above, order is not just the opposite of conflict and can take many forms, including those compatible with violent conflict. I adopt Staniland's approach to political order which focuses on the structure and distribution of authority: "who rules, where, and through what understandings."[69] Political order in this conceptualization is essentially a set of relationships between the ruler, other relevant elite actors, and the population; and is ultimately about bargaining, coalition formation, and legitimation.

Political orders differ in the degree and form of legal monopoly, or in other words, how much social control they have or even would like to have. Some rulers aspire towards legal centralism, others settle for hybrid legal orders in which state statutory law is intermixed with custom and religious legal systems. I link the regulation of social life through dispute resolution with the regulation of political power through the management of alternative legal systems.

[67] Finkel, Evgeny. *Ordinary Jews: Choice and survival during the Holocaust.* Princeton University Press, 2017; Petersen, Roger. *Resistance and rebellion: Lessons from Eastern Europe.* Cambridge University Press, 2001; Marks, Zoe. "Gender, Social Networks and Conflict Processes." *feminists@ law* 9, no. 1 (2019).

[68] Toft, Monica Duffy. 2009. *Securing the peace: The durable settlement of civil wars.* Princeton University Press, 2009; Walter, Barbara. *Committing to peace: The successful settlement of civil wars.* Princeton University Press, 2002.

[69] Staniland, "States, insurgents, and wartime political orders": 247.

The Politics of Legal Pluralism

The standard view, derived from Max Weber's work, suggests that rulers should seek to monopolize social control and oppose alternative non-state legal institutions. As Yüksel Sezgin puts it: "the ability to establish a monopolistic control over the legal affairs of a subject population has come to be viewed as an inseparable aspect of stateness."[70] Yet, political leaders adopt different approaches toward non-state legal systems. Most generally, a ruler who governs a society under legal pluralism has three broad potential policy approaches toward non-state legal systems:

1) suppression, 2) promotion, and 3) tolerance or nonintervention.[71]

The *suppression strategy* is the most consistent with the Weberian ideal of state-building. Gradual suppression of non-state legal systems was a path to state-building for many European states. Ataturk's abolishment of Sharia law in Turkey and Nyerere's ban of customary law in Tanzania are more recent examples of the suppression strategy.

The *promotion strategy* requires active government support for non-state legal systems. This support can be either formal – through the official recognition of non-state legal forums and constitutionalization of them, like in Namibia, Ghana, Uganda, or Israel – or informal, through *de facto* support, for instance, of the provision of material and symbolic benefits to non-state authorities and concessions in the cases of jurisdictional conflicts.

The *tolerance or nonintervention strategy* occurs when the government in charge of state law neither suppresses nor promotes non-state legal systems. This approach describes a situation in which state and non-state legal institutions function in parallel, like the state and traditional authorities in contemporary Afghanistan.

What factors determine the approach a leader would take? The most obvious factor is *state capacity*. Some states just do not have the coercive capacity to eradicate non-state legal forums and lack the administrative

[70] Sezgin, *Human rights under state-enforced religious family laws in Israel, Egypt and India*: 20.
[71] There are more nuanced typologies of potential government strategies toward non-state legal systems, but these typologies can be generalized into suppression, promotion, and tolerance. See Sezgin, *Human rights under state-enforced religious family laws*; Swenson, "Legal pluralism in theory and practice"; Ubink, *Traditional authorities in Africa*.

capacity to build an effective state legal system.[72] Weak state capacity is therefore likely to be associated with either tolerance or promotion approaches. A version of this argument is the *path dependence* explanation, which proposes that places with established forms of non-state authority in the past, often as a result of colonialism, will continue to have them subsequently.[73]

Leaders' or more broadly regimes' *ideology* also affects the adoption of an interventionist approach: either suppression or promotion.[74] From the standpoint of a progressive ruler, the presence of customary or religious law might be seen as a legacy of colonialism, an indicator of backwardness, and a form of discrimination against religious, ethnic, and other social groups. These considerations motivated some post-independence political leaders to suppress non-state legal institutions and unify the legal system. Examples of this ideology-driven approach can be found across the world from India and Indonesia to Tunisia and Nigeria. The Marxist-leaning leaders who ruled Tanzania, Ethiopia, Guinea, and Mozambique were especially radical in their attempts to eradicate "the rudiments of the past." In contrast, if a leader holds a strong traditionalist or religious ideology, they are likely to preserve legal pluralism and promote legal systems based on religion and custom. Rulers might also promote legal pluralism if they hold an exclusionary ideology that aims to "preserve and reinforce existing ethnic, sectarian, and linguistic divisions among their subjects."[75] Most colonial regimes and contemporary Israel and Lebanon exemplify this situation.

[72] Herbst, Jeffrey. *States and power in Africa: Comparative lessons in authority and control.* Princeton University Press, 2000; Hooker, *Legal pluralism*. For a comprehensive overview of the concept of state capacity and the analysis of compliance with state rules as its manifestation, see Berwick, Elissa, and Fotini Christia. "State capacity redux: Integrating classical and experimental contributions to an enduring debate." *Annual Review of Political Science* 21 (2018): 71–91.

[73] De Juan, Alexander. "'Traditional' resolution of land conflicts: The survival of precolonial dispute settlement in Burundi." *Comparative Political Studies* 50, no. 13 (2017): 1835–1868.

[74] Pisani, Elizabeth, and Michael Buehler. "Why do Indonesian politicians promote shari'a laws? An analytic framework for Muslim-majority democracies." *Third World Quarterly* 38, no. 3 (2017): 734–752; Sezgin, Yüksel, and Mirjam Künkler. "Regulation of 'religion' and the 'religious': The politics of judicialization and bureaucratization in India and Indonesia." *Comparative Studies in Society and History* 56, no. 2 (2014): 448–478.

[75] Sezgin, *Human rights under state-enforced religious family laws in Israel, Egypt and India*: 29.

A policy toward non-state legal systems can also be a response to *popular demand*. In a democratic polity in which the median voter prefers legal institutions based on tradition and religion, a ruler is likely to promote them in order to win the popular vote. Kate Baldwin refers to this idea as "the most simple" explanation for political promotion of traditional authorities in the wake of democratization across different African counties. It goes as follows: "rural dwellers have inherent preferences for a strong chieftaincy, and therefore, governments that depend on rural support will empower traditional leaders as a direct response to rural preferences."[76] Donna Lee Van Cott similarly attributes the resurgence of informal justice in Latin America to the intense pressure from indigenous organizations.[77] Politicians might also promote legal pluralism to win the support of traditional and religious elites, who can act as brokers for electoral mobilization.

State capacity, ideology, and popular demands all matter for the politics of legal pluralism. However, existing explanations of the persistence of legal pluralism rare out the conditions of nested sovereignty and conflict environment. I argue that under these conditions, local rulers' policies toward non-state legal systems can be best understood as a part of their quest for political control in the periphery.[78]

Legal Pluralism and Political Control in the Periphery

In the most general terms, legal pluralism can be presented as the struggle for social control between state and society. However, as I outlined above, this view is too simplistic. "State" and "society" can hardly be taken as unitary actors. The conditions of nested sovereignty especially complicate the picture. The cast is simply too multifarious, including at the very minimum 1) the metropole or the federal center, 2) the local ruler or intermediary of the center in the periphery, 3) local elites who function as communal authorities in charge of non-state dispute resolution as well as other elite groups, and 4) the general population with diverse preferences for social order.

---

[76] Baldwin, *The paradox of traditional leaders in democratic Africa*: 64. Baldwin's own analysis highlights a much more complex role of chiefs as development brokers.

[77] Van Cott, "A political analysis of legal pluralism in Bolivia and Colombia."

[78] Hassan, Mattingly, and Nugent defined political control as an umbrella concept that covers "any tactic through which the state seeks to gain compliance from society." The authors note: "In more authoritarian regimes, however, political control is often in service of the survival of the ruling elite." I use the concepts of political control and political survival interchangeably. See Hassan, Mai, Daniel Mattingly, and Elizabeth Nugent. "Political control." *Annual Review of Political Science* 25 (2022): 6.1–6.20.

In the past, imperial and colonial authorities often promoted legal pluralism due to weak state capacity or ideology, or as a part of a divide-and-rule policy. At present, many central political authorities are driven by similar motivations as well as by popular demand. However, contemporary states are also bound by the image of stateness and as a result are more likely to prefer the promotion of state law as the law of the land to ensure control over the periphery. Contrastingly, communal elites in peripheries are more likely to promote non-state legal systems. Sandwiched between the metropole and the communal elites are local state rulers. These rulers have to strategically reconcile demands of the state and those of the communal elites and segments of the population in these peripheral regions. Thus, they form the central focus of my analysis. This is in line with the historical analysis of nested sovereignty that has highlighted the crucial role of imperial intermediaries and the notion that all state-building is local.

Local rulers in the periphery are caught in what international relations theorist David Lake has called the State-Builder's Dilemma.[79] Lake emphasizes that local rulers have to make a trade-off between loyalty to the interest of the metropole and legitimacy in the eyes of the local population. The radical version of this dilemma under legal pluralism occurs when the metropole demands a strict monopoly for state law and the local population demands non-state justice based on tradition and religion. Lake's focus is on the central state-builder, for whom there is no solution to the dilemma. In contrast, I focus on the local ruler. For the local ruler, the solution to the problem rests on their relative dependency on the metropole versus popular support. If a ruler has room to maneuver, then the promotion of legal pluralism might be their best bet. Legal pluralism can increase a local ruler's legitimacy and curb the enthusiasm of the central authorities to intervene in their domain.

However, in addition to managing vertical power relations – upward with regard to the center and downward with regard to the population – the local ruler also has to navigate horizontal relations with other local elites. From these other elites, the ruler has to form coalitions of support. At the same time, these other elites can politically challenge the ruler and destabilize the local political order. We thus run into another crucial dilemma. If a ruler empowers non-state legal forums, say to make the population happy or to keep the central authorities at bay, these forums may be hijacked by potential challengers to their rule or even become the

---

[79] Lake, David. *The statebuilder's dilemma: On the limits of foreign intervention.* Cornell University Press, 2016.

challengers themselves. In other words, the strategy of promoting legal pluralism can have a "Frankenstein" effect. William Reno formulated this sentiment in its most general way. He wrote that the key reason that leaders prefer weak formal and informal institutions "lies in their fear that enterprising rivals could use control over successful institutions" to challenge their rule.[80] This dilemma calls one to consider the local ruler's coalition formation and the balance of power between the local ruler and other elites. Thus, I propose focusing on three key areas in which legal and political orders overlap and where a local ruler's political survival is determined: legitimation, boundary control, and coalition-building.

Typically, the first thought that comes to mind when we want to explain a ruler's promotion of non-state legal systems is that of legitimacy. The reasoning here is that non-state legal institutions rooted in custom and religion ensure a local ruler's control over the masses because they often enjoy high legitimacy. Yet, legitimacy is a "mushy" concept that can lure social scientists into a trap of tautological explanation.[81] In the case of the promotion of non-state legal systems, understanding legitimation is relatively straightforward. It is an appeal to authority — such as religion or tradition — external to the claimant making an appeal. In other words, a local ruler "borrows" legitimacy from religion and tradition. This reasoning relies on the assumptions that tradition and religion enjoy high support among the population, and that this support is independent from the government's promotion of the authorities in charge of religious and traditional institutions. If these assumptions are not met, then reference to legitimacy falls into the category of circular explanation.

Second, political power within nested sovereignty necessitates the establishment and maintenance of local autonomy – insulation from challenges from the center. This is a key consideration for the subnational regimes in federal polities that need to protect themselves from interventions by the central government. But it is also relevant for postcolonial nation-states because external actors, such as former metropoles, international organizations, and corporations, all play important roles in local state–society relations and struggles for power.

[80] Reno, William. "Shadow states and the political economy of civil wars." In Mats Berdal and David M. Malone (eds.), *Greed and grievance: Economic agendas in civil wars.* Boulder, CO: Lynne Rienner, 2000: 53.

[81] Wedeen, Lisa. *Ambiguities of domination: Politics, rhetoric, and symbols in contemporary Syria.* University of Chicago Press, 1999: 12.

Edward Gibson, who developed a theory of *boundary control*, claims that "In any large-scale system of territorial governance political institutions are entangled across space. Strategies of political control are thus never limited to any single arena."[82] In other words, the rulers must navigate challenges from local opposition as well as the threat of external intervention. In order to survive these two types of threats, Gibson argues, the leaders of subnational regimes are constantly engaged in strategies of boundary control – e.g., maximization of incumbent influence over local politics and prevention of external intervention in local affairs.

I argue that boundary control can also be achieved by the promotion of legal pluralism. The promotion of legal pluralism serves as a tool of "parochialization of power" in Gibson's terms. In the case of a postcolonial national political unit, a ruler who promotes customary or religious law distances their country from the former colonial power or "international community" that usually stands for "the rule of law," commonly understood as Western statutory law. In the case of a subnational political unit, a local ruler who promotes customary or religious law increases the autonomy of their region from the federal center that stands for the national legal system. For instance, in Nigeria, politicians from the Northern states at different points in time promoted Sharia as a means of ensuring their autonomy from the center, which was dominated by Christian administrative and economic elites.[83]

Third, support for non-state legal systems can serve as a tool in the ruler's coalition-building and more broadly, relations with other elite actors. Support for non-state legal systems can be used to co-opt the communal authorities into the ruler's political machine. In other words, governments can strengthen traditional and religious authorities to create powerful brokers who can use coercion, deference, and material incentives to mobilize support for the rulers.[84]

---

[82] Gibson, Edward. *Boundary control: Subnational authoritarianism in federal democracies.* Cambridge University Press, 2013. Gel'man and Ross applied the framework of subnational authoritarianism to explain political development in Putin's Russia. See Gel'man, Vladimir, and Cameron Ross, eds. *The politics of sub-national authoritarianism in Russia.* Ashgate Publishing, Ltd, 2010.

[83] Kendhammer, Brandon. *Muslims talking politics: Framing Islam, democracy, and law in Northern Nigeria.* University of Chicago Press, 2016; Laitin, David. "The Sharia debate and the origins of Nigeria's second republic." *The Journal of Modern African Studies* 20, no. 03 (1982): 411–430.

[84] Pisani and Buehler, "Why do Indonesian politicians promote shari'a laws?"

In this light, it is not surprising that cooptation of communal elites has been a common strategy for many political leaders across time and space. For example, Daniel Mattingly presents a comprehensive account of how the Chinese state uses communal elites and associations such as clan lineages and religious groups in order to ensure informal political control in rural areas.[85] This strategy, moreover, is not limited to authoritarian states. For instance, in post-Suharto Indonesia, state elites accommodate Islamist movements by enacting Sharia regulations in order to increase their symbolic capital, gain economic benefits, and mobilize the electorate.[86] In South Africa the ruling party African National Congress supports customary law arbitration by chiefs because chiefs are effective agents of electoral mobilization.[87] Similar alliances have been historically common in many other sub-Saharan African countries, where chiefs have been placed in charge of both dispute arbitration and electoral mobilization.[88]

However, not all elite actors are prone to cooptation. State-building from above often takes the form of elite competition. Grzymala-Busse and Jones centered this insight in their definition of state formation as "elite competition over the authority to create the structural framework through which policies are made and enforced."[89] Therefore, it is crucial to consider *the balance of power* or relative strength of the local ruler *vis-à-vis* potential elite challengers and the composition of these potential challengers. I assume that if their rule is consolidated and there are no viable challengers, a local ruler is likely to promote non-state legal systems to gain additional legitimacy, increase its autonomy from the metropole, and co-opt communal elites. China and the dominant party regime in South Africa illustrate the point that strongly consolidated regimes engage in the promotion of legal pluralism and non-state authorities.

If the ruler dominates the potential challengers in terms of political power, but a potential challenge is still viable, the ruler can be expected to

[85] Mattingly, Daniel. *The art of political control in China.* Cambridge University Press, 2020.
[86] Buehler, Michael. *The politics of Shari'a law: Islamist activists and the state in democratizing Indonesia.* Cambridge University Press, 2016.
[87] De Kadt, Daniel, and Horacio A. Larreguy. "Agents of the regime? Traditional leaders and electoral politics in South Africa." *The Journal of Politics* 80, no. 2 (2018): 382–399.
[88] Boone, *Property and political order in Africa*; Cruise O'Brien, Donal. *The Mourides of Senegal: the political and economic organization of an Islamic brotherhood.* Oxford. Clarendon Press, 1971.
[89] Grzymala-Busse and Jones Luong "Reconceptualizing the state": 531.

abstain from promoting non-state legal institutions or even to suppress them out of the fear that these alternatives forums of power might be hijacked by a challenger or pose a challenge themselves. For example, in Egypt, Nasser abolished religious courts in part to "break down the independent political power of religious authorities who had opposed his revolutionary agenda."[90] In turn, if the ruler is rather weak or challenged, then their approach toward legal pluralism is conditional on who is behind the challenge. If traditional authorities support the challenge, the ruler is likely to try to suppress them. If the challenge comes from elsewhere, the ruler can promote non-state legal authorities in order to build an alternative ruling coalition. For instance, in Sudan in 1983 President Nimeiri imposed Sharia law in "a futile attempt to save his failing presidency" after economic crises and a challenge from the liberal opposition.[91]

All dimensions of the politics of legal pluralism are closely interdependent. For example, the greater the ruler's control over the population and elites, the more autonomy the ruler can ensure from the metropole. In order to separate these factors and analyze the role of the balance of power on the strategic use of legal pluralism, I focus on the transformative effects of conflict. Conflict presents a shock to entrenched political systems. It influences the dimensions of political order such as autonomy from the center, legitimacy, and the ruler's coalition-building. Focusing on these changes allows one to observe the relationships between different components of political order, and thus further explore the seemingly intractable dilemmas of state-building.

Legal Pluralism and Political Control after Conflict

Separatist conflict as a culmination of the confrontation between center and periphery is likely to make local autonomy the key political issue. Therefore, the strategies of boundary control become vital. If the separatists win, they will typically want to ensure their victory by institutionally promoting legal systems that are outside of the center's system of justice. If the separatists lose, the postwar local rulers imposed by the center will have to signal at least some autonomy to show that they are not just puppets. For example, the imposition of Sharia law by the Indonesian

---

[90] Sezgin, *Human rights under state-enforced religious family laws in Israel, Egypt and India*: 9.
[91] Massoud, *Law's fragile state*: 213.

state became the guarantee of local autonomy in Aceh in the context of the prolonged separatist conflict.[92]

Conflict also affects the nature of the elite coalitions that rulers need to secure their political survival. Perhaps the most important elite transformation is driven by the *militarization of authority*. Conflict ultimately increases the role that the military plays in politics: it may bring military personnel to top political positions or make them key members of the ruling coalition.[93] Professional militaries in many countries hold secular modernist views and might therefore push against non-state legal systems. Separatist conflict, however, brings to the political arena non-state armed actors too – warlords and former rebels.[94] The incorporation of these actors into governmental processes in many post-conflict societies leads to the rise of a distinct type of government official that I call *rebel-bureaucrats*. These former rebels usually are not socialized through standard military or bureaucratic routines and might hold strong religious and communal identities developed during the conflict. Such officials are thus often less likely to follow the letter of the law and to prefer non-state dispute resolution. A ruler's policy toward non-state legal systems has to take into consideration the preferences of this "constituency with the guns."

Conflict outcomes at the macro-level can alter the coalition-formation process by changing the relative strength of the local ruler *vis-à-vis* the potential challengers. If the separatist conflict ends with a decisive military victory on one side, then the local regime established in the aftermath is likely to be consolidated. If the conflict ends with a negotiated settlement or a stalemate, the peripheral ruler is likely to face many serious elite challengers and may end up quite weak. In other words, conflicts, depending on the mode of the resolution, can produce very strong and very weak rulers who are both likely to engage in the promotion of legal pluralism albeit for different reasons. Nevertheless, a top-down imposition of legal order is an endeavor with far from certain results. To a large degree it depends on lay individuals' legal beliefs and behavior. In the next section, I explore state-building lawfare from the bottom-up.

---

[92] Aspinall, Edward. *Islam and nation: Separatist rebellion in Aceh, Indonesia.* Stanford University Press, 2009: 209–213.

[93] Eibl, Ferdinand, Steffen Hertog, and Dan Slater. "War makes the regime: Regional rebellions and political militarization worldwide." *British Journal of Political Science* 51, no. 3 (2021): 1002–1023.

[94] Driscoll, *Warlords and Coalition Politics*; Mukhopadhyay, Dipali. *Warlords, strongman governors, and the state in Afghanistan.* Cambridge University Press, 2014; Marten, *Warlords*; Staniland, "States, insurgents, and wartime political orders."

SOCIAL ORDER: LEGAL POLITICS FROM BELOW

Social order is one of the most fundamental social science concepts that deals with the question "what is it that glues societies together and prevents them from disintegrating into chaos and war?"[95] Social order is often understood in two related ways: as predictable patterns of behavior and as cooperation. Some scholars use the concept of social order very broadly to encompass "a web of all social, political, and economic institutions that characterize a society."[96] I take a narrow view of social order as the distribution of social control that comes from the aggregate of individual beliefs and behavior toward resolution of everyday disputes. The intricate link between law and social order has been emphasized by theorists since Plato and Aristotle. In some recent studies, dispute resolution was also highlighted as a major component of social order. For instance, David Skarbek has stressed that adjudication of disputes is "perhaps the most important form of governance" that prison gangs provide for the social order of the criminal underworld.[97] My understanding of social order starts from the question of how people relate to law and choose between forums of justice.

How Do People Choose among Forums of Justice?

How and why do people turn to law? How do people choose between state and non-state legal systems? Law and society scholarship documents that disputing is a complex multi-party and multistage process. For example, Laura Nader and Harry Todd distinguished three stages: the grievance stage in which an individual recognizes their injury, the conflict stage in which the individual confronts the other party, and the dispute stage in which the conflict is brought to the public arena for adjudication.[98] Related is the influential pyramid model of disputing that goes through naming, blaming, and claiming stages.[99] Disputing can take many different avenues: lumping it, self-help, informal negotiation, alternative dispute resolution. Formal litigation is always a tiny fraction of the

---

[95] Elster, Jon. *The cement of society: A survey of social order.* Cambridge University, 1989: 1.
[96] North, Wallis, and Weingast, *Violence and social orders.*
[97] Skarbek, *The social order of the underworld,* 146.
[98] Nader and Todd, *The disputing process.*
[99] Felstiner et al., "The emergence and transformation of disputes."

disputing forms. Legal pluralism further complicates the picture: individuals can draw on multiple alternative legal systems to resolve their disputes. I thus focus on people's choice of arbitration systems – whether state or non-state – along with what they say about these multiple systems.

Law as seen from below is often represented by the closely related concepts of *legal mobilization* and *legal consciousness*. Legal mobilization is primarily about behavior – employing law to express a grievance, desire, or demand.[100] Legal consciousness encompasses legal beliefs, popular understandings of right and wrong, perceptions of legal entitlements, and moral foundations behind the pursuit of redress.[101] Under legal pluralism, these beliefs and behaviors reflect the everyday choices made between alternative forums of justice. This bottom-up perspective allows scholars to emphasize the agency of lay individuals against a backdrop of large structural forces behind legal pluralism, such as colonialism.[102]

Legal beliefs and behaviors are in a complicated relationship though.[103] Behaviors are collectively negotiated through interaction and are context dependent, "meaning that they belong to situations as much as individuals."[104] Thus, legal behavior does not always follow from legal consciousness. Acknowledging this complexity, I assume that legal beliefs and behavior under legal pluralism are in part shaped by both normative considerations and instrumental forces.

Normative considerations are driven by beliefs about what are appropriate behaviors given a situation, role, and identity. What ought to be done is the guiding principle. This principle is informed by beliefs,

---

[100] McCann, Michael. *Rights at work: Pay equity reform and the politics of legal mobilization.* University of Chicago Press, 1994; Zemans, Frances. "Legal mobilization: The neglected role of the law in the political system." *American Political Science Review* 77, no. 3 (1983): 690–703.

[101] Ewick, Patricia, and Susan S. Silbey. *The common place of law: Stories from everyday life.* University of Chicago Press, 1998. I follow primarily what Ewick and Silbey call "liberal" tradition that suggest that consciousness emerges out of the aggregated attitudes of individuals (p. 36).

[102] Sartori, Paolo. *Visions of justice: Sharī'a and cultural change in Russian Central Asia.* Brill, 2016: 9. Sartori insightfully applied the concept of legal consciousness to the social order of Muslim subjects of colonial Central Asia under the Russian rule.

[103] Lehoucq, Emilio, and Whitney Taylor. "Conceptualizing legal mobilization: How should we understand the deployment of legal strategies?" *Law & Social Inquiry* 45, no. 1 (2020): 166–193.

[104] Jerolmack, Colin, and Shamus Khan. "Talk is cheap: Ethnography and the attitudinal fallacy." *Sociological Methods & Research* 43, no. 2 (2014): 178–209.

routines, habits, and social norms. Normative choices are often based on fast, automatic, instinctive, and emotional cognition. For example, many individuals often opt out of using courts in order to preserve good relations with their family members, neighbors, and communities.[105] Normative choices are especially likely to prevail in the domain of moral issues.

The appropriateness of a legal system is determined by perceptions of procedural fairness and by group identification.[106] If these group affiliations are associated with distinct legal systems, then this implies that the salience of such affiliation will influence legal preferences and behavior. For instance, people with a very strong religious identity might always choose religious law, irrespective of any practical considerations. Identity and legal consciousness are thus mutually constitutive.[107]

The normative perspective on legal choices corresponds to insights from cultural theories of law. Sally Merry highlighted that state law and non-state legal systems are not just a set of rules and enforcement mechanisms, but also "a system of thought by which certain forms of relations come to seem natural and taken for granted."[108] One of the founders of this tradition Clifford Geertz showed how the understanding and the use of law and custom reflect cultural codes for interpreting the world, and construct facts, truth, justice, responsibility, and causality.[109] Relatedly, John Bowen showed how state law, Sharia and customary law in Indonesia serve as repertoires of reasoning about how "family" is to be understood and reproduced.[110] Thus, in this perspective, legal choices reflect norms, social meanings, patterned social interactions, and other aspects of reality that are taken for granted.

In contrast to the normative approach, *the instrumental approach* is about interests. It assumes that if alternative legal systems lead to divergent outcomes, individuals will be inclined to engage in forum-shopping

---

[105] Merry, Sally Engle. *Getting justice and getting even: Legal consciousness among working-class Americans.* University of Chicago Press, 1990; Hendley, Kathryn. *Everyday Law in Russia.* Cornell University Press, 2017.

[106] Tyler, Tom R. "The psychology of procedural justice: A test of the group-value model." *Journal of Personality and Social Psychology* 57, no. 5 (1989): 830; *Why people obey the law.* Princeton University Press, 2006.

[107] Chua, Lynette J., and David M. Engel. "Legal consciousness reconsidered." *Annual Review of Law and Social Science* 15 (2019): 335–353.

[108] Merry, "Legal Pluralism": 889.

[109] Geertz, Clifford. "Local knowledge: Fact and law in comparative perspective." *Local Knowledge: Further Essays in Interpretive Anthropology* 175 (1983): 215–234.

[110] Bowen, *Islam, law, and equality in Indonesia*: 8.

and choose the legal system that best serves their own interests. Forum-shopping is pervasive in many contexts, from international trade arbitration to choosing customary forums in western Sumatra.[111] The concept of self-interest is potentially so inclusive as to be "too big to fail." I operationalize it as following the logic of consequences – getting the most favorable judgment or verdict in a dispute. Individual self-interest is idiosyncratic, but group interests can serve as a good proxy. Legal pluralism has large distributional consequences along group lines determined by age, class, and social status. For instance, customary law gives a lot of power to older generations. Therefore, it is plausible to assume that older people will be more likely to support customary law.

The most important group interest under legal pluralism is gender. As I discussed above, gendered family law disputes have large distributional consequences. There is empirical evidence that when women have the option to choose, they are indeed more likely to prefer the state dispute resolution system to traditional justice.[112] Intersectionality of gender with race, political position, age, and class surely complicates this picture. But in general, women and other groups marginalized by religious and customary law have an instrumental motivation to rely on state law.

Instrumental considerations include not only the favorability of the expected outcome, but also calculations of the costs. Scholars have explained the marked preference for customary justice forums over state judiciary by their accessibility – in terms of travel and material costs – among other more normative factors like perceived transparency and congruence with local values.[113] Costliness of access to formal state law demands attention to the role of resources, from material to social capital, in determining legal choices.

Social pressure is the major cost that individuals have to bear in mind when making legal choices. For this book, the most important consideration is that families and communities led by powerholders who are the

---

[111] Busch, Marc. "Overlapping institutions, forum shopping, and dispute settlement in international trade." *International Organization* 61, no. 4 (2007): 735–761; von Benda-Beckmann, Keebet. "Forum shopping and shopping forums: Dispute processing in a Minangkabau village in West Sumatra." *The Journal of Legal Pluralism and Unofficial Law* 13, no. 19 (1981): 117–159.

[112] Cooper, Jasper. "State capacity and gender inequality: Experimental evidence from Papua New Guinea." *Unpublished Manuscript* (2018); Sandefur, Justin, and Bilal Siddiqi. "Delivering justice to the poor: theory and experimental evidence from Liberia." In *World Bank Workshop on African Political Economy, Washington, DC, May*, vol. 20, 2013.

[113] Lubkemann et al., "Neither state nor custom."

beneficiaries of customary and religious law, impose social sanctions, including sanctions as severe as ostracism and violence, upon individuals who utilize state law. Community cohesion determines the effectiveness of such social pressure.

I assume that legal choice is based to a significant degree on the relative prevalence of normative versus instrumental considerations: norms, identities, and routines versus interests, resources and costs. I argue that legacies of conflict can affect the balance of these considerations and therefore shape legal choices. In particular, experiences of conflict might actualize group interests though the wartime transformation of social roles, especially in gender relations; redistribute material and social capital; raise the salience of ethnic and religious identities; and change the effectiveness of social pressure by influencing community cohesion. This framework allows me to formulate two major logics for understanding the role of legacies of conflict in individual legal choices. I turn to these two logics next.

How Conflict May Affect Legal Choices

Recent political science scholarship has consistently concluded that experiences of conflict affect ethnic, religious, and political identities.[114] Laia Balcells has shown that victimization experiences during the Spanish civil war led to the rejection of the state. Lisa Blaydes, drawing on research in Iraq, argues that when state repression is collective and severe, individuals come to believe that they share a "linked fate" with their fellow group members, which increases group identity and solidarity. Noam Lupu and Leonid Peisakhin trace how the intensity of family victimization during the forced deportation of Crimean Tatars affected Tatar ethnic identity and attitudes towards the Russian state. Arturas Rozenas and his coauthors find a similar pattern at the community level: they show that communities that were subjected to indiscriminate violence during Stalin's deportation campaign in western Ukraine during the

---

[114] Balcells, Laia. "The consequences of victimization on political identities: Evidence from Spain." *Politics & Society* 40, no. 3 (2012): 311–347; Blaydes, Lisa. *State of Repression: Iraq under Saddam Hussein.* Princeton University Press, 2018; Lupu, Noam, and Leonid Peisakhin. "The legacy of political violence across generations." *American Journal of Political Science* 61, no. 4 (2017): 836–851; Nair, Gautam, and Nicholas Sambanis. "Violence exposure and ethnic identification: Evidence from Kashmir." *International Organization* 73, no. 2 (2019): 329–363. Rozenas, Arturas, Sebastian Schutte, and Yuri Zhukov. "The political legacy of violence: The long-term impact of Stalin's repression in Ukraine." *Journal of Politics* 79, no. 4 (2017): 1147–1161.

1940s are now significantly less likely to vote for "pro-Russian" parties. These studies support *the logic of alienation*: individuals who experience violence become alienated from the perpetrators of the violence. States are often the primary perpetrators of violence during civil wars. It is thus plausible to assume that such victimization will lead to alienation from state law.

The impact of victimization on attitudes toward the state versus its alternatives is conditional on which side inflicted the harm and also on the subjective attribution of blame. Victimization is then translated into alienation through a process of collective identity formation. I assume that individual blame attribution and collective identity formation are mutually reinforcing and serve as filters between victimization and alienation. The formation of a collective identity allows victimized individuals to overcome fear and actively reject the state.

Alienation logic dominates the recent political science literature. However, in addition to the psychological trauma and change in the salience of communal identities that lay in the foundation of alienation logic, conflict also fundamentally reshuffles societal structures and challenges or outright destroys preexisting forms of social control. Here I once again build on Migdal, who points out that armed conflict, along with revolutions, migration, natural disasters, and epidemics, is the major source of disruption of non-state social orders.[115] Importantly, conflict does not only weaken non-state authorities – the supply side of justice provision; it can also form the demand for state law by disrupting the existing social hierarchies and thus actualizing group interests. I thus contrast the alienation logic with *the logic of disruption of social hierarchies*.

I focus on gender hierarchies in particular. As mentioned above, family disputes that determine control over female sexuality are the key areas of contestation between the state and other social forces. As a result, gender typically features as the central group interest in legal pluralist contexts. Another reason is that armed conflict often has a transformative effect on gender relations. Historical research has shown that the World Wars led to women's empowerment in both economic and political spheres in advanced industrial counties such as the United States and the United Kingdom.[116] For instance, Russian women gained suffrage and equal

[115] Migdal, *Strong Societies and weak states*: 270.
[116] Goldstein, Joshua. *War and gender: How gender shapes the war system and vice versa.* Cambridge University Press, 2003.

legal rights after World War I and the Revolution of 1917. Recent studies have also shown that civil wars too can disrupt and reorder gender relations, spurring women's political representation.[117] For example, Aili Mari Tripp's analysis shows that the largest increase in women's political representation has happened in those African countries that have experienced the most enduring and intense conflicts.

The literature outlines several potential mechanisms behind conflict-induced women's empowerment. These factors are interconnected and the lines between them are quite porous. The first is *a demographic shift*, i.e., changes in the sex ratio or household composition due to the loss of men in armed conflict. As a result, one should expect a link between the share of women and share of female plaintiffs in state courts.

The second mechanism is *a cultural shift* caused by an increase in experiences of agency among women. During a conflict, women often play important combat roles as well as roles in the support networks of the rebellion.[118] Women also engage in social movements against violence. Elisabeth Wood highlights that as a result of war, women often become the interlocutors between their families, communities, and the military actors.[119] This heightened sense of agency potentially changes women's image of their potential roles and their group interests. A realization of their group interests can in turn switch women's preferences toward state law.

The third potential channel of change is *an economic shift*. Conflict kills men and distracts them from economic activities. As a result, women often become the principal breadwinners in their households. This gives women resources to pursue their rights in state courts, which is a costly endeavor. In addition, the experience of inhabiting the breadwinner position is likely to heighten women's self-esteem and thus strengthen the cultural shift mechanism. Tripp puts it the following way:

economic disruptions had consequences for women's status in the household, which in turn affected women's political standing in the community, and both

---

[117] Berry, Marie. *War, women, and power: From violence to mobilization in Rwanda and Bosnia-Herzegovina.* Cambridge University Press, 2018; Cockburn, Cynthia. *The space between us: Negotiating gender and national identities in conflict.* London, UK: Zed Books, 1998; Tripp, Aili Mari. *Women and power in post-conflict Africa.* Cambridge University Press, 2015; Viterna, Jocelyn. *Women in war: The micro-processes of mobilization in El Salvador,* 2013.

[118] Parkinson, Sarah Elizabeth. "Organizing rebellion: Rethinking high-risk mobilization and social networks in war." *American Political Science Review* (2013): 418–432.

[119] Wood, "The social processes of civil war."

of these types of changes had ideational and symbolic outcomes in terms of what became part of the realm of the possible for women in many other spheres.[120]

The fourth mechanism is *an institutional shift* made possible by legislative changes that aim to improve women's rights and cause a proliferation of women's rights organizations. Quotas for women in the positions of power are perhaps the most widely known of these formal institutional changes. However, others include the passage of land rights for women and legislation against gender-based violence. Taken together, these mechanisms of change suggest that experiences of conflict increase the likelihood that women will choose state law over alternative legal systems.[121]

It is worth noting that not all forms of victimization can be expected to lead to women's empowerment. For example, sexual violence may alienate women and their communities from the perpetrators but also diminish women's status in their communities.[122] It is also important to note that conflict often spurs hypermasculinity, including violence against women and a backlash against women's potential advancement.[123] As a result of this backlash – when women are "forced back to kitchens and fields" – there should be no observable gender differences in legal preferences and behavior.

War-induced transformation of gender relations is just a part of the more general process of transformation of social hierarchies. All kinds of hierarchies are ruined in the process of community disintegration that war often brings. Violence, displacement, and the polarization of political identities diminish community and family social control, as well as weaken generational and clan hierarchies. As a result, families and communities are less able to force their members to rely on customary and religious justice systems. This can lead to more individuals turning to the

---

[120] Tripp, *Women and power in post-conflict Africa*: 35.

[121] I understand women's empowerment in a rather thin way – that is, as an outcome of the process of transformation of gender roles characterized by an increase in women's sense of agency, social status, material resources, and access to political and legal institutions. Feminist scholarship has developed a richer understanding of women's empowerment as "the process by which women redefine gender roles in ways which extend their possibilities for being and doing." The latter approach also stresses that "struggles for empowerment tended to be collective efforts." See Mosedale, Sarah. "Assessing women's empowerment: Towards a conceptual framework." *Journal of International Development* 17, no. 2 (2005): 243–257.

[122] García-Ponce, Omar. "Women's political participation after civil war: Evidence from Peru." Unpublished manuscript, 2017.

[123] Berry, *War, women, and power*; Pankhurst, Donna. *Gendered peace: Women's struggles for post-war justice and reconciliation.* Routledge, 2012.

state. When individuals go to state courts in large numbers, it constitutes what I call state-building from below.

The logic of alienation, of course, assumes the opposite – that communities that experience violence will become more cohesive, reinforce their hierarchies, boundaries, and sense of belonging, and thus experience a bolstering of non-state social control. At the same time, the logics of conflict-induced alienation and disruption of hierarchies are not necessarily incompatible. It is entirely plausible that conflict reshapes the identities of some people and thus pushes them toward non-state legal systems, while at the same time disrupting social hierarchies and so allowing other individuals to pursue their interests in state courts.

The social ordering of legal pluralism from below and the political ordering from above are obviously interconnected. For instance, the salience of group identities affects both individual choices among alternative legal systems and the local ruler's legitimation strategies. If conflict leads to alienation from state law, a local ruler can gain legitimacy by promoting non-state legal systems. In contrast, if conflict leads to the disruption of traditional hierarchies, the local ruler can build their legitimation by either siding with the empowered women and other marginalized groups or by attempting to reestablish the pre-conflict social order to win the support of men and other privileged groups.

* * *

The theoretical sketch presented in this chapter analyzed the process of state-building in the periphery in terms of lawfare. It looked at the competing orders of social control and political power. Legal pluralism, nested sovereignty, gender cleavage, and separatist conflict were taken as key factors in state-building at the periphery. Legal pluralism was seen to reflect the fragmented social control. Struggles for social control are especially contested in gender relations and the family law domain, which makes gender the key societal divide. Nested sovereignty, whether in the form of empire or federalism, reveals the heterogenous nature of the state and the contradictions of center–periphery relations. Separatist conflict fractures sovereignty even further and actualizes gender divide. It also politicizes group identities, brings new groups such as former rebels into the political arena, and redetermines the distribution of political power among the peripheral rulers, the metropole, and local challengers. I thus argued that state-building on this shaky ground can be productively analyzed as legal politics from both above and below.

The view from above focuses on governmental strategies toward non-state legal systems. I contrasted the role of state capacity, ideology, and popular demand with the logic of local political control. I outlined how the promotion of non-state systems can help local rulers win legitimacy, increase autonomy from the center, and build a coalition out of elite groups. In turn, the view from below pictures social order as the aggregate of individual choices regarding state versus non-state legal systems. I contrasted normative and instrumental forces behind legal choices and outlined two logics as to how conflict might affect social ordering. The logic of alienation postulates that individuals and communities who experience state violence in the course of a separatist conflict will heighten their commitment to religion and tradition and ultimately reject state law. The logic of disrupted hierarchies states the opposite: experiences of conflict will weaken non-state social control and thus lead to an unintentional state-building from below driven by those who benefit from state law.

Of course, this theoretical sketch does not claim to provide definitive answers to the fundamental, enduring – perhaps even philosophical – questions raised here: what drives individual interests, what holds a society together, how are identities built, how do governments control societies, etc.? These questions will always be unanswerable. This book is just one small addition to the library that precedes it. Furthermore, what I have borrowed from this library was to a large degree shaped by what I experienced in the field. In short, this chapter presented a carefully curated and stylized theoretical framework. The next chapter presents ethnographic narratives from my immersion in Chechen social life which form the foundation of my understanding of the local knowledge and local perspectives of the theoretical phenomena I studied.

2

The Field

Ethnography of Legal Pluralism in Postwar Chechnya

The head of the Council of Elders of the Chechen Republic, Said-Abdulla Akhamadov, is an energetic man in his sixties who wears a splendid tall *papakha* (sheepskin hat). Right after we met, he told me: "Oh, you have a difficult topic, young man. You will never fully understand our customs and our religion." However, there were people who said that basically the opposite is true. For example, Khamzat, a lawyer in his thirties, told me:

People who say that you can't properly study custom and Sharia because you are not a Chechen are wrong. In fact, you, as an outsider, can ask questions about traditions and religion that I, as a Chechen, can't ever ask. The issues of tradition and religion are not up for questioning. If I meet an elder and start asking questions about a particular custom, he will ask me if I am a fool. In contrast, if a guest asks a question about our culture, of course we all will be glad to talk for hours.

I suspect that both positions have some truth in them. As an outsider, I was able to ask almost any questions I wanted. As a person not socialized in the culture, I was never able to fully grasp all the particularities of the customary law and of Sharia as it is practiced in Chechnya.

This chapter analyzes the strengths and limitations of my fieldwork by presenting ethnographic narratives about immersion in Chechen family and social life, researcher positionality and subjectivity, and the ethics of the study. I understand ethnography as a sensibility, a commitment to "glean the meanings that the people under study attribute to their social and political reality."[1] Some readers might expect to see such materials in

[1] Schatz, Edward, *Political ethnography: What immersion contributes to the study of power.* University of Chicago Press, 2009: 5.

59

an appendix, as they disrupt the flow of the argument. I however ask you to read the chapter as a part of the story. Here I follow Georgi Derluguian's book *Bourdieu's Secret Admirer in the Caucasus* that starts with ethnographic descriptions that aim to instill "some practical sense of the complex and perhaps exotic environments we shall be investigating."[2] I also follow Katherine Cramer's *The Politics of Resentment*, where the author explains that "knowing how I went about collecting these data is important for understanding what I learned from them."[3] The chapter thus serves two purposes. First, it presents the methodological reflections that are necessary to situate the study. These reflections tell the story of how I formulated the research question and gathered evidence to answer it. Second, it provides the key substantive insights – insiders' perspectives on legal pluralism, conflict, and the foundations of Chechnya's social and political orders. Thus, ethnography in my case is not just a method of data gathering, but a constitutive element of my study that grounds its theoretical abstractions.[4]

"ENOUGH GIRLS!" OR AN IMMERSION

During my fieldwork, I developed a particularly strong connection to one person, who became my host and my guide in the matters of war, legal pluralism, and all other things I was curious about in the field. Originally, I heard about Satsita Israilova from one of my colleagues in the community of researchers of the Caucasus, who described her as "the leader of civil society in Chechnya."[5] Satsita was the director of the Chechen National Library. The library was situated in a modernist glass and steel building, one of the largest in the city center of Grozny. It was famous for hosting numerous conferences, roundtables, art exhibits, and clubs where people discussed books or practiced speaking in English.

I arranged an interview with Satsita during one of my early field trips to Chechnya. The interview was held in her office in the library. When I told Satsita that I was interested in adat, Chechen customary law, her eyes lit up. Satsita told me that for her entire life her favorite activity had

---

[2] Derluguian, Georgi. *Bourdieu's secret admirer in the Caucasus: A world-system biography*. University of Chicago Press, 2005: 29.

[3] Cramer, Katherine. *The politics of resentment: Rural consciousness in Wisconsin and the rise of Scott Walker*. University of Chicago Press, 2016: 23.

[4] Wedeen, Lisa. "Reflections on ethnographic work in political science." *Annual Review of Political Science* 13 (2010): 257.

[5] Satsita encouraged me to share her story under her real name in my academic writings.

been to question elders about Chechen traditions. As a result, Satsita had acquired great knowledge of adat. Our conversation lasted for several hours, and in the end, she asked me where was I staying in Grozny. That time I was staying in a rented apartment in the very center of the city. When she heard my response, Satsita said that this was a shame: "You are a guest. Next time you come, you will stay with me." I gratefully accepted her invitation and stayed with Satsita during my subsequent trips to Chechnya. My relationship with Satsita, who semi-jokingly adopted me as her son, became an extremely important part of my study. First and foremost, she shared with me her extensive knowledge of adat and Chechen history. Soon I found out that Satsita's family had an important role in this history.

History Is Personal

Satsita's grandfather, Khasan Israilov, organized one of the major rebellions against the Soviet authorities in the mountainous parts of Chechnya in the 1940s. Khasan's life trajectory is emblematic of the great historical transformations that took place in Chechnya in the first part of the twentieth century. He received a good Islamic education and also obtained a law degree from a university in southern Russia. In 1929, Khasan joined the Bolshevik party. He was writing prose and poetry and worked as a journalist for one of the leading newspapers of the Soviet Chechen Republic. In the early 1930s, Khasan was arrested for his critical articles about the corruption of local-level officials, but soon he was released. After his release, Khasan went to study in Moscow at the Communist University of the Toilers of the East. Other students at that time included Deng Xiaoping, Ho Chi Minh, and Jomo Kenyatta, as well as intelligentsia from the North Caucasus.

Upon his return to the Caucasus, Khasan worked as a prosecutor in one of the mountainous districts of Checheno-Ingushetia. However, he remained critical of the regime. In 1940, he wrote a letter to the Soviet leadership in which he claimed that the Soviet government aimed to annihilate the Chechen people, and announced a rebellion that lasted for four years in the form of small-scale guerrilla attacks. In 1944, Khasan was killed by NKVD (KGB) agents. One of Khasan's sons, Magomed, refused to surrender and continued to fight along with dozens of other rebels in the mountains of the borderland region of Georgia. Magomed's group of rebels surrendered only in 1957 with a guarantee of amnesty from the Soviet authorities. Magomed started a civilian life and married Sero, a woman from the Pankisi Gorge. Sero gave birth to three daughters. The parents named the third daughter "Satsita," which in Chechen means "enough girls!" The spell worked and Sero then gave birth to a son. But Magomed never saw his son's birth – he was assassinated by KGB agents on the street in front of his house. Sero was left with four young children and the status of being the wife of an enemy of the Soviet people.

Satsita's family history illustrates some of the core manifestations of adat. Originally Sero refused Magomed's proposal to marry him. She loved another man from her village. But Magomed, the former rebel, decided to try his fortune and kidnapped Sero. Teymuraz, Sero's father, was extremely angry, but forced Sero to marry Magomed to avoid any possible speculations about the family's honor.[6] Sero never loved Magomed. However, after she became a widow when she was just twenty-seven, she refused endless offers to remarry, even from the man from her village whom she loved. Why? Because another marriage would have meant leaving her children with their father's family. Instead, she appealed to the elders of Magomed's family and asked their permission to leave the children with her and let her stay in her husband's house as his widow. The elders agreed to her plea. Magomed's relatives avenged his death in accordance with adat: they killed a brother of the KGB agent who they thought was responsible for his assassination. Thus, bride kidnapping, blood revenge, and adat norms regarding children were intertwined in Satsita's life from the very beginning.

Satsita's life trajectory illuminated for me life in Chechnya during the late Soviet Union, the troubled times of the Chechen national revolution and the de facto independent state of Ichkeria, and especially the wars. Satsita never left Chechnya during either war and her recollections of the wartime period largely shaped my knowledge of civilian experiences during the Chechen wars. For instance, from Satsita's stories came the vivid image of how she, her mother, and their neighbors hid from artillery shelling in a basement near their house in the fall of 1999 and winter of 2000. The nonstop shelling forced them to live in this basement for

---

[6] On the similar role of discourses of honor and shame in forcing families to accept marriage through bride abduction in post-Soviet Central Asia, see Werner, Cynthia. "Bride abduction in post-Soviet Central Asia: Marking a shift towards patriarchy through local discourses of shame and tradition." *Journal of the Royal Anthropological Institute* 15, no. 2 (2009): 314–331.

several months, and the only food they had was canned tomatoes. This story has an epilogue. One morning Satsita and I were taking a cab from her small house in the outskirts of Grozny to the library in the city center. The driver refused to take the money for the ride. He said to Satsita that he remembered her: she had allowed this man, his wife, and their nine children to stay in their basement for several weeks in the winter of 2000, even though the canned tomatoes were almost gone. This encounter taught me the power of shared lived experiences of conflict. It also suggested that even though Satsita is in every way a unique character, her life story resonates with the experiences of other people of her generation.

Satsita grew up in Grozny, a city with a sizeable Russian population. The category of "Russians" included ethnic Russians, Ukrainians, Armenians, and Jews. Chechens and Ingush were minorities in the city. In Satsita's school there were as many Chechens as Russians though. Like many other Chechens who had lived in the Soviet Union, Satsita remembered that period as a time of inter-ethnic friendships and intercultural exchange. However, at the same time, Satsita also remembered numerous incidents of discrimination. For example, one of her teachers referred to all Chechen students as "bandits" and to Satsita as "the granddaughter of the main bandit."

Family history turned from a burden into a potential resource with the Chechen revolution of 1991. The story of Khasan Israilov, who had belonged to the Chechen intelligentsia and rebelled against Soviet power, became attractive to the emerging Chechen nationalist movement. Ichkeria's officials even renamed one of the streets in Grozny after him. In turn, Satsita, by then a young woman, received numerous marriage proposals from those who wanted to marry the granddaughter of the famous rebel. She declined all of them. In the early 1990s Satsita finished her college degree and started to work as a librarian. Her mother lovingly grumbled that Satsita spent most of her time reading "Russian Korans." This occupation was not a usual one for a young Chechen woman. The library system at the time mostly employed Russian speakers. However, soon after the revolution of 1991, most of them left the region, including Satsita's boss Iosif Asailovich. As one of the few who did not leave, Satsita became the head of the Grozny library system at the age of twenty-seven.

The time of the revolutions, political struggles, and wars was not especially suitable for library work. During the post-Soviet period, Satsita fought endless attempts to expropriate the Grozny city library building and turn it into a restaurant. In this struggle, she even ended

up in the office of Dzhokhar Dudayev, the First President of the independent Chechnya, whom she remembers from their meeting in his office as a
tired and lonely man. Dudayev helped to keep the city library open.

During the wars, Grozny was extensively bombed and almost all of the
libraries in the city burned down. Satsita experienced it as a personal
tragedy and walked around the city to collect books from the ruins. She
then stored them in the basement of her own house. There were tens of
thousands of books stored there. As she recalled, the first book in this
collection was Plutarch's "Lives of the Noble Greeks and Romans,"
which she had found in the ruins of the destroyed headquarters of the
famous Chechen warlord Salman Raduyev. In the immediate aftermath of
the Second Chechen War, in February 2000, Satsita reopened the City
Library of Grozny, which for a long time remained the only venue open to
the public in the destroyed city. Both the Russian army and the rebels
called Satsita crazy but let her keep the library running. The library
became a magnet for those who stayed in the city and served the crucial
role of maintaining social ties. Few came to read – people mostly needed
communication and some normalcy in their life. Satsita organized art
exhibits, roundtables, and poetry readings. Due to her efforts to save
the books and keep the library open during both wars, Satsita became a
legendary figure in Grozny.

On Local Knowledge

Having Satsita as my host was a tremendous advantage for my study.
Satsita's references helped me to secure many interviews with representatives of the Chechen intelligentsia, scholars, and many prominent former
politicians. Satsita also helped me with the logistics of the study. I received
an informal office in the library, where I held some of my interviews and
wrote my field diaries. Satsita also asked librarians across Chechnya to
help me with my study. Libraries exist in every town and village in
Chechnya, and she knew the librarians in almost all of them. Because of
that, when I needed to go to a village, I always had an initial contact there.

Being in the field for a long time and living with Satsita were immensely
helpful for understanding the basics of family relations in Chechen society. During my stay with Satsita, I met many of her relatives, neighbors,
and colleagues, who all shared with me their life stories and cases of
disputes resolved according to one of the alternative legal systems. Out of
the 150 employees of Satsita's library, perhaps 90 percent were women,

with many of whom I had numerous conversations. These conversations helped me to partially overcome my inability to access women interviewees, which I further discuss below. Overall, the knowledge that I gained from conversations with Satsita's relatives, neighbors, and colleagues was almost as important for my understanding of everyday disputes in Chechnya as the insights from my interviews.

Satsita sometimes disagreed with my interpretations. Her own example contradicts one of the major conclusions of this book, that war "empowered" women to use state law. Conflict had indeed empowered Satsita. Her fearless activism during the war made her one of the leaders of the Chechen intelligentsia. She occupies an important position. But she did not embrace Russian state law. In fact, she is a self-described "die-hard adat supporter." This is evident from her everyday behavior: Satsita always stands up when a man walks into her office – even if this man is twenty years old and works *for* her as a driver. As she would say, "This is our tradition." This attitude also manifests in high-stakes situations: in one of her personal disputes, Satsita abstained from going to court even though this would have brought her a lot of money, and instead behaved according to adat. Thus, Satsita was a constant reminder for me to clearly see the heterogenous patterns in women's legal consciousness and behavior.

Outside of Satsita's house and the library, when I was not traveling to different locations outside of Grozny, I usually spent time in the Center for Contemporary Art – an art café where intellectual Chechen youth gather in the evenings. The café hosted exhibits, live music concerts, and public lectures. People also gathered to play board games, drink tea, and talk. This was basically the only place of its kind, and I became a regular there. Both men and women gathered at the café. Because of that, some of my respondents considered the café regulars "too liberal." But for me this was a perfect setting to socialize with the young Chechen men and women. I spoke with them about their families, contemporary Chechen literature and music, family relations, and dating. I wouldn't have asked similar questions in the setting of a formal interview. Many people at the café gave me advice on my study and connected me to their relatives, colleagues, and friends. I visited the native villages of some of my interlocutors, went to their families' weddings and funerals, and we went together to coffee shops, shopping malls, and fast-food restaurants, and watched football together. These moments were very useful for gathering the "metadata," using Lee Ann Fujii's terms: anecdotes, rumors, conspiracy theories, and telling moments of silence, as well as nonverbal elements of communication, such as dress, gestures, and facial expressions.[7] In post-conflict and authoritarian contexts, these metadata can reveal a lot. Since I was a regular at the café, many people grew used to me. When I returned to the field after months of being away, a common reaction was "We haven't seen you in a while, where have you been?" In some sense, I was becoming a local. But in many other regards, I was an outsider. The interplay between my outsider identities and local knowledge shaped my study in important ways.

POSITIONALITY AND SUBJECTIVITY

When I decided to study the North Caucasus, I had no connection to the region – no family history, no friends or acquaintances. Essentially, I remained an outsider even after spending many months in the region. There were different markers of my outsider status, but perhaps one of the clearest ones was on my face – I wore glasses, which is considered "unmanly" in Chechnya and the neighboring regions. Another visible marker was my relatively long curly hair, which was in stark contrast with the short hairstyle that was standard among men in the region. Thus, even by glancing at me, almost everyone was able to identify me as an outsider. In what follows, I analyze how my outsider status shaped the study. This task is not only analytical, because, as Zachariah Mampilly rightly puts it, "recognizing our own positionality allows us to grant our field subjects the basic dignity they deserve."[8]

"This Cat Is Handsome"

The largest barrier for me in the field was the fact that I didn't speak the Chechen language. As a result, I wasn't able to read many social interactions that I observed, and thus missed important elements of social relations. Two Chechens will almost always talk to each other in Chechen in a private setting. Chechen is a part of the Nakho-Dagestani language family, which is unrelated to the Indo-European family.[9] It is very difficult to learn it outside of the natural language environment. Even

---

[7] Fujii, Lee Ann. "Shades of truth and lies: Interpreting testimonies of war and violence." *Journal of Peace Research* 47, no. 2 (2010): 231–241.

[8] Mampilly, Zachariah Cherian. "The Field is everywhere." In Krause and Szekeley, *Stories from the field*: 277–285.

[9] Aliroyev, Ibragim. *Yazyk, istoriia i kultura Vainakhov* [Language, history and culture of Vainakh People]. Grozny, 1990.

Chechen families who live outside of Chechnya have a hard time transmitting the language to their children. For outsiders it is an even more complicated task. For a long time, the only phrase in Chechen that I knew was *Khara tsitsig khaza du*, which meant "This cat (male) is handsome." Since many Chechen households have cats, the phrase proved to be a useful icebreaker. Overall, though, my language skills in Chechen never served any other function than entertaining my interlocutors. Over the time I spent in Chechnya, I learned basic phrases, but it seemed impossible to learn the language anywhere close to being able to use it as a research tool. Therefore, I relied on Russian, my native language.

Russian is often the default option for communication in public settings in Chechnya; it is the language of bureaucracy, education, and academia. This was true even during the independence period of the 1990s – the vast majority of newspapers that were published then, though staunchly anti-Russian in content, were published in the Russian language. The Cyrillic alphabet poorly transmits Chechen phonetics and, as a result, few Chechens, even those who are perfectly fluent, can read in Chechen. At the same time, almost everyone is fluent in Russian. I encountered only one interlocutor who did not speak the Russian language at all – a 115-year-old man in one of the mountainous villages. His neighbors were happy to translate. Because Russian is the second language for Chechens, many speak a literary version. The Chechen intelligentsia does not miss an opportunity to highlight the fact that the giants of Russian literature Mikhail Lermontov and Leo Tolstoy both spent time in Chechnya. In fact, one of the villages in Chechnya is named after Tolstoy.

Research as "a Truly Islamic Endeavor"

Religion was a recurring identity concern during my study. Chechnya is a very religious society; almost no one will say he or she is an atheist. Many of my interviews and conversations – with imams, university professors, and police officers alike – ended with a question of whether I had considered converting to Islam. There is a simple reason for this. In Islam there is a principle that inviting people to the religion is a meritorious activity. In addition, many people were sure that through studying Sharia I would find my way to Islam. I always remained sensitive to religious issues and carefully listened to the proselytizing speeches. Reading the Koran and academic books on Islam in general, and Islamic law in particular, as well as interviewing clerics across the North Caucasus for several years, made me somewhat knowledgeable about the basics of the Islamic faith. This knowledge in turn allowed me to better structure numerous conversations about religion and show respect for my interlocutors.[10]

The religious conversations became especially heated after the Charlie Hebdo attack in Paris in January 2015. In response to the Charlie Hebdo caricatures of the Prophet Muhammad, Ramzan Kadyrov called for a mass rally in support of the Prophet Muhammad. Almost the entire population of Chechnya gathered for the rally in the main square of Grozny. At the rally, and during the entire fieldtrip that coincided with the Charlie Hebdo attack, I had numerous conversations about it. Even the most liberal among my respondents supported violence against the caricaturists. Another religiously-colored controversial issue that often came up in my interviews and mundane conversations with people in Chechnya was homosexuality. Most of my interlocutors expressed extreme hostility and embraced violence against gay people, justifying it with religious references.[11] In conversations about Charlie Hebdo and the issue of gay rights, I always tried to persuade people away from the violent positions. But otherwise, my numerous conversations about religion were mostly philosophical. And several of my religious interlocutors stated that even though I am not a Muslim, research, the pursuit of knowledge, is "a truly Islamic endeavor."

Between Two Empires

Being *not* Chechen and *not* Muslim was one thing, being Russian was another. Despite the extreme brutality of the Russo-Chechen wars, I never encountered any hostility towards me personally or Russians in general. Many people with whom I spoke hated Boris Yeltsin, who started the Chechen wars, and the generals and the soldiers of the Russian army who committed war crimes, but never Russians as a nation. In fact, many people were nostalgic for the times of the Soviet Union, when Chechnya was a multiethnic republic and many Russians lived there. I benefited from the fact that I was from St. Petersburg, which most of my interlocutors saw as "the city of intelligentsia, where people are cultured and

---

[10] Richard Nielsen similarly highlighted the importance of religious knowledge, in his case the ability to recite Koranic verses, for research on religious authorities and activists. See Nielsen, Richard. 2020. "Recite! Interpretive fieldwork for positivists." In *Stories from the field*: 36–46.

[11] These conversations happened before reports of the wave of state-sponsored violence against gay people in Chechnya that began in 2017. See Elena Milashina "Ubiystvo chesti" [An honor killing]. *Novaya Gazeta*. N 34. April 3, 2017.

kind," in contrast to Moscow and other regions of Russia. My association with St. Petersburg did not provoke hostility even when I went to Aldy, the village in the outskirts of Grozny where special forces from St. Petersburg committed indiscriminate mass killing of civilians during a *zachistka* (sweep operation) in 2000. Moreover, even though I was an outsider in many respects, my interlocutors and I still shared a common language and shared cultural references that to a large degree were preserved even among the post-Soviet generations despite the decade of military conflict.[12]

In fact, without a Russian passport, it would have been nearly impossible to do my fieldwork. Given the political context in Chechnya and Russia overall, my affiliation with an American university was a more problematic identity than my Russian nationality. After the United States put Ramzan Kadyrov on their sanctions list due to human rights violations, the authorities of Chechnya turned bitterly anti-American. Despite the repeated advice of my trusted interlocutors in Chechnya to avoid mentioning America altogether, I always informed people whom I met that I was a researcher at a university in the United States. At the same time, I obtained letters of endorsement for my study from two research universities in Moscow – the Higher School of Economics and the Academy of Public Administration. Both schools are connected to the Russian federal government and the latter even has "The President of Russia" in its full name. Affiliation with government-connected Russian universities and an American university at the same time formed an ambiguous identity and endowed me with local legitimacy to carry out the study.

Another manifestation of my strategic positionality was the framing of my research as the exploration of custom, religion and law, rather than a study of conflict, state-building, and political power. Traditions and religion are seen as the domain of culture, rather than the domain of politics, and are therefore less sensitive. Law is also perceived as a legitimate topic. In the end, even the most repressive authoritarian regimes maintain an image of their own legality.[13]

---

[12] Nostalgia for the socialist past is a common feature of post-socialist spaces, including the Muslim-majority peripheries of the Soviet Union in Central Asia. See De Soto, Hermine, and Nora Dudwick, eds. *Fieldwork dilemmas: Anthropologists in postsocialist states.* University of Wisconsin Press, 2000.

[13] See also Massoud, Mark Fathi. "Field research on law in conflict zones and authoritarian states." *Annual Review of Law and Social Science* 12 (2016): 85–106.

In a few situations, my identity of a scholar associated with a prestigious American university put me in the spotlight. On one occasion, I appeared on Chechen national television, a situation that I used to further legitimize my study in the eyes of the Chechen authorities. On another occasion, the media affiliated with the *Muftiat* (religious authorities) of the neighboring republic of Ingushetia widely publicized my interview with the Mufti on social media. The Ingush Mufti had a conflict with the governor of Ingushetia and used the fact that a researcher from a famous university had come to meet him to boost his credentials. In this case, I was directly inserted into the political struggle. Interpreting similar situations, Romain Malejacq and Dipali Mukhopadhyay conclude that power relationships between the researcher and their "subjects" are far from unidirectional.[14] The ambiguity of a researcher's power is perhaps best exemplified by the status of the guest.

"You Are Our Guest First of All"

My fieldwork was facilitated by the strong norm of hospitality that is deeply rooted in the societies of the North Caucasus.[15] The guest has a nearly sacred status. I was a guest, therefore almost everyone I met in the field offered me their protection and help. At the same time, guest status made me dependent on my hosts, less free in my movement and ability to communicate with others. As William Reno put it, "The guest belongs to the host."[16] On many occasions, especially in the rural areas, people invited me to spend a night or at least come for a meal in their house. What were supposed to be semi-structured interviews turned into real feasts and hours-long conversations. The guest role was ultimately more important than my gender, nationality, and personality. A telling detail is that I was almost never allowed to pay in cafés when I met with my interlocutors there, by men and women, old and young, rich and poor alike. The guest status overshadowed practical considerations and my objections.

---

[14] Malejacq, Romain, and Dipali Mukhopadhyay. "The 'tribal politics' of field research: A reflection on power and partiality in 21st-century warzones." *Perspectives on Politics* 14, no. 4 (2016): 1014.

[15] On the role of hospitality among Chechens, see Aliroyev, Ibragim, and Zulai Khasbulatova. Gostepriimstvo i Kunachestvo [Hospitality]. In Soloviyeva, Lubov, Zulai Khasbulatova and Valery Tishkov (eds.) *Chechentsy* [The Chechens]. Moscow, 2012.

[16] Cited in Malejacq and Mukhopadhyay, "The 'tribal politics' of field research": 1018.

At the same time, a few people were suspicious of me because they assumed I was working for some intelligence agency, with varying options: FSB because I was a Russian, CIA because I was affiliated with an American university, or Mossad because I had curly hair and as a result, many people assumed I was Jewish.[17] Conspiracy theories are quite widespread in Chechnya and an outsider curious about Chechen society can face distrust. This is of course fully understandable. During the decade-long conflict, Russian secret services and denunciations solicited by them were central to the systematic repressions in Chechnya. Anthony Marra's novel *A Constellation of Vital Phenomena*, fiction based on extensive documentary evidence, vividly captures the ubiquitous presence of the FSB and their informants in Chechen society during the war period.[18] Since the war, the pro-Russian Chechen authorities have been framing the conflict as a result of the foreign intelligence agencies' manipulations. Thus, Chechens have every reason to distrust outsiders who inquire about their lives. However, as I found out, the norm of hospitality can overcome the inclination towards conspiracy theories. Idris, a rich businessman in his fifties, who held strong traditionalist views, told me that he firmly believed that I was "a spy who works for the CIA or Freemasons or something like that. But in the end, that does not matter – I will talk to you anyway. Because you are our guest first of all, and then a spy or whoever you are."

Another particularly helpful feature of the Chechen social context was the high level of connectedness of the society. For instance, to establish my first contacts, when I knew nobody in the region, I went to a wrestling club in my native city St. Petersburg, where my friend was a coach. I knew that wrestling, and martial arts in general, are very popular in the Caucasus, so I asked my friend if he had any people from the Caucasus in his club.[19] He told me that there were plenty and I could talk to any of

---

[17] On the blurred lines between ethnography and intelligence-gathering, see Jesse, Driscoll, and Caroline Schuster. "Spies Like Us." *Ethnography* 19, no. 3 (2017): 411–430. On the role of rumors about researchers in the field, see Fujii, "Shades of truth and lies."

[18] Peter Krause reports similar suspicions from his subjects among Palestinians in several Middle Eastern countries. He writes that "Palestinians, as a people without a state, face significant suspicion and repression everywhere they reside. Therefore, they have interactions with intelligence and security officials at far higher rate than most populations." Krause, Peter. "Navigating born and chosen identities in fieldwork." In *Stories from the field*: 259.

[19] See also Emil Aslan Souileimanov on boxing as an entry point to study Chechen diasporas. Souileimanov, Emil Aslan. "Building trust with ex-insurgents." In *Stories from the field*.

them. This is how I secured my first interview. My first informant, Magomed, happened to have an uncle who was the head of one of the municipal districts in the Caucasus, whom I interviewed later in the field. This became one of the central tools of my research: in the densely connected societies of the North Caucasus, everyone knows everyone, and references from the right people could open almost any door. The connections were not necessarily based on kinship. Making connections through relatives was common, but ties of friendship or professional association were no less prevalent. For example, during my first research trip to Chechnya, I was hosted by a poet, to whom I had been introduced by another poet.

Despite spending a lot of time with Lema, my host-poet, a man in his forties, I never really saw his wife. Lema was an intellectual who expressed liberal progressive ideas, but gender separation of social space in his household was very strict. Lema's wife cooked the food for us in the "women's part" of their small apartment, but it was Lema's son Ahmet, ten years old, who brought the dishes to the main room where we were sitting. I needn't mention that I wasn't able to talk about dispute resolution with Lema's wife. I never asked to talk with her – it was implied that this wasn't appropriate. This illustrates perhaps the major identity factor that shaped my study: gender.

Gender Matters

Chechnya is a patriarchal society, perhaps the most conservative one in terms of gender regimes in the former Soviet Union. Being a male researcher, I was thus on the one hand enabled to talk with men, but on the other hand restricted in access to non-elite female interlocutors. Georgi Derluguian's explanation of how Anna Politkovskaya's reporting of Chechen conflict benefited from her gender is relevant here: "she can gain access to the inner spaces of Chechen women, which remain off limits to a male sociologist like myself. Thus, Politkovskaya could document the massive and possibly routine incidence of rape committed against both Chechen women and Chechen male prisoners by Russian security personnel."[20] Anthropologist Iwona Kaliszewska, doing

---

[20] Derluguian, Georgi. "Introduction: Whose truth?" In Politkovskaya, *A small corner of hell*: 22.

fieldwork with her baby in her arms, provided another example of using her own gender to gain access to both male and female subjects to study sensitive topics in Chechnya and neighboring Dagestan.[21]

On the other hand, had I been a female researcher, I potentially would have had limited access to male-dominated spheres, especially religious institutions.[22] In addition, Russian and Western female researchers and journalists with whom I met in the Caucasus had to spend large portions of their work answering questions about their private life ("Why not married?" "Why no kids?"), to which I was exposed in only a limited manner. They also had to be cautious in their relationships with male counterparts, while I was never treated in a sexualized manner.

Critical inquiries into gender matters and family relations face wariness in Chechen society. For example, in 2019 the North Caucasus branch of Radio Liberty reported the reactions of three prominent female Chechen human rights activists to the media scandal regarding a young Chechen woman who had allegedly been forced by her family to leave a shelter in Moscow and then brought to Chechnya.[23] All three experts stated that Chechen customary law does not discriminate against women. They correctly claimed that arranged and early marriages are extremely rare in modern Chechnya, that many Chechen women receive higher education, and that gender roles vary significantly across social strata and across families. The experts criticized outsiders – Russian human rights organizations, liberal media, and experts on the region – for turning the case into a scandal and hyping "barbaric Chechen traditions" in general.[24] These concerns, widely shared in Chechen society, made me cautious when discussing gender relations in Chechnya and writing about them. However, the insights from different sources of evidence collected on the ground made me confident in the arguments I put forward in this book.

---

[21] Kaliszewska, Iwona, and Maciej Falkowski. *Veiled and unveiled in Chechnya and Daghestan.* London, 2016.

[22] Western female academics are often treated in conservative gender environments as a "third gender" with access to both male and female worlds. See Schwedler, Jillian. "The third gender: Western female researchers in the Middle East." *PS: Political Science and Politics* 39, no. 3 (2006): 425–428.

[23] Garmazhapova, Alexandra. Kavkaz dlya mnogikh prevratilsya v hayp. [The Caucasus became hype for many]. Kavkaz.Realii. July 17, 2019.

[24] These criticisms echo questioning of "whether Muslim women need saving." See Abu-Lughod, Lila. "Do Muslim women really need saving? Anthropological reflections on cultural relativism and its others." *American Anthropologist* 104, no. 3 (2002): 783–790.

Out of the seventy-eight semi-structured interviews that I rely on, only fourteen were with female interlocutors. This was largely due to the fact that the majority of my interviewees were authorities in charge of the alternative legal systems. Customary and religious authorities are exclusively male. Men also dominate the state judiciary and law enforcement agencies. Nevertheless, the interviews with female academics, lawyers, police officers, NGO members, and journalists were very helpful for understanding how the alternative legal systems work. Female interlocutors shared with me their personal experiences of disputes adjudicated within the alternative systems and also cases in which they worked as lawyers.

My exploration of gender relations in Chechnya was facilitated by the strong network of civil society organizations that work on issues of women's empowerment and combating gender-based violence in Chechnya. I was surprised by the presence of this vibrant community of NGOs under the repressive conditions of Kadyrov's Chechnya. I spent many hours in the offices of these NGOs, where their workers shared with me information about their projects and gender issues in Chechnya. For example, lawyers from one NGO told me about their experiences with representing Chechen women in state courts and shared with me transcripts of court hearings on child custody and inheritance disputes. Thus, even though I had little access to female disputants, interviews with the lawyers and NGO workers allowed me to gain important insights on women's perspectives on legal pluralism, for example, the contested constructions of "the moral woman" in the state courtrooms and the places of religious arbitration.

The strict separation of male and female social spaces that I encountered in the poet's house was the exception rather than the norm in Chechnya. Over the course of my fieldwork, I interacted with many women who worked in the government, NGOs, and universities. I became friends with some local female scholars and journalists. Women were the absolute majority of the interviewers who carried out the survey that I organized in Chechnya. These were of course not the "average" Chechens, but university-educated, mostly urban intelligentsia. My inferences about attitudes and behaviors of ordinary Chechen women are based on the analysis of a representative household survey and state courts' comprehensive case records.

Secondary literature on gender in Chechnya, written by local academics who had better direct access to local women, also became an essential research source for me.[25] During my many meetings and conversations with Chechen female academics, they shared with me the results of their studies and their candid observations on gender issues in contemporary Chechnya. Characteristic of the state of gender relations in contemporary Chechnya, young men who served as university security guards always checked that female professors wore appropriate headscarves and that their skirts were long enough when we entered the university campus.

I treat subjectivity defined by my gender, religion, nationality, university affiliation, ideology, and other born and chosen identities not as biases to acquiring objective truths, but as a constitutive part of the research. For example, my own gendered fieldwork taught me a lot about the role of gender in the social order in contemporary Chechnya. In Katherine Cramer's words, "I was using myself as a scientific tool."[26] Field observations and immersion into Chechen daily life allowed me to develop local knowledge – perspectives of lived experiences of legal pluralism, conflict, and key elements of social and political orders.

GROUNDING THEORY

Originally, I went into the field to explore the politics of Sufism, a mystical and hierarchical branch of Islam that plays a major role in the political life of Chechnya and the neighboring regions of Ingushetia and Dagestan. I interviewed Sufi religious authorities and their followers, as well as their opponents and critics. During these interviews, I realized that Sufis had great political power; for example, they mobilized their followers during elections and rallies. But no insider would talk about these issues with me because of the secretive nature of the Sufi orders. At the same time, while

---

[25] Bersanova, Zalpa. "Sistema tsennostei sovremennykh Chechentsev" [The system of values of contemporary Chechen society]. In Dmitry Furman (ed.) *Chechnia i Rossiia: Obschchestva i gosudarstva* [Chechnya and Russia: Societies and States]. Moscow: The Andrey Sakharov Fund, 1999; Khasbulatova, Zulai. *Vospitanie detey u Chechentsev: Obychai i traditsii* (XIX–early XX) [Child Rearing among Chechens: Customs and traditions (nineteenth–early twentieth centuries)], 2007. Kurbanova, Lida. *Problemy i processy gendernoi samoidentifikatsii Chechentsev* [Problems and processes of gender identification among the Chechens]. Krasnodar, Russia, 2012. Nanaeva, Baret. *Traditsionnoye obschestvo Chechentsev: Sotsiokulturnyy analiz* [Traditional society of Chechens: Socio-Cultural analysis]. Moscow: ISPI RAN, 2012. Zaurbekova, Galina. "Gendernyi aspect voiny v Chechne" [Gender aspect of the war in Chechnya]. In *Chechenskaia Respublika i Chechentsy* [Chechen Republic and Chechens]. Moscow: Nauka, 2006.

[26] Cramer, *The politics of resentment*: 34.

interviewing these religious authorities, I was able to observe the lines of disputants who came to ask them to adjudicate their conflicts.

Living Law

On one occasion, I was interviewing an imam in a mosque in the ancient Dagestani city of Derbent. This imam used to be an officer in the Red Army who fought with mujahidin in Afghanistan in the 1980s. While we were having tea and talking about his unusual path to religious authority, three men came in and asked for the imam's attention. The imam invited me to observe their meeting. The men, all in their thirties, came from a mountain village. They asked the imam for a Sharia trial of a man from another village who had borrowed money from one of them and failed to return it in time. The imam promised to arrange mediation with the borrower and noted that, should it fail, he would conduct the Sharia trial.

On another occasion, I was interviewing a village elder. During the interview, his phone rang. After a short conversation in Chechen, he immediately left his house. The man on the phone had asked the elder to solve a dispute regarding a minor car crash. What seemed paradoxical was that the man who had called was an officer of the Russian Road Traffic Safety Police. Even though his agency was in charge of dealing with car crashes, when he became involved in a road dispute himself, he appealed to a village elder. The elder solved the problem by referring to the customary law, presumably developed long before the advent of the automobile.

Observations of the resolution of these quotidian disputes in nonstate legal systems organized on the foundation of religion and tradition made me interested in the issue of legal pluralism. Thus, ethnographic serendipity lays the very foundation of this study. It was also important that most people with whom I talked in Chechnya immediately recognized the relevance of the study of legal pluralism. In fact, many local scholars in the Caucasus explore legal pluralism, usually in historical perspective.[27] But even beyond academic circles, all my interlocutors

---

[27] Akhmadov, Musa. *Chechenskaia traditsionnaia kultura i etika [Chechen traditional culture and ethics]*. Grozny: Vainakh, 2006; Albogachieva, Makka, and Irina Babich. "Pravovaia kultura Ingushey: Istoriia i sovremennost" [Legal culture of Ingushs]. *Istoriia gosudarstva i prava* 19 (2009): 33–39; Albogachieva, Makka, and Irina Babich. "Krovnaia mest' v sovremennoy Ingushetii" [Blood revenge in contemporary Ingushetia]. *Ethnographicheskoye Obozreniye* 6 (2010): 133–140; Bersanova, Zalpa. "Obychai krovnoy mesti i praktika primireniia v sovremennoy Chechne" [The custom

could easily relate to the problem of legal pluralism. Everyone has a story of a dispute – personal, or involving a family member or a neighbor. Most people also have strong views on the alternative legal systems.

Adat supporters are numerous among the Chechen intelligentsia: academics, poets, writers, teachers, etc. Adat is also strong in the rural areas, especially in the mountains. Musa, an elder from one of the villages, emphasized that adat is "the essence of the Chechen nation." Another elder, Visait, who is also a professor of biology, argued that adat is a "perfect form of democracy." And Khakim, who works as a teacher in a high school, attributed the benefits of adat to its flexibility: "Adat is a common law, it is based on precedent, like in America." Mansur, Khakim's son, who was present during our conversation with his father, subsequently told me that he did not share his father's traditionalist views; he was a proponent of Sharia. This is indicative of the fact that Sharia has a very strong appeal in Chechnya, especially among the youth. Ibrahim, a businessman in his thirties, put it as follows: "First and foremost we are Muslims, and therefore we must live according to Sharia." Many people in Chechnya sincerely believe in Sharia rule of law, even if they have different visions of what exactly it entails.[28] Adat and Sharia are deeply interconnected, but people often prefer one of the two. For example, Jabrail, a man in his forties who works as a government official, said: "Sharia is law. Adat is lawlessness. The side that has more pistols is always right."

Many Chechens reject Russian state law on ideological grounds. Isa, a businessman from the town of Urus-Martan, stated: "Those who go to Russian court are outcasts. And they are a tiny minority. Because everyone knows that if a person goes to a Russian court, he does not want justice, he just wants to win. Such people get very little respect." Abdullah, a young male lawyer, said in a group discussion that "Sharia and adat are more humane. These norms are guided by the ideas of justice

---

of blood revenge and the practice of reconciliation in contemporary Chechnya]. *Vestnik Vosstanovitelnoy Yustitsii* 8 (2011): 50–53; Khasiev, Said-Magomed. *Chehentsev drevniaia zemlia [The ancient land of Chechens]*. Saint-Petersburg: Seda, 1994. Mezhidov, Jamal, and Ibragim Aliroyev. *Chechentsy: Obychaii, traditsii, nravy: Sotsialno-filosofskiy aspekt [Chechens: Customs, traditions, manners]*. Grozny: Kniga, 1992; Misrokov, Zamir. *Adat i Shariat v Rossiyskoy pravovoy sisteme. Istoricheskiye sud'by yuridicheskogo pluralizma na Severnom Kavkaze [Adat and Sharia in Russian Legal System: The History of Legal Pluralism in the North Caucasus]*. Moscow State University, 2012; Saidumov, Dzhambulat. *Sud, pravo i pravosudiye u Chechentsev i Ingushey (XVIII–XX). [Courts and law among Chechens and Ingushs]*. Grozny, 2012.

[28] A comprehensive account of the desire for Sharia rule of law can be found in Massoud, *Shari 'a, Inshallah*.

(*spravedlivost*). One can say that they represent the spirit of the law. And Russian state law is only the letter of the law."

Quite often even state officials are against state law, as I document throughout the book. Mikail, a man in his thirties who works as a lawyer, told me a story of how his client was stopped by the road traffic police. Police officers demanded a bribe from him. He wrote an official complaint to the prosecutor's office. The police and the prosecutors pressured him: "What's wrong with you? Why all this legal talk? Did you learn it from the Russians?" Subsequently they mobilized elders who persuaded this client to withdraw his complaint.

Despite the presence of strong normative commitments, there is pervasive forum shopping: people choose a dispute resolution system based on the outcome they expect to obtain. For example, Israil, a federal judge in his sixties, described the process as follows:

Often people try several things: first they will go to an imam. If they don't like his decision, they might say, we don't like this imam – let's go to another imam. If another imam also won't give them what they want, they appeal to the court.

Zelimkhan, a prominent Grozny-based intellectual, confirmed that "people use the norm that is beneficial for them. When the norms collide, the side that has the deeper pockets wins." Many of my interlocutors shared instrumental reasons other than just personal benefit for choosing a particular forum. For example, Madina, a female law student at Chechen State University, said that Russian state law is very slow and inefficient, while adat is fast, easy, and accessible. Others emphasized differences in enforcement.

Enforcement in adat and Sharia is based on social pressure. Families and communities in Chechnya push individuals to rely on customary and religious institutions of dispute resolution and ostracize individuals who bring their disputes to the police and courts. For example, several religious leaders mentioned that if a disputant does not comply with the results of religious arbitration, an imam can announce that the community is not to attend the disputant's family wedding or funeral, implying their loss of social status.

An example from the town of Urus-Martan illustrates the power of social pressure as an enforcement mechanism. Khozh-Ahmed, a government official in his sixties, ordered a group of female workers to repair the façade of his house. He said they did a poor job and he refused to pay them. The women brought the case to the local imam for Sharia arbitration. Khozh-Ahmed was skeptical of this Sharia trial: he said,

I know these so-called judges. They are all former combine-harvester drivers. Then they learned a few phrases in Arabic and now they are judges. I showed up to this trial and the so-called judge was saying complete nonsense, that I have to pay for the weight of the material that they used. I didn't agree with this. But the elder of my family advised me to comply with the ruling. He said that if I don't comply, they will start spreading rumors throughout the entire village that I did not pay because of my high position. So, I complied. This whole system works based on the force of public opinion. This is their only measure of enforcement. But it is quite effective, because everyone knows each other.

Overall, my observations and interviews highlighted the role of normative commitments, pervasive forum shopping and the role of enforcement in the functioning of living law in Chechnya. Chapter 5 develops this descriptive account of legal pluralism.

Orientalism

Exploration of customary law and Sharia is always on the verge of falling into the traps of orientalist romanticization and essentialization. As I document in Chapter 3, orientalism largely defined the approach of the Russian Empire and the Soviet Union towards the people of the North Caucasus. Quite tellingly, "the rudiments of the past" in the form of such traditions as blood feuds and bride kidnappings were part of the representation of the Caucasus in Soviet popular culture, most notably in comedy films. Some Chechens also actively participate in the essentialization of their nation. The 1990s witnessed a dramatic rise in Chechen romantic nationalism and neo-traditionalism. Thus, I always had to bear in mind Valery Tishkov's warning of the danger of "forging Chechens from ethnographic references."[29] For example, when I asked authorities in charge of alternative legal systems about the cases that they have to adjudicate, almost all of them started to talk about blood revenge or bride kidnappings, even though feuds and kidnappings make up only a tiny share of the disputes they adjudicate. Furthermore, even the cases of blood revenge and kidnappings that people usually shared with me were

---

[29] Tishkov, Valery. *Chechnya: Life in a war-torn society*. University of California Press, 2004: 219–222.
   See also Hughes, James. *Chechnya: From nationalism to jihad*. University of Pennsylvania Press, 2007: 2–9.

very dramatic and contained a lot of symbolic elements. For instance, one interlocutor narrated the following case:

This story happened in the midst of the First Chechen War in the village of Bamut, situated on the border between Chechnya and Ingushetia. One man, called Ilyas, was irritated by his neighbor's dog's constant barking. One day the dog also bit Ilyas's son, who had been teasing it. Ilyas got very angry and shot the dog right in the neighbor's yard. According to the Chechen customary law – adat – to kill a dog in someone's yard is equivalent to murder. And according to adat, murder must be avenged with murder. So, when the dog's owner Jabrail learned about the killing of his dog, he took his gun and killed Ilyas. The spiral of violence continued: Ilyas's relatives retaliated and killed Jabrail. Then Jabrail's clan killed another person from Ilyas's clan. After seven people had been killed, the two sides decided to find a way to resolve the feud. State institutions were not functioning in the midst of the war, so the two sides went to the village imam for arbitration according to Sharia. In Islam, unlike in adat, the dog is an unclean animal, and there is no such thing as collective responsibility, so the imam failed to find any solution for reconciliation. With no resolution coming from the imam, the two sides called for a gathering of respected elders. The elders deliberated for two days and finally found a solution according to adat: they found the dog guilty of initiating the feud, and since it had been killed, elders decided to punish the dog's "clan," its puppies, and applied one of the harshest form of punishments reserved in adat – they expelled the puppies from the village. After that, the dispute finally came to an end.

This case is fascinating. It shows the power of adat and the complicated relationship between alternative legal systems. However, first of all, it is not clear if the case actually happened and is not a legend. When I retold this story to one of my trusted interlocutors, his reaction was "This is either made up, or these people in Bamut are crazy nuts!" In other words, even though the case illuminates many elements of the Chechen customary law, it is hardly typical. Thus, I always had to differentiate the descriptions of actual dispute resolution practices from the normative accounts. I found a very similar reflection on fieldwork in Ekaterina Sokirianskaia's study on Chechen clans. She wrote "I noticed that during interviews when asked questions about traditional institutions people would often talk about how things ought to be, not how they really are."[30] In order not to fall into the traps of essentialization, it is crucial to situate the accounts of legal pluralism in larger social and political orders.

---

[30] Sokirianskaia, Ekaterina. *Governing fragmented societies: State-Building and political integration in Chechnya and Ingushetia (1991–2009).* Ph.D. dissertation, Central European University, Budapest, 2009: 117.

Elements of Social Order

Writings on Chechnya have always been preoccupied with *teips* or *taips*, Chechen clans. References to *teips* explained virtually everything that was happening in Chechnya. For example, Anatol Lieven tells a fascinating story of how Russian security services relied on spurious theories about Chechen *teips* when they were planning the first military operation in 1994 that turned out to be a disaster.[31] In the 1990s, there was a resurgence of traditionalism and clans started to organize congresses, and some even came up with *teip* heraldic symbols. Ekaterina Sokirianskaia's study, based on extensive ethnographic fieldwork, showed that explanations of Chechen politics through references to clans and other forms of neo-traditionalism in the 1990s were empirically false.[32] Since at least the early nineteenth century, Chechen *teips* have been loosely organized symbolic groups. James Hughes concluded that "the modern notion of *teip* is largely an invention of Russian nineteenth-century military colonizers and bureaucrats who forced the Chechens into an artificial, territorialized notion of *teip* identity."[33] Nowadays, some of the Chechen *teips* have tens of thousands of people and therefore are largely "imagined communities." But the power of imagination should not be underestimated – especially if it is Ramzan Kadyrov's imagination. Kadyrov has been actively revitalizing the importance of *teip* belonging by promoting his own *teip* named *Benoi* and using threats of collective punishment against the *teips* of his opponents.

Many people with whom I spoke talked about the crucial role that *teips* play in contemporary Chechnya. For example, Salman, a male lawyer in his late fifties, said that "all 100,000 men from my *teip* are always ready to support me in a difficult situation." On the other hand, some others, especially in Grozny, presented a much more modest account of the significance of *teips* in contemporary Chechnya. As Zelimkhan, a historian in his fifties, told me, "*Teips* are largely irrelevant now. Even in the case of blood revenge, only brothers and maybe cousins will be involved. The second cousins are too distant relatives already."

---

[31] Lieven, Anatol. *Chechnya: Tombstone of Russian power.* Yale University Press, 1998: 335.

[32] Sokirianskaia, *Governing fragmented societies.*

[33] Hughes, *Chechnya*: 3. See also Mamakaev, Magomet. *Chechenskiy teip (rod) v period ego razlozheniia. [Chechen clan in the period of decay].* Grozny, 1973.

Extended family, *dozal,* rather than the notorious *teip,* is the principal form of social organization in contemporary Chechnya. The extended family includes three to four generations of blood relatives and is known in Chechen as "people of one house." In rural and semi-urban areas extended families often live together in walled or fenced compounds consisting of several houses connected to each other and sharing a common yard, which in rural areas often has apple and pear trees. The moral economy of Chechen extended families allows them to overcome poverty stemming from the low incomes of individual family members. The official average monthly salary in Chechnya at the time of my research was about $150–200, one of the lowest in the Russian Federation.[34] However, when combined with welfare payments for the retired, disabled, and children, and remittances from other family members who work in Russia or perhaps even live in Europe, it allows Chechen extended families to maintain a decent quality of life. Building a large house is therefore the most important investment, and judging by the houses, Chechnya appears to be a prosperous region.

Each extended family has a patriarch, a senior man who makes key decisions – about marriage, inheritance, and disputes with other families. Senior women also have a lot of power over junior women and children. Chechen family life is regulated by a strict set of norms. For example, there is a norm that bans husband and wife from calling each other by name. Thus, they have to come up with joking names for each other. The wife also cannot call the male relatives of her husband by name. Another norm bans parents from holding their children on their lap in front of older relatives. All these norms form a complex system of etiquette that signals respect and highlights generational and gender hierarchies.

A strong sense of belonging is also attached to territorial communities, usually ancestral villages or peri-urban settlements, where the family has been living for several generations. Even the majority of those who live in the cities have houses and land in the villages. One might not live in "their" village anymore, or even never have lived there, but preserve the normative attachment. Chechens have a strong preference for being buried in their village – even those who live in diasporas in Europe overcome every difficulty to bury their dead in their home village cemetery. Chechen communities vary in size – some are as large as fifteen to

---

[34] According to the Russian statistical agency, the average income in Chechnya in 2015–2016 was approximately 21,000 Rub ($320). My observations and conversations in the field suggest that this number was inflated.

twenty thousand people, but most settlements are of several thousand residents. Members of communities usually know each other or at least know families who live in their settlement. They meet regularly at weddings and funerals. Usually, the entire community, or at least delegates from all extended families, attends weddings and *tezet*, wakes that last for three days. Men also regularly meet at the Friday prayer. The community is important, because family status is determined in the interactions with families from one's community. Gossip plays a big role here. Communities are also central in the distribution of land and public goods provision. For example, I was told that communities raise funds for constructing mosques, building or repairing of roads, and even bringing in good doctors and teachers.

Another key element of the Chechen social fabric is religion. Even though in the Soviet era religion was banned and only a few practiced some basic religious rituals, Chechnya experienced a dramatic religious revival in the post-Soviet period. In the early 1990s, mosques reopened across all Chechen settlements, many people went to perform Hajj in Mecca, some Chechens went to study Islam in Arab countries, and Muslim missionaries in turn came to Chechnya. The war played an especially big role in the rise of religiosity in Chechnya. The experiences of conflict, when existential threat was a permanent state of daily life for all Chechens, created a dire need for the promise of eternal life and ultimate justice. In addition, the war destroyed the Soviet urban secular classes of nomenklatura and intelligentsia, many of whom left Chechnya. Another factor was that almost an entire generation of Chechen children was left without regular secular education. At the same time, Islamic education, however limited, was widely available. Finally, the postwar Chechen government of Ramzan Kadyrov actively pursued the policy of Islamization of all spheres of Chechen life in its quest for legitimacy. Islam became a hegemonic cultural frame.

The religious sphere in Chechnya is divided between the Sufi and the Salafi versions of Sunni Islam.[35] There are two main Sufi orders in Chechnya, Qadiri and Nakshbandi, but they are also divided into

---

[35] Akaev, Vakhit. *Islam: Sotsiokulturnaia realnost' na Severnom Kavkaze. [Islam: Socio-cultural reality in the North Caucasus].* Rostov-on-Don, 2004; Akaev, Vakhit. *Sufiyskaia kultura na Severnom Kavkaze. Teoreticheskiy i prakticheskiy aspekty* [Sufi culture in the North Caucasus: Theoretical and practical aspects]. Grozny, 2011; Knysh, Alexander. "Contextualizing the Salafi–Sufi conflict (from the Northern Caucasus to Hadramawt)." *Middle Eastern Studies* 43, no. 4 (2007): 503–530; Yemelianova, Galina. "Sufism and politics in the North Caucasus." *Nationalities Papers* 29.4:

numerous suborders, *virds*. Belonging to Sufi *virds* cuts across clan belonging. These social categories – clan, family, community, and Sufi *vird* – are perhaps the most significant social markers in contemporary Chechnya. At the same time, many Chechens reject Sufism and tacitly criticize Sufi practices such as famous Qadiri *zikrs* – rituals of remembrance of God and Prophet Muhammad that resemble collective dances in circles. Salafi ideas are widespread among young people, which leads to acute generational conflicts in Chechnya and elsewhere in the North Caucasus.[36] Knowledge of this religious divide was very valuable for navigating conversations with the representatives of different generations in Chechnya.

The government of Ramzan Kadyrov has been actively promoting the Sufi version of Islam in Chechnya, which is recognized as the "traditional" or "official" Islam. In turn, the Salafi versions of Islam in Chechnya are pejoratively labeled as "Wahhabism" and their adherents are heavily persecuted. Visible markers of Salafism such as a long beard without mustaches, or short pants, invite government repression. Repression against Salafi adherents, human rights groups, independent journalists, lay regime critics, and marginalized groups, such as drug users and homosexuals, is the foundation of the political order in Kadyrov's Chechnya. However, the regime cannot be reduced to coercion alone.

The Political Order

Chechnya is currently part of the Russian Federation, and Russia under Vladimir Putin is an authoritarian regime. But there is authoritarian and then there is *authoritarian*. Ramzan Kadyrov, the Head of the Chechen Republic, basically a governor of one of the regions of Russia, openly refers to himself, and is referred to by his subordinates and lay people during official government meetings and on Chechen national TV, as

---

661–688; Vatchagaev, Mairbek. "Virdovaia structura Chechni i Ingushetii" [Sufi structures of Chechnya and Ingushetia]. *Prometey* 26 (2009).

[36] Starodubrovskaya, Irina. "Sotsialnaia transformatsia i mezhpokolencheskiy konflikt (na primere Severnogo Kavkaza)" [Social transformation and intergenerational conflict (the case of the North Caucasus)]. *Obschestvennye Nauki i Sovremennost'* 6 (2016): 111–124; "Krizis traditsionnoy severokavkazskoy sem'i v postsovetskiy period i ego sotsialnye posledstviia" [The Crisis of traditional North Caucasian Family in the post-Soviet period and its social consequences]. *Jurnal Issledovaniy Sotsialnoy Politiki* 17, no. 1 (2019).

Padishah – "Master King" in Persian.[37] This is something totally unimaginable for Vladimir Putin or any other regional leader in Russia.

Ramzan Kadyrov was appointed the President of Chechnya by Vladimir Putin in 2007, effectively succeeding his father Akhmat-hajji Kadyrov, a former separatist religious leader who switched sides and became the pro-Russia administrative leader of Chechnya in the early 2000s but was killed in a terrorist attack in 2004. Ramzan, who became the President of Chechnya when he was just thirty, managed to brutally suppress the insurgency and consolidate his rule by eliminating all viable potential challengers. Under Ramzan Kadyrov, all elections in Chechnya end with an official turnout of 99 percent and a pro-government vote of the same 99 percent.

Kadyrov's rule is almost a perfect illustration of Weber's concept of sultanism as the highest form of neopatrimonialism. The ruler owns his territory. Kadyrov's blood relatives and people from his native village of Khosi-Yurt (alternatively known as Tsentaroy) occupy key government positions at all levels. People close to Ramzan Kadyrov are given special car plates with the three letters KRA, which stand for Kadyrov Ramzan Akhmatovich. These plates serve as a license to drive without following any rules, as I've learned on one of my rides with government-connected interlocutors. Kadyrov's family owns numerous businesses across Chechnya: markets, business centers, taxi parks, gas stations. Any successful business faces a high risk of expropriation. Kadyrov is exceedingly rich and displays his wealth through palaces, racing horses, a private zoo, and expensive presents to his loyalists. On many occasions, I observed a seemingly endless motorcade of Kadyrov's expensive bullet-proof cars running through the city at enormous speed.

All employees in the public sector and all private businesses in Chechnya have to provide regular donations to the private foundation named after Akhmat Kadyrov. The size of the "voluntary donations" is around a third of the salary of public employees and varies across businesses.[38] Funds from the parallel taxation system are spent on the construction of mosques, support for the poor during Ramadan, payment for their Hajj trips and *kalym* (bride money), but also for the organization of mass sports events, mostly in martial arts, and lavish entertainment events

---

[37] As my interlocutors put it, Chechens have never had royal figures, and therefore there is no Chechen word for king.

[38] Tumanov, Grigoriy. "Rabota na vsnos" [Work for donations]. Kommersant N 94, June 1, 2015.

that feature Western celebrities like Jean-Claude Van Damme, Mike Tyson, and Hilary Swank.

There are numerous displays of the cult of Ramzan Kadyrov and his father in Chechnya. All towns and villages are filled with the gigantic banners of Ramzan, Akhmat, and Vladimir Putin. Ramzan's and Akhmat's portraits hang in every single government office, but also in every single grocery store, many cars, and even some private houses. The main streets of almost every Chechen town and village are named after Akhmat-hajji Kadyrov. Grozny's football club was renamed to Akhmat. The Kadyrovs' native village of Khosi-Yurt was renamed to Akhmat-Yurt. There are youth organizations named after Akhmat and Ramzan, and sports competitions and schoolchildren's poetry readings in honor of Akhmat and Ramzan. Grozny's main mosque is named after Akhmat and the main mosque in the town of Argun is named after Ramzan's mother Aymani. Aymani's birthday has become an official government holiday – Chechen Women's Day. All public servants in Chechnya had to follow and like Ramzan's Instagram account, until it was shut down when he was placed on the U.S. sanctions list.

The Kadyrovs' cult can be productively analyzed with the framework that Lisa Wedeen developed to explain the cult of Hafiz al-Assad in Syria. The cult is a strategy of domination based on compliance. Wedeen wrote that "the regime produces compliance through enforced participation in rituals of obeisance that are transparently phony both to those who orchestrate them and to those who consume them."[39] Thus, the cult is a disciplinary device that provides the guidelines for accepted speech and behavior. The disciplinary power is best illustrated by the spread of the practice of forced public apologies to Ramzan Kadyrov. When locals complain – about officials' corruption or lack or poor quality of government-provided public goods – or make any critical remarks about the Kadyrovs or Putin, they are forced to make a public apology that is aired on Chechen national television.

The cult invites transgressions, as Wedeen suggested. Intelligentsia often share anecdotes about their uneducated rulers. The fact that Kadyrov is an honorary member of the Russian Academy of Natural Sciences makes people jokingly call him "our academician." Because of the ubiquitous presence of the political banners, some in Grozny joke about "the city of icons: the Father (Akhmat), the Son (Ramzan), and the

[39] Wedeen, *Ambiguities of domination*: 6.

Holy Spirit (Putin)." Some transgressions are more confrontational. In one village, the locals have been burning down Akhmat's banner at the entrance gate of their village almost every week for several years. But overall, the repressions and the cult are very effective in producing compliance. As a result, throughout my fieldwork I have heard numerous odes to Ramzan and his father. On one occasion, I met with a respected cleric, and we talked for several hours – mostly about the independence period of the 1990s. Then the next day he called me back and asked for another meeting. During the second meeting, he gave a long panegyric to Kadyrov, whom we did not even mention during the first interview. People are afraid, and they have good reason to be.

One's security in Chechnya is at the government's pleasure. For instance, during my fieldwork, the human rights organization "Committee Against Torture," which had an open conflict with Ramzan Kadyrov, suffered numerous attacks by unidentified militias. The organization's office in Grozny was burned down. A car with the NGO's employees and journalists from Russia and Europe was attacked on the road. The unidentified militias beat the activists and journalists and burned their car. Over time, Kadyrov's regime has created an unprecedented atmosphere of fear in Chechnya. Drawing a parallel with Linda Green's description of war-torn Guatemala, it is possible to say that in postwar Chechnya, "rather than being solely a subjective experience, it [fear] has penetrated the social memory. And rather than being an acute reaction, it is a chronic condition ... Fear destabilizes social relations by driving a wedge of distrust between members of families, between neighbors, among friends."[40] Most of my interlocutors stated that people were more afraid during this "peace" than they had been even in the most difficult periods of war. Talking about violence contains danger in itself, because the government heavily polices narratives about Stalin's deportation of Chechens and about the post-Soviet wars.

Experiences of Violence

As a sign of intractable conflict, the streets of Grozny and the roads of the Republic are always filled with heavily-armed security personnel. However, there are few other visible manifestations of violence. Grozny

---

[40] Green, Linda. "Living in a state of fear." In Antonius Robben and Carolyn Nordstrom (eds.) *Fieldwork under fire: Contemporary studies of violence and survival*. Berkeley: University of California Press, 1995.

was completely destroyed during the wars, but there are almost no physical signs of war left in the capital. Even critics agree that Ramzan Kadyrov managed to effectively rebuild a republic that was laying in ruins. The new Grozny city center copies Dubai; it is full of tall concrete and glass buildings and shopping malls. Unlike many other post-conflict sites, for instance Sarajevo, where the authorities decided to preserve some holes from bullets and bombs as symbols of the horrors of the war, the government of Chechnya completely erased everything that could point to the history of conflict. There are no special monuments for victims of the war – only to Akhmat Kadyrov and the pro-Russia police officers that were killed in the counterterrorist operations.

Commemoration of Stalin's deportation of Chechens to Central Asia in 1944 is also strictly regulated, because collective commemoration of the crimes of the Soviet and the Russian governments against the Chechen people seems dangerous to the Chechen regional authorities. For example, after the civil society activist Ruslan Kutaev organized a roundtable on February 23, the day of the deportation, in 2014, he was arrested and sentenced to four years' imprisonment for alleged drug possession. The politics of memory in Kadyrov's Chechnya is almost like a minefield.

Nevertheless, my interlocutors often shared with me their experiences of violence. In both Chechnya and Ingushetia, I had numerous conversations with elders who had survived the deportation of 1944 or were born in Central Asia before the Chechens and Ingush were allowed to return to the Caucasus in 1957. In almost all these conversations, we went through respondents' memories of the deportation and life in exile. For instance, Khamzat, an elder from the village of Starye Atagi, told me that he was seven when he was deported along with his father, mother, two brothers, and sister. Their family was deported to a remote mountainous area in Kazakhstan, where they were forced to work at a sawmill.

The conditions were unbearable. My father bribed some administrator of the sawmill camp and they allowed us to leave the camp and go to the city nearby. There was no transportation. We, children, did not have any shoes and had to walk through the forest for four days in severe cold in self-made shoes. During the trip my sister died. Soon both of my brothers and my father died too.

The acclaimed Ingush writer Issa Kodzoev, who survived the deportation as a child, told me how all thirteen of his closest relatives perished in Central Asia. Personal stories of loss characterized narratives about the deportation and the war.

Conversations about the war happened all the time. Even at the art café, where talking about the war was formally prohibited, on some occasions people started to spontaneously recollect their childhood war-time memories. One night, for example, two young men started to talk about how they had played with bombshells. They discussed the kinds and parameters of the bombs with such profound knowledge and detail that I was amazed. For this generation of Chechen children, shells and bullets were their only toys.

Many people started talking about the war even if I did not ask them about it. In fact, almost no one was able to speak about their life without mentioning it. For example, Shirvani, an elder in one of the Chechen villages, told me that for him the experience of war was first of all about humiliation. His house was repeatedly invaded by both Russian soldiers and rebels. Shirvani remembered how one day his wife made some bread for Russian soldiers, who raided their house in the morning, and the same night the rebels entered their house and said: "We've heard that you feed the feds [Russian soldiers] here, old man!" Shirvani responded that his family had no choice when armed men came – whether Russian or Chechen. Shirvani said that for him it was especially painful that he had to offer excuses to younger Chechen men, who invaded his house and talked disrespectfully to him and his wife. For him, this was a clear violation of the Chechen customary code of behavior that he embraced. Similarly, Vakharsolt, an elder from a village that experienced intensive bombing and counterinsurgency operations during the Second Chechen War, told me that for him the most vivid memories of the war were the images of the soldiers who walked through his house "with their boots covered in mud" and "constantly swearing." For Shirvani, Vakharsolt, and many other people with whom I talked, these experiences of humiliation were almost as painful as the killings that they witnessed.

The war had a profound impact on the mental health of generations of Chechen men and women. For instance, Suleiman, a lecturer of law at one of the local universities, told me that

Everyone here is a little bit crazy. The war made us crazy. When I was a kid, I came very close to being dead. I was eight years old, maybe. I went to swim in the river which was separated from our village by a small forest. When I was walking through this forest, I heard a click beneath my foot – by then everyone in Chechnya knew that this click meant that I had stepped on a landmine. I tried to shout out for help – but no one heard me. I stood on the same place for maybe five hours. At some point, I had no energy left and took my leg away. The mine did not work. I guess I was too emaciated and the bomb just did not consider me a human. You have to be forgiving to our people after all that.

When talking about the war, many people remembered funny episodes. According to one of my respondents, dark humor became very popular in Chechnya as a coping strategy during the wars. "It was horror everywhere, so we needed to confront it with laughs." Another respondent, Saipudi, told me that for him the most memorable episode of war was the episode described in the following story:

I was fighting in the resistance movement. During the First War, at some point the Feds [the Russian army] had already captured Grozny, but we [the rebels] still controlled Staraya Sunzha – the village right next to the city. Our men were tired and hungry and we decided to send one of us to the city to find some food. I volunteered. I went to Grozny and after some walking around I saw several sheep by the roadside. I took one sheep and turned back. However, soon after, heavy shelling started. I had to hide and hugged the sheep to protect it. When the shelling ended, we kept walking. On a bridge next to the old tram depot, I heard noise from coming troops and their armed vehicles. We – the sheep and I – were in an open spot. There were no buildings around, so I jumped in a rocket crater in the bridge to hide. The sheep jumped into the same crater. I decided that it was too risky to leave our shelter and we sat there in this small crater for hours, the two of us – the sheep and I. At night we finally went out and we made it back. When my men saw me, they were very happy – they'd thought that I was surely dead. When they saw that I'd brought the sheep, they became even more excited, expecting to have some good kebab. However, I prohibited them from touching the sheep. It had become my comrade! I gave it to a family in the village and asked them to protect it. Unfortunately, I did not find this family after the war, so I do not know what that sheep's fate was after our meeting.

Such stories allowed me to better understand the experiences of those who had fought and those who had tried to survive in different civilian roles. But even more importantly, my immersion in Chechen social reality taught me that the entire population was profoundly affected by the war and living under postwar dictatorship. In the next section, I discuss the ethics of study under these conditions.

RESEARCH ETHICS IN A POST-CONFLICT AUTHORITARIAN CONTEXT

Research in the shadow of violent conflict and under authoritarian conditions is always an ethically challenging task. Summarizing ethnographies of civil wars, Elisabeth Wood wrote that "violence and terror often leave behind a legacy of salience, fear, and uncertainty that can be deeply corrosive of self-confidence, trust, and hope."[41] Conflict also exacerbates power disparities between researchers and participants in their studies.[42] Therefore, a researcher has to be extra careful to ensure research participants' safety, dignity, and autonomy.

Managing Risks

Following the guidelines from earlier immersive studies of conflict-affected and authoritarian societies, I developed the following protocol.[43] First, I always briefed my informants about the purpose of my study, explained the potential risks, and orally requested their consent to take part in the study.[44] I assured anonymity and confidentiality of my records. I explained that I was studying the interrelationships among custom, religious arbitration, and Russian state law and how they were transformed in the post-Soviet period. I told my interlocutors that my ultimate goal was writing an academic book. I also talked about my own life trajectory, where I was born and raised, where I went to school, and about my previous research in the Caucasus. As I've mentioned above, I always informed study participants that I was affiliated with both American and Russian universities.

As a rule, I avoided asking any political questions about Ramzan Kadyrov, Vladimir Putin, or other sensitive issues such as repressions in contemporary Chechnya. I also took special care in asking questions about wartime experiences. Many conversations and interviews touched upon political subjects, but they usually happened only after two or three meetings. I often consulted my trusted interlocutors to help me determine what questions to ask and not to ask and what the risks were for potential participants in particular locations and situations. Following other researchers who work in authoritarian and conflict-ridden post-Soviet

[41] Wood, Elisabeth Jean. *Insurgent collective action and civil war in El Salvador.* Cambridge University Press, 2003: 40.
[42] Cronin-Furman, Kate, and Milli Lake. "Ethics abroad: Fieldwork in fragile and violent contexts." *PS: Political Science & Politics* 51, no. 3 (2018): 607–614.
[43] I followed the protocols developed in the following studies: Derluguian, *Bourdieu's secret admirer in the Caucasus;* Driscoll, *Warlords and coalition politics in Post-Soviet states;* Fujii, Lee Ann. *Killing neighbors: Webs of violence in Rwanda.* Cornell University Press, 2009; Shesterinina, Anastasia. *Mobilizing in uncertainty: Collective identities and war in Abkhazia.* Cornell University Press, 2021; Wood, *Insurgent collective action and civil war in El Salvador.*
[44] The study was approved by Columbia University's IRB commission.

contexts, I never recorded the interviews.[45] During the interviews, I made notes. My terrible handwriting doubled as a form of encryption. Every evening, I wrote field diaries that became the foundation of this chapter. In the notes, diaries, and in the text of the book, I never attributed any identifying information to my interlocutors. I use aliases other than when quoting the respondents in official positions who wanted to be named and did not express any politically sensitive information or opinions.

I obtained permissions from the local authorities to carry out my research. I met with many government officials during my fieldwork, but most crucially during one of the early field trips I met with one of the deputies of the Prime Minister of the Chechen Republic. As in many other situations, I organized that meeting through a network of previously established connections. That high official met me for maybe ten minutes, listened to my speech about my study of the use of Chechen customary law and religious norms to adjudicate disputes, and said: "Study whatever you want. These are good topics." Clearly, affiliation with Russian academic institutions and framing my research as an exploration of law, custom, and religion was instrumental in getting favorable treatment from the authorities.

I assumed that my communications in Chechnya were under constant surveillance, given the high coercive capacity of local security services. In response, every day of my fieldwork, I called my mother and in very plain language explained to her what I did during the day, emphasizing learning about Chechen customary practices such as bride kidnappings, blood revenge, funerals, and weddings. I never communicated any sensitive information about my study participants. I assumed that I was speaking not only to my mother, but also to some lieutenant in the local branch of the FSB. This was another way of framing the study as a study of culture, harmless for the authorities. I never lied. My study indeed focused on custom, religion, and law. But where to put the emphasis was important.

Thinking about Benefits

The potential risks for my study participants were relatively clear, but what about the benefits? Usam Baysaev, a well-known Chechen human rights activist living in Europe, once wrote on social media that

[45] Derluguian, *Bourdieu's secret admirer in the Caucasus*; Driscoll, *Warlords and Coalition Politics in Post-Soviet States.*

For people who want to get an academic degree, we are an ideal object. First, despite the small numbers, for a long time we have been a factor in world politics. In the good and the bad sense. In short, there is interest in us! Second, we are terra incognita. These two factors lure researchers of different sorts to us like flies to honey.

There is bitter truth in this statement. Indeed, writing about Chechnya is beneficial for scholars like me, but gives little to the people whom we write about.

Despite the fact that there are many writings about Chechnya, field research in the region is rare. My study thus can be justified by the need for grounded perspectives on the legacies of conflict and post-conflict political development.[46] However, an even more powerful justification comes from the active support of this study from the people I've met in Chechnya and elsewhere in the Caucasus. Even though I stated that there were no tangible benefits associated with the study, for the vast majority of my interlocutors, the idea of exploring customs, religion, and experiences of conflict was absolutely enough.[47] Many people were very curious to read the book based on my study. My long-term presence in the field, acquired knowledge about Chechen customs and Islamic religion, and references from respected local intelligentsia all showed that I was serious about the study.

During the later stages of my fieldwork, when I met with some of my original informants for follow-ups, I presented them with the results of the quantitative analysis of the survey data and court records. My interlocutors were curious to learn the results of the analysis and offered useful interpretations of the data.[48] Of course, I was not able to discuss the results with all interlocutors, but mostly with local scholars and members of nongovernmental organizations. Not all agreed with the

---

[46] Ekaterina Sokirianskaia's dissertation on clans in Chechnya and Ingushetia and Sasha Klyachkina's dissertation on local governance in Chechnya, Ingushetia, and Dagestan are rare examples of studies based on immersive fieldwork in the region. See Sokirianskaia, *Governing gragmented societies*; Klyachkina, Alexandra. *Reconfiguration of subnational governance: Responses to violence and state collapse in the North Caucasus.* Ph.D. dissertation, Northwestern University, 2019.

[47] According to Wood, the willingness of study participants in conflict-affected contexts "to talk about their personal and community histories at length with a researcher" is common to ethnographies of civil wars. Wood, Elisabeth Jean. "The ethical challenges of field research in conflict zones." *Qualitative Sociology* 29, no. 3 (2006): 378.

[48] This practice is known as "giving back," "the repatriation of data" or "member-checking." Importantly, I did not share any parts of my qualitative data.

interpretations I put forward in this book. Curiously enough, among people with whom I discussed the impact of conflict on legal pluralism, roughly half believed that the war strengthened the role of adat, and the other half that it completely disrupted the traditional social order. These conflicting interpretations from my trusted interlocutors were in themselves invaluable information that suggested the potential for multiple channels that link conflict with post-conflict social order.

Challenges

My fieldwork inevitably had to rely on a network of trusted sources in response to the challenging security situation.[49] This network was large, and I had multiple "entry points" in the field. Ultimately, I was able to meet and interview actors across the ideological spectrum and the former wartime fronts: government officials and pro-government fighters (*kadyrovtsy*) and former secessionist leaders and rebels. Nevertheless, through the time I spent in the field, I developed strong feelings towards particular actors, which undoubtedly colored my observations and my analysis.[50] Empathy towards the individuals victimized by the conflict was the strongest emotional basis of the study.

It is noteworthy to emphasize that I was not pursuing "extreme fieldwork" and by and large there was never any immediate danger involved in my study. However, the repressive and violent political conditions of the North Caucasus created a stressful environment.[51] During the period of my study, the Russian media constantly reported episodes of insurgent attacks and counterterrorist operations in Chechnya and the neighboring regions of Dagestan and Ingushetia. On the ground, however, the situation differed dramatically from the media's portrayal.

There was no active sustained insurgency in Chechnya during the time of my study (2014–2016), only episodic attacks. Despite the presence of heavily armed security personnel, overall, it was quite safe. Crime was almost entirely absent – many people told me that you could leave a car

---

[49] Malejacq and Mukhopadhya, "The 'tribal politics' of field research."

[50] For discussions of empathy in conflict research, see Shesterinina, Anastasia. "Ethics, empathy, and fear in research on violent conflict." *Journal of Peace Research* 56, no. 2 (2019): 190–202.

[51] On the emotional challenges of fieldwork in conflict settings, see Driscoll, Jesse. *Doing global fieldwork.* Columbia University Press, 2021.

unlocked and no one would take it, and I was easily able to walk around Grozny at any point at night. But there was always a potential danger from the regime. This taught me that there is a difference between a perception of a place as dangerous from a distance and the understanding of more specific manifestations of danger on the ground.

Perhaps the scariest episode of my fieldwork happened during one of my early fieldtrips, when I lived in a rented apartment. At seven in the morning, I heard loud knocking on my door. Through a peephole I saw a group of armed men in camouflage in front of my door. I did not open it, moving silently to pretend that the apartment was empty. To my surprise, the men left. They went upstairs and started to knock on other doors in the building. Clearly, they had not come for me. As I was told later, this was a standard procedure of the Chechen police who regularly check apartments in the city center. I was not sure what exactly they were checking. But I was scared.

Some people whom I met at various points during my trips were later killed. Others were jailed. One man who had hosted me once was kidnapped for ransom. These things, along with anxiety about my own security during the trips, made field research stressful. At the same time, my fieldwork was an extremely insightful and rewarding experience. I made good friends, some of whom became almost like a second family. And I have learned a lot. The power of the field transformed my study and transformed me. Even when I left the North Caucasus, I continued to learn and shape my study through continued conversations with the interlocutors whom I had met in the field, meeting members of the vast Chechen diasporas, getting feedback from Chechen scholars at conferences, and reading news and discussions on social media. I entered the field but would never leave it.[52]

* * *

Said-Magomed Khasiev, the late great Chechen ethnographer, told me this when we met at the National Museum of the Chechen Republic: "Many people here understand ethnography as a study of cultural artefacts: sheepskin hats, carpers, daggers. Anything that is old, traditional.

---

[52] On ethics beyond the field site in unstable political contexts, see Knott, Eleanor. "Beyond the field: Ethics after fieldwork in politically dynamic contexts." *Perspectives on Politics* 17, no. 1 (2019): 140–153.

But ethnography is about people!"[53] In this chapter, I followed this wisdom and paid attention to people and their perspectives on history, conflict, and state-society relations. This chapter adopted the lenses of both positivist and interpretivist approaches to ethnography. As a positivist and realist, I was seeking to develop grounded perspectives on the key elements of my theory: social and political orders, legal pluralism, and conflict.[54] When I put on an interpretivist hat, I focused on sense-making and co-production of knowledge between the researcher and study participants through reflections on positionality and subjectivity. These tasks were clearly interrelated, as explorations of my own subjectivity revealed a lot about the social world. Reflexivity was also a guiding ethical principle of this research and a facilitator of its analytical transparency.[55] In general, in this book, ethnography is envisioned as a bridge between theory and evidence. Ethnographic sensibility helped me to ground my theory and also informed all the methods of the study: historical analysis, case studies, observations, interviews, and even survey research. In the next chapter, I present an analysis of the historical evidence on state-building in Chechnya through the lens of legal pluralism.

[53] "Here" reflects the dominant Soviet understanding of ethnography as the description of material culture. On Soviet ethnography see Tishkov, Valery et al. "The crisis in Soviet ethnography [and comments]." *Current Anthropology* 33, no. 4 (1992): 371–394. Slezkine, Yuri. "The fall of Soviet ethnography, 1928–38." *Current Anthropology* 32, no. 4 (1991): 476–484. Hirsch, Francine. *Empire of nations: Ethnographic knowledge and the making of the Soviet Union.* Cornell University Press, 2005.

[54] On the realist ethnography, see Allina-Pisano, Jessica. "How to tell an axe murderer: An essay on ethnography, truth, and lies." in Schatz, *Political ethnography*: 53–73.

[55] On reflexivity and transparency see Jacobs, Alan et al. "The Qualitative transparency deliberations: Insights and implications." *Perspectives on Politics* 19, no. 1 (2021): 171–208.

PART II

LAWFARE AND POLITICAL ORDER

3

The Chechen Way

Lawfare under Imperial and Soviet Rule

The history of Chechnya is usually told and written as a history of warfare.[1] In this chapter, I will instead narrate the key formative periods of Chechen history through the lens of lawfare. As we shall see, the interrelationship among custom, Sharia, and Russian/Soviet state law was central to the struggles for political control in the region. For instance, in 1860, after the defeat of the major anti-colonial resistance movement, the Russian Viceroy of the Caucasus Prince Aleksandr Baryatinskiy, in his *Proclamation to the Chechen People*, declared that the Russian Empire would allow its subjects to preserve their justice based on custom and religion:

The rulers that will be placed above you will govern according to adat and Sharia, and the justice will be enacted in the people's courts, composed of the best people elected by you and appointed with the consent of our officials.[2]

In 1920, none other than Joseph Stalin, who was at that time the Soviet minister for Nationalities Affairs, speaking in Dagestan, echoed his imperial predecessor in his appeal to the peoples of the North Caucasus, promising to preserve Sharia:

---

[1] Characteristically, a curated collection of the archival documents on Chechens and the Russian colonial authority that covers both the imperial and the Soviet periods consists primarily of military reports. See Kozlov, V.A. et al. *Vainakhi i imperskaia vlast: problema Chechni i Ingushetii vo vnutrennei politike Rossii i SSSR (nachalo XIX–seredina XX veka)* [*Vainakhs and Imperial Authority: Chechnya and Ingushtia in domestic politics of Russia and the USSR (early nineteenth–mid-twentieth century)*]. Moscow: ROSSPEN.

[2] Cited from Bobrovnikov, Vladimir. *Musulmane Severnogo Kavkaza: Obychai, pravo, nasilie.* [*Muslims of the North Caucasus: Custom, law and violence*]. Moscow: Vostochnaia Literatura, 2002: 167.

We have also been informed that the enemies of Soviet power are spreading rumors that it has banned the Sharia. I have been authorized by the Government of the Russian Socialist Federative Soviet Republic to state here that these rumors are false. The Government of Russia gives every people the full right to govern itself on the basis of its laws and customs. The Soviet Government considers that the Sharia, as common law, is as fully authorized as that of any other of the peoples inhabiting Russia.[3]

Soon after, the Soviet government changed its tone and brutally repressed non-state justice in the Caucasus. This chapter will survey the imperial "divide and rule" accommodations and the Soviet imposition of legal "modernization" as different modes of the metropole's political management of legal pluralism in the North Caucasus. It highlights the role of the violent transformations during the Caucasian War and Stalin's deportation of the Chechen people to Central Asia as the formative periods in the development of legal pluralism in the region.

THE IMPERIAL LEGAL PLURALISM

Pre-colonial Social Order

Legal pluralism existed in the North Caucasus throughout its entire recorded history, but it was intensified and politicized as a result of Russian colonization in the nineteenth century. Before the colonization, Chechens and the related Ingush people did not have a centralized state. Territorial communities were the principal social organizations; they were governed according to the customary law, adat.[4] Since Chechen society was politically fragmented, there was no unified system of adat. Different communities had their own versions of adat, even though the core principles were common across all Chechen societies. As in other clan-based stateless societies throughout the world, Chechen adat assumes that the subject of the law is collective – the extended family and clan or the community, rather than the individual. Banishment of the individual from the family and clan or the community is therefore the worst form of punishment, because it leaves one without legal protection. Blood revenge

---

[3] Ibid.: 219.

[4] Dalgat, Bashir. *Rodovoi byt i obychnoye pravo Chechentsev i Ingushey [Family life and customary law of Chechens and Ingushs]*. Moscow: IMLI RAN, 2008 [1934]; Leontovich, Fedor. *Adaty kavkazskikh gortsev [The customs of the Caucasian mountaineers]* Vol. 2. Odessa, 1882.

as the ultimate regulator of inter-family and inter-clan relations also highlights the collective nature of customary law.

There is little evidence on the functioning of customary law in Chechnya prior to Russian colonization and anti-colonial struggles.[5] Chechen culture was largely oral and adat norms were not codified. Nevertheless, there are several widely shared views on Chechen adat among local historians and legal scholars.[6] According to these scholars, adat was carried out by elders. Chechen clans and communities delegated an elder to a representative institution called *Mekh-Khel* (the Council of the Land), which convened regularly and had judicial, legislative, and executive authority. Communities had their own local courts (*khels*). These courts had an even number of members and their decisions were based on the principle of unanimity.

From the mid- to late nineteenth century, Russian military officers and academic ethnographers (often the same people) wrote down the adat norms of the peoples of the North Caucasus and attempted to systematize them. However, these attempts were bound to be incomplete due to the flexible and context-dependent nature of adat.[7] Most of the norms of Chechen adat were reconstructed based on the oral testimonies of elders recorded by Russian ethnographers. For example, one of the first ethnographic descriptions of Chechen society, *The Chechen Tribe*, was published in 1872 by Umalat Laudaev, a man of Chechen origin who served in the Russian military. Laudaev's account is clearly biased against the "savage Chechens," but he nevertheless made several important observations. First, he claimed that Chechens never had any aristocracy or monarchy and were all equal. Second, he described Chechen society as "anarchic" and based on the rule of force. In particular, Laudaev noted that adat justice relied heavily on oath and had no enforcement. As a result, strong families and clans disregarded adat rulings and abused weak ones. Laudaev also described several cases of dispute resolution according to adat. For example, he described the following dispute:

---

[5] This is in contrast to the presence of numerous primary sources on customary law and Sharia in neighboring Dagestan. See Bobrovnikov, *Musulmane Severnogo Kavkaza;* Gould, Rebecca, and Shamil Shikhaliev. "Beyond the Taqlīd/Ijtihād dichotomy: Daghestani legal thought under Russian rule." *Islamic Law and Society* 24, no. 1–2 (2017): 142–169. Kemper, Michael. "Adat against Shari'a: Russian approaches toward Daghestani 'customary law' in the 19th century." *Ab Imperio*, no. 3 (2005): 147–173.

[6] For a review, see Saidumov, *Sud, pravo i pravosudiye u Chechentsev i Ingushey.*

[7] Bobrovnikov, *Musulmane Severnogo Kavkaza*: 130; Kemper, "Adat against Shari'a."

A man was walking down a river bank with his stick, while a shepherd was sitting on the edge of the cliff of this bank. The man accidentally dropped his stick; the shepherd flinched from the unexpected noise, fell into the river and died. The shepherd's relatives blamed the man for murder. The Elders gathered to resolve the dispute and decided that the shepherd's blood cost forty cows. The payment of the blood price was divided equally between the man, his stick, and "the timid soul" of the shepherd. So, as a result, the man paid only a third of the blood price and gave his stick to the relatives of the shepherd.

This example highlights two major features of Chechen adat. First, adat does not distinguish between intentional and unintentional crimes. Second, adat is based on a nuanced compensatory logic: basically, every transgression has a price.

Relying on ethnographic materials, Maksim Kovalevsky, a famous Russian sociologist of the second half of the nineteenth century, wrote the seminal treatise *Law and Custom in the Caucasus.* Among other things, Kovalevsky and his student and colleague Bashir Dalgat emphasized that adat in Chechnya and elsewhere in the Caucasus had been significantly changed under the influence of Islam.[8] Islamization occurred in Chechnya relatively late, between the fifteenth and the eighteenth centuries.[9] With the adoption of Islam, Chechens started to adopt Sharia norms, but the use of these norms in Chechnya was highly selective. Usually, Sharia norms were used when they did not contradict adat regulations. Anna Zelkina highlighted four main differences between Sharia and Chechen adat. First, adat was based on the principle of collective responsibility, while Sharia was based on the principle of individual responsibility. Second, in contrast to Sharia, adat had no differentiation between premeditated and unintentional criminal acts. Third, in Sharia punishment and inflicted harm had to be proportional to one another. Finally, in Sharia a dispute was adjudicated by a third party, while in adat adjudication was carried out by the most respected elders of the parties involved in the dispute.[10]

Russian colonization and the related Caucasian War (1817–1864) brought major transformations to legal pluralism in Chechnya. During the initial period, the Russian colonization policy in the North Caucasus

---

[8] Dalgat, *Rodovoi byt i obychnoye pravo Chechentsev i Ingushey*; Kovalevsky, Maksim. *Zakon i obychai na Kavkaze [Law and custom in the Caucasus].* Moscow, 2012 (1890).

[9] Gammer, Moshe. *Muslim resistance to the Tsar: Shamil and the conquest of Chechnia and Daghestan.* Taylor & Francis, 1994.

[10] Zelkina, Anna. *In quest for God and freedom: The Sufi response to the Russian advance in the North Caucasus.* New York University Press, 2000.

was carried out by General Aleksei Yermolov, who served as High Commissioner of the Caucasus from 1816 to 1827. In an attempt to pacify and incorporate the Caucasus, Yermolov applied brutal terror against any insubordination. He was especially harsh in his repression against the Chechen population. Yermolov's colonization caused deep resentment and motivated numerous acts of armed resistance in Chechnya.[11]

Anti-colonial State-Building: Warfare and Lawfare

The most notorious rebellion in Chechnya started in 1840, when Chechens invited Sheikh Shamil, a famous religious and military leader from neighboring Dagestan, to lead an insurrection. Elected as the Imam of Dagestan and Chechnya, Shamil declared jihad against the Russian invaders. Shamil managed to organize effective guerrilla warfare against the Russian Empire for several decades. Even more importantly, he managed to build the first centralized state in the mountainous parts of Chechnya and Dagestan. Shamil's state, or Imamate, which functioned from 1834 to 1859, was a military theocracy. The state had an elaborate government apparatus, a system of taxation, and a unified legal system.

Shamil's struggle was as much a struggle against the local allies of Russian colonialism – customary authorities and feudal nobles – as against the empire itself. Shamil's predecessor, Imam Gamzet-Bek, had ordered the assassination of the entire family of Avar khans. Shamil was no less brutal towards his political opponents among the communal elites. As a result, warfare during the colonization can be characterized as a civil war between anti-colonial religious movements and the loyalists of the Russian imperial project headed by traditional authorities. Adat and Sharia were contraposed in this struggle.

Sharia was the ideology and political basis of Shamil's state.[12] The imamate had several levels of government, and Sharia arbitration had a system of appeal. Each village in the imamate had a qadi, an Islamic judge who was in charge of resolving disputes. On the province level, Sharia

---

[11] On Russian colonization of the North Caucasus, see Gammer, Moshe. *Muslim resistance to the Tsar*; Gapurov, Shahrudin. *Rossiia i Chechnia: posledniaia tret' XVIII – pervaia polovina XIX veka [Russia and Chechnya: late eighteenth–early nineteenth century]*. Grozny: Academy of Sciences, 2009; Khodarkovsky, Michael. *Bitter choices: Loyalty and betrayal in the Russian conquest of the North Caucasus*. Cornell University Press, 2011.

[12] Bobrovnikov, *Musulmane Severnogo Kavkaza*: 137.

was carried out by a mufti. The imam, as the head of state, had supreme judicial authority. Guided by Sharia, Shamil enacted a set of laws, *nizams*, that regulated issues of governance, taxation, and social behavior.

Shamil actively tried to suppress or change adat norms in his state and especially in Chechnya, where they were much more powerful than in Dagestan. He abolished the *Mekh-Khel* and prohibited local customs of blood revenge, bride kidnapping, and large bride prices. In accordance with Sharia, Shamil also obliged women to cover their heads and faces, and prohibited alcohol consumption, smoking, music, and dances. At the same time, Shamil exploited some adat norms for his own purposes. For example, he resolved a land dispute between the Chechen community of Kharachoy and the neighboring Dagestani community of Andi based on a customary agreement engraved on stone and dating back to the seventeenth or eighteenth century.[13] Local qadis also considered local customs when making their rulings.

Shamil's jihad and state-building efforts had many parallels in other colonial peripheries. Shamil's contemporaries often compared his struggle to that of Amir Abdelkader, who led a resistance against French colonialism in Algeria from 1832 to 1847. Striking parallels can also be found in many other places. For example, in the 1920s the Berbers of the Rif region in northern Morocco organized jihad against the Spanish colonial power. The struggle was led by the tribal noble Abd El-Krim. In addition to successful warfare, Abd El-Krim engaged in lawfare which was very similar to Shamil's state-building. According to Jonathan Wyrtzen, legal Islamization was one of the primary mechanisms Abd El-Krim used to consolidate his state:

He centralized and monopolized control of the juridical system by banning tribal customary law (*izref* or *urf*) and unifying a shari'a based judiciary ... Abd El-Krim's campaign to eradicate customary law in the Rif and replace it with shari'a ... undercut local tribal autonomy and centralized state control in a hierarchically organized system of government appointed judges ... Married women, widows, and divorcees were prohibited from singing or dancing, and the length of wedding celebrations was reduced from seven to three days.[14]

If one were to substitute Abd El-Krim with Shamil and Rif with the Caucasus in this description, they would get the story of state-building lawfare in Chechnya and Dagestan. The prevalence of parallels with other

---

[13] Ibid.: 140.   [14] Wyrtzen, *Making Morocco*: 126–127.

regions highlights the general pattern of the nexus of anti-colonial warfare and lawfare in the Muslim peripheries of the Western empires.

The Caucasian War led to the destruction of the traditional Chechen moral economy, mass population resettlements, the loss of a large share of the male population, and the strengthening of the role of Islam and Sharia.[15] All these factors undermined the power of clans and elders and thus transformed social relations in Chechnya. The Caucasian War also produced an ideological divide between and within Chechen families. Some were supportive of Shamil's Islamic order based on Sharia, while others took the side of Chechen traditionalism and customary law.

After a series of military defeats, Shamil surrendered to the Russian Viceroy of the Caucasus, Prince Aleksandr Baryatinskiy, in 1859. Shamil was exiled to central Russia, where he was treated as a celebrity and was given a good pension by the Russian Tsar. Many Chechens with whom I spoke viewed Shamil's surrender as a betrayal of the struggle. This theme is very prominent in discussions of legal pluralism, because some traditionalists and proponents of adat view Shamil and the imposition of Sharia in Chechnya, which they associate with him, in a negative light. However, others embrace Shamil and his legacy. For example, in the 1990s the authorities of an independent Chechnya actively used Shamil's image in framing their struggle. Today, Shamil remains a polarizing figure in Chechnya.[16]

The Imperial Accommodation

After the defeat of Shamil's resistance, the Russian administration effectively utilized Shamil's government structure and even his state personnel.[17] Thus, Shamil's state-building and especially his unification of the justice system eased the task of the Russian colonial enterprise. Famous Soviet-era Chechen writer Abuzar Aidamirov wrote about how the new Imperial authority was legitimized in Chechnya by the former rebel communal authorities in his historical novel *The Long Nights*:

---

[15] Sokirianskaia, *Governing fragmented societies.*
[16] On the controversial representation of Shamil in Chechen literature, see Gould, Rebecca. *Writers and rebels: The literature of insurgency in the Caucasus.* Yale University Press, 2016.
[17] Bobrovnikov, *Musulmane Severnogo Kavkaza*: 107–108. This section heavily draws on Bobrovnikov's analysis.

Sharia is now being interpreted in favor of the authorities. If ten years ago, mullahs were saying that all non-Muslims were enemies of Allah, now they say that the Russian Tsar and his henchmen are enemies no more. Now they say that the Tsar is the God-given ruler of Earth, and all his officials govern in accordance with God's will. And those who would rise against the Tsar, his officials, and the rich will burn in hell.

Not everyone accepted Russian colonial rule: many Chechens, along with other North Caucasian *muhajirs* (immigrants), moved to the Ottoman Empire. In turn, the Russian Empire brought colonists and Cossacks to the lowlands of the North Caucasus. The authorities in St. Petersburg then listed Chechnya as part of the ethnically diverse Terek region (*Terskaya oblast*). Colonial state penetration in the region remained weak. Facing low legibility of the indigenous population and limited resources, the metropole came up with a hybrid of direct and indirect rule.

In 1860, the newly established Terek region was placed under a civil-military administration (*voenno-narodnoye upravleniye*) which included a bifurcated system of justice. Military courts dealt with high crimes of treason, rebellion, murder, and theft of state property.[18] People's courts (*narodnye sudy*) in the towns and villages tried both civil and criminal cases based on adat and Sharia. The Russian administration formalized legal pluralism and introduced a division of jurisdictions: personal law issues, including marriage, divorce, and inheritance, as well as religious property, were under Sharia jurisdiction; petty crime and property disputes were regulated by adat. In practice, alternative legal systems were weakly differentiated. In the rural areas, the same people often formed the court that adjudicated family disputes, petty criminal cases, and land disputes according to a mix of Sharia and adat.

Throughout the colonial period, imperial authorities actively promoted adat to counterbalance Sharia, which they viewed as a major threat to Russian dominance in the North Caucasus. The colonial administration also preferred customary law because the officials assumed that they could adjust and manipulate the customs due to their relative flexibility. Perceptions of adat in the Russian Empire were based on romantic orientalist visions of the Caucasus. The image of "the noble savages"

---

[18] In 1871 the Terek region was transferred to the Russian civil administration and military courts were replaced with civil ones. However, during the era of conservative counter-reforms in 1888, the entire administration of the region was placed under the military. This formed the military-police regime that governed the region until the revolution.

was widely popularized in Russian literature and art.[19] Ethnographic writings led to an understanding of the Caucasus through the ideas of premodern kinship (*rod*), community (*obschina*) and popular justice (*narodnoye pravo*). Under the guidance of the benevolent empire these institutions were supposed to evolve towards embracing modern state law and civil society.[20] The imperial policies were clearly driven by civilizational ideology. The administration attempted to eradicate certain "archaic customs" that directly contradicted Russian law. For instance, blood revenge was strictly prohibited and equated with murder. In contrast, Sharia norms based on scripture were perceived to be much more difficult to adjust or manipulate. However, as historian Robert Crews has shown, imperial scholars of Islamic law profoundly changed the way Sharia was practiced among Muslim subjects of the empire.[21]

Of course, legal pluralism in the Russian Empire did not begin with the conquest of the Caucasus. According to Jane Burbank, inclusive state legal pluralism, differentiated legal systems for different collectivities such as ethnic groups and religious communities, had been the cornerstone of the Russian "imperial rights regime" since at least the sixteenth century.[22] She wrote that "an imperial dimension of Russian legal thinking was the assumption that all peoples possessed their own customs and laws. Incorporating these distinctive customs and laws into official governance was a means to enhance order and productivity in each region of the empire."[23]

Over time the empire moved towards legal centralization. The North Caucasus, however, remained an exceptional region in the Imperial legal regime. It was heavily policed and governed in a militarized way. Some other regions with large Muslim populations, for example Crimea and Kazan province, were incorporated into the centralized Russian legal order as a result of the liberal judicial reform of 1864. As Stefan Kirmse shows, after the reform, some Muslim Tatars in these provinces eagerly

[19] Grant, Bruce. *The captive and the gift: Cultural histories of sovereignty in Russia and the Caucasus.* Cornell University Press, 2009; King, Charles. *The ghost of freedom: A history of the Caucasus.* Oxford University Press, 2008; Tolz, Vera. *Russia's own orient: The politics of identity and oriental studies in the late imperial and early Soviet periods.* Oxford University Press, 2011.
[20] Bobrovnikov, *Musulmane Severnogo Kavkaza:* 151–152.
[21] Crews, Robert. *For Prophet and Tsar.* Harvard University Press, 2009.
[22] Burbank, Jane. "An imperial rights regime: Law and citizenship in the Russian Empire." *Kritika: Explorations in Russian and Eurasian History* 7, no. 3 (2006): 397–431.
[23] Ibid.: 401.

went to Russian courts to seek redress and advance their interests. Some of the litigants were women who brought disputes related to divorces, inheritance, forced marriages, and bride kidnappings to Russian courts. Unlike these other peripheries, however, the North Caucasus remained the "bastion of legal fragmentation" in the Russian Empire until the revolution.[24]

Another bastion of Russian colonial legal pluralism was Central Asia, conquered in the second half of the nineteenth century. There, the empire employed a mix of direct and indirect rule through the protectorates of Khiva and Bukhara. The colonial administration strategically "preserved" local Sharia courts for the settled population and applied adat for the nomads.[25] In addition, there were courts presided over by Russian justices of the peace and Russian military officials. Paolo Sartori shows that Central Asians learned different notions of morality from dealing with these different courts. Many started to file complaints with Russian authorities about the corruption, ignorance, and incompetence of the Muslim judges. Ultimately, some locals started to engage in forum shopping and "profit from legal diversity."[26]

Similar processes of the strategic use of different courts were also present in colonial Chechnya. Gradually, more Chechens started to join the Russian imperial military and administrative services. In return, the colonial government gave their new servicemen large plots of land expropriated from Chechen communities. That led to a sharp rise in inequality among Chechens, who had previously relied on collective forms of property rights. The colonial administration also involved Chechnya in the national and global capitalist economy. In the late nineteenth century, Chechnya witnessed the development of the oil industry, and its capital Grozny became one of the main industrial centers of the North Caucasus. The colonial administration, military service, and capitalism weakened traditional forms of social control in Chechnya and led to a rise in the use of imperial law and police. However, the balance among the three legal systems that regulated the daily life of ordinary Chechens was largely preserved outside the modern sectors of the economy. The Imperial

---

[24] Kirmse, Stefan. *The lawful empire: Legal change and cultural diversity in late Tsarist Russia*. Cambridge University Press, 2019: 73.

[25] Sartori, Paolo. *Visions of justice: Sharī'a and cultural change in Russian Central Asia*. Brill, 2016: 5.

[26] Ibid.: 6.

system of formalized legal pluralism in the North Caucasus ended only with the Russian Revolution of 1917.

Lawfare Amid Revolution and Civil War

After the 1917 Revolution, Chechnya became a part of a short-lived confederation called the Union of the Mountaineers and subsequently the Mountainous Republic (1917–1920). It was organized by the intelligentsia of different nationalities of the North Caucasus and was first headed by the Chechen oil industrialist Abdulmajid "Tapa" Tchermoeff. The union was rather weak, and real political power was contested at the local level.

During the revolution, calls to establish Sharia law were among the most prominent political slogans across the North Caucasus. Liberal Chechen lawyer Akhmetkhan Mutushev, who was elected as the head of the Chechen Executive Committee, wrote that "Right from the start, the Chechen people badgered us, their revolutionary committee: 'Give us Sharia!'"[27] The revolutionary period witnessed constant power struggles between the national elites, who held liberal and socialist ideologies, and religious authorities.[28] In response to the demands of religious authorities, the First Congress of the Mountainous People of the North Caucasus that took place in May 1917 established Sharia courts (*sharsudy*) in major cities of the region. Village courts were also reorganized on the basis of Sharia. At the same time, different political forces understood Sharia in different ways. For instance, the proponents of the radical agrarian reform justified their proposal with reference to "Sharia, which defends the interests of the proletariat." Their opponents used Sharia to justify the opposite: preservation of large landholdings.[29] Some proponents of Sharia attempted to discredit influential socialists by claiming that they "give the wives the husbands' rights; among them it is not the husband,

---

[27] Muzaev, Timur. *Souz Gortsev. Russkaia Revolutsiia i narody Severnogo Kavkaza [The union of the mountaineers. Russian Revolution and the peoples of the North Caucasus].* Patria, 2007: 23.

[28] Vatchagaev, Mairbek. *Souz Gortsev Severnogo Kavkaza i Gorskaia Respublika. Istoriia nesostoyavshegosia gosudarstva 1917–1920 [The union of the peoples of the Northern Caucasus and the mountainous republic. The history of would to be state 1917–1920].* Litres, 2018: 42–54.

[29] Muzaev, *Souz Gortsev*: 90. Such "bending" of Sharia towards contradictory ends has been common in many other historical contexts. See Massoud, *Shari 'a, Inshallah*.

but the wife who initiates a divorce."[30] This quote highlights that lawfare around gender and family law was a key cleavage even during the revolutionary struggles for political power fought along class lines.

The collapse of the Tsarist regime led to violent conflicts between Chechens and the Cossacks over land and a dramatic rise in crime. Robberies became endemic in Chechnya and paralyzed its economic life. Religious authorities decided to seize the moment and called for the broader enactment of Sharia law in order to combat disorder. As a result, according to historian Timur Muzaev, power in Chechnya became split between the lawyers and the sheikhs.[31] The camp of the Sharia proponents was also bitterly divided among the followers of different influential Sufi sheikhs.

The Russian civil war led to further fragmentation of political authority. The government of the Mountainous Republic introduced military Sharia courts. Both the Whites and the Reds, when they took control over the region, organized their own Sharia courts that often functioned as military tribunals.[32] In addition, Uzun-haji, one of the most influential sheikhs, established the North Caucasian Emirate, "an independent Sharia monarchy" that controlled the mountainous parts of Chechnya and Dagestan.[33] Thus, in accordance with my theoretical outline, the extremely fragmented political field of the revolutionary period in Chechnya led to Sharia outbidding: competitive appeals that challenged the legitimacy of Islamic law. We'll see a similar process in Chechnya in the 1990s. Ultimately, these alternative state-building projects of the revolutionary period were suppressed by the Bolsheviks, who took full control over the North Caucasus by the early 1920s. The new era of Soviet legal pluralism began.

LEGAL PLURALISM DESPITE SOVIET RULE

Red Legal Pluralism

Initially, the Bolshevik government built a surprising coalition with Islamic clerics, most notably the powerful Sufi sheikh Deni Arsanov, and established Soviet Sharia courts. The decisions of these courts could be appealed only in the Supreme Court of the Russian Republic. In the

---

[30] Ibid.: 140.   [31] Ibid.: 114.   [32] Bobrovnikov, *Musulmane Severnogo Kavkaza*: 227.
[33] Vatchagaev, *Souz Gortsev Severnogo Kavkaza i Gorskaia Respublika*: 243.

early years of Soviet rule, Sharia courts in Chechnya were very powerful and adjudicated up to 80 percent of all cases.[34]

However, with the consolidation of Soviet authority in the mid-1920s, the government banned Sharia courts and started to suppress customary institutions as "relics of the past" throughout the North Caucasus. The government's action was driven by ideologies of modernization and anti-clericalism. Many religious and traditional authorities were repressed, including respected clerics and elders. However, the government's attempts to eradicate adat and Sharia never fully succeeded. The establishment of the Soviet justice system in Chechnya was a challenging project. In Chechen understanding, the Soviet justice system "stipulated strict penalties for minor offences, while not punishing murderers sufficiently. Consequently, minor offences were hardly ever reported and blood feuds were carried out regardless of the Soviet courts."[35] As a result, Chechen society continued to live under a legal symbiosis of Soviet justice, adat, and Sharia.

As in the cases of other ethnic minorities who were perceived as "backward," the Soviet government encouraged cultural development and promoted local institutions of state power in Chechnya. The government organized mass education campaigns in the 1920s and 1930s, published dictionaries, schoolbooks, and collections of folklore in the Chechen language, and created theaters, newspapers, and libraries.[36] However, the affirmative action that the Soviet government implemented towards other minority ethnic groups was quite limited in Chechnya.[37] Tellingly, in the 1930s the Chechen Autonomous Oblast had the lowest percentage of titular nationals in the total government apparat among all regions of the North Caucasus: in 1933 it was just 11 percent.[38] Furthermore, local Chechen party cadres and nascent national intelligentsia were heavily repressed during the 1937–1938 purges.[39] Khasan Israilov, whose story I narrated in Chapter 2, was among those arrested, though unlike many, he was released.

[34] Bobrovnikov, *Musulmane Severnogo Kavkaza*: 228.
[35] Sokirianskaia, "Governing fragmented societies": 82.   [36] Tishkov, *Chechnya*: 22.
[37] Avtorkhanov, Abdurakhman. *Imperiia Kreml'ia: Sovetskiy tip kolonialisma [The Kremlin's Empire: The Soviet type of colonialism]*. Prometheus Verlag, 1988; Bugaev, Abdulla. *Sovetskaia Avtonomiia Checheno-Ingushetii [The Soviet autonomy of Checheno-Ingushetia]*. KEP, 2012.
[38] Martin, Terry. *The affirmative action empire: Nations and nationalism in the Soviet Union, 1923–1939*. Cornell University Press, 2001: 173.
[39] Tishkov, *Chechnya*: 23.

Stalin's collectivization program, initiated in 1929, largely failed in Chechnya. Chechens sabotaged the program by organizing collective farms based on extended family units. For example, in Shatoy district, the village of Shali alone witnessed registration of eighty-seven collective farms, but by 1943, such farms accounted for only 4 percent of the district's cattle.[40] According to historian Pavel Polian, this was "at best a parody of collectivization."[41] These can all be interpreted as signs of the low legibility of the Chechen population to the high modernist Soviet state.

Deportation: Social Order vs. State Repression

Repressions and collectivization sparked several major rebellions and widespread banditry in Chechnya during the early Soviet period (1921–1941). A telling fact is that from September 1937 to September 1938, 11,691 weapons were seized from the population, including artillery pieces.[42] Stalin responded to the perceived Chechen disloyalty with his characteristic "ultimate solution." On February 23, 1944, "Operation Lentil" began. The entire Chechen and Ingush nations were deported to Central Asia for alleged collaboration with Nazi invaders. This was despite the thousands of Chechens and Ingush having been mobilized to fight in the Soviet Army. The Autonomous Checheno-Ingush Soviet Socialist Republic was abolished.

The deportation was staggeringly harsh. It took place in the midst of a severe winter. People were forced to walk to the transportation centers and then were packed into overcrowded train cars, where they spent several weeks of travel. Those deemed non-transportable were shot dead by the NKVD squads. Likewise, more than 700 people in the mountainous village of Khaibakh who were not able to walk to the transportation center were gathered in a stable and burned alive. On the way, people died from cold, hunger, and infectious diseases. Those who died were thrown from the train cars. Almost a third of the population perished on the way.[43]

---

[40] As quoted in Tishkov, *Chechnya*: 24.
[41] As cited in Sokirianskaia, *Governing fragmented societies*: 82.
[42] Westren, Michael Herzeg. *Nations in exile: "The Punished People" in Soviet Kazakhstan, 1941–1961*. Ph.D. dissertation. University of Chicago, 2012: 74.
[43] Tishkov, *Chechnya*.

Conditions in Central Asia were also extremely difficult. Deported people were sometimes abandoned in the empty steppe. They were treated by the Soviet authorities and local population as "traitor-nations" and "bandits." Within the ethnic order of Central Asia, Chechens and other groups from the North Caucasus were at the very bottom, with the dominant Slavic groups at the top and the local Central Asian nationalities in the middle. Chechens and Ingush were especially subject to discrimination by the state and by local communities. According to the Soviet police archives, Chechens and Ingush faced extreme violence, even lynching and pogroms.[44]

Deportation further weakened the clan structure of Chechen society, but strengthened national identity. Birgit Brauer wrote, "one of the side effects of the deportations was that ... Chechens became much closer and stronger as a people. Their families and villages may have been torn apart, but their defiance against these circumstances led to the development of a national identity."[45] Deportation also led to traditionalization and the increased power of elders and religious authorities. Historian Michael Herzeg Westren showed that traditional authorities became power brokers between the Soviet authorities and isolated and closed communities of Chechens and Ingush. He documents how imams and family authorities would control the population, increase work discipline, and participate in elections. However, at the same time, other traditional authorities "called for sabotage of work, disruption of housing construction and the destruction of state cattle, and declared that stealing government or kolkhoz property was not subject to Sharia law."[46]

During the deportation, traditional authorities established a sort of shadow government. They provided social welfare for their communities and settled disputes within them. In the reports of the Soviet Ministry of Interior, these courts were called "Khel", "Shariat", or "third-party courts." This highlights the fact that these informal courts combined elements of customary and religious legal systems. The central aim of these courts was the resolution of inter-family feuds. For example, Westren reports the following case where the police (MVD) outsourced conflict resolution within a Chechen community to a prominent Chechen religious leader.

---

[44] Westren, *Nations in exile*: 251–252.
[45] Brauer, Birgit. "Chechens and the survival of their cultural identity in exile." *Journal of Genocide Research* 4, no. 3 (2002): 399.
[46] Westren, *Nations in exile*: 292.

In October 1949, in Karaganda city, a mass fight occurred between several Chechen clans as a result of a blood feud. Dozens of participants were recruited into the struggle from surrounding districts. When the dust settled, six were badly crippled by knife wounds and hospitalized. It started in the settlement of Mel'kombinat, when Khusen Buraev walked past Akhmed Tokaev without greeting him, which the latter took as an offense. After several days, the Tokaevs and their relatives the Dzhabrailovs kidnapped a girl relative of Buraev, Khasi Toseuva, for one of the Dzhabrailovs to marry. The Buraevs and their allies the Toseuvs went after the Dzhabrailovs and threatened one of the participants, who revealed the location of the stolen girl, and the latter was returned home. Several days later, Akhmed Tokaev and his brother encountered Khusen Buraev, who was drunk, in a tea cafeteria. They picked on him, and an argument started. Akhmed Tokaev hit Buraev in the face with an open palm, which is considered a great insult among Chechens. Buraev returned home, gathered his relatives from surrounding districts, armed themselves with knives, broke into the Tokaev apartment, and attacked them. The mullah Arsanov stepped in and persuaded all sides to leave the matter alone. The organizers of the fight were not prosecuted by the Karaganda MVD, which instead imposed only administrative sanctions, and the case was not turned over by the Kazakh MVD to the oblast to make arrests, as part of their deal with Arsanov, who, in reconciling the two sides, requested in return that no one be arrested.[47]

The informal courts also punished those who collaborated with the state and especially those who denounced their co-ethnics. For example, "in May 1952, one Ata Bibulatov was sentenced by Soviet courts for the theft of a stick of dynamite, after evidence was provided against him by Magomet Kudusov. The elder courts subsequently sentenced Kudusov for this betrayal of the community ... and punished him with a fine of 6,000 rubles to be paid to Bibulatov's family in compensation."[48] Chechen communities also excluded and ostracized those who embraced the Soviet way of life. In some cases, "apostates" from the Chechen communities faced violence.

Soviet reports consistently highlighted the persistence and power of "backward, feudal" customs among the Chechens and Ingush. The customs became even more strictly enforced during the exile, compared to how they had been practiced in the Caucasus. This was a way of preserving culture, but also an instrument to block the penetration of the Soviet state into Chechen society. My interviews provide support for this narrative. Prominent Chechen ethnographer Said-Magomed Khasiev told me that in exile elders made an edict regarding the strong norm of ethnic endogamy for women (not marrying non-Chechens), which is

[47] Ibid.: 296.   [48] Ibid.

largely preserved now. This is in line with the idea that the invention of tradition often happens in periods of rapid social change.[49]

At the same time, deportation exposed Chechens to Soviet institutions and forced them to learn the Russian language. According to Valery Tishkov, deportation is a moment when "history essentially begins for the modern generations of Chechens."[50] The memory of deportation, perceived as genocide, constitutes a central tenet of Chechen and Ingush identities.

After Exile: Slow Sovietization

In 1957, the Chechens and Ingush were allowed to return to their native land. After they were deported, Checheno-Ingushetia had been resettled with workers from central Russia; as a result, the Checheno-Ingush ASSR became a multiethnic republic. The Russian-speaking population lived in Grozny and in the northern part of Chechnya. Chechens mostly resettled in the rural areas. Upon their return, Chechens faced the structural problem of unemployment.[51] Many positions in the economy were occupied by the Russian-speaking settlers. Chechens were completely excluded from the industrial oil sector and the government, and were largely employed in agriculture and trade. High unemployment forced Chechen and Ingush men to leave the republic for seasonal jobs (*shabashka*) in the rest of the Soviet Union.[52]

Chechens were explicitly discriminated against in Chechnya after their return. Until the very end of the Soviet Union, Checheno-Ingushetia always had a Russian-speaking first secretary of the Communist Party (the most important political position). There were no Chechens in prominent positions in the KGB, and few in top positions in the police and other government institutions. Even in the regional library system, there were only a few ethnic Chechens out of more than a hundred employees at the end of Soviet rule in 1990. The Chechen language was not taught in schools and universities and was discouraged if not de facto prohibited in public spaces. Many of my interviewees who grew up in the Soviet Union recalled how their teachers or random passengers on trams in Grozny

[49] Hobsbawm, Eric, and Terence Ranger, eds. *The invention of tradition*. Cambridge University Press, 1983.
[50] Tishkov, *Chechnya*: 21.   [51] Bugaev, *Sovetskaya Avtonomiia Checheno-Ingushetii*.
[52] Derluguian, *Bourdieu's secret admirer in the Caucasus*.

cursed them for speaking Chechen in public. The common phrase was: "Speak in a normal language, not your barbarian one!"[53]

Despite social exclusion and discrimination, Chechens started to slowly integrate into the Soviet system. At the same time, custom and Sharia kept playing major roles. For example, in a report to Moscow in 1959 based on interviews conducted in Checheno-Ingushetia, two inspectors concluded that "the customs of blood revenge, *kalym* (bride price), forced marriages, polygamy, and secret courts (based on adat custom) are much more prevalent than one could have assumed."[54] The authors of the report describe the following case:

In the village of Urus-Martan, citizen Tayupov, in revenge for a minor injury, decided to harm citizen Talkhigov (who was a relative of the person who had injured him) and stabbed him in the hip. Talkhigov fell and hit a rock. Lacking proper medical help, he died. Talkhigov's family declared blood revenge and as a result eighteen men from Tayupov's family, including the village head, are hiding, not working, fearing a revenge killing. It is known that the Talkhigovs are hunting the village head, and not the actual murderer, because he is more of an equal to the murdered in significance.

Thus, despite the enormous Soviet state capacity and ideological work against "the relics of the past," customary and religious norms persisted. My interviews provide ample empirical evidence for this assertion. For example, in the late Soviet period the uncle of Khava, one of my interviewees, was killed in his native village. He argued with a drunk neighbor and the neighbor stabbed him in the back. There was a trial, but apparently the murderer had influential relatives, so the court acquitted him. In response, the victim's brother shot the murderer right on the steps of the court. The police that were present decided not to arrest the brother and asked village elders to resolve the case. The elders agreed that the brother did nothing wrong, and the state did not intervene. This case happened in the early 1980s, at the zenith of Soviet rule.

When Soviet rule weakened during perestroika, customary norms became even more prominent. Khozh-Ahmed, one of my interviewees, who had worked in the prosecutor's office in the 1980s, said that de-Stalinization and glasnost created a demand for justice in Chechen society. Many Chechens and Ingush appealed to the prosecutor's office to

---

[53] For a similar narrative, see Vatchagaev, Mairbek. *Chechnya: The inside story. From independence to war.* Open Books, 2019.
[54] Kozlov et al., *Vainakhi i imperskaoa vlast*: 934.

release materials on repressions during Stalin's time. People were seeking those who wrote the denunciations and wanted revenge. A wave of blood feuds swept through Chechnya. Relatives were killing relatives, because those who had denounced their neighbors often tried to marry into their families, expecting that one day they might have to account for their deeds. However, that did not stop the avengers. Khozh-Ahmed recalled:

Six men came to the house of my neighbor. They asked if he had prayed, which meant, was he ready to die? My neighbor asked: "Who are you and what did I do? I don't even know you." These men replied that my neighbor's uncle had denounced their grandfather and the grandfather was executed. They wanted to avenge him. My neighbor tried to explain that he did not even know his uncle – this uncle perished during the deportation. But the men were adamant and shot my neighbor nevertheless.

Thus, even during Soviet times when the state had very high coercive capacity and modernist ideology, legal pluralism persisted in Checheno-Ingushetia, at least to some degree.

* * *

This chapter tells the history of Chechnya through the history of trans-formations of legal pluralism in the region. The anti-colonial state-build-ing project of Imam Shamil and subsequent Russian colonization brought legal pluralism to the previously stateless social order that relied on the fragmented system of customary law. The Russian Empire institutional-ized legal pluralism as part of a divide and rule strategy and a response to low state capacity and following orientalist ideology. In this regard, Russia did not differ much from other empires of that time, which also promoted legal pluralism in order to control their colonies.

When the center weakened and collapsed after the Russian Revolution of 1917, local actors in the Caucasus attempted to mobilize Sharia law for competing political projects. Even the Bolsheviks, who ended up becom-ing the new center, initially built a surprising coalition with religious leaders and established Red Sharia courts. Upon the consolidation of Soviet rule, the central government attempted to eliminate custom and Sharia in the region. The Soviet drive to ensure legal centralism was fueled by the ideology of modernization and increased state capacity. However, the project ultimately failed because of Stalin's forced deportation of the entire Chechen nation to Central Asia in 1944. State violence strengthened the Chechen national identity and alienated Chechens from state law. After the return to the Caucasus in 1957, Chechens remained marginalized in the Soviet state-building project and preserved customary and religious institutions. As the next chapter will show, when the state weakened and subsequently collapsed, the role of non-state legal systems became even more prominent as a result of local struggles for political control.

4

"There Are No Camels in Chechnya!"

Lawfare during the Independence Period

Sultan-haji Mirzaev is one of the most famous Chechen clerics of the post-Soviet period. During the turbulent period of the 1990s he was the head of the Supreme Sharia Court of the independent Chechen Republic of Ichkeria. Subsequently, he was Mufti, the principal religious authority, during the pro-Russian Kadyrov administration. I am meeting the retired Sultan-haji in one of his houses in rural Chechnya. The house is big, but not luxurious. Sultan-haji explains that he has three wives, and he moves around between three houses in three different communities to give each wife proper attention. He readily jumps into a debate with the Chechen ethnographers who previously told me that Chechen customary law does not allow polygamy. Sultan-haji says, "These ethnographers are talking nonsense. They are nerds who can't satisfy one wife, so they spread fairy tales that adat does not allow polygamy."

Sultan-haji's relatives bring us a large plate of hot *khingalsh* – traditional flatbread with pumpkin. Sultan-haji himself is writing a doctoral dissertation about the political philosophy of Kunta-haji Kishiev – the most influential Chechen Sufi sheikh of the nineteenth century, whom he compares to Leo Tolstoy. Thus, he is sympathetic to my academic inquiry. In contrast to many people in contemporary Chechnya, he is willing to talk about the turbulent period of the 1990s. He narrates with some nostalgia that "Despite the fact that society became more cohesive during the war, there were many internal conflicts. Theft, bride kidnappings, kidnappings for ransom, property disputes – we had everything. Many people came to me for resolution." He goes on to describe one case:

Three rebels came to their native village from the mountains where they were fighting. And they saw a young guy with a young woman in a new Lada car engaged in some romance. The rebels got very angry and threw the guy from the car, saying, "While we are fighting, you are having fun here". They took that young man's car. But the young man had a powerful clan behind him. The clan people came to the relatives of the rebels and demanded they buy a new car and give a huge amount of cash as compensation for the offense. The two sides came to me. I spoke with the rebel guys – they agreed to return the car but refused to pay the compensation. But the leader of the offended clan, who was an imam and also a high-status criminal (*blatnoy*) at the same time, said, "We have the power, let them pay the full price!" When the rebels heard this, they just went back to the mountains and did not return anything. These clan people kept coming back to me and asking for additional arbitration, but I told them to get out of my house.

This case presents a picture of the complex legal hybrid that emerged in the de facto independent Chechnya of the 1990s amid armed conflict. The modern Chechen government heavily polices narratives about that period. Writing on it is censored in the state archives and libraries. It is supposed to be forgotten. However, many people with lived experience of the 1990s shared their memories with me, which allowed me to reconstruct the history of lawfare during the critical periods of Chechen independence and armed conflict.

The de facto independent state of Ichkeria existed from 1991 to 1999. It effectively seceded from the Russian Federation in the aftermath of the collapse of the Soviet Union. Neither Russia nor any other state except for Afghanistan under the Taliban recognized Ichkeria. However, this period of Chechen history is qualitatively different from the imperial and Soviet periods, because local rulers ceased to be just intermediaries of the center and instead engaged in building an independent state. Lawfare played a major role in this process, as I document below. The time of independence can be divided into three periods: Dudayev's pre-war rule in 1991–1994, the wartime social and political orders during active warfare (1994–1996 and 1999–2000), and the interwar period of 1996–1999, which ended with the start of the Second Chechen War and the forced reintegration of Chechnya into the Russian Federation.

INDEPENDENCE AND THE REVIVAL OF TRADITION
AND RELIGION

Perestroika and glasnost, as implemented by Mikhail Gorbachev in the second half of the 1980s, brought nationalist and religious revival to Chechnya. A significant part of the national intelligentsia that emerged in Chechnya in the late Soviet period organized into proto-political movements and clubs with a nationalist agenda.[1] In 1990, supporters of Chechen independence from Russia organized the all-Chechen Congress, which elected Dzhokhar Dudayev, the only Chechen who held the rank of general in the Soviet military forces, as its leader. In September 1991, amid mass demonstrations in support of Chechen independence, Dudayev's supporters ousted the communist leadership and took power in the republic. In a short period of time, Dudayev was elected as the President of Chechnya and declared its independence from Russia. President Dudayev came up with a new name for his new state: the Chechen Republic of Ichkeria (ChRI).

The Chechen national movement and its first steps towards state-building were organized in the European tradition of nationalism. In March 1992, the newly elected Chechen Parliament adopted the Constitution of ChRI. Khussain Akhmadov, the chair of the Chechen Parliament in 1992–1993, stated, "There was no mention of traditional institutions and very little emphasis on religion in that first constitution. All MPs had the Constitutions of the United States and of European countries on our desks. We produced many decent laws. We were oriented towards a European democratic model."[2] Similarly, Vakha Murtazaliev, the former Military Prosecutor General of ChRI, told me, "When we were writing the Constitution, we had copies of the Constitutions of Lithuania and Georgia in front of us."

Ichkeria's first president, Dzhokhar Dudayev, shared these secular and modernist views. In an interview he said: "I would like Chechnya to be a constitutional secular state."[3] The Ichkerian Constitution of 1992 pronounced Islam to be the official religion, but at the same time stated the principle of freedom of religion. Dudayev was wary of the influence of religious and traditional communal elites and even issued a presidential decree to minimize and control intrusion by private actors and religious

[1] Derluguian, *Bourdieu's secret admirer in the Caucasus*; Gakaev, Jabrail. *Ocherki politicheskoy istorii Chechni (XX vek) [Essays on political history of Chechnya]*. Moscow, 1997. Gakaev, Jabrail. 1999. *Put' k chechnskoy revolutsii. [The path to Chechen revolution]*. In Dmitry Furman (ed.) *Chechnia i Rossiia: Obschchestva i gosudarstva [Chechnya and Russia: Societies and States]*. Moscow: The Andrey Sakharov Fund, 1999; Hughes, *Chechnya*.
[2] Sokirianskaia, *Governing fragmented societies*: 159.
[3] As quoted in Hughes, *Chechnya*: 66.

institutions into the court system.[4] There were nevertheless activists at the Congress of the Chechen People, the organization that had installed Dudayev as the president of Ichkeria, who demanded implementation of Sharia law. Dudayev rejected these demands. According to Taimaz Abubakarov, who was a finance minister in the Ichkerian government, Dudayev said:

The Koran and Sharia are holy, and it's pointless to talk about them in vain. Everything has its time. There are a lot of Muslim countries in the world, but only a few of them live strictly according to Sharia. Besides, not every Chechen is a Muslim. We all know this well. The roots of Islam in Chechnya were greatly undermined by the Communists, and it is impossible to restore them in an hour or a year. I respect your perseverance, but I consider it premature. If today we declare Sharia law, tomorrow you will demand that I begin to cut off the heads and hands of sinners. But you don't realize that tomorrow it will be a rare participant of the Congress of the Chechen People who keeps his head and hands. You are not ready for this now, and nor am I. Let us, therefore, establish the order based on the Koran in our souls, and the order based on the Constitution in our public life.[5]

While the executive and legislative branches of the ChRI were radically transformed, the judiciary remained organized much the same way as it had been during the Soviet period. Many Russian cadres who had worked in courts and law enforcement agencies left Chechnya after the declaration of independence, but former Soviet judges, prosecutors, and police officers who were of Chechen nationality largely kept their positions. Most of these cadres were skeptical of the idea of independence and few supported Dudayev. This is not surprising, given that these people had been indoctrinated by the Soviet state and also remained connected to the Russian federal judicial and law enforcement agencies. I spoke with six men who had served in both the Soviet and Ichkerian legal systems, and they all universally acknowledged hostility towards the idea of independence, and towards Dudayev personally, in the ranks of the law enforcement cadres.

The legal system and the law enforcement agencies in the independent Chechnya faced a strong challenge as a result of Dudayev's decision to

---

[4] Presidential decree No. 6. January 8, 1992. Cited in Klyachkina, *Reconfiguration of subnational governance*: 202.

[5] Abubakarov, Taimaz. "Mezhdu avtoritarnost'iu i anarkhiey. Politicheskiye dilemmy Prezidenta Dudayeva" [Between authoritarianism and anarchy: Political dilemmas of President Dudayev]. In Dmitry Furman (ed.) *Chechnia i Rossiia: Obschchestva i gosudarstva* [Chechnya and Russia: Societies and states]. (Moscow, The Andrey Sakharov Fund, 1999.

release all prisoners from the Soviet prisons. Coupled with the dramatic proliferation of weapons taken from Soviet military bases by crowds of Dudayev supporters during the revolution of 1991, the release of criminals led to skyrocketing crime. This further increased the judicial and law enforcement community's hostility towards Dudayev's rule. However, the confrontation between the president and the legislative branch of the government was even harsher.

In 1992–1993, Dudayev clashed with the Parliament over ministerial appointments and accountability. In response to the political crisis, Dudayev dissolved the Parliament. In order to counterbalance it, Dudayev decided to promote the all-Chechnya Council of Elders – a neotraditional "parliament" of self-appointed elders that took the historic name of *Mekh-Khel*. Dudayev also toured Chechnya and met with elders in the rural areas that became his strongholds. In turn, Dudayev's support emboldened and politicized the neotraditionalists. The head of the *Mekh-Khel*, Said-Magomed Adizov, became preoccupied with organizing political rallies, political lobbying, and business affairs rather than resolving disputes.[6]

Neotraditionalism also rose from below. Many *teips* (clans) organized congresses of their members. Some of these congresses gathered thousands of people. The revival of the salience of *teip* membership was a radical change for some Chechens who lived in cities and did not even know to which clan they belonged. During the Ichkeria period this became a big issue. One large clan went so far as to create heraldic symbols that they put on their cars.

Simultaneously with the rise of nationalism and neotraditionalism, Chechnya also witnessed a religious revival. During the Soviet period, religion had effectively been banned. In the 1930s, many Chechen Islamic scholars and imams were repressed, and religious institutions shut down. In the late Soviet period, in Chechnya there were just six official mosques staffed "by no more than twenty mullahs."[7] The restrictions on religion in Chechnya were very harsh even by Soviet standards – there were hundreds of open mosques in neighboring Dagestan.

Liberalization of religious life during perestroika, and especially after the declaration of Chechen independence, changed the picture dramatically. Mosques opened in every town and almost every village in Chechnya. Thousands of Chechen pilgrims went on hajj to Mecca.

---

[6] Sokirianskaia, *Governing fragmented societies*: 182. [7] Hughes, *Chechnya*: 12.

Some Chechen students went to study Islam in Egypt, Syria, Yemen, and other Arab states. At the same time, the role of religion in politics was quite small. One prominent sign of religious expression that became emblematic of the independent Chechnya was the loud Qadiri *zikrs*, collective rituals of the remembrance of Allah and the Prophet Muhammad that resemble dances in circles. These were performed by Dudayev's supporters in the squares of Chechen cities and villages during rallies in support of Dudayev. However, Dudayev himself remained a secular Soviet man. Georgi Derluguian notes relatedly that "The key figures of the Chechen revolution in 1991 were a military pilot, a writer, a journalist, industrial managers, engineers, professors, policemen, a few inevitably shady businessmen – but there was not a single traditional peasant, clan elder, or Islamic preacher among them."[8]

Most importantly for this study, the re-emergence of religion, tradition, and customs had only a limited impact on dispute resolution practices and the maintenance of social order. For instance, several of my respondents who worked in the police during the early Ichkeria period recalled that the police became more lenient in cases of bride kidnappings and blood revenge. In these types of conflicts, the police often asked elders and imams to help to arrange a reconciliation between feuding families, relying on adat and Sharia norms. But outside of these special cases, Soviet laws were applied. Then, the eruption of armed conflict with Russia in 1994 changed all spheres of life, including dispute resolution.

WAR AND LEGAL PLURALISM

The history of the Chechen wars (1994–1996 and 1999–2009) has been extensively documented,[9] so here I will only briefly outline the conflict. The First Chechen War (1994–1996) started as a result of a confrontation between the leadership of the secessionist Chechen Republic of Ichkeria, headed by Chechen President Dzhokhar Dudayev, and the authorities of

---

[8] Derluguian, "Introduction. Whose truth?": 17.

[9] Dunlop, John. *Russia confronts Chechnya: Roots of a separatist conflict.* Cambridge, 1998; Evangelista, Matthew. *The Chechen wars: Will Russia go the way of the Soviet Union?* Brookings Institution Press, 2002; Gall, Carlotta, and Thomas De Waal. *Chechnya: Small victorious war.* Pan Original, 1997; Hughes, *Chechnya*; Kramer, Mark. "The perils of counterinsurgency: Russia's war in Chechnya." *International Security* 29, no. 3 (2005): 5–63; Lieven, *Chechnya*; Zürcher, Christoph. *The Post-Soviet wars: Rebellion, ethnic conflict, and nationhood in the Caucasus.* New York: NYU Press, 2007.

the Russian Federation, headed by President Boris Yeltsin. There were many factors that contributed to the escalation of the conflict, including the Chechen collective trauma of the deportation, the presence of a large number of sub-proletariat young men in Chechnya, and Yeltsin and Dudayev's internal political struggles.[10] In particular, Yeltsin and his hawkish advisors were looking for "a short, victorious war" to raise his ratings.[11] At the same time, Daniel Treisman argued that the main factor behind the Russian intervention was the security threat resulting from the disintegration of state institutions and lawlessness in Dudayev's Chechnya.[12]

The Russian government declared an emergency situation in Chechnya and started a full-scale military invasion into the secessionist region in December 1994. The Chechen side was represented by Dudayev's paramilitary forces and volunteers, who mobilized in response to the Russian military intervention. Most Chechen fighting units were small at around fifteen to twenty people, lacking clear hierarchy and coordination, and formed on the basis of neighborhoods and extended family.[13] Mairbek Vatchagaev, a Chechen historian who was at one point also an official in the ChRI government, told me that "people were motivated by patriotism. Everyone fought – rich and poor, villagers and PhD candidates." The Russian anthropologist Valery Tishkov painted a more complicated picture and highlighted the fact that in addition to patriotism, Chechen fighters were motivated by a desire to protect their families, competition for social status, greed inspired by plundering, the lure of danger, and "a certain satisfaction in wreaking violence on others."[14]

The Russian army had a significant advantage in manpower, weapons, and military equipment, but was poorly managed and lacked motivation and morale. The Chechen fighters were much more motivated and knew the terrain better, both the natural and the social. The First War ended with a peace agreement between the Russian state and Chechen rebels in 1996 after the rebels, successfully employing guerrilla warfare strategies, captured Grozny.

During the interwar period, 1996–1999, Chechnya was a de facto independent state. After the assassination of Dudayev by the Russian

---

[10] Derluguian, *Bourdieu's secret admirer in the Caucasus*; Hughes, *Chechnya*.
[11] Evangelista, *The Chechen wars*: 37.
[12] Treisman, Daniel. *The return: Russia's journey from Gorbachev to Medvedev*. Simon and Schuster, 2011: 292.
[13] Lieven, *Chechnya*: 345.   [14] Tishkov, *Chechnya*: 106.

army in 1996, an Ichkerian government was formed on the basis of free and fair elections won by Aslan Maskhadov, one of the most prominent leaders of the rebels and a political moderate. Maskhadov's government was sabotaged, however, by other field commanders, who attempted to gain power by other means after losing the election.[15] In 1999, Shamil Basayev, the notorious Chechen field commander and Maskhadov's main challenger, invaded the neighboring Russian region of Dagestan, supposedly in order to establish an Islamic state there. This was used as *casus belli* by Russia, now led by Vladimir Putin, who launched a second military campaign against Chechnya.

The active combat phase of the Second War (1999–2000) ended in the rebels' military defeat and reintegration of Chechnya into the Russian state. It was followed by a long-lasting insurgency (2000–2009) and a brutal counterinsurgency campaign.[16] After the active phase of the war ended in the early 2000s, the Kremlin outsourced local governance and the counterinsurgency campaign to its local loyalists, headed by the Kadyrov family, who had defected from the rebels and joined the pro-Kremlin forces during the course of the war. The Chechen conflict was characterized by extensive victimization of civilians; I document civilian experiences of conflict and its legacies in Chapter 7. Another principal feature of the conflict was its gendered nature, which I analyze in Chapter 8. Here I focus on the functioning of legal pluralism during the conflict.

---

[15] Merlin, Aude. "The postwar period in Chechnya: When spoilers jeopardize the emerging Chechen state (1996–1999)." In N. Duclos (ed.), *War veterans in postwar situations: Chechnya, Serbia, Turkey, Peru, and Côte d'Ivoire*. Macmillan, Palgrave, 2012: 219–239; Wilhelmsen, Julie. "Between a rock and a hard place: The Islamisation of the Chechen separatist movement." *Europe-Asia Studies* 57, no. 1 (2005): 35–59.

[16] Kramer, "The perils of counterinsurgency"; Le Huérou, Anne, Aude Merlin, Amandine Regamey, and Elisabeth Sieca-Kozlowski. *Chechnya at war and beyond*. New York: Routledge, 2014; Lyall, Jason. "Does indiscriminate violence incite insurgent attacks? Evidence from Chechnya." *Journal of Conflict Resolution* 53, no. 3 (2009): 331–362; Lyall, Jason. "Are coethnics more effective counterinsurgents? Evidence from the second Chechen war." *American Political Science Review* 104, no. 1 (2010): 1–20; Souleimanov, Emil Aslan, and David S. Siroky. "Random or retributive: Indiscriminate violence in the Chechen wars." *World Politics* 68 (2016): 677; Toft, Monica Duffy, and Yuri M. Zhukov. "Denial and punishment in the North Caucasus: Evaluating the effectiveness of coercive counter-insurgency." *Journal of Peace Research* 49, no. 6 (2012): 785–800; Toft, Monica Duffy, and Yuri M. Zhukov. "Islamists and nationalists: Rebel motivation and counterinsurgency in Russia's North Caucasus." *American Political Science Review* 109, no. 2 (2015): 222–238.

Blood Revenge and Violent Mobilization

What role did legal pluralism play during the war? Political scientists Emil Aslan Souleimanov and Husseyn Aliyev published a series of papers and a book in which they attributed Chechen mobilization against the Russian army to the customary norm of blood revenge and more generally to the honor culture that in addition to retaliation also includes hospitality and the code of silence.[17] Taken together these cultural traits created a "value asymmetry" between Chechen rebels and the Russian army that determined the success of insurgency. I believe that this culturalist explanation is mistaken, even though it is shared by a number of the authors' interlocutors in the Chechen diaspora. In showing why this is the case, I will focus on blood revenge, since it is at the center of Souleimanov and Aliyev' account. Other factors are less developed; for example, the authors' claims that Chechens have a code of silence "similar in nature to the South Italian custom of omertà"[18] lack systematic evidence.

Souleimanov and Aliyev define blood revenge as "revenge against the perpetrator of an offense, a member of a group associated with the offender through blood kinship, or a broader group associated with the offender but not necessarily related to him through blood kinship."[19] This broad definition conflates blood revenge, a mechanism of collective responsibility based on customary law, with revenge in a more general sense. Revenge in a general sense is a powerful motivator of violent mobilization. Valery Tishkov wrote: "No propaganda was as likely to turn an ordinary Chechen into a *boyevik* (rebel) as the destruction of his home or the loss of his family."[20] Scholars have shown similar dynamics in other contexts.[21] But revenge in a general sense is qualitatively different

---

[17] Souleimanov, Emil Aslan, and Huseyn Aliyev. "Blood Revenge and violent mobilization: Evidence from the Chechen Wars." *International Security* 40, no. 2 (2015): 158–180; "Asymmetry of values, indigenous forces, and incumbent success in counterinsurgency: evidence from Chechnya." *Journal of Strategic Studies* 38, no. 5 (2015): 678–703; *How socio-cultural codes shaped violent mobilization and pro-insurgent support in the Chechen wars.* Springer, 2017.

[18] Souleimanov and Aliyev, "Asymmetry of values, indigenous forces, and incumbent success in counterinsurgency."

[19] Souleimanov and Aliyev, "Blood Revenge and violent mobilization": 159.

[20] Tishkov, *Chechnya*: 155.

[21] Balcells, Laia. *Rivalry and revenge.* Cambridge University Press, 2017; Kalyvas, *The logic of violence in civil war*; Petersen, Roger 2001. *Resistance and rebellion: Lessons from Eastern Europe.* Cambridge University Press; Wood, *Insurgent collective action and civil war in El Salvador.*

from blood revenge. Blood revenge is driven by deterrence logic, and not by grievances.

Many influential anthropological works show that in stateless clan-based societies, the custom of blood feuds serves as a tool for maintaining social order.[22] Chechen and Ingush scholars also emphasize deterrence and social order maintenance as the key functions of blood revenge.[23] When one member of a clan kills someone or engages in another serious transgression like rape, he and his clan will be targeted in retaliation. If a clan does not retaliate for the murder or humiliation of its member, it loses its credibility in interclan relations. It will be considered weak, and thus vulnerable to other possible transgressions.

Because deterrence of this type requires shared expectations of retaliation, it can operate only among members of communities that share those expectations – and know that others share them as well. Consequently, in the Chechen context, blood revenge can only be applied to Chechens and Ingush people, as well as some ethnic groups with established relationships with Chechens. This includes groups in the neighboring region of Dagestan, and across the border in the country of Georgia. However, blood revenge cannot be applied to Russians. Russians are simply outside the relevant community.

My interviews provide some telling quotes regarding the idea of extending blood revenge to Russians. For example, Vakha Murtuzaliev, the former Minister of Justice in the Ichkeria government, said, "Blood revenge is between Chechens. How can you declare blood revenge against a Russian? They won't understand it." Sultan-haji Mirzaev, whom we met in the beginning of this chapter, claimed, "People avenged their relatives, but that was not blood revenge. Russians are not even Muslims!" Murat, a high-level government official of Ichkeria, said, "It is a misunderstanding that Chechens applied blood revenge to Russian soldiers. Some avenged their relatives, like in the Budanov case,[24] but that

---

[22] Chagnon, Napoleon. "Life histories, blood revenge, and warfare in a tribal population." *Science* 239, no. 4843 (1988): 985–992. Evans-Pritchard, E. E. *The Nuer.* Oxford, 1944; Gluckman, Max. "The peace in the feud." *Past and Present* 8, no. 1 (1955): 1–14.

[23] Albogachieva and Babich, "Pravovaya Kultura Ingushey"; Albogachieva and Babich. "Krovnaya mest v sovremennoy Ingushetii"; Bersanova, Zalpa. "Obychai krovnoy mesti i praktika primireniya v sovremennoy Chechne" [The custom of blood revenge and the practice of reconciliation in contemporary Chechnya]. *Vestnik Vosstanovitelnoy Yustitsii* 8 (2011): 50–53.

[24] Colonel Yuri Budanov was found guilty of the murder (and credibly accused of rape) of the 17-year-old Chechen teenager Elza Kungaeva. In 2011, soon after he was released from Russian prison, Budanov was shot dead in Moscow.

was not blood revenge. Blood revenge is strictly regulated." Abdulla Bugaev, deputy head of the interim pro-Russian government of the Chechen Republic in 1995–1996, stated that "Blood revenge is a mechanism of protection of individual and family rights in our society. It has nothing to do with emotions." These quotes highlight the crucial role of community ("between Chechens," "not even Muslims"), the role of common knowledge ("they won't understand it"), and norms of customary law ("blood revenge is strictly regulated").[25]

One possible explanation for the radical difference in perceptions about the link between blood revenge and violent mobilization in the Chechen wars between Souleimanov and Aliyev's account and my interlocutors' accounts is that their study is based on the interviews with members of the Chechen diaspora in Europe. It could be, for example, that people in Chechnya who live under the repressive regime of Ramzan Kadyrov and who are also currently citizens of Russia are forced to say that blood revenge cannot be applied to Russians, and others outside that context might offer systematically different responses. However, the interviews I conducted with members of the Chechen diaspora in Europe casted doubt on this explanation. In particular, I interviewed three men who directly participated in conflict. Only one of my interlocutors provided support for Souleimanov and Aliyev's account – but even in that one case the support was partial. Alvi, a man in his late forties, was a former fighter who participated in the Second War. Alvi claimed that in principle it is possible to kill a Russian as an act of blood revenge, "but only the one who is directly responsible for the murder of your family member. You cannot kill another guy, that is meaningless." This suggests that contrary to Souleimanov and Aliyev's claims, even Chechens who accept the possibility of extending blood revenge to *individual* Russians do not accept the idea that blood revenge can extend to "a broader group associated with the offender." All other diaspora interlocutors said that it is wrong to assume that blood revenge was a driver of mobilization during the conflict. Adam, one of the field commanders who participated in both the First and the Second Wars told me that "the idea that people fought because of blood revenge is nonsense! How can you commit blood

[25] Ingush ethnographer Makka Albogachieva makes a similar observation: "One more very important characteristic for blood feuds should be noted: it applies only to those nations that have a similar rule." Albogachieva, Makka. "Blood feud in Ingushetia: Differences in adat and sharia." In Voell and Kaliszewska (eds.) *State and legal practice in the Caucasus: Anthropological perspectives on law and politics.* Ashgate Publishing, Ltd, 2015: 52.

revenge against Russians? Blood revenge is only between Chechens."
Adam also said that emotions (or in Souleimanov and Aliyev's terms
grievances) play absolutely no role in blood revenge. "Blood revenge is
always done with a cold heart."

Moreover, explaining mobilization in guerrilla warfare through the
custom of blood revenge drastically overpredicts mobilization.
According to my interviews, the number of fighters on the Chechen side
in the Second War was significantly lower than in the First War, despite
the fact that victimization of civilians was much more widespread in the
Second War. According to Saipudi, a former fighter in his fifties, "Only
experienced fighters (*boyeviki so stazhem*) and Islamic radicals (*wahha-
bisty*) fought in the Second War." Of course, some people joined the fight
driven by the desire to avenge their dead relatives. Even so, the overall
numbers were lower than in the First War and gradually decreased over
the course of the Second War. By 2007–2008 only a few dozen insurgents
were still fighting. Thus, the motive of retaliation (revenge in a common
sense) largely exhausted itself after several years of conflict. By contrast,
the custom of blood revenge is obligatory. Blood can be avenged even
after a hundred years, and the revenge cannot be abandoned without a
formal reconciliation procedure.

Nevertheless, the custom of blood revenge did play a major role in
post-Soviet Chechnya, especially during the conflict. As I mention above,
independent Chechnya witnessed a radical decrease in law enforcement
agencies' coercive capacity, as well as the liberation of criminals and
proliferation of arms. These factors combined made violent crimes,
including murder, robbery, and kidnapping, very common in Chechnya.
According to my interviewees, during that time the threat of blood
revenge served as insurance against violent crimes. In other words, when
state capacity weakened, the deterrence logic of blood revenge became
especially prominent. Russian-speaking minorities, who in that period
constituted a significant share of Chechnya's population, were not protected by the institution of blood revenge. As a result, they overwhelm-
ingly became the targets of violent crimes. Thus, the institution of blood
revenge can explain discriminatory violence against non-Chechen minorities in post-Soviet Chechnya.

In addition, the institution of blood revenge had a significant effect on
the dynamics of the conflict. The first stage of the conflict, which started in
1992, was an inter-Chechen power struggle. On one side were supporters
of President Dzhokhar Dudayev, and on the other was the military wing
of the opposition to Dudayev, which was backed by Moscow. Clashes

between militias ended with several people being killed. At the culmination of the confrontation in 1994, the main opposition newspaper, *Revival*, warned that the relatives of those killed might choose to engage in blood revenge, which could lead to full-scale civil war.[26]

Avoidance of large-scale inter-Chechen conflict was also an imperative for Aslan Maskhadov, who was elected the President of the Chechen Republic of Ichkeria in 1997 after the end of the First War. Despite Maskhadov's overwhelming victory in free and fair elections, his power was constantly challenged by other warlords and radical Islamist groups.[27] In several cases, conflicts between Maskhadov's supporters and his rivals turned violent and put Chechnya on the verge of civil war. However, in all conflict situations Maskhadov abstained from using violence. According to my interviews with people from Maskhadov's inner circle, his reasoning for not using violence was that he did not want to fight against his former brothers-in-arms. But my respondents acknowledged that the threat of spiraling violence as a result of blood feuds between families of political rivals was also an important consideration. Thus, the custom of blood revenge can be considered one of the factors that prevented consolidation of the independent Chechen state, because it hindered the ability of the Chechen government to use legitimate force to establish a stable social order.

During the Second Chechen war and counterinsurgency, inter-Chechen feuds became very common. The Russian army attempted to use the feuds for its own tactical purposes. For example, Anna Politkovskaya reported that Russian security agents set up a paramilitary detachment composed of members of one of the most influential families of Chechnya – the descendants of Sufi Sheikh Deni Arsanov – to execute a hit on Ruslan Gelayev, one of the most prominent field commanders of the separatists, in response to the shooting of several members of the family. Politkovskaya wrote:

Now these militants are under the auspices of a Main Intelligence Department (MID) unit deployed in the Staropromyslovsky district of Grozny. They live in its barracks and are supplied with food and arms. The reason for this merger is one of

---

[26] Vozrozhdenie. "Samosud nepriemlem" [Mob Law is unacceptable]. N 39, January 1994.
[27] Merlin, "The postwar period in Chechnya"; Muzaev, Timur. *Chechenskiy krisis 99: Politicheskoe protivostoianie v Ichkerii [The Chechen Crisis of 99: Political confrontation in Ichkeria].* Panorama, 1999; Osmaev, Abbaz. *Obschestvenno-politicheskaia i povsednevnaia zhizn' Chechenskoy Respubliki v 1996–2005. [Society, politics, and everyday life in Chechen Republic in 1996–2005]* Ph.D. dissertation, Makhachkala, 2010.

the goals of the MID unit – eliminating Gelayev and his people. For that, you can't find better allies than these blood avengers.[28]

Legal Pluralism and Wartime Social Order

Outside the domain of blood feuds, the role of customary law during the conflict was rather limited. As Khakim, one of the elders I spoke with, said, "The men with guns became the law. People stopped listening to the elders." Yet the customary norms were able to constrain the behavior of armed actors to some degree. Magomed-Said, a prominent elder from eastern Chechnya, told me a story from his village. He had learned that a warlord from the area had kidnapped a local twelve-year-old girl as a bride from their village. He and a delegation of other elders came to the warlord and told him:

"A marriage is a great thing. Congratulations! But you have to follow the custom. You went to the household without an invitation. There is a fine for that. You walked a girl through the village *maidan* [central square], there is a fine for that." And we went on and on with little details. In the end, the wedding happened, but the warlord paid a huge bride price to the family and the community. After that kidnappings stopped in the village for several years.

The war also brought Sharia back into Chechen public life. During the Soviet period and the early post-Soviet years of Ichkeria, Sharia norms were applied in the private domain, mostly related to marriage and funerals. Formal Sharia arbitration first appeared in Chechnya among certain rebel groups during the war. Anatol Lieven reported that "The growth of Shariat courts and punishments in the separatist-held areas of the mountains from the spring of 1995 onwards reflected partly the greater conservatism of these areas, but it also appeared to spread chiefly from the Chechen fighting groups, and to have been motivated above all by military considerations."[29]

Zelimkhan Yandarbiyev, one of the leaders of the rebels, described the process of formation of rebel Sharia courts in the following way:

The most important event in public life happened in April [of 1995] in the village of Vedeno. For the first time in a half a century, a Sharia court was formed there,

---

[28] Politkovskaya, Anna. *A dirty war. Russian reporter in the Caucasus.* Random House, 2009: 138, 181.
[29] Lieven, *Chechnya*: 365.

and then spread to other districts of Chechen Republic of Ichkeria ... Sharia was coming back into the life of the Chechen nation. Sharia's role in civic life in general and especially in state, societal, and military discipline, as well as the moral foundations of the society, was highlighted by many foreign journalists.[30]

The resurgence of Sharia arbitration in Ichkeria was facilitated by the repatriated members of Chechen diaspora from the Middle East, foreign fighters, and Islamists from the neighboring republics of the North Caucasus who joined the jihad against Russia.[31] Some of these men had knowledge and lived experience of Islamic law, and all of them had strong ideological beliefs where Sharia was a central element. Their influence is difficult to explore systematically though: in contemporary Chechnya, everything connected to foreign fighters is a sensitive topic. In turn, media accounts and secondary sources tend to exaggerate the influence from Arab countries because of the prominence of the Arab foreign fighter commander Khattab during the First War. From the scattered accounts of the Ichkeria period in my interviews, I got a sense that foreign preachers and Islamists from the neighboring Dagestan played a significant role in spreading Sharia ideology and running Sharia institutions in the interwar period. However, the demand for Sharia also had local roots. The suffering of the war dramatically increased religiosity among the population. As Rosa, a female representative of Chechen intelligentsia in her fifties, said, "I was a secular person before 1994. But it is hard to remain an atheist under the bombs that fall on your head. Religion helped me a lot to go through this hell." During the war, when state institutions of law and order basically did not function, some people started to rely on religious arbitration to resolve their disputes. But the official introduction of Sharia in Chechnya was not brought by demand from below, but rather imposed from above.

THE INTERWAR PERIOD: SHARIA OUTBIDDING

In 1996, when Dudayev was assassinated by the Russian army, Vice-President Zelimkhan Yandarbiyev became the acting president. In August 1996, Chechen rebels organized a major offensive operation, captured Grozny, and forced the Russian government to sign a peace agreement,

---

[30] Yandarbiyev, Zelimkha. *Checheniia: Bitva za svobodu.* [Chechnya: Struggle for freedom]. Lviv, 1996: 362.
[31] Bakke, Kristin. "Help wanted? The mixed record of foreign fighters in domestic insurgencies." *International Security* 38, no. 4 (2014): 150–187.

the Khasavyurt Accords. After the peace agreement, which ended the First War, Ichkeria scheduled a presidential election.

Acting President Yandarbiyev was challenged by other candidates, including two of the most prominent rebel commanders, Aslan Maskhadov and Shamil Basayev. Facing imminent electoral defeat, Yandarbiyev announced the establishment of Sharia law in Chechnya. Most people with whom I discussed Yandarbiyev's decision considered it to be a political maneuver. It was clear that Yandarbiyev was going to lose to the more popular rebel leader Aslan Maskhadov. Yandarbiyev appealed to his brothers-in-arms to quit the race and allow him to be the president in the spirit of unity, but these appeals had no effect. In response, Yandarbiyev, who in the early period of Chechen separatist movement was a leading intellectual figure among the secular nationalists, announced the introduction of Sharia law.

Yandarbiyev's promotion of Sharia law was an attempt to win the support of two powerful constituencies: war veterans, the rebels who had just won the war against Russia, and foreign fighters and foreign donors from the Gulf. However, according to my interviews, Yandarbiyev's state-wide imposition of Sharia law was met with skepticism even among some former rebels, who by and large supported Islamist ideas. One of my interlocutors, Alvi, put it the following way: "We all knew that Sharia was sacred. But no one knew exactly what it was." Another respondent, Adam, a former rebel commander, was very harsh in his assessment of the introduction of Sharia: "Yandarbiyev deliberately screwed us over (*podlozhil nam svin'u*) with his Sharia idea. No one knew how to implement it, so the only thing he achieved was that he undermined our state."

All my respondents agreed that imposition of Sharia was a purely strategic act in Yandarbiyev's struggle for power. Because of the sacred status of Sharia, newly elected President Aslan Maskhadov had to comply with its partial imposition. Promotion of adat and Sharia was also used to ensure more autonomy vis-à-vis Moscow – something that can be conceptualized as boundary-making. According to Vakha Murtuzaliev, who at some point served as the Minister of Justice in the Ichkeria government, the promotion of Sharia was needed because "otherwise we lived according to the Russian laws. So it made no sense that we wanted to be independent. By emphasizing the use of Sharia, we emphasized that we are not part of Russia anymore."

As a result of this lawfare, for almost three years (1996–1999) there were two parallel formal systems of justice in Chechnya: Soviet state law and Sharia, with the informal customary normative system in the background. Implementation of Sharia was difficult. First, Chechnya lacked specialists in Islamic law who could serve as qadis. Second, many Sharia norms were unknown to the population. Third, it was unclear what to do with the remaining Soviet courts, prosecutors, and police.

The criminal situation in Chechnya deteriorated in the interwar period and became even worse than it had been prior to the conflict. The republic was left in ruins. There were no jobs in the industrial sector or in agriculture. Many among Chechnya's administrative, academic, and art elites left the region. The black market bloomed – people were selling weapons, drugs, and smuggled crude oil. Drug abuse and alcoholism spread among people who had gone through the enormous stress of war. A grim indicator of state failure was that "child mortality reached a level unprecedented in the post-Soviet world – more than 100 babies out of 1,000 under one year old died.[32]

The veterans of the "national resistance movement", as the war was officially called in the Chechen press, became a mass of armed unemployed men who felt entitled to privileges in return for their sacrifice.[33] Some of them turned into state officials of the independent Chechen state. Valery Tishkov quoted one of his informants, Visit M., on the rebels-turned-bureaucrats after the First War:

After the war everyone rushed to seek official posts ... but most of them are ignorant or ill-qualified for the jobs. They've never worked in government, have no proper notion of official service, and confuse a state institution with their own houses. All their relatives form long lines at their doors, seeking government posts. African chiefs may behave that way, but that just isn't a modern state, it's tribal life.[34]

Field commanders did not disarm and were not incorporated into the national army. Many of them became warlords who established control over large territories within Chechnya. At some points, Maskhadov's government controlled only Grozny and several loyal rural districts.[35] Chechnya became a lawless territory. The infamous kidnappings for ransom proliferated across Chechnya and became its most successful business.[36] Murders, robberies, and other violent crimes also became endemic. Chechnya's main daily newspaper, *Grozny's Worker*,

[32] Tishkov, *Chechnya*: 189.   [33] Merlin, "The Postwar Period in Chechnya."
[34] Tishkov, *Chechnya*: 145.   [35] Wilhelmsen, "Between a rock and a hard place."
[36] According to the figure provided by the Russian Ministry of Interior, between 1992 and 2000, there were 1,815 cases of kidnappings with a peak in 1996. See Zürcher, *The Post-Soviet Wars*: 105.

consistently published crime reports on its front page. According to the data published by the newspaper, in 1997 alone Chechnya had 353 murders. With a population of approximately 600,000 people or even less, Chechnya was hence characterized as a place with one of the highest homicide rates in the world. Most of the murders and other serious crimes remained unsolved.

In this dire criminal and political situation, there were calls to radically reorganize the legal and political foundations of the independent Chechen state. Khozh-Akhmed Noukhayev, a politician, businessman, and mafia boss, published an article in the leading Chechen newspaper *Grozny's Worker* with a proposal to reorganize the state according to adat. All state institutions were supposed to represent different Chechen clans – *teips*. In the archive of the newspaper, I found many positive responses to this utopian neotraditionalist platform – mostly from intelligentsia that had little say in political decision-making.

Other proposals demanded strict implementation of Sharia as the only possible solution to the lawlessness and rampant crime. Sharia courts were established in all districts of Chechnya. The disputants could appeal the decision of the Sharia district court at the Supreme Sharia Court of the Chechen Republic of Ichkeria. To enforce the decisions of these courts, the government established the Ministry of Sharia National Security (MShGB). As Derluguian pointed out, formation of these institutions "cannot be ascribed so much to Islamic traditions as to Islam becoming the last resort of desperate politicians and society when the promises of the 1991 revolution were replaced by grim reality."[37] In a similar vein, analyzing judicial and political innovations in independent Chechnya, Valery Tishkov highlighted that "the Chechen revolution both destroyed the former Soviet system of rule and simultaneously indulged in an unrealized project of restoring an imagined order (based on clan structure and religion) that had never previously existed or, at the very least, had not existed since Chechnya's incorporation into the Russian state."[38]

Sultan-haji Mirzaev, who headed the Supreme Sharia Court, described to me their work in the following way:

Even though in principle, the source of law for us was the Koran, actually we judged according to Soviet laws. All Sharia courts had a secular judge, who worked as the qadi's deputy, and several prosecutors who carried out all paperwork for the cases. This was necessary. How were we, imams, supposed

---

[37] Derluguian, "Introduction. Whose truth?": 22.   [38] Tishkov, *Chechnya*: 223.

to know the court procedures? We had to learn by doing. The prosecutor's office helped us a lot.

Vakha Murtuzaliev seconded Mirzaev's narrative: "In the 1990s we had a mixed system: Soviet law, adat and Sharia. But the Soviet system was dominant: it was dominant even in the work of Sharia courts."

Sharia courts started to rule on everything from drinking alcohol to regulation of oil production. Chechen historian Timur Muzaev documented that at some point, nine out of ten cases heard in Sharia courts were labor disputes, causing the government of Ichkeria to prohibit Sharia courts from taking them.[39] The Sharia courts were supposed to implement the new civil and criminal codes that were adopted in 1996. The chaotic process of adopting these codes led to profound confusion and mistakes. Most notoriously, the civil and criminal codes of the ChRI were copied from Sudanese originals.[40] However, in Sudan, people live according to the Maliki School of Islamic jurisprudence (*mazhab*), while in Chechnya, the population adheres to the Shafii *mazhab*. In addition, the translated codes did not adjust Sudanese realities to the Chechen social context. As a result, many fines were reported in camels. For instance, for a murder of a man, the murderer's family was supposed to provide the compensation of one hundred camels. One of my interlocutors laughed when he remembered this and said: "There are no camels in Chechnya!" Such discrepancies between the new legal codes and Chechen social reality led to numerous jokes.

Many Sharia provisions were unknown to the Chechen population and alien to their value system, which was based on the norms of adat. For example, Rosa, who was a young state official in the Ichkeria government, shared with me her reminiscence of getting to know Sharia law:

One day they [the government] published the new Criminal Code in the main government newspaper. We all heard about it and we were very curious. I got the newspaper and read the entire thing. It was pure Kamasutra! There were the provisions regarding rape. In our culture, it is shameful to discuss all those dirty things. In Chechen adat, if a man even touches a woman's arm, this is a gross offense to her entire family. And rape is something unthinkable. And in that newspaper, they were discussing what rape is: to what percentage a penis has to go inside a woman. Chechens would never discuss these details. I felt dirty. I realized that I didn't need this Sharia.

[39] Cited in Klyachkina, *Reconfiguration of sub-national governance*: 213.
[40] Bobrovnikov, *Musulmane Severnogo Kavkaza*. Presumably, these codes were adopted because Sudan was the latest country to implement Sharia legal norms.

Another interlocutor, Denilbek, a man in his fifties, remembered that

the Sharia proponents started to use public flogging for some offenses, like drinking alcohol and so on. In our adat, such a thing is extremely shameful – a man cannot beat another man like cattle. In response, the relatives of those who were punished this way attempted to avenge the offenses against their relatives' honor. This could have spiraled into mass violence very fast.

Public executions became closely associated with Sharia. In 1997, a Sharia court sentenced to death a pair of lovers, a man and a woman, who had killed the woman's husband. They were shot in public by a squad in a square in Grozny. This caused an outcry from many within Chechnya, as well as from the Russian and Western media, who reported on "the barbaric practices of the Chechen Islamic radicals."

Many of my respondents expressed strong negative opinions about the functioning of Sharia courts in the interwar period. Valid, a man in his forties, said:

These Sharia courts and Sharia patrols were bandits, nothing else. They were very powerful in my village, Urus-Martan. These bearded men were stopping cars and if they found that a man and a woman who were in the car weren't related, they demanded bribes. The price for this was $100.

The corruption of Sharia courts and patrols was highlighted by other respondents as well. For instance, Asya, a woman in her fifties, told me a story of gross abuse by the men who served in the Sharia guard. A man killed her Russian neighbor to get her apartment. Other neighbors told this story to the police. He was arrested, but then several jeeps with armed members of the Sharia patrol came to the police post and freed him. This case highlights the contested and often confrontational relations between secular state institutions that remained from the Soviet Union and the newly established Sharia institutions. For almost two years these institutions functioned in parallel.

One of my high-level respondents, who was in a leadership position within the ChRI Ministry of the Interior, told me that he and his colleagues, many of whom were Soviet police officers, did not consider Sharia courts and patrols to be legitimate institutions: "These things were unconstitutional. Also, they were mostly neophytes who did not know much religion and knew nothing about law and police work."

Perhaps the best critical description of the parallel functioning of the secular and Sharia legal orders and their competition is given in German Sadulaev's novel *Shali Raid*. Even though it is fiction, it is based on multiple real stories from interwar Chechnya. Tamerlan, the novel's main character, serves in the state police office in his native town of Shali. Their office has to both work in parallel and compete with the local Sharia guard office. Tamerlan says:

Those Sharia courts were real trouble. They formed their own parallel structures. They didn't need us to enforce their rulings – they relied on Islamist rebels, Wahhabi units, advised by their commanders from Saudi Arabia. These guys were not subordinate to President Maskhadov as they were supposed to be. Their normative basis was Sharia. A system of Muslim law based on Koran, hadith, and commentaries of Islamic scholars, mostly from medieval ages. The older, the more authoritative. These norms were created by Arab nomads, desert tribes, camel riders. God damn it! I wasn't able to get on board with the idea that these archaic norms were to be applied here at the end of the twentieth century.

Many of my respondents who served in courts or law enforcement agencies during the Ichkeria period shared the sentiments of Sadulaev's fictional character.

Maskhadov's rule was constantly challenged by other prominent war-lords who formed political parties and movements, published newspapers that criticized the president, organized mass protest rallies, and even engaged in violent clashes with the president's supporters.[41] Maskhadov's legitimacy was based on the secular institution of elections, so in order to undermine this legitimacy the opposition actively promoted the Islamist agenda. The strict implementation of Sharia law and abolition of all secular institutions became the opposition's main demand.

For two years, Aslan Maskhadov resisted the demands to fully implement Sharia law. However, in February 1999, in an unexpected political maneuver, Maskhadov announced the introduction of full Sharia rule in Chechnya. Maskhadov took the initiative away from the opposition, leaving them without their main demand. However, as Maskhadov's former advisor Mairbek Vatchagaev acknowledged, this decision also ultimately undermined Maskhadov's rule. He was elected in accordance with the Constitution of the ChRI, and the introduction of Sharia basically canceled the Constitution and left Maskhadov's office without any legitimacy. In addition, the Parliament of the ChRI did not agree with the decree, ruled it unconstitutional, and gave Maskhadov a vote of no confidence. In place of the ChRI Parliament, Maskhadov announced the formation of a *shura*, an Islamic council. The opposition formed an

---

[41] Muzaev, *Chechenskiy krisis 99*: Osmaev, *Obschestvenno-politicheskaia i povsednevnaia zhizn' Chechenskoy Respubliki.*

alternative *shura*. According to Georgi Derluguian, "Eventually, every powerful man in Chechnya, starting with President Aslan Maskhadov, scrambled to acquire a degree of Islamic discourse and representation—beards grew longer, prayers became conspicuous, women were expelled from the remaining offices."[42] The internal political conflict and Sharia outbidding were stopped only by the start of the Second Chechen War when the Russian army invaded in September 1999.

Many judges, prosecutors and police officers who worked in Soviet times and during the pro-Russian administrations imposed during the war (1995–1996) were ousted in 1999, which further weakened the judicial system of the independent Chechen state. For example, Khozh-Ahmed, a former prosecutor, told me that "The Sharia court gave me a death sentence for collaboration with the occupying government. I had to leave Chechnya." Bekhan, another former judicial official, told me that he was arrested: "Their so-called Sharia court arrested me and put me in prison. But I had a strong clan behind me, so they had to release me."

At the same time, some of my other respondents expressed strong support for the ChRI Sharia courts. For example, Khalid, a religious authority, told me that "Ichkeria's Sharia courts maintained order. They were strict, even harsh, but they were just. And people listened to them. It was a hard time, but these courts served the nation and God well." Another interlocutor, Isa, a man in his forties, said that "If not for these courts, it would have been chaos. The authorities provided special courses and trained these judges. They took many important cases, even the cases of kidnappings for ransom." Some of my respondents were afraid to openly discuss their perception of Sharia courts during the Ichkeria period, as this topic is particularly sensitive. This made it even more surprising to find praise for the Ichkeria Sharia courts from Ramzan Kadyrov. In one of his interviews, Kadyrov said, "During the Ichkeria times we had harsh laws; Sharia courts judged in a very strict manner. But that was necessary. The price for heroin in Chechnya was two times lower than in the neighboring regions!"

* * *

This chapter told the story of top-down lawfare in Ichkeria. It thus contributed to our understanding of the unrecognized de facto

---

[42] Derluguian, Georgi. "Che Guevaras in turbans." *New Left Review* (1999): 10.

states.[43] The collapse of the Soviet Union in 1991 led to the separatist movement and de facto independence of Chechnya. The Chechen national revolution was characterized by the resurgence of traditionalism and religion. The war that broke out between the federal center and Chechen separatists in 1994 reduced state capacity to rubble. The ideology of political Islam became dominant among Chechen politicians. After the end of the First Chechen War in 1996, the victorious separatist leaders enacted Sharia. However, promotion of legal pluralism in the de facto independent Chechnya was driven not by ideology, demand from the population, or state capacity, as in the past, but rather the rationale of establishing local political control. In fact, most of my respondents emphasized that Sharia in Ichkeria was imposed from above; large segments of the population were skeptical of the idea of living under Sharia law. The establishment and promotion of non-state legal systems was used by incumbents to increase their legitimacy by association with religion and tradition, to distance from the Kremlin, and as a concession to the powerful constituency of former rebels. At the same time, the incumbents were wary of strengthening the non-state judiciary too much. In general, the political field in Chechnya in the 1990s was fragmented and incumbents were afraid that powerful legal systems based on tradition and religion would become arenas of political contestation and ultimately be hijacked by the opposition. The rulers turned to promotion of Sharia and adat only when they were directly challenged and needed to reinforce political control regardless of the costs. In the next chapter, I develop the pattern of the use of legal pluralism for political control with a case study of postwar Chechnya under Ramzan Kadyrov.

---

[43] For comparative perspective, see a fascinating account of the functioning of the unrecognized state of Biafra through the lenses of law: Daly, Samuel Fury Childs. *A history of the Republic of Biafra: Law, crime, and the Nigerian civil war.* Cambridge University Press, 2020. On the unrecognized states in Eurasia, see Bakke, Kristin, Andrew M. Linke, John O'Loughlin, and Gerard Toal. "Dynamics of state-building after war: External-internal relations in Eurasian de facto states." *Political Geography* 63 (2018): 159–173; Caspersen, Nina. *Unrecognized states: The struggle for sovereignty in the modern international system.* Polity Press, 2013; King, Charles. "The benefits of ethnic war: understanding Eurasia's unrecognized states." *World Politics* 53, no. 4 (2001): 524–552; Kolstø, Pål. "The sustainability and future of unrecognized quasi-states." *Journal of Peace Research* 43, no. 6 (2006): 723–740.

5

"We Will Use Every Resource!"

Jurisdictional Politics in Postwar Chechnya

Madina Umaeva, a twenty-three-year-old who lived in the village of Druzhba in the eastern part of Chechnya, died on June 12, 2020. Madina's death caused a major public controversy that involved her extended family, police, religious authorities, and even Ramzan Kadyrov, the powerful head of the Chechen Republic assigned by the Kremlin to rule the region in 2007.[1] Madina's parents divorced when she was just nine months old. In accordance with the dominant interpretation of Chechen custom, Madina was raised by her father's family. In 2013, sixteen-year-old Madina married Vishadzhi Khamidov. They had three children. Vishadzhi is officially mentally disabled, but his family connections helped him to secure a position at the center for special forces training situated in Kadyrov's native village and headed by Kadyrov's cousin. Vishadzhi regularly beat Madina and she often ran away from him, but always returned, pressured by both extended families. On the day of her death, Madina used some children's welfare money to buy a new television, which caused a conflict with her mother-in-law. When Vishadzhi came back from work, he joined the conflict on his mother's side. Madina ended up dead. Vishadzhi Khamidov's family claimed that Madina fell down the stairs. The doctor who came to examine the body wrote a report stating that the cause of death was unknown. In violation of Russian law, no postmortem examination was conducted. Then, against Chechen tradition, Madina was buried the same night.

---

[1] Elena Milashina. "Chto sluchilos s Madinoy Umaevoy?" [What happened to Madina Umaeva?]. *Novaya Gazeta*, July 6, 2020. Taus, Serganova. "Bylinka na kholodnom vetru." [A blade of grass on cold wind]. *Dosh Journal*. July 9, 2020.

A message claiming that Madina had been killed and a video of the unusual nighttime burial went viral on Chechen social media. Madina's mother Khutmat Davletmurzaeva filed a petition on her daughter's murder with the Investigative Committee of the Russian Federation in the Chechen Republic. Following the mother's petition, an autopsy of Madina's body was conducted and a criminal investigation opened. The story then took an unexpected turn. Ramzan Kadyrov gathered the extended families of Madina and Vishadzhi, the greater neighborhood, religious authorities, and all senior republic law enforcement officials in a large hall in the city of Gudermes. Kadyrov addressed the gathering: "I, the *padishah* ["king of kings" in Persian] have gathered you all in front of Allah to figure out who is to be blamed." He then chastised Khutmat Davletmurzaeva, Madina's mother, for initiating the autopsy, which was "against Sharia." "Russia is telling us to do the autopsy, but we are doing everything to avoid it!" He asked her extended family, "Aren't there any men in this family? Why didn't you stop this woman? Now people in the West say that there is no justice in Chechnya, that we abuse women." Khutmat Davletmurzaeva and her male relatives were forced to apologize to Kadyrov. The autopsy declared Madina's death to be of natural causes, and the criminal investigation was closed. However, the public in Chechnya remained convinced that Madina had been killed. In an effort to change public opinion, Chechen television made a special report that portrayed Madina as a promiscuous woman and suggested that her murder had been an "honor killing," thus justifying it through reference to custom.

This story conveys the extensive use of references to custom and Sharia by the Chechen authorities headed by Ramzan Kadyrov. It also reflects the subversion of Russian state law in Chechnya, especially in the gendered domain of family relations, the eastern part of the republic, which constitutes Kadyrov's power base, and in regard to the actions of those connected to the law enforcement agencies, the core of Kadyrov's coalition of support. Ramzan Kadyrov often contrasts his rule with the de facto independent Chechnya-Ichkeria in the 1990s, highlighting his loyalty to Russia. At the same time, many observers argue that de facto autonomy from Russia is almost as high under Kadyrov as it was during the years of Chechen independence – and that his power is greater than that of Ichkeria's authorities ever was.[2] In this chapter, I will argue that

---

[2] Yaffa, Joshua. "Putin's dragon. Is the ruler of Chechnya out of control?" *The New Yorker*, February 1, 2016.

strategic promotion of non-state legal systems plays a major role in Kadyrov's autonomous political order.

Ramzan Kadyrov has publicly acknowledged his support for Sharia and adat on many occasions. French journalist Pierre Avril reported that Kadyrov told him, "In my opinion, Sharia law is above the laws of the Russian Federation."[3] On another occasion, Ramzan Kadyrov admonished members of the Chechen diaspora who went on a rally against his rule in Vienna. He publicly proclaimed, "We will use every resource: the law, tradition, religion!" This quote highlights the fact that Kadyrov understands non-state legal systems as sources of power that can be used in an instrumental manner against his opponents. This chapter will first document the political use of legal pluralism in Ramzan Kadyrov's Chechnya and then explain how the politics of legal pluralism have been shaped by conflict. The final part of the chapter compares lawfare in Kadyrov's Chechnya with legal politics in the neighboring regions of Ingushetia and Dagestan.

LEGAL POLITICS IN KADYROV'S CHECHNYA

State Encroachment into Custom and Sharia

In the spirit of Sharia implementation, Ramzan Kadyrov effectively banned alcohol sales in Chechnya, introduced "modest" dress codes for women in all public spaces, and encouraged polygamy. Kadyrov's government has regularly referred to the adat norm of collective responsibility in its practices. During the counterinsurgency phase, the government persecuted the relatives of rebels in order to force them to surrender. For example, in 2004, Chechen security forces arrested forty relatives of the prominent rebel commander Magomed Khambiev – including women and old people – and held them hostage to force Khambiev to abandon fighting. Subsequently, when the large-scale insurgency was crushed, the government used collective punishment against the relatives of critics of the regime. For example, in 2016, Chechen state television reported on the gathering of the *Chinkhoi* clan that publicly denounced its member Ahmed Zakayev, the leader of the rebel government-in-exile who lives in London. The report stated, "Collective responsibility is one of the traditional institutions of self-regulation in Chechen

---

[3] Avril, Pierre. "Tchétchénie: les deux faces du régime Kadyrov." *Le Figaro*, May 27, 2010.

society. By denouncing the relative, members of his family and his clan confirm that from this moment they can't be responsible for his actions."

In a similar vein, the government has been punishing the relatives of young men and women who went to fight in Syria and Iraq or who participated in the sporadic insurgent attacks in Chechnya. Since 2008, the government of Chechnya has extensively employed the practice of burning down the houses of the family members of alleged insurgents. After a violent insurgent attack in December 2016, the government organized congresses of the elders of several settlements, which decided to expel from Chechnya the relatives of the insurgents who fought in Syria. Likewise, the day after the insurgent attack on Grozny in 2017, which I witnessed in the field, the government arrested more than one hundred relatives of the insurgents. They were all immediately fired from their jobs. The government also stopped giving pensions and welfare payments to these people.

Kadyrov's government often uses references to customary law and Sharia in its attempts to regulate women's behavior and appearance.[4] One infamous case is depicted in Joshua Yaffa's report on Chechnya in *The New Yorker*. Yaffa claimed that "the republic is now governed by diktats inspired by Sharia jurisprudence and Kadyrov's personal interpretation of *adat*. In 2010, after vigilantes drove around Grozny firing paintballs at uncovered women, Kadyrov said that he wanted to 'give an award' to the men."[5]

All these descriptions highlight one common feature: the government of Chechnya is heavily involved in interpreting, enforcing, and even inventing customary and religious norms. This is in fundamental conflict with the core principles of the self-regulation of Chechen society, which had been preserved despite almost two centuries of imperial and Soviet rule. Chechen customary law is the social order of the stateless society. For instance, the principle of blood revenge as the ultimate regulator of conflicts and a deterrence mechanism makes sense only in the absence of a third-party institution of law enforcement. In the post-conflict period, it has become the government that dictates what custom and Sharia are and

[4] Lokshina, Tanya. 2014. "Virtue campaign for women in Chechnya under Ramzan Kadyrov: Between war backlash effect and desire for total control." In Anne Le Huérou, Aude Merlin, Amandine Regamey, and Elisabeth Sieca-Kozlowski (eds.) *Chechnya at war and beyond*. New York: Routledge, 2014: 236–255.

[5] Yaffa, "Putin's dragon."

carries them out. Yaffa reported a Chechen woman's perception of this change:

When I was a young girl, my grandfather made me wear a head scarf, she said. I was afraid of him. He explained to me, "You are a Chechen girl, and so you will wear a head scarf." But today we don't have such grandfathers, and instead their role is played by the Department of Spiritual and Moral Education.[6]

The government of Chechnya does not promote legal pluralism, where alternative autonomous legal systems would function in parallel, but rather aims to establish control over all three parallel legal systems. One of my respondents, Khalid, a respected *alim* (religious scholar) with a degree in Islamic law from Al-Azhar, the most prestigious center of Islamic education in the world, told me that the government prohibited him from adjudicating disputes according to Sharia and directed him to transfer all disputants to the imam of his village, who had received a mediocre Islamic education and was not fluent in Sharia norms. This highlights the way that the government co-opts some elders and Islamic authorities and delegates them power to adjudicate disputes but restricts the functioning of non-state legal systems if the authorities in charge of them are not sanctioned by the government. Even though the Chechen government controls the functioning of the non-state legal systems to a high degree, these non-state forums still enjoy limited autonomy, which is a rare thing in Kadyrov's Chechnya. Ultimately, the resolution of particular disputes according to Sharia and adat is left to the discretion of qadis and elders.

At the same time, the promotion of legal pluralism gives more discretionary power to the ruler. If there is one legal system, everyone has to obey its regulations, including the ruler. If there are multiple parallel legal systems, the ruler as the most resourceful actor can strategically cherry-pick principles across legal systems and avoid the restrictions each of them imposes. The use of legal pluralism to increase discretionary power can be seen in Kadyrov's counterinsurgency policies. Collective punishment is one of the principles of Chechen customary law, but it is against both Russian law and Sharia. Another example is the government-sponsored introduction of polygamy, which is rooted in Sharia but is against Russian law and Chechen customary law. Max Weber emphasized discretion as the single most important feature of the extreme form of patrimonial authoritarian regime that he called *sultanism*. He wrote:

---

[6] Ibid.

Where domination is primarily traditional, even though it is exercised by virtue of the ruler's personal autonomy, it will be called patrimonial authority, where instead it operates primarily on the basis of discretion, it will be called sultanism.[7]

Kadyrov perhaps would approve of the classification of his regime as sultanism given that he insists on his subordinates calling him "Padishah." Jonathan Littell, French writer and journalist, who worked in Chechnya for a long time, captured the selective promotion of non-state legal system in the following way: "Chechnya's present governing class's desire for Sharia, or rather an à la carte neo-Sharia, seems very strong." He went on to describe the hybrid social reality:

The archaic structures remain, in the underpinnings of people's behavior, but piled over them is a thick layer made up of a mixture of fast cash, business, mobile phones, Porsche Cayennes and Hummers, despotism, a total absence of restraint, and a half-reinvented and half-radicalized religion, with neo-traditional kitsch sprinkled over it. And all with the blessings of the Kremlin.[8]

The Kremlin, which imposed Kadyrov on Chechnya, perceives the prevalence of customary and religious arbitration negatively because it violates the monopoly of Russian law in the region. When Vladimir Putin was asked at his 2016 press conference about the practice of collective punishment of the relatives of the alleged insurgents, and relatedly whether Russian law functions in Chechnya at all, he unequivocally denounced practices that go against Russian law. Putin said:

In Russia everyone has to follow the law. No one can be considered guilty until the court verdict ... No one, including the leadership of the Chechen Republic, has the right to extrajudicial measures. Moreover, the law enforcement agencies are doing a preliminary examination of the case of the burning down of those houses in Chechnya ... Kadyrov had no right to say what he said about burning the houses. ... Life is difficult, but we all have to follow the law. If we leave the boundaries of law, this will lead to chaos.

Alvi Karimov, Kadyrov's press secretary, then immediately claimed that Ramzan Kadyrov has never violated Russian Constitution and state law and that reports of collective punishment were based on a wrong translation of what Kadyrov said. In the end, Kadyrov was not punished, but Putin's public message was clear. Kadyrov's power comes first and

---

[7] Weber, Max. *Economy and society: An outline of interpretive sociology.* University of California Press, 1978 (1922): 1020.

[8] Jonathan Littell. "Chechnya, Year III. Ramzan Kadyrov." *London Review of Books*, November 19, 2009.

foremost from Putin. This consideration reaffirms the need to solve the puzzle: Why does the government of Ramzan Kadyrov promote legal pluralism?

Like Father, Like Son?

One plausible explanation is that of path dependency: that Ramzan Kadyrov simply follows the patterns of governance that had been adopted by the local rulers that preceded him. Kadyrov effectively inherited his position of President of Chechnya from his father Akhmat-haji Kadyrov. Kadyrov Senior was appointed by Vladimir Putin to head the provisional administration of the Chechen Republic on June 12, 2000. In October 2003, Akhmat-haji was elected President of the Chechen Republic, but his presidency was short-lived. In May 2004 he was killed in a terrorist attack in Grozny.

Akhmat-haji Kadyrov is a perfect example of an intermediary in the imperial politics of state-building. Born in Kazakhstan during the Chechen exile to a very modest peasant family, he received an Islamic education in a Bukhara medrese and the Tashkent Institute of Islam. During perestroika, he founded the first Islamic Institute in Chechnya in the town of Kurchaloy. Akhmat Kadyrov welcomed Dudayev's revolution and became one of the leading clerics of the separatist Chechen Republic of Ichkeria. In 1995, he was elected the Mufti of Ichkeria and declared jihad against Russia. After the First Chechen War, he supported the new president Aslan Maskhadov and enjoyed the position of being one of the leaders of de facto independent Chechnya.

Over time, however, Akhmat Kadyrov became the key figure in the internal conflict within the Chechen secessionist movement. A devout Sufi, he became wary of the growing influence of Islamic radicals, referred to as Wahhabis. On many occasions he spoke out against Wahhabis and, together with some traditionalist field commanders, led a confrontation with the Islamic radicals. In June 1999, Akhmat Kadyrov even tried to organize a coup and was declared military *amir* (ruler). Referring to Sharia, he tried to eliminate Maskhadov's presidency and rule himself.[9] The coup attempt failed. When the Second War started shortly after, he defected from Ichkeria and joined the pro-Russian forces. The Ichkerian Sharia court sentenced him to death for treason. The Kremlin appreciated

---

[9] "Mufti Kamikadze." Kommersant-Vlast. 20 June, 2000.

its new ally, especially for his influence among the traditionalist Chechen commanders and lay fighters.

The Kremlin's choice of Akhmat-haji Kadyrov to lead the new pro-Russian administration was unexpected. Previously, Moscow had relied on local cadres with a very different profile. Take, for example, Doku Zavgayev, the only head of region of Chechen nationality in the late Soviet period (he ruled in 1989–1991). Zavgayev was a lifelong party apparatchik from the Northern — most Russified — part of Chechnya and married to a Russian woman. Zavgayev was brought back to Chechnya and appointed to lead the pro-Russian administration during the First War in 1996. Or take Salambek Khadjiyev, another leader of the pro-Russian administration during the First Chechen War. He had been a scientist and the deputy minister of oil industry of the Soviet Union. Khadjiyev was a typical representative of the high Soviet Chechen intelligentsia, adamantly pro-Moscow and against the separatist project. Akhmat-haji Kadyrov was a very different character, an Islamic cleric, from a village, speaking rusty Russian and wearing traditional Chechen *papakha* on all occasions – and, of course, the man who declared jihad against Russia. Yet he was chosen over Moscow Chechen intelligentsia, wealthy Chechen businessmen, and pro-Russian military commanders. The Mufti of Ichkeria became the President of Chechnya. This illustrates the point that traditional non-state authorities often become the king-makers or even the rulers themselves in imperial state-building projects. Alexei Malashenko, a well-known expert on Russian Muslim regions, compared Putin's bet on Kadyrov with the tactics of the Bolsheviks in Central Asia in the 1920s. At that time, facing the resistance of local insurgents (*basmachi*), the Soviets made a deal with some field commanders and gave them administrative positions in the new government.[10] This tactic severely weakened the insurgency. This was also the case in Chechnya.

Initially, Akhmat-haji Kadyrov's power in Chechnya was very weak. The Russian army was able to establish control over the major cities and optimistically declared the end of the war in Chechnya in June 2000. In reality, though, the war went on for another six to seven years in guerrilla form. For a long period of time, Kadyrov's administration controlled only

---

[10] Alexei Malashenko. "Kak Chechnya stala osobennoy" [How Chechnya became special]. *Vedomosti*, December 10, 2019. On the general pattern of ethnic defection in civil wars, see Kalyvas, Stathis. "Ethnic defection in civil war." *Comparative Political Studies* 41, no. 8 (2008): 1043–1068. On proxy rule in Chechnya in comparative perspective, see Hughes, *Chechnya*: 118.

the city of Gudermes and nearby eastern districts. Grozny was no man's land. The real power in Chechnya was in the hands of the numerous Russian *siloviki* – the Ministry of Defense, the FSB, the GRU, and the MVD.[11] Kadyrov's administration was seen as merely a façade. He also had to face the Kremlin's other local intermediaries. Different agencies and factions among the *siloviki* all had their own Chechen proxies, warlords who had fought on the Russian side. Gradually, Kadyrov Senior managed to increase his power, diminish the rule of federal security agencies, and contain their local proxies. Yet his rule was never consolidated; there were always other powerful political players, who could challenge Akhmat Kadyrov's political (and physical) survival.

Most importantly for the story that this book tells, Akhmat-haji Kadyrov did not actively promote Sharia and customary law during his three years' tenure as ruler of Chechnya. Despite the fact that he himself was a cleric and a traditionalist, Kadyrov centered his legal politics on strengthening Russian state law. Kadyrov Senior made the reestablishment of the Russian legal system in Chechnya one of the top priorities of his administration. Two federal judges whom I interviewed acknowledged that Kadyrov personally reached out to them and asked them to move from central Russia to take judicial posts in Chechnya. The same was true for the prosecutor's office. For Akhmat Kadyrov, strengthening Russian law was a preliminary step to restraining the lawless behavior of federal *siloviki* and potentially bringing them to justice for war crimes. In the early 2000s these were the main concerns of the Chechen population. For Akhmat Kadyrov, state law was the only possible way to win local legitimacy.

At the same time, Kadyrov Senior claimed that Sharia courts were discredited, and he did not want Chechnya to be an Islamic Republic. In an interview with Anna Politkovskaya in 2000, he said that he was now "an official, not a cleric" and that he thought that "Islam should occupy the same place with us as it does in Ingushetia and Dagestan."[12] That meant a very modest place. He also did not publicly embrace customary law or try to create any sort of elders' courts.

In 2003, Akhmat-haji Kadyrov defended a Ph.D. dissertation in political science on "the genesis, nature, and ways of resolution of Chechen

---

[11] Evangelista, *The Chechen wars;* Taylor, *State building in Putin's Russia.*
[12] Politkovskaya, Anna. *A Dirty War. Russian reporter in the Caucasus.* Random House, 2009: chapter 23.

conflict."[13] To put it mildly, there is a reasonable doubt that Kadyrov wrote the dissertation himself – having a Ph.D. title is a popular thing among Russian officials, and in most cases, dissertations for high-profile officials are ghostwritten. Yet, it is still quite interesting that his dissertation did not put forward Sharia and adat as means of conflict resolution. The dissertation vigorously defended the Russian Constitution and state law.

Curiously, in his dissertation, Akhmat Kadyrov presented an analysis of the survey of the Chechen population conducted at the military checkpoint between Chechnya and North Ossetia. Methodologically this analysis is dubious, but the interpretations of this survey evidence is of great value. The results of Akhmat Kadyrov's survey suggested that the Chechen population rejected the idea of independence and wanted to live as a part of the Russian Federation. Most interestingly for my analysis, Akhmat Kadyrov's dissertation reported the responses to the question "do you believe that Chechen people should live according to Sharia law?" The result of the survey indicated that only 14.5 percent agreed with this proposition, more than 70 percent disagreed, and 15 percent did not respond or said that they didn't know. The author claimed that this result is driven "not by the beliefs in the anachronistic nature of this form of government, but the results of the previous authorities' performance. Chechnya learned the results of the Sharia law: medieval public executions and the youth that did not attend school for more than five years." He also wrote that people were told by these authorities "we will build an Islamic state. In a year, there will be another Saudi Arabia here. They were promised golden cups with camel's milk. This is how they were killing our people..." Kadyrov further claimed that Islam for Chechens is a "ritual, tradition, identity, rather than conscious faith. ... Islam (submission in Arabic) and its Sharia law did not sit too well with independent, freedom-loving Chechen spirit."[14]

Reading these narratives coming from the former religious leader is puzzling. However, they illustrate one of the key points of my theory of state-building lawfare: the regime of Kadyrov Senior was not consolidated, and he could not risk the creation of independent sources of power

---

[13] Kadyrov, Akhmat. *Rossiysko-chechenskiy konflikt (genezis, suschnost', puti reshenia)* [*Russo-Chechen conflict: Genesis, nature, and paths to resolution*]. Ph.D. dissertation, Russian Academy of Sciences, 2003.

[14] Ibid.: 130. I don't think the survey numbers reported in Kadyrov's dissertation are valid and can be contrasted with the results from my survey. But the interpretations of these data are of great interest.

based on custom and religion. His power came solely from the Kremlin. Thus, strengthening the Russian state law was in his best interests. Ramzan, who inherited his father's post in 2007 after a short interregnum, always claims that he follows the path of his father in every aspect. Yet Ramzan's jurisdictional politics is very different from his father's. Perhaps, then, Ramzan changed the policy towards non-state legal systems because he realized that it was impossible to eradicate them? In other words, perhaps weak state capacity can explain the persistence and power of non-state legal systems in Ramzan's Chechnya?

"The Death of Custom" or On State Capacity

Adat and Sharia persisted in Chechnya to some extent despite decades of Soviet attempts to eliminate these systems of dispute resolution. However, the insights from my research cast doubt on the state capacity explanation for the prevalence of legal pluralism in contemporary Chechnya. I analyze the sudden abolition of the customs of bride kidnapping, early marriage, and blood revenge to show that the government in fact has great power to intervene and either encourage or discourage customary and religious practices.

Bride kidnapping is one of the most (in)famous Chechen customs. According to a human rights report published in 2010, as many as one in four marriages in Chechnya began with the woman being kidnapped and forced to wed against her will.[15] Sometimes bride kidnapping is consensual, mostly when the women's parents do not approve of the marriage, but in many cases kidnappings are not consensual. Bride abductions in Chechnya became endemic during the conflict, and especially after the end of the Second Chechen War. Marha, a female lawyer in her forties, told me:

After the war there were many men with weapons. They did whatever they wanted. They saw a beautiful girl for the first time in their life on the street and then immediately abducted her in the presence of her mother and father. No one was able to stop them – they had guns.

According to the estimates of a local NGO, about 90 percent of marriages that resulted from abductions ended in divorces. Bride

---

[15] Radio Free Europe. "Despite official measures, bride kidnapping endemic in Chechnya." October 21, 2010.

kidnapping also had detrimental consequences for the abducted women's psychology, health, and social status within their new families. Some girls were kidnapped when they were thirteen years old or even younger. The custom of bride kidnapping was embedded in the local culture and widely accepted as legitimate.[16] However, by 2015 the practice had effectively been eradicated in Chechnya. Zaur, a clerk at the Justice Department, told me, "Maybe there will be one or two cases in the whole republic, but several years ago there were hundreds if not thousands of such cases." How did it happen that one of the most notorious Chechen customs was abolished in such a short period of time?

According to one prominent human rights activist in Chechnya, the abolition of the custom of bride kidnapping was the result of a deliberate legal mobilization effort. Chechen activists managed to build a surprising coalition among Chechen Islamic clergy, European human rights activists, and the metropole personified by Vladimir Putin. First, human rights activists tried to exploit the fact that bride kidnappings severely violate the principles of the Koran. Sharia explicitly requires that legal marriage needs consent from both parties. A marriage without consent or performed under coercion is considered void and may be annulled on those grounds. Moreover, abduction of a person is also strictly prohibited in Sharia. In 2008–2009, human rights activists attended all public events organized by the Chechen Muftiat, the religious administration of the republic, and consistently asked the same question: What is the position of Sharia on bride kidnapping? My interlocutor recalled that even though representatives of the clergy were Chechen men who either supported bride kidnapping or did not want to speak against it, they had to publicly acknowledge that the practice was against the Koran and Sunna.

Second, human rights activists promoted the agenda of fighting bride kidnapping on the international level. In the 2000s, there were many conferences devoted to the problems of human rights in Chechnya, and activists raised the issue of bride kidnapping at many of them. As a result of this international campaign, Vladimir Putin was repeatedly asked about bride kidnapping in Chechnya at his meetings with foreign leaders. At some point, according to my respondents, Putin allegedly called Ramzan Kadyrov and asked him to stop bride kidnapping by any means.

[16] Kurbanova, *Problemy i protsessy gendernoy samoidentifikatsii chechentsev.*

Even though Kadyrov's militia fighters were the most common bride abductors, as they had absolute power and almost no accountability, Kadyrov obeyed and publicly denounced the practice of bride kidnapping. Islamic leaders in Chechnya followed Kadyrov and also denounced it. In addition, Kadyrov promised to prosecute kidnappers under Russian law, and at the same time introduced an informal fine against bride kidnappers: one million rubles (approximately $30,000 at that time). Chechen custom also imposed a fine for kidnapping, but it was almost ten times smaller. Thus, the Chechen government combined all three sources of authority: religious reasoning, formal legal enforcement, and a customary fine practice.

These policies had an immediate effect: kidnappings basically stopped. At the time of my interviews, all respondents recognized this as a major achievement of Ramzan Kadyrov. Most officials in the government and the Muftiat also condemned the practice and praised Kadyrov for eliminating it. As one imam put it, "Thanks to Allah, thanks to Ramzan, we got rid of this stupid custom!" Some government officials with whom I discussed this radical change blamed Ichkerian separatists for the spread of bride kidnappings. Others among my interlocutors denied that bride kidnapping had ever been a legitimate Chechen custom.[17] They attributed this practice to the bad influence of neighboring peoples, for example, the Dagestanis or Cossacks. Finally, as Kadyrov had promised, some abductors were prosecuted. During my fieldwork, I was told about several criminal cases in which kidnappers received long prison sentences.

Almost at the same time, in 2014, Ramzan Kadyrov effectively banned the early marriages that had also proliferated in the postwar period. Early marriage was a practice justified by religious norms, rather than customary law. It was common for brides to be fourteen or fifteen years old, still schoolgirls. Kadyrov made it a rule that no one could marry before they reached eighteen years of age and had finished high school. Enforcement of the new rule was expected from the clerics, not just state officials. This was important because many Chechens do not register their marriages with the state and only go through a religious ceremony. Imams were prohibited from performing *nikah* (the marriage ceremony) for underaged

---

[17] In Central Asia, the historical authenticity of the "tradition" of nonconsensual bride abductions is also a contentious issue. See Werner, "Bride abduction in post-Soviet Central Asia."

brides. Those clerics who defied the rule were fired. The reasoning of the government was not the protection of women's rights, but that early marriages often lead to divorces, which is bad for the moral order. In addition, the government demanded that both bride and groom provide a medical certificate that they were HIV-negative to the imam before the *nikah* ceremony. Without these certificates, imams would not perform the ceremony. This intensive government penetration into the regulation of marriage – an institution that was considered sacred, private, and largely off-limits to the state, even in Soviet times – indicates that the regional state in Kadyrov's Chechnya does not lack capacity in the regulatory sphere.

A third illustration of the limitation of the state capacity argument is the effective termination of the custom of blood revenge in Kadyrov's Chechnya. As I have noted throughout the book, blood revenge is the cornerstone norm of the customary law. According to adat, murder must be avenged with murder. Chechenization of the Second War, when pro-Moscow Chechens were put in charge of the counterinsurgency, led to numerous blood feuds between Chechen families. Ramzan Kadyrov and his associates earned many blood enemies themselves. Yunus, a high-level police officer and prominent agent of Kadyrov, put this fact in a memorable way. At one point during our lunch in a small café, Yunus placed his gun on a table. He explained that he always carries the gun with him: "I've been serving in the police for a while – do you know how many blood enemies I have at this point?"

In 2010, Ramzan Kadyrov created a commission for national reconciliation. The commission was staffed with respected elders and religious leaders, including the Mufti. In just one year, according to then-Mufti Sultan-haji Mirzaev, the commission managed to reconcile more than 400 feuding families. The majority of these feuds were the product of the killings during mopping-up operations. The commission appealed to the Sharia norm that advises would-be avengers to forgive their blood enemies "for Allah" and to accept monetary compensation instead. Of course, the reconciliation process was backed by government force, but appeals to Sharia, which have very high legitimacy in Chechen society, helped to freeze, if not to end, the practice of blood revenge in Chechnya.

My interlocutors have different perspectives on the question of whether the feuding families actually reconciled. Some argue that since they pledge on the Koran, they can't take their words back and the feuds are over. Others argue that nobody forgave anyone, because "all these reconciliations were forced by *kadyrovtsy*." Amir, a man in his thirties, said, "People will avenge not only killings, but also humiliation during these so-called acts of reconciliation." There is also the issue of a large Chechen diaspora. Diaspora Chechens did not reconcile with their enemies and, according to my interviews, many of them are waiting until Kadyrov's regime is weaker in order to come back and avenge their relatives.

Also, while Kadyrov's regime is actively forcing Chechen families to reconcile, Kadyrov himself and his closest associates reject the idea of leaving the custom of blood revenge behind. As I mentioned in the introduction, in 2019, long after the reconciliation policy was put in place and blood feuds were effectively banned, Magomed Daudov, the Speaker of the Chechen Parliament and Kadyrov's close associate, declared blood revenge against popular anti-government blogger Tumso Abdurakhmanov for speaking ill of Akhmat-haji Kadyrov. On another occasion, in 2017, *kadyrovtsy* declared blood revenge on the families of the insurgents who had killed police officers. This was a strange twist of the custom, because the insurgents were themselves killed during the attack.

In any case, whether the customs of bride kidnapping and blood revenge and the practice of early marriage have indeed been completely eradicated, or just temporarily put on hold, potentially to return in the long run, is less important for my analysis. What is more important is that the evidence of the sudden "death" of these notorious customs, directed by the government of the Chechen Republic, shows that the government has enough coercive capacity to eradicate customary and religious norms. Thus, state capacity is a poor explanation for the top-down legal politics in Chechnya. Given this, I suggest we look for a political explanation for the promotion of non-state legal systems in Ramzan Kadyrov's Chechnya.

LEGAL PLURALISM FOR POLITICAL CONTROL

Legitimation

I argue that the promotion of legal pluralism in Chechnya helps to solve three crucial problems of political control: legitimation, boundary control, and coalition-building. First, promotion of legal pluralism increases the government's legitimacy by associating it with traditional and religious sources of power. Borrowing legitimacy from alternative sources – traditional, charismatic, and rational-legal – the ruler might combine their comparative advantages and selectively use references to them for different audiences. As I outlined, Ramzan Kadyrov's regime is largely based on military force and repression, but even the most repressive authoritarian regimes need popular belief that the ruler's powers are legitimate. The case of Madina Umaeva, introduced in the beginning of this chapter, showed that Chechen regional authorities care a great deal about public opinion.

Ramzan Kadyrov especially emphasizes his Islamic credentials and his commitment to Sharia justice. By organizing government-sponsored qadi courts in each district of Chechnya, Kadyrov follows the logic of "religious outbidding":[18] he presents himself as even more Islamic than his main opponents, the Islamist rebels.[19] Islam and Sharia have almost unquestioned legitimacy in postwar Chechnya, so associating his government with Sharia increases support for Kadyrov, especially among the youth. Qadi courts are not the only example of Kadyrov's strategy of constructing a Chechen-Islamic cultural hegemony: he has built mosques in every village in Chechnya, opened an Islamic University in Grozny, sponsored madrasas, a competition of *khafiz* who memorize the Koran, and television broadcasts about Islam, and obliged all government employees to wear traditional Islamic dress.[20] After the Charlie Hebdo attack in January 2015, Kadyrov organized a rally of one million people "in support of the Prophet Muhammad." Islamic symbols play a crucial role in the functioning of Kadyrov's government, and the presence of Islamic courts is an important part of the government-imposed cultural hegemony.

Likewise, association with Chechen customary law promotes Kadyrov's legitimacy among traditionalists. Even though Kadyrov relies on young people in his government – most offices are occupied by people under the age of thirty-five – in public he always pays respect to elders and emphasizes his commitment to Chechen traditions. For instance, Kadyrov organizes congresses of his *teip, Benoi*, invests in rebuilding the ancient Chechen towers in the mountains, and polices the adherence to Chechen customs at weddings. The government has banned "European wedding dresses" and also regulated "the appropriate dance moves" for wedding dances. Some traditionalists applaud these initiatives because "[this]

---

[18] Toft, Monica Duffy. *Securing the peace: The durable settlement of civil wars.* Princeton University Press, 2009; Snyder, Jack. *From voting to violence: Democratization and nationalist conflict.* New York, 2000.

[19] Islamist ideology became dominant among Chechen insurgents during the insurgency phase of the Second War in the early 2000s. See Hughes, *Chechnya*; Toft and Zhukov, "Islamists and nationalists"; Wilhelmsen, "Between a rock and a hard place."

[20] Laruelle, Marlène. *Kadyrovism: Hardline Islam as a tool of the Kremlin?* IFRI, 2017.

allows us to preserve our traditions, our culture!" as Zaur, one of my male interlocutors, who is an elder in his family, put it.

Kadyrov's legitimation through jurisdictional politics is explicitly gendered. As I documented above, the government has been promoting and sometimes inventing rigid conservative patriarchal interpretations of customary law and Sharia. The promotion of polygamy, honor killings, regulation of women's dress, and the crackdown on divorces are the major elements of Kadyrov's jurisdictional politics. Government involvement in the case of Madina Umaeva is not an isolated incident of top-down lawfare. In Chapter 8, I will relate this top-down lawfare with conflict-induced women's mobilization of state law. The larger point is that the legitimation of political order in postwar Chechnya is based on the traditionalization of social order. Here I concur with Janet Elise Johnson, who claims that "there is a gendered core in Kadyrov's warlordism."[21]

Boundary Control

At the same time, Kadyrov promotes non-state legal systems as a means of increasing his autonomy and indispensability to the metropole. Kadyrov was imposed on Chechnya by the Kremlin and to a great extent relies on the Kremlin's monetary transfers and military aid. According to a common expression used by Kadyrov's opponents, "Kadyrov's regime in Chechnya rests on Russian bayonets." However, many powerful players in the Kremlin despise Kadyrov and dream of his removal. Quite often, as I observed in the field, rumors spread that Kadyrov would soon be removed from office. In this light, promotion of customary law and Sharia works as a boundary-control mechanism. It signals that the head of Chechnya is not like a governor in other Russian regions: this position requires the ability to navigate multiple legal systems. In other words, it implies that Moscow cannot appoint an outsider to govern Chechnya, as it did in neighboring Dagestan in 2017, because this outsider would have to deal with polygamy, blood revenge, clans, and so forth. Emphasizing these unique essentialist elements of the Chechen political landscape strengthens Kadyrov's position by preventing oversight and intervention from the center and signaling that none but he is able to do the job.

---

[21] Johnson, Janet Elise. "Fast-tracked or boxed in? Informal politics, gender, and women's representation in Putin's Russia." *Perspectives on Politics* 14, no. 3 (2016): 652.

Ramzan Kadyrov's speech in the aftermath of the Madina Umaeva's death controversy is illustrative here. One of the key points that Kadyrov emphasized was that Russian central authorities have been forcing the Chechen regional authorities to do postmortem examinations, especially during the coronavirus pandemic, but the authorities of Chechnya actively resisted this demand from the center, justifying their resistance with the claim that autopsy is against Sharia. This can be interpreted as either pandering to the population preferences, or as a powerful signal to the Kremlin regarding Chechnya's autonomy.

Coalition-Building

Third, Kadyrov's government uses legal pluralism for coalition-building. Kadyrov's electorate is one person – Vladimir Putin, who appointed him and to whom Kadyrov is personally loyal. However, in order to succeed at his main task, political stability, Kadyrov has to rely on a broader coalition of supporters. Promoting non-state legal systems allows Kadyrov to incorporate religious and traditional authorities into his coalition. At the same time, by recognizing informal non-state forums of justice, Kadyrov establishes regulation over them. Thus, he prevents the formation of elites with a source of power independent from him. In my interviews, respondents revealed that the Chechen authorities extensively screen candidates for both customary and religious positions for their political loyalty. The government promotes the "right elders," most of whom are either active or retired government or security personnel. Even after that, all religious activities are under strict surveillance. But in addition to this stick, there is also a carrot: both religious and customary authorities are on the government payroll. These authorities not only resolve disputes, but also monitor the social behavior of their "constituency" and mobilize the population for the government's needs. For instance, on one occasion, I witnessed how a qadi of one of the districts called people in his native village to ensure that they were coming to a government-sponsored rally. Thus, the controlled elites help to further control the masses.

The strategies of political control in Ramzan Kadyrov's Chechnya have been fundamentally affected by conflict. Most notably, the war transformed the coalition-formation dimension of jurisdictional politics. Kadyrov tailored his strategy of political control based on legal pluralism to the post-conflict political topography of Chechnya and to the powerful constituency of former rebels.

The Regional Core

In terms of political topography, Chechnya is conventionally divided between the more Russified North and the mountainous traditionalist South. I will analyze this divide in the next chapter. Politically, the division between the West and the East of Chechnya is much more important. In the postwar period, the eastern region of Chechnya became the stronghold of the Chechen government headed by Kadyrov family, while the western region is largely considered less loyal to the government. Almost all key government officials in postwar Chechnya are from one of the four eastern regions of Kurchaloyevsky, Gudermessky, Shalinsky, and Nozhay-Yurtovsky.[22] This division was highlighted in all my interviews related to the war and its legacies. Elders from several eastern villages confirmed in a group discussion that "we [eastern Chechnya] are indeed the base of Kadyrov's regime." In contrast, the West is considered to be less controlled by the regional authorities. My respondents in the western areas acknowledged that locals are not very fond of the government and that this relationship is reciprocal. For example, according to one interview, in one of the western villages, people for many years – up to 2012 – kept burning down the huge banner picturing Akhmat-haji Kadyrov almost every week. Every week the government posted a new one.

My interviews suggest that the government is much more likely to initiate criminal and civil cases in western and other non-core communities than in the core communities in the east. This illustrates the well-known principle *to my enemies, the law*. For example, a prosecutor from one of the districts outside of the regime's regional core told me that their district annually receives a quota for corruption cases. In response, the district administration gathers its employees and they cast lots to determine who will be the "corrupted official" that year. Other interviewees suggested that criminal and civil cases initiated by the government largely serve as a mechanism for extortion. This claim is supported by the interviews presented in a report "Chechnya: The Inner Abroad." According to an expert interview,

---

[22] Malashenko, Aleksei. *Ramzan Kadyrov: rossiyiskiy politik kavkazskoy natsionalnosti* [*Ramzan Kadyrov: Russian politician of Caucasian nationality*]. Moscow: ROSSPEN, 2009.

None of the rule-of-law institutions work in compliance with the Russian law, not only in law enforcement, but also in civil law. Land code, social and commercial law function through administrative management by local officials who have turned it into a tool for extortion and a source of self-enrichment.[23]

The government uses law to force the population to pay taxes and utility tariffs that are arbitrarily set very high. In contrast, in the core eastern communities, state law is barely used by the government or the people. A telling fact is that for several years there were almost no court cases in Kadyrov's native village of Khosi-Yurt (now renamed Akhmat-Yurt after Ramzan's father).

In this light, it is more understandable why Kadyrov went out of his way to defend Vishadzhi Khamidov – Madina Umaeva's husband and the alleged culprit in her death — from appearing in Russian state court. Khamidov's family is from Gudermes region – one of the eastern districts of Chechnya that form Kadyrov's power base. After Madina Umaeva's death, Vishadzhi not only avoided prosecution, but also received a new house from Ramzan Kadyrov as a present. Perhaps even more important for this outcome was that Khamidov worked in Chechen law enforcement, in the elite special forces training center situated in Kadyrov's native village. Law enforcement cadres, many of whom were former rebels, constitute the core of Ramzan Kadyrov's coalition of support. Like the spatial division between the East and the West, the political role of law enforcement officials is a direct product of the Second Chechen War.

Rebel-Bureaucrats

Conflict transforms the structural composition of elites that a ruler needs in order to have a stable ruling coalition. After the end of the Second Chechen War in the early 2000s, when the Kremlin delegated regional power to Akhmat-haji Kadyrov, he announced a broad amnesty for the rebels, and many fighters surrendered and were given amnesty. The majority of these former rebels joined the Chechen police force and other government agencies.[24] For example, the Speaker of the Chechen Parliament, the former warlord Magomed Daudov, fought the Russians until 2004, then surrendered, joined Kadyrov's inner circle, and became

---

[23] "Chechnya: The inner abroad." The International Crisis Group, Report No. 236. June 30, 2015: 28.
[24] Malashenko, *Ramzan Kadyrov*.

one of the most powerful Chechen political leaders. According to my interviews, the majority of the personnel in the Chechen police and other law enforcement agencies had been rebels at some point. Some of these people were opportunists, but many of them had fought for nationalist or Islamist ideals. These rebels-turned-bureaucrats often did not receive any formal legal education or indoctrination into the state legal practices. As a result, many state officials in Chechnya hold a strong attachment to their religious and ethnic identities and prefer Sharia and adat over state law.

Interviews and field observations provide ample direct evidence for the phenomenon of the anti-state bureaucrats. For example, Ruslan, the prosecutor in a mountainous Chechen district, told me,

> We are sitting and talking here about law. But, say, if someone offends my father, even verbally, I will definitely kill him in revenge. This is part of our adat. Adat developed for centuries; it is stronger than any written law. If I don't follow adat, other families will think that our family is weak, and they won't give us their daughters to marry, and they'll show other signs of disrespect.

State officials in charge of law enforcement often directly contradict the norms of Russian law. For example, many interviewees emphasized how Chechen men in law enforcement defy their responsibilities in gender-related cases if they go against their beliefs. For instance, in one case, according to Leila, a lawyer in her forties, a woman tried to file a lawsuit against relatives who had seized her property, but the male court clerk did not accept her documents because, he said, "It is bad to litigate against your relatives."

It is noteworthy that there is also a sizable share of "legalists" among the judicial and law enforcement personnel in Chechnya, who follow the letter of the law and value it over the norms of custom and religion. Many of these legalists received their education and indoctrination into the legal profession in the Soviet Union. Some younger cadres whom I would also call legalists received a good education in Chechnya or in other regions of Russia in the post-Soviet period. But the top government officials are the rebel-bureaucrats, who prioritize custom and Sharia. The government's policy of promoting non-state legal systems can be understood as a concession to this important constituency of the ruling coalition.

The conflict also directly affected the structure of local political competition, which, as I propose, determines the viability of the strategic promotion of legal pluralism. The Second Chechen War ended with the military defeat of the rebels and consolidation of power by Ramzan Kadyrov thanks to the "Russian bayonets" and his skills in outmaneuvering and literally eliminating his potential rivals.[25] Thus, the ultimate outcome of the war was that the government of Ramzan Kadyrov was left without any viable potential local opposition and therefore was able to promote legal pluralism without fearing that the non-state legal forums would be hijacked by local challengers at some point. In other words, the high degree of regime consolidation allowed Ramzan Kadyrov to engage in lawfare to further strengthen his rule at home and to increase his autonomy from the metropole. To further explore the role of political control versus state capacity, popular demands, and ideology in the politics of legal pluralism, I put lawfare in postwar Chechnya into comparative perspective with the treatment of customary and religious systems in the neighboring regions of Ingushetia and Dagestan.

COMPARATIVE LEGAL POLITICS IN THE NORTH CAUCASUS

Ingushetia: Lawfare in the "Brother-Nation"

As I outlined in the Introduction, Ingushetia is arguably an ideal case for comparison with Chechnya. Like the Chechens, the Ingush people belong to the Vainakh ethnic group; they share customs and social structures.[26] Chechens and Ingushs often refer to each other as "brother-nations." The difference between Chechen and Ingush languages is similar to that between British and American English. The Ingush people live under the same arrangement of legal systems as Chechnya's population: Russian state law, Sharia, and adat. Until 1992, Checheno-Ingushetia was a single federal unit within the USSR and subsequently Russia, but in 1992 they split in two: Chechnya proclaimed independence from Russia while Ingushetia remained within the Russian Federation. As a result, Ingushetia was not directly exposed to post-Soviet armed conflict, and its post-Soviet political trajectory can be treated as a counterfactual for the macro effects of warfare on Chechen legal politics.[27]

---

[25] Marten, *Warlords.*   [26] Albogachieva and Babich, "Pravovaya kultura Ingushey."

[27] In 1992, Ingushs were engaged in an intense ethnic conflict with Ossetians over the disputed territory of Prigorodny district. The conflict lasted for one week and led to killings and the displacement of many Ingushs. It is also noteworthy that the war in Chechnya had spillover effects on Ingushetia: the influx of more than one hundred thousand refugees from the conflict in Chechnya undoubtedly had an effect on the local economy and societal relations of Ingushetia. Political developments in Chechnya also affected the politics in Ingushetia. Thus, the cases are interdependent, and I do not claim

In 1992 when Chechnya and Ingushetia split, General Ruslan Aushev, a hero of the Soviet war in Afghanistan, became President of Ingushetia. Aushev was immensely popular. In his first elections he received 99 percent of the vote; in 1998 he was re-elected with 65.5 percent. Aushev was a secular leader who did not support the use of adat and Sharia in Ingushetia. The President suppressed the People's Congress of Ingushetia, a popular neotraditionalist movement, and closed the Islamic center in one of the towns in Ingushetia. Aushev enjoyed wide popularity and did not want to promote alternative centers of power. Isa Tsechoev, a prominent religious leader, told me that "Aushev left almost no power to the Muftiat. He acted like a tsar."

Over time, opposition to Aushev's rule emerged. One opposition leader, the rich businessman Idris Abadiev, actively promoted neotraditionalism and customary institutions; the opposition umbrella organization was named the Council of Teips. The opposition stressed the need to strengthen the adat principle of governance that asserts that no one should be an authoritarian leader, but rather that councils of elders should make the important decisions. However, domestic opposition was not a very strong threat to Aushev's rule. Thus, his rule represented a balance of power where the ruler is powerful but does not want to risk the potential "Frankenstein effect" of promoting non-state legal systems.

The situation changed when Aushev entered a feud with the Kremlin. In 1999, Aushev's opposition to the looming renewal of the Chechen conflict led to a confrontation with the federal center. The Kremlin started to support the opposition within Ingushetia. This was a serious challenge. In response, Ingushetia's authorities started to actively promote legal pluralism. Most notably, in 1999, Aushev issued a decree that gave official status to the Sharia court established by the Muftiat of Ingushetia in May that year. Almost at the same time, he issued another that legalized polygamy.[28] This was an unexpected maneuver for the

---

that my comparison is a "natural experiment" in any way. For other comparative analyses of Chechnya and Ingushetia see Bakke, *Decentralization and intrastate struggles*; Klyachkina, *Reconfiguration of sub-national governance*; Sokirianskaia, *Governing fragmented societies*.

[28] *Zakon o shariatskom sude [The law on Sharia court]* (1999); *O nekotoryh voprosah gosudarstvennoy registratsii zaklucheniya brakov [On some questions of state registration of marriage]* (September 19, 1999). See Albogachieva and Babich, "Pravovaya kultura Ingushey." Previously, in 1997, the Ingushetia legislature had made the provision that the Justice-of-the-Peace courts in Ingushetia would judge in accordance with the principles of adat and Sharia.

Soviet general and secularist. According to Isa Tsechoev, "In the late 1990s strong opposition emerged to Aushev's rule. His people decided to mobilize religion to secure his power. He himself was a deeply secular man. He was an atheist and he had never tried to hide that." Thus, promotion of non-state legal systems by Ruslan Aushev can be interpreted as a tool of boundary control. The promotion of custom and religious law sent a strong signal to the Kremlin that Ingushetia deserved more autonomy, and that the Kremlin should not intervene in its politics by supporting the opposition. Ultimately, however, in 2001 Aushev had to resign under pressure from the Kremlin, and his successor Murat Zyazikov rolled back Aushev's decrees on polygamy and the Sharia court.

From 2008 to 2019 Ingushetia was governed by another general, Yunus-Bek Yevkurov, whose rule was also characterized by a shift in terms of support for legal pluralism. At the beginning of his tenure, Yevkurov tolerated an informal Sharia arbitration system organized by a state-sponsored religious organization, the Muftiat. The opposition tried to use this forum for their own goals – very much in accordance with the "Frankenstein" idea: in 2011, the opposition sued Yevkurov in the Sharia court for electoral falsifications during the Russian parliamentary elections. Idris Abadiev, who was one of the opposition leaders, recalled, "They had to close down the Muftiat to avoid accepting our appeal for Sharia justice."

However, in 2016 the relationship between Yevkurov and the Muftiat deteriorated as a result of political and economic conflicts. This led to an intense confrontation between the secular and religious authorities in Ingushetia. In 2018 religious authorities held a Sharia trial of Yevkurov for his intervention in religious affairs. Not surprisingly, Yevkurov spoke out against increasing the power of religious arbitration and religious norms. For instance, he argued against polygamy, in stark contrast to Kadyrov, who always promotes the idea. In the end, the government went as far as to attempt to suppress non-state law: it legally liquidated the Muftiat and its Sharia arbitration.

Analysis of the Ingushetia case shows that non-state legal forums, both customary and religious, can be strategically used by local rulers. When rulers are relatively strong, but still face some potential challenge, they either disregard or tolerate the non-state forums. However, when rulers are challenged, they respond by intervening in the politics of legal pluralism. When the challenge came from the outside, the ruler of Ingushetia (Aushev) promoted legal pluralism to increase local autonomy. By contrast, when local non-state authorities were behind the challenge, the ruler of that time (Yevkurov) attempted to suppress legal pluralism. Evidence from Ingushetia further supports the idea that the promotion of non-state legal systems can be considered a tool of political control and that the use of this tool is linked to the balance of political power.

Dagestan: Legal Pluralism from Below

Dagestan is another natural comparative case for studying Chechnya. The two regions share a history of Russian colonization in the nineteenth century and were united in anti-colonial struggle. Both share the legacies of Soviet rule, high levels of Islamic religiosity, and an emphasis on the importance of family and community belonging. However, there are also fundamental differences. The majority of Dagestan's population did not directly experience Stalin's deportation to Central Asia and post-Soviet armed conflict. Dagestan is also ethnically diverse, and its political field is extremely fragmented. In fact, Dagestan is famous for all kinds of complexity and diversity. With thirty-four officially recognized ethnolinguistic groups, it is by far the most ethnically heterogeneous of Russia's republics.

Historically, Dagestan has been a major center of Islamic knowledge and culture: Islam was brought there as early as the seventh century. As a result of the profound Islamization of society, customary law remained in Dagestan mostly in the form of rites and ceremonies and thus cannot be considered a legal system as it is in Chechnya and Ingushetia.[29] Thus, in Dagestan in the post-Soviet period there have been two parallel systems of justice: Russian state law and Sharia.

In the 1990s, Dagestan went through a profound Islamic resurgence. Many observers highlighted Dagestan as the most Islamized region of post-Soviet Russia.[30] As in Chechnya, the religious sphere in post-Soviet Dagestan has been divided between Sufis and Salafis. Adherents of Sufism, and in particular the followers of the sheikh Said-Afandi of Chirkey, control official religious institutions in the Republic. The Salafis, who are pejoratively referred to as "Wahhabis," have been persecuted by the state, and in 1999 Salafism was officially banned.

The confrontation between Sufis and Salafis had culminated in 1998, when the followers of militant Salafism proclaimed "a separate Islamic territory governed by Sharia laws" in four rural settlements of Dagestan

---

[29] However, customary norms are used in the redistribution of land in several post-Soviet Dagestani communities. See Bobrovnikov, *Musulmane Severnogo Kavkaza*.
[30] Ibid.: 264.

known as the Kadar Zone. The local state administration and law enforcement were disbanded and inhabitants who disagreed with the new "Islamic order" were forced to leave. The "Islamic territory" was short-lived, though, as in 1999, the federal authorities suppressed it with military force. The Kadar zone was widely covered in Russian media and is the most well-known instance of the imposition of Sharia law outside of the independent Chechen Republic of Ichkeria. However, there were other instances of the emergence of Sharia institutions that did not involve violent conflict and therefore are less known. For example, Russian scholar Dmitry Makarov documented the bottom-up establishment of Sharia in the village of Kirovaul. Notably, the village has a cleavage between Sufis (Tariqatists) and Salafis (Wahhabis), but they cooperated in the establishment of the Sharia institutions. Makarov wrote:

> The gathering of Kirovaul inhabitants voted in May 1998 for the establishment of the sharia court and sharia guard to fight alcohol and drug abuse, theft and moral laxity. Tariqatists and Wahhabis got equal representation among the 6 judges (the 3 most competent scholars from each side) and the guard, which consisted of some 40–50 people. Leaflets informing the population about the principles of the sharia structures' activity were posted on the mosques' walls. The sharia guard have started patrolling the village streets, especially at night. All those picked up in the street for appearing drunk or committing theft are being brought before the court, which determines an appropriate punishment in accordance with the sharia. Of course, such measures as the cutting off of hands or throwing stones have never been applied, and the only punishment in use is beating with a stick. The number of blows depends upon the nature of the transgression. There are no public floggings in Kirovaul. All punishments are executed in the madressa building in the presence of the judges and guard members only. However, the names of the punished become immediately known all over the village.[31]

Vladimir Bobrovnikov also documented the establishment of Sharia institutions in certain other rural communities of Dagestan, both traditionalist Sufi and fundamentalist Salafi. Despite the intense conflict, their Sharia institutions function quite similarly. Bobrovnikov notes that Sharia courts in rural Dagestan are usually presided over by the imam of the main mosque. These courts deal with family disputes, petty crime, and land disputes, and often function as a notary service.[32] My observations and interviews in Dagestan in the mid-2010s showed that Dagestan still

---

[31] Makarov, Dmitri. "Enacting the Sharia laws in a Dagestani village." *ISIM newsletter* 1, no. 19, 1998. See also the discussion of this evidence in Bobrovnikov, *Musulmane Severnogo Kavkaza*: 276–277.

[32] Bobrovnikov, *Musulmane Severnogo Kavkaza*: 277.

has two parallel systems of Sharia arbitration: some forums of religious justice are affiliated with the Muftiat, the official religious authorities of the republic, which belong to the Sufi tradition, while other forums are organized by the Salafi communities. The radical Islamist insurgents that were active in the region in the 2010s also had their own Sharia courts.[33] It is also noteworthy that, in contrast to Chechnya and Ingushetia where the presence of legal pluralism is all but ubiquitous, post-Soviet Dagestan exhibits tremendous spatial and social diversity of relationships between state and non-state legal systems: some villages and some economic spheres, such as construction, are governed in strict accordance with Sharia, while in others Sharia is not used at all.[34]

Most importantly for my analysis, despite the common use of Sharia for resolving everyday disputes and the bottom-up emergence of Sharia institutions in some Dagestani communities, appeals to formally implement Sharia law have been virtually absent among Dagestani regional authorities throughout the post-Soviet period – a stark contrast with Chechnya and even Ingushetia. None of the six heads of post-Soviet Dagestan have promoted Sharia law. This seems surprising given the high religiosity of the region and demands for introduction of Sharia by powerful religious actors, for example, by Said-Muhhamad Abubakarov, the Mufti of Dagestan, who was assassinated in 1998. However, it is not surprising in light of the argument advanced in this book. Unlike Kadyrov's Chechnya, with its consolidated authoritarian regime with no viable challengers, the Dagestani political scene has always been fragmented between different political cliques. Thus, the rulers of Dagestan have always faced the threat of a challenger. In these conditions, promoting non-state forums of power would be a risky

---

[33] Yarlykapov, Ahmet "Adat, Shariat i rossiyskoye pravo na sovremennom Severnom Kavkaze" [Adat, Sharia and Russian law in contemporary North Caucasus]. *Rossiya i Musulmanskiy Mir* 271 (2015).

[34] Kazenin, Konstantin. "Sotsiologiia islamskogo i obychnogo prava v postkonfliktnom uregulirovanii" [Sociology of Islamic and traditional law in post-conflict regulation]. *Mir Islama*, no. 2 (2013): 112–136; "Perspektivy institutsionalnogo podkhoda k yavleniiu poliyuridizma na primere Severnogo Kavkaza" [Prospects for an institutional approach to the phenomenon of the polyjuridicism on the example of the North Caucasus]. *Ekonomicheskaya Politika* 3 (2014): 178–198; "Uregulirovaniye konfliktov na Severnom Kavkaze: rol' neformalnykh pravovykh mekhanizmov" [Conflict management in the North Caucasus: The role of informal legal mechanisms]. *Obschestvennye Nauki i Sovremennost* 2 (2016): 144–154; Varshaver, Evgeny, and Ekaterina Kruglova. "Koalitsionnyi klintch protiv islamskogo poriadka: Dinamika rynka razresheniia sporov v Dagestane" [Coalition clinch against Islamic order: Dynamics of the market of dispute resolution institutions in Dagestan]. *Ekonomicheskaya Politika* 3 (2015): 87–112.

strategy because these non-state forums might turn against the ruler. In fact, the political history of Dagestan provides evidence for this assertion.

In 2016, the official religious authorities in Dagestan unexpectedly decided to challenge the secular authorities in the regional legislative elections. The Muftiat and its supporters formed their own party, People Against Corruption, which gathered many prominent Sufi religious leaders. This party quickly gained momentum and many observers predicted that it would defeat the United Russia Party, which represented the secular authorities. Ultimately, the government of Dagestan forced the religious authorities to withdraw from the race with the help of Moscow. In retaliation for their disloyalty, the government of Dagestan subsequently suppressed Sharia forums in several mountainous areas that were the regional core of support for the religious authorities.

This explains why even though Dagestan has a prominent Islamic tradition and its population is no less religious than Chechnya's, Dagestani regional authorities have never engaged in jurisdictional politics and promoted legal pluralism. While the regional authorities would have potentially increased their legitimacy by promoting Sharia, they were afraid that non-state justice would be hijacked by one of the numerous power players in Dagestani politics; thus, the benefits of this policy would be outweighed by its costs. Furthermore, when the religious authorities challenged the secular government, the government's response was the suppression of informal dispute resolution based on Sharia. This again provides support for the idea that government policies towards alternative legal systems reflect strategic calculations, rather than state capacity, ideology, or response to the demands of the population.

* * *

This chapter has shown that Ramzan Kadyrov has been promoting non-state legal systems in order to win support from segments of the population, increase his autonomy from the federal center, and build a coalition of support from non-state authorities and former rebels who turned into bureaucrats in the postwar period. In this regard, Kadyrov's politics of legal pluralism are similar to those pursued by the leaders of independent Chechnya-Ichkeria in the 1990s. As Chapter 4 showed, the leaders of Ichkeria also wanted to gain legitimacy, distance themselves from the metropole, and incorporate communal elites and rebels with strong religious normative commitments into their coalitions. The difference is that Kadyrov enjoys a political monopoly and promotes non-state legal systems without fear that they might turn against him. By contrast, Ichkeria's rulers always faced this potential "Frankenstein" effect, and turned to the strategy of promoting legal pluralism when they were severely weakened in the process of political competition. Thus, armed conflict can produce both excessively strong local rulers and excessively fragmented local political fields – both configurations of power in the periphery conducive to lawfare for political control.

This chapter casts doubt on alternative explanations, namely the roles of path dependence, weak state capacity, ideology, and popular demand in explaining the persistence and power of non-state legal systems in postwar Chechnya. All these factors played major roles in state-building lawfare in Chechnya in the past, as the previous chapter suggested. However, when the state-building project is directed by the peripheral leaders, the quest for political control is of primary concern, and other factors have limited explanatory power.

To elaborate, the evidence that Ramzan Kadyrov's policy towards non-state legal systems is radically different from the policy of his father, who was a cleric and traditionalist, yet strengthened Russian state law and abstained from promoting Sharia and adat, is troubling for the path-dependence argument. Meanwhile, the narrative of how Ramzan Kadyrov was able to effectively "cancel" the customs of bride kidnapping and blood revenge – the most notorious Chechen customs – indicates that the state capacity explanation is also limited.

Another potential explanation is that Kadyrov's policy of promoting legal pluralism reflects his ideological beliefs.[35] This is plausible indeed. In fact, Kadyrov himself can be characterized as a rebel-bureaucrat. He spent his youth fighting alongside his father, who was a Mufti of Ichkeria, known for declaring jihad against Russia. One objection is that ideological commitment assumes internal consistency and therefore promotion of one legal system. Religious ideology should be associated with promotion of Sharia, and traditionalism should be associated with promotion of customary law. Kadyrov, however, promotes both Sharia and custom and also extensively uses Russian state law. This syncretic blend can perhaps be considered ideology, but it has strong internal contradictions. In addition, even if in Ramzan Kadyrov's case, ideology and political strategy are observationally equivalent, other cases of legal politics in the North Caucasus highlight the limits of ideological explanations.

[35] Laruelle, *Kadyrovism*.

The "traditionalist" and cleric Akhmat-haji Kadyrov strengthened Russian state law. In turn, Dzhokhar Dudayev and Aslan Maskhadov of Ichkeria, discussed in the previous chapter, and Ruslan Aushev of Ingushetia, all secular legal centralists, promoted non-state legal systems when struggles for political control with internal and external opponents forced them to do so.

Finally, one may also argue that the policy of promotion of non-state legal systems is a response to popular demand. My interviews and field observations show that there is indeed strong popular support for Sharia and adat in Chechnya. However, as I showed in the comparative section of this chapter, there has been a comparable demand from the populations of post-Soviet Ingushetia and Dagestan, and the politics of legal pluralism promotion in these neighboring regions has been radically different. To further explore the demand side of state-building lawfare, in the next part of the book, I focus on individual legal preferences and behavior and how conflict has affected them.

PART III

LAWFARE AND SOCIAL ORDER

6

Laws in Conflict?

Hybrid Legal Order in Contemporary Chechnya

Many experts on Chechnya and locals in my interviews said that there is only one law in Chechnya: "what Ramzan said." The grim state of the rule of law in postwar Chechnya is undoubtedly true. For example, in October 2016 Ramzan Kadyrov publicly criticized particular court decisions and demanded the resignation of the judges who made them along with the Chief Justice of the Chechen Supreme Court. However, Chief Justice Murdalov did not resign. One of Kadyrov's closest associates, Magomed Daudov, a former rebel commander nicknamed Lord who was the Speaker of the Chechen Parliament at that time, went to the judge's office with his armed men and beat up the judge. The fact that the Speaker of the Parliament personally beat up the head of the Supreme Court was widely acknowledged as an indication of the poor condition of Russian state justice in Chechnya.

However, Chechnya is not just a lawless place. State and non-state legal systems have some autonomy. Kadyrov cannot possibly control everyday dispute resolution, even though he sometimes directly intervenes in particular cases. The fact that the alternative legal systems in Chechnya are not just a façade can be illustrated by the following paradox. Russian penal code allows for convicts to petition for parole after they have served a part of their sentence. Most convicts in Russian prisons use this opportunity. However, in Chechnya, those who serve time for murder or manslaughter never appeal for parole, even when they legally can do so. The reason is that if a murderer does not serve the full sentence according to state law, then it complicates interfamily negotiations regarding blood revenge according to custom and Sharia. If such a convict is released on parole, then the family of the murdered can withdraw their forgiveness and kill the released. Therefore, such convicts don't even file for parole.

Following the ethnographic narratives of living law presented in Chapter 2, this chapter outlines the functioning of the alternative legal systems with a special focus on the authorities in charge of them. I then sketch the most common disputes in which legal systems clash, analyze preferences for alternative forums in these situations, and explore patterns of variation in legal behavior based on court cases data.

STATE AND NON-STATE LEGAL SYSTEMS

State Judiciary

De jure, Russian state law is the law of the land in postwar Chechnya. The functioning of state law is systematically recorded. In this section, I combine my observations of legal practices and interviews with state officials, lawyers, plaintiffs, and NGO workers to describe the functioning of the state legal system in Chechnya.

The re-establishment of the state judicial system was one of the priorities of the Russian government once its army gained control of the territory in early 2000. The Russian federal judicial system officially started to function in Chechnya in 2001 amid an ongoing active insurgency. From 2009 to 2016, as I mentioned in the introduction, the reestablished Russian state courts in Chechnya heard more than 500,000 cases.

The Russian state judiciary is organized into several levels. The Supreme Court of the Chechen Republic is in charge of major crimes (for a long time, mostly those related to insurgency and terrorism). The Arbitration Court of the Chechen Republic is in charge of adjudicating economic disputes. The second level of the federal judiciary is the *rayon* (district) courts. There are fifteen district courts in Chechnya, which operate in all municipal districts and cities. They deal with civil, criminal, and administrative cases. Finally, the lowest level of the state system is the Justice-of-the-Peace courts. These courts deal with family disputes, property and labor disputes, and petty crimes. There are sixty-six JP Court districts in Chechnya. In contrast to the rest of Russia, where the majority of judges, especially at the lower levels, are women,[1] the overwhelming majority of judges in Chechnya (approximately 85 percent) are men. For

---

[1] Volkov, Vadim, Aryna Dzmitryieva, Mikhail Pozdnyakov, and Kirill Titaev. *Rossiyskiye sud'i kak professionalnaya gruppa: sotsiologicheskoe issledovanie. [Russian judges as professional group: A sociological study]*. St. Petersburg: European University Press, 2012.

instance, in 2011, among sixty-six Justices-of-the-Peace, only thirteen were women.

Law enforcement in Chechnya is carried out by the prosecutor's office and police. Russian security agencies, such as the FSB, also have a heavy presence in the republic. In Russian political discourse, those in charge of law enforcement are collectively called *siloviki*. According to some estimates, Chechnya has more *siloviki* per capita than any other Russian region.[2] The ubiquitous presence of the state in Chechnya can be illustrated by the large posters with the photo, name, and contact information of local police inspectors (*uchastkovyi*) that hang in all town districts and all villages in Chechnya. Police posts and courts usually occupy typical new two-story buildings. Sometimes they share a building with local administration. On all administrative buildings in Chechnya, including those of the police and the courts, there are always two flags – Russian and Chechen – and three portraits – of Putin, Kadyrov the senior (Akhmat-haji), and Kadyrov the junior (Ramzan).

In the immediate aftermath of the war in the early 2000s, the majority of the judicial and law enforcement cadres in Chechnya were ethnic Russians appointed from other regions of Russia. However, by the time of my research in 2014–2016, the vast majority of positions within the state legal system were occupied by local cadres, ethnic Chechens. For example, in 2017, only two of fifteen members of the Council of Judges of the Chechen Republic were non-Chechen ethnic Russians. Overall, the share of ethnic Chechen in judicial positions is about 85 percent. Most judges who are not ethnically Chechen serve in the Grozny Military Court. Some of the local cadres went through Soviet educational programs and served before the 1990s; however, the majority are too young for this. Appointing young cadres is one of the key features of Ramzan Kadyrov's government. Kadyrov himself became president immediately after turning thirty. Throughout his tenure, he has preferred appointing young men to government positions. In the nominally gerontocratic Chechen society, this sends a powerful signal by a young leader.

The authorities in charge of the state legal system in Chechnya belong to the federal agencies; therefore, in principle, Kadyrov has no power over the appointments of judges and prosecutors. However, he manages to heavily, if informally, influence the appointments of judges and law enforcement officers in "his republic."

---

[2] "Strana spetznaz" [The Special ops country]. *Novaya Gazeta*, July 25, 2011.

The state judicial system has been actively used by Kadyrov's government as a means of repression, along with a wide variety of extrajudicial repressive tools. The vast majority of high-profile cases in the Supreme Court of the Chechen Republic were brought against former insurgents. Given that Kadyrov's forces were also mostly former insurgents, the prosecution of former insurgents was highly selective. In addition, Kadyrov used the state legal system to intimidate civil society activists, human rights organizations, and independent journalists. In a series of cases that were widely covered in Russian and Western media, state courts in Chechnya convicted civil society activist Ruslan Kutaev, journalist Zhelaudi Geriev, and Oyub Titiev, who was the head of the Chechen branch of a Human Rights Center "Memorial." All three of these cases were fabricated and involved gross violations of procedural rules.

Open conflicts between Kadyrov and legal authorities have been extremely rare. In one prominent case heard in 2013, Federal Judge Vakhid Abubakarov recused himself from the case of a man charged with murdering police officers during the insurgency. The accused had been tortured, and the judge wanted to investigate the torture. However, the Deputy Minister of Interior, a close associate of Kadyrov, called Judge Abubakarov and demanded that he "avoid complications and make the judgment that he was supposed to make." The judge reported the call and recused himself. This was widely interpreted as a rebellion of this judge against Kadyrov. But the judge managed to remain in his position despite the pressure.

The state judicial system in Chechnya is perceived to be very corrupt. I spoke with many low-level clerks in the judicial system who acknowledged that the system is based on corruption: resolution of almost every criminal and civil case has a price. Moreover, positions in the judiciary and law enforcement are for sale. Said, a young lawyer, told me that after graduation he wanted to become a prosecutor, but the price for the job was 1.5 million rubles (25,000 USD at that time). His family did not have that money and he decided to enter a law firm. However, the private legal sphere is not free from corruption either. According to Khasan, a man in his thirties, who works as an attorney, "A lawyer in our republic is a broker. He takes money from the side he represents and bargains with the prosecutor and the judge. The side that pays more, wins."

My observation of court practices confirmed the prevalence of corruption. In several cases that I observed in federal district courts, participants told me afterwards that they had to pay the judge or prosecutor to get a more lenient decision. For example, the relatives of the defendant in the murder case described in the opening pages of this book were expected to pay two million rubles (approximately $30,000 at that time) to reclassify the case as one of excessive self-defense.

Despite the fact that Kadyrov's government uses the state judiciary as a tool of repression against political opponents and despite the fact that the system is profoundly corrupt, in the vast majority of cases, the system still follows the rules of procedure and the legal statutes. Because judges and state enforcement cadres are formally working in federal agencies, they are incentivized to follow the rules because there is always the possibility of oversight by the federal center.[3] In addition, as I wrote in the previous chapter, the large share of the judicial and law enforcement personnel in Chechnya are "legalists" who were educated in law during the Soviet Union or in the law schools of other regions of Russia in the post-Soviet period. These cadres try to follow the letter of the law when political constraints allow.

Local state courts were even able to partially address injustices committed by the Russian state during both Russo-Chechen wars. Chechnya never received any systematic transitional justice. The criminal prosecution of perpetrators of war crimes in Chechnya has been a very rare exception. Yet, as Emma Gilligan shows, local courts in Chechnya in the period from 2009 to 2015 were able to satisfy civil demands for monetary compensation for moral harm inflicted during the conflict, despite the hostile political environment.[4] Gilligan attributes the success of this legal mobilization for moral compensation to "the rise of a professional class of lawyers inside Chechnya" and "the way in which local lawyers and the judiciary deployed regional and international human rights law to build legitimacy within their own domestic legal institutions." Gilligan's analysis of court cases shows that Russian state courts in Chechnya are not just "kangaroo courts."

Thus, one can conclude that there is a dual state legal system in Chechnya: one that is used as a mechanism of repression and another that serves, even if imperfectly, the judicial function. Ernst Fraenkel originally introduced the concept of the *dual state* to analyze the functioning of law in Nazi Germany.[5] He showed that even under

---

[3] On the Russian law enforcement institutional machinery, see McCarthy, Lauren. *Trafficking Justice: How Russian police enforce new laws, from crime to courtroom.* Cornell University Press, 2015.

[4] Gilligan, Emma. "Chechen compensation cases: War crimes, domestic litigation, and moral harm in the Russian Federation." *Journal of Comparative Law* 37, no. 2 (2020): 37.

[5] Fraenkel, Ernst. *The dual state: A contribution to the theory of dictatorship.* New York, 1969. See also Meierhenrich, Jens. *The remnants of the Rechtsstaat: An ethnography of Nazi law.* Oxford University Press, 2018.

dictatorships, most aspects of the courts operate in a fairly normal and routine manner. In other words, despots are rarely interested in particular divorces or car accidents, and therefore, the court system in general operates according to the rules. Kathryn Hendley applied the concept of a dual legal system to Putin's Russia. She wrote:

> The legal system, as it has evolved over the past decade, is best conceptualized as a dual system under which mundane cases are handled in accordance with the prevailing law, but cases that attract the attention of those in power can be manipulated to serve their interests. To put it more simply, justice is possible and even probable, but it is not assured.[6]

In Chechnya, the sphere of law in which the government intervenes is perhaps even larger than in Nazi Germany or Russia as a whole, but mundane cases adjudicated in accordance with the letter of the law remain prevalent. Family law disputes represent such mundane cases, where direct intervention of the authorities is rare. However, the domain of family law also represents the arena in which state and non-state legal systems are most often in conflict. Before I outline these conflicts, I sketch the functioning of the customary and religious forums.

How to Become an Elder?

Despite the fact that only state law officially functions in Chechnya, customary law and Sharia remain powerful legal systems. Furthermore, as I document throughout the book, Kadyrov's government has been actively promoting the semiformal institutions of adat and Sharia. The status of government-sponsored councils of elders and qadi courts is ambiguous. They are not recognized as judicial institutions; even so, elders and qadis have formal positions within the state bureaucracy. For instance, qadis are appointed as deputies to municipal mayors. Elders also sometimes occupy government positions.

Elders are supposed to carry out customary law. Every Chechen extended family has an elder who, at least nominally, is in charge of important family decisions, such as marriage, divorce, and especially blood revenge. Chechen clans – *teips* – also usually have a nominal head, but some clans are very large, up to a hundred thousand people, and therefore clan elders often have purely symbolic authority. Some of my

---

[6] Hendley, Kathryn. "Assessing the rule of law in Russia." *Cardozo Journal of International and Comparative Law* 14 (2006): 351.

interlocutors even went as far as to say that "there are no real elders in Chechnya anymore, this is all fairy tales" and therefore "there is no adat as a legal system anymore." However, the majority of people I spoke with in Chechnya could easily point out the elder of their family and name respected elders in their communities.

How do people become elders? An elder is not necessarily the oldest male member of the family, even though being old is important. Elder is a position of respect; therefore, historically elders were successful warriors, knowledgeable in religion, or just "righteous" people – in short, those who enjoyed the respect of their family and community. According to Musa, an academic historian in his sixties, these idealistic visions of the origins of elders became largely irrelevant during the Soviet period. He claimed that the Soviet authorities realized the power of elders and started to promote their own candidates as village elders. Often these elders were former party apparatchiks, heads of collective farms *kolkhoz*, or police officers. However, reputation still plays a crucial role for an elder. For example, in the eastern part of Chechnya, many remember an elder with a very unusual last name: Weissert. He was a Volga German who was deported with his people to Central Asia during World War II. There he fell in love with a Chechen woman who had also been deported. Willy Weissert converted to Islam, adopted an Islamic name Ahmet, and married this woman. After the Chechens were allowed to come back to the Caucasus, he went with them. He was a good worker and spent substantial time and effort learning the Chechen language and customs and the Islamic religion. Chechens greatly respected his efforts and know-ledge, and soon he became involved in dispute resolution according to adat across all of Chechnya.[7] Now his son plays the same role.

In Kadyrov's postwar Chechnya, the position of elder was semiformalized. The government established councils of elders at the regional, district, and village levels. Loyalty to the government is the main prerequisite for getting this position. Elder positions are unpaid, but often combined with sinecures. For example, the head of the Council of Elders of the Chechen Republic, Said-Abdulla Akhamadov (who appeared in the beginning of Chapter 2) also serves as a head of the hunting agency of the republic. He claims to be a *qureishit*, a descendant of the Prophet Muhammad, which gives him additional legitimacy. Said-Abdulla told

---

[7] Weissert's story is so unusual that it has already been covered in several academic and journalistic accounts on Chechnya. See Derluguian, *Bourdieu's secret admirer in the Caucasus*; Lieven, *Chechnya*; Politkovskaya, *A dirty war*.

me that the regional council of elders deals primarily with blood feud cases. Council members are also involved in "moral education" – lecturing the youth about the repercussions of alcohol and drug abuse, as well as radical versions of Islam (Salafism). Councils of elders at the district and community levels serve largely the same functions. Thus, it is evident that the regional authorities created a state-like hierarchy for the customary organizations.

During one of my fieldtrips, I was allowed to participate in a meeting of the council of elders in one of the lowland districts of Chechnya. Usually, their discussions are held in Chechen, but for me the elders made an exception and spoke in Russian. Altogether nine elders participated in the gathering all wearing sheep hats. They represented their village councils. The meeting was held in a mosque. Before the start of the meeting, the elders performed *movlid*, a Sufi ritual (that resembles singing) that honors Prophet Muhammad. These details clearly show the interconnectedness of religious and customary authority in Chechnya.

I asked the council members to tell me what they were doing before becoming elders to try to see any patterns in their life trajectories. Their responses indicated no particular pattern: one elder was the son of the aforementioned Weissert, the others were a driver, a kolkhoz worker, a forester, a welder, a railway worker, a factory worker, a former police officer, and a former imam. All of them praised Kadyrov and emphasized that there is perfect harmony among state law, adat, and Sharia.

State-sponsored elders have considerable symbolic resources, but people prefer to rely on their family elders for dispute resolution. Sometimes they also refer to knowledgeable people. For instance, many people apparently used to come for dispute resolution to the famous Chechen ethnographer Akhmad Suleimanov, who knew adat very well.

In contemporary Chechnya, adat does not have a specialized system of dispute resolution and enforcement; instead, extended families serve as decentralized institutions of interpreting adat norms and enforcing them. Ilyas, a man in his 40s, eloquently put it: "In adat everyone is a judge." Here there is a direct parallel with Pierre Bourdieu's writing about Kabyls' customary law:

because each agent has the means of acting as a judge of others and of himself that custom has a hold on him: indeed, in social formations where, as in Kabylia, there exists no judicial apparatus endowed with a monopoly of physical or even symbolic violence and where clan assemblies function as simple arbitration tribunals, that is, as more or less expanded family councils, the rules of customary law have some practical efficacy only to the extent that, skillfully manipulated by the holders of authority within the clan they "awaken", so to speak, the schemes of perception.[8]

Similarly, all Chechens have their own ideas about what adat is, which are developed though their socialization process. Customary law is practiced and enforced though these shared norms. Often the people who make the principal decisions within extended families in the name of adat are powerful state officials or rich businessmen. Therefore, the authority of elders is often symbolic and used to justify the decisions of powerful members of families and communities.

Kadi Justice?

Max Weber used the term *kadi justice* (*Kadijustiz*) to contrapose judicial discretion to the rational-legal system of the rule of law. In Kadyrov's Chechnya, the official Islamic justice system is centralized and tightly controlled, and therefore quite distant from Weber's picture of *kadi* justice.

The highest religious authority of Chechnya is the Mufti, who heads the Muftiat, an organization that regulates and directs all religious affairs. Technically, the Muftiat is an NGO, but it operates more like a government ministry. The Muftiat appoints *qadis*, or Islamic judges, to each district. Qadis are officially the deputies to the head of each district municipality. The Muftiat also appoints all imams to mosques across Chechnya, even though the Shafii legal school demands imams to be elected by the community. If disputants opt for religious arbitration, they will first go to an imam. If that resolution does not work, they will then go to a qadi, and if that does not work, they can appeal to the Mufti. This layered system of religious justice presents an informal equivalent to an appeal system.

Imams and qadis are usually young men. Most of them have received some Islamic education. Some were educated in the Arab countries, mostly Egypt, Syria, and Yemen, while others received their education in the Islamic universities in Grozny, the village of Kurchaloy, or in some other Russian Muslim region. One *qadi* described to me the process of how qadis and imams are selected: "The Muftiat asks a candidate

---

[8] Bourdieu, Pierre. *Outline of a theory of practice.* Cambridge University Press, 1977: 17.

questions regarding the war in Syria and regarding Sufi orders to see who is loyal and who could be a troublemaker." Obviously, only loyal people get appointed as imams and qadis. Sometimes appointed imams are young, quite inexperienced, and not very knowledgeable. In one village, most of my interviewees said that the imam had no authority in the village. In places like that, people often rely on Sharia resolution that operates independently from semiformal government-sponsored Sharia institutions. Disputants ask knowledgeable people for adjudication even though those people lack any formal religious positions. Many Chechens went to study abroad at Islamic universities in the 1990s, but in contemporary Chechnya many of them are seen as potentially disloyal and therefore cannot get a formal religious position. Nevertheless, they have good religious education. I met with two people who spent four and seventeen years respectively at Al-Azhar, the most prominent Islamic education center, which is situated in Cairo. They both told me that many of their relatives and acquaintances prefer to go to them rather than to a poorly educated imam.

However, in other places, qadis and imams are knowledgeable, respected, and sometimes arguably more powerful than bureaucrats in secular positions. For instance, in one of the mountainous districts of Chechnya, the qadi combines his religious position with being head of the council of elders. This qadi has been an imam in his village for more than twenty years and knows everyone in the village. He is Chechen, but his distant ancestor was an Arab, which increases his religious credibility. Another powerful qadi in a lowland district explained his prominence by his connection to Kadyrov's inner circle. This qadi told me that before he turned to religion he was "a simple Soviet hooligan." He served in the Soviet military, and when he was discharged he studied religious education. According to this man, he is involved in hundreds of disputes every year.

Interlegality

Adat, Sharia, and even state law are deeply interconnected and profoundly influence each other, as the case on the opening pages of the Introduction documents. Quite often, Chechen cadres in the Russian state judicial and law enforcement system follow the principles of adat and Sharia. For example, Kuri, a young male clerk at the Department of Justice praised a judge in the following way: "He is a good judge. He is trying to implement Sharia whenever he can. I mean when this does not directly contradict state law." In some situations, state officials defer to communal authorities instead of doing their job. The words of Ansar, an Islamic arbiter, illustrate the point:

Judges, prosecutors, police officers – they are all Chechens in the end. They come to us with disputing sides and say: we don't want to initiate criminal proceedings, why don't you ask for resolution from the respected people. Let them decide.

In other cases, though, elders and religious authorities refer disputes to the state organs. For example, Khava, a female police officer, told me that in her village,

One man stole a car in the neighboring town. The owner found out about who stole it and came to the most respected elder of the family of the hijacker to demand justice. The elder decided to turn the hijacker to the police, and no one questioned his decision, because he had such high respect.

References to customs and religion are prevalent in state court hearings, especially in family disputes. Imams and elders sometimes participate in them as witnesses and experts. For example, in one child custody case, an imam came to testify on behalf of the mother. The central point of the imam's testimony was that she was a "moral woman." He also specified that "her family, both on her father's side and on her mother's side are decent people." Witnesses from the other side claimed that "the mother lives in violation of Chechen mentality" (euphemism for violating adat norms). When a female lawyer who represented the father's side asked the imam if, according to Sharia, the mother, the plaintiff in the case, was allowed to travel outside of Chechnya without the approval of her husband, the imam rebuked her by saying that "according to Sharia you should stay at home and not be in the courtroom now." At the same time, state officials sometimes testify in Sharia arbitrations. In one adjudication I witnessed, the qadi invited a traffic police officer as a witness to a car accident.

Some of my interlocutors, even authorities who are in charge of dispute resolution, often confused adat, Sharia, and state law norms. Ruslan, a man in his thirties who works as a prosecutor told me:

People simply don't understand the difference between law and custom. For example, one woman comes to me and say – please, help me to get the custody documents for my sister's son so that I can get the benefits from the government. I said – what are you talking about – this is against the law, this is fraud. And she said – but why? We are the one family anyway! – Our people have no sense of how Russian law works.

This should not be interpreted as an indication of just naivete or low legal knowledge; instead, this is a reflection of the profoundly complex hybrid legal order that emerged in postwar Chechnya. Most of my interviewees highlighted that there is a "perfect harmony" in the functioning of the state and non-state legal systems. This can be considered as a "public transcript." However, my field observations helped me to uncover common disputes in which the alternative legal systems directly and explicitly clash.

THE MOST COMMON DISPUTES

Private Domain

Arguably the most common type of disputes in which alternative legal systems are in direct conflict is child custody. In case of divorce, according to the dominant interpretations of adat, children must stay with their father, because they belong to their paternal extended family. According to Sharia, however, children should stay with their mother until they are seven years old and after that decide for themselves with whom to stay. Russian state law, on the other hand, gives preference to the mother in the vast majority of cases (even though there is no clear legal norm). So, the forum one chooses largely determines the outcome one gets. As a result, child custody cases are often bitterly contested. In some cases, women who go through divorce decide to leave their children with their former husbands in order to have an opportunity to remarry as there is a strong norm that a woman cannot bring her children to another family. But in other cases, women decide to fight for their children.

Zaindi, the head of one large rural municipality and a man in his early thirties, told me that child custody disputes have been very prevalent in his village. Usually, children stay with their father. In one case, he narrated:

A stepmother was terrorizing the children and literally torturing them by putting needles under their skin. The husband was drinking and did not care. We intervened and took the kids from this family and gave them to the mother. Both the father's and mother's extended families were against this, because it is wrong according to adat. But I said that if they don't agree with our decision, they will face troubles. We are the state! So, it worked.

The increase in the level of aggression after the conflict caused domestic violence to spread in Chechnya. According to women rights activists, reasons given for wife-beating include disobedience, using the phone or social networks, or even poor cooking. This issue is considered very sensitive: many of my interviewees claim that "there is no such problem in Chechnya." In adat, wife-beating is considered to be very shameful for a husband and can be retaliated against by the wife's relatives. If the wife's relatives bring her back to her parents' home, this is also considered shameful for men. According to one of my interlocutors, this serves as "a means to contain domestic violence." In Sharia, there are very strict regulations concerning when and how a man can beat his wife. In Russian law, domestic violence can be punished by prison sentences if the injuries are severe. In general, domestic violence is rarely brought to third-party adjudication.

While domestic violence is often left without any third-party involvement, disputes that arise from bride kidnapping necessarily require the involvement of authorities and referral to one of the alternative legal systems for reconciliation. According to Isa, a man in his thirties, "customary" Chechen bride kidnapping has many symbolic and ritual elements. If any of them are violated, adat allows relatives of the victim to kill the abductor or another person in his extended family, or to try to publicly shame the abductor by capturing him and releasing him in the middle of the village without his pants, which is the worst possible insult.

As I documented in the previous chapter, Kadyrov's government effectively prohibited the custom of bride kidnapping, but it semiofficially supports honor killings. Honor plays a central role in Chechen culture. If a woman somehow "puts shame" on her family, her male relatives can kill her. According to adat, "the right to kill" belongs to the father and brothers. A husband cannot kill his wife even if he witnesses her infidelity, because she does not belong to his extended family. According to Sharia, both a man and a woman can be punished for infidelity by death, but the requirements for evidence of guilt are very strict: one needs four eyewitnesses in order to accuse someone of infidelity. Nevertheless, the so-called honor killings find support among some of my interlocutors. For example, one man told me that "if my neighbor kills his daughter who somehow puts shame on his family, I'll be happy for him." This man himself had four daughters.

According to a prominent female human rights activist, quite often the so-called honor killings happen due to economic reasons. She told me a story from her own village, where a man learned that his old female relative bequeathed her house to her granddaughter, his niece, and not him. He killed the young woman and pronounced that "she put shame on her family." In other cases, honor killings are used to hide sexual violence: a male federal judge in his sixties told me a story of a brother who killed his sister to cover incest. Very few cases of honor killings get prosecuted. In Chapter 8, I briefly describe one such case.

Another common area of conflict of laws is polygamy. Kadyrov's government has been actively promoting polygamy in postwar Chechnya. The Chechen government expressed concerns about the "reproduction potential of the nation" and about "public morals" because of the perceived gender imbalance as a result of war. In response, the government issued an informal decree according to which all government employees had to take second wives. High-level bureaucrats and business-men were strongly encouraged to have multiple additional wives. Before the enactment of this unofficial governmental policy, polygamy among Chechens was rare. In fact, according to local ethnographers, Chechen adat does not allow polygamy except in case of a wife's infertility. Russian law does not recognize polygamy. Polygamy often leads to divorces and also seriously complicates inheritance disputes.

In the dominant interpretations of adat, women do not have any inheritance rights. In this regard, Sharia is more beneficial to women. There is a special "science of shares" in Sharia allowing women to inherit property, although their shares are smaller than men's. For example, a widow would inherit 1/4 of her late husband's property if they did not have children and 1/8 of it if they did. Daughters also inherit their father's property, but their shares are half the size of those of sons. Russian law assumes gender equality in inheritance rights. Zaur, a local male state official in his thirties, said that "Property must stay with the son. Wife and daughters should be supported by their family. Only if a woman has no brother, or if she is from a weak family, she will go to a court." He said this last part with strong disdain. In addition, as Adam, another male middle-aged interlocutor put it:

if a woman gets inheritance in a Russian court, the society will not recognize this right. For instance, if a woman decides to sell the house that she inherited this way, a normal buyer will first come and talk to the male heirs and they will explain the situation. So, no one will deal with such a woman.

A case from one of the women rights NGOs confirms this narrative. Marem became a widow when she was sixty. She did not have a son. The relatives of her husband forced her out of the house where she lived for more than forty years. She appealed to the court and won the case. But she is afraid of moving to the house and stays in a rented apartment.[9]

---

[9] Brulé documents that inheritance, especially land inheritance, is the key domain of gender regimes across the world. See Brulé, Rachel. *Women, power, and property: The paradox of gender equality laws in India*. Cambridge University Press, 2020.

Public Domain

The roots of property disputes unrelated to inheritance often come from the absence of documents or conflicting documents over apartments in Grozny and land plots in villages in the aftermath of the conflicts. It was especially common in Grozny for those who were leaving the city to sell their apartment to multiple buyers simultaneously. Adat proposes an equal split of the property if it is impossible to establish to whom it belongs. According to Sharia, such disputes are solved by taking an oath on the Koran. Russian law assumes resolution of such disputes will be based on verification of the relevant documents. Khalid, a man in his early forties, recalled that

there were numerous property disputes after the war. But they were quite efficiently managed based on elders' witness testimonies. It is believed, that if you don't trust an elder's testimony, you offend his whole family.

Car accidents are also resolved through multiple different forums. In addition to road police and courts, imams and elders also adjudicate such disputes. Particularly contested are accidents that involve cattle. Chechen qadis even issued a *fatwa* specifying that if an accident happens during the daytime, the car owner is responsible; if it happens at night, the cattle owner is responsible.

In disputes regarding debt, the major point of distinction is that Sharia prohibits interest. Chechen adat allows interest, but this norm is not well known. Interest rate disputes face strong disapproval in Chechnya. One of my interlocutors, Zaindi, a male state official, said that "I am against those who give with an interest. I won't talk to such person – he is not a true Chechen."

There is no Islamic banking in Chechnya. Therefore, according to Said-Magomed, who works in the Muftiat,

qadis have to adapt to the Russian realities. If a man got a loan and does not pay it back justifying it through the references to religion, we ask him to pay, because otherwise it seems that he uses the norms of religion for his profit.

Abdullah, another middle-aged religious arbiter, said that "there are many cases about debts and changes in currency rates. I rule that the debt has to be paid back in the same currency as it was given. But I also award compensation for inflation." Thus, even though there is no infrastructure for Islamic banking, there is quite a complex informal system for arbitrating difficult technical disputes.

The most difficult disputes to resolve are caused by murder. According to the Chechen custom of blood revenge, murder must be avenged by the subsequent murder of the perpetrator, or one of their male relatives if the murderer escapes. Ibrahim, one of my trusted interlocutors, recalled that in his village

there was a man who always had a Mauser pistol on him. Apparently, someone in his family killed a man and that man's family chose him for revenge. In cases like that, avengers sometimes try to choose the most successful and strong representative of the feuding family. This man was forgiven only when he turned seventy. Perhaps the other family could have killed him but decided not to use their right. In fact, the right to kill is more important than the act of revenge.

Adat does not differentiate between intentional and unintentional murder: blood must be avenged in every case. As a result, there are many blood revenge disputes as a result of car accidents. Even if the person who died in the accident is responsible for its occurrence, their family has a right to kill the other side. Though, in cases of unintentional murder, families usually settle on forgiveness.

If a family does not retaliate for the intentional murder or humiliation of a member, it will lose its credibility in interfamily relations. It will be considered weak and thus subject to other possible transgressions. Vakha, a former government official in his sixties, told me that when he was a boy, his family got into a feud. His father had a dispute with another farmer's family who offended him by taking his gun by force. The father's brothers insisted on killing two members from the other side, because taking someone's gun is a gross offense. Instead, they captured the other man, took off his pants and shot these pants with their pistols. "This was worse than killing him. After that incident, no one messed with our family, because they knew that we are capable of harsh revenge."

Blood revenge is also allowed in Sharia, but responsibility in Sharia is individualized, so relatives of the murderer cannot be targeted in retaliation. Most importantly, even though Sharia allows revenge, it prefers reconciliation. To facilitate reconciliation, the murderer's family must pay monetary compensation to the victim's family. Russian law considers blood revenge and other customs such as bride kidnapping as vestiges of the past and does not recognize them. In contemporary Chechnya, murders are usually prosecuted by the formal legal system. But if two families do not reach reconciliation, the family of the victim will kill the murderer when he is released from prison.

Overall, there is informal coordination among the three legal systems: high-cost economic cases and criminal cases are mostly resolved through state law, while family disputes are mostly determined by Sharia and adat. Also, there is an informal hierarchy of legal systems: people usually start dispute resolution through adat; if that does not work, they go to a religious forum; and if that does not work, they go to the state authorities. However, this informal coordination and hierarchy is quite weak, and in many situations, alternative legal systems contradict each other and lead to drastically different dispute resolution outcomes. In the next section, I will explore the preferences for alternative legal systems in situations in which these systems are in conflict.

LEGAL CONSCIOUSNESS UNDER LEGAL PLURALISM

Legal pluralism is an elusive phenomenon. Because *de jure* state law alone functions in Chechnya, there is no systematic data on Sharia and adat arbitration. All my attempts to get records of arbitration according to adat or Sharia failed. One of my interviewees explained to me that in Russia there is a criminal charge for "usurpation of judiciary role," and therefore non-state justice authorities do not record arbitration. Because of this elusive nature, it is a real challenge to capture systematic variation in the use of state and non-state legal systems. In response, I explore legal consciousness – preferences for state law *vis-à-vis* alternative systems based on religion and custom, relying on an original face-to-face survey of Chechnya's population.[10]

Choosing among Forums

To explore preferences for alternative legal forums, I relied on a vignettes approach. I designed ten vignettes based on my qualitative research, involving the most common disputes in contemporary Chechnya as highlighted above: (1) child custody, (2) domestic violence, (3) bride kidnapping, (4) honor killing, (5) polygamy, (6) inheritance, (7) property, (8) car accident, (9) debt, and (10) murder. Each vignette is a composite of multiple actual cases.[11] Each dispute is modeled to provide respondents with a conflict among the legal systems: all three legal systems would be

---

[10] See details of survey design and implementation in Lazarev, Egor. "Laws in conflict: Legacies of war, gender, and legal pluralism in Chechnya." *World Politics* 71, no. 4 (2019): 667–709. Also on survey research in Chechnya, see Khaikin, Sergei, and Natalia Cherenkova. "Izuchenie obschestvennogo mnenia Chechenskoy Respubliki" [Studying Public Opinion in the Chechen Republic]. *Mir Rossii* 12, no. 3 (2003): 3–34.

[11] Before conducting the survey, I discussed each vignette with lawyers, alims (Islamic scholars), and leading Chechen ethnographers to ensure their validity in capturing social conflicts in Chechnya.

expected to lead to divergent outcomes. The questions that follow the vignettes asked respondents to choose the best forum for dispute resolution among state law, Sharia, and adat. The vignettes and likely substantive resolutions are presented in Table 6.1.

Responses to the vignettes are presented in Figure 6.1. The figure clearly shows that there is a wide variation in preferences for alternative legal systems in Chechnya. The figure shows that people prefer Sharia in the majority of hypothetical disputes, especially in family matters. Demand for state law is particularly high for cases of property dispute over an apartment, a car accident, and murder. Adat is the most common choice for instances of bride kidnapping, which is not surprising given that it is a practice often associated with the customary norm.

I aggregated responses across all ten vignettes into indices of preferences for state law, Sharia, and adat by calculating the number of times respondents selected each forum or chose the "don't know" option. I normalized these variables so that they took values from 0 to 1. Descriptive statistics show that the likelihood of choosing state law in a dispute is approximately 33%, Sharia is 36%, and adat is 21% (with the remainder "don't know").[12] I use these indices as the dependent variables in my analysis. See Figure 6.2 for the aggregated results.

The survey also measured actual experience with using institutions across all three legal systems. Descriptive statistics show that 15% of my sample reported going to the police or courts to solve disputes at least once during the last three years, 19% appealed for adjudication to an imam or qadi, and another 19% asked elders to solve their dispute. Measures of the reported use of a legal system are highly correlated with support for it in hypothetical disputes.[13]

I asked a set of questions about legal knowledge across forums. For knowledge of Russian law, I asked what the legal age of marriage in Russian Federation is. The correct answer is eighteen, and it was a relatively easy question: 82% of respondents answered correctly. For knowledge of Sharia, I asked how much of her husband's property a widow would be entitled to if the couple did not have children. The correct answer is 1/4. This was a relatively difficult question; only 22% answered correctly. For

---

[12] Klyachkina ran a similar survey in Chechnya in 2018 and found comparable patterns, with slightly higher preference for Sharia and slightly lower preference for adat. See Klyachkina, *Reconfiguration of Sub-national Governance*: 238.

[13] This finding is in line with the idea that "veterans of the judicial process" are more likely to have positive attitudes toward the legal system. On similar patterns elsewhere in Russia, see Hendley, *Everyday law in Russia*.

TABLE 6.1 *Vignettes of the most common disputes*

Issue	Vignette	State Law	Sharia	Adat
Child custody	Aslan decided to divorce his wife Seda after thirteen years of marriage. Aslan and Seda had two children: a six-year-old boy and a four-year-old girl. Both sides wanted to keep the children and could not resolve this dispute between themselves.	children stay with the mother	children stay with the mother until they are seven years old and then decide for themselves with whom to stay	children stay with the father
Domestic violence	Mansur severely beat his wife because he thought that she cooked dinner badly. He beat his wife almost every week, but the last episode was especially bad: he broke his wife's arm.	husband should be imprisoned or sentenced to correctional labor	husband should pay his wife a fine	wife's relatives should retaliate and beat the husband
Bride kidnapping	In one of the mountainous villages of Chechnya, a young man named Ruslan kidnapped a local young woman to marry her against her will.	Ruslan should be imprisoned	Ruslan should be punished with forty strokes	Ruslan should pay a fine and if the woman's relatives won't accept it, he should be forced to go in the middle of the village without his pants

(continued)

TABLE 6.1 (continued)

Issue	Vignette	State Law	Sharia	Adat
Honor killing	Musa heard rumors that his wife Rosa cheated on him. Musa became extremely angry upon finding out about this and killed his wife.	Musa should be tried in court and imprisoned	Musa should be tried for murder in Sharia court because he had no witnesses to his wife's infidelity	Rosa's relatives should retaliate and kill Musa
Polygamy	Suleiman, an unemployed man from Grozny, had lived with his wife Khava for fifteen years. They had four children. Now Suleiman wanted to take a second wife, but Khava was firmly against it.	Suleiman can't take a second wife because it is unlawful	Suleiman can take a second wife	Suleiman can't take a second wife because it is against custom
Inheritance	Khasbulat, who recently passed away, was survived by his daughter and his son. They both claimed rights to his house and land plot.	disputants divide the property equally	son receives two-thirds, daughter receives one-third	son receives everything
Property	Zaur and Zelimkhan had documents for the same apartment in Grozny. Both claimed that their documents were valid and that they bought the apartment from the previous owners who left during the war.	conduct notary expertise	swear on the Koran	the apartment should be divided into two equal parts

Car accident	Andarbek's car crashed into a cow on a section of road without a special sign for a livestock path. The accident happened in daylight. Said, the cow's owner, and Andarbek had a dispute about compensation.	Said should cover the costs, because there was no special sign for cattle crossing	Andarbek should cover the costs because the accident happened in the daytime	disputants should split the costs
Debt	Sultan, a businessman from Gudermes, lent 1 million rubles to his nephew Vakha on the condition that he pay it back in a year with 15 percent interest. After a year, Vakha was able to repay only a part of the debt and refused to pay the interest.	Vakha should repay both the loan and interest rate	Vakha should return the loan but not the interest	both loan and interest should be forgiven because Vakha is Sultan's nephew
Murder	During a mass fight, Ali hit Shamil with his fist. Shamil fell down and died.	Ali should be tried in court	Ali's relatives should pay compensation and ask for reconciliation	Shamil's relatives should kill Ali in revenge

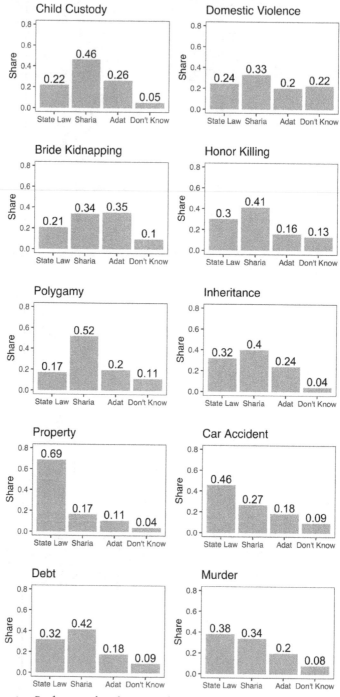

FIGURE 6.1 Preferences for alternative legal systems in the most common disputes

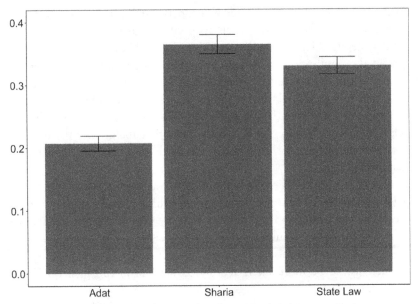

FIGURE 6.2 Aggregated preferences for alternative legal systems in the most common disputes

knowledge of adat, I asked whether a Chechen woman can initiate divorce according to adat. The correct answer is yes, and in fact this norm is a particular Chechen institution – no other ethnic group in the Caucasus has this institution. However, knowledge of it was rather low (44%), and the responses might actually reflect respondents' attitudes toward gender equality rather than actual knowledge of the norm. My interviews and field observations suggest a similar pattern of low legal knowledge. For example, very few interlocutors were able to correctly say that the population of Chechnya follows the *Shafii* legal tradition. Many people confused the norms of adat and Sharia. Nevertheless, most people did have quite strong opinions on what legal systems should be used, when, and why.

What Explains the Differences in Legal Preferences?

What explains the variation in the preferences for alternative legal systems? To answer this question, I first explored these differences across issue domains. In order to do that, I classified the vignettes as either belonging to family law and the private domain (child custody, domestic violence, bride kidnapping, honor killing, polygamy, and inheritance) or to the public domain (car accident, property, debt, and murder). I then created a set of statistical models to predict choices among alternative legal systems.[14] The results showed that the likelihood of choosing state law in the family domain is approximately 20 percentage points lower than in disputes outside of it. The likelihood of choosing both Sharia and adat was substantially larger in the family domain. This finding confirms the logic of the normative choice approach and is also in line with the relational distance hypothesis, which states that the greater the distance between the disputants, the higher the likelihood they will bring their dispute to court.[15]

Second, I explored the role of individual characteristics as predictors of legal preferences. These characteristics were also recorded by the survey. Descriptive statistics showed that 52% of my sample were women. Since state law formally assumes gender equality, while non-state legal systems are often far less favorable to women, I expected that in gendered disputes women would be more likely to rely on state law, and men on Sharia and adat.

The average age of my sample is thirty-five years old. To test whether age affects legal preferences, I created a categorical variable that distinguished "youth" (18 to 30 years old), who comprised approximately 42% of the sample; "middle-aged people" (30 to 50), who also comprised around 42%; and "older people" (50–82), who comprised 15%. Because customary law gives a lot of power to elders, it is plausible to expect that older people will be more likely to rely on adat, while younger people will be more likely to rely on Sharia and state law. Another consideration is that different generations went through different socialization processes, which might have affected their legal consciousness.[16]

In the sample, 46% lived in urban areas. I expected that urban dwellers would be more inclined to rely on state law because of its accessibility and because social pressure to rely on custom and Sharia is more effective in rural communities. Indicators of education and income showed considerable variation. I expected that richer and more educated individuals would be more likely to rely on state law, because wealth and education provide the resources and knowledge that are necessary for having access to state law. To analyze the role of connections and access to formal state

---

[14] I used multinomial logistic regression models. See Lazarev, "Laws in conflict" for details.
[15] Black, Donald. *The behavior of law*. Emerald Group Publishing, 1976.
[16] Gallagher, *Authoritarian legality in China*.

institutions, I included a variable for employment in government as an indicator of official status within the formal state system. Approximately 18% of the sample were government officials, which reflects the postwar situation that many jobs, especially outside of urban centers, derive from state administration. It is plausible to expect that government officials will be more likely to rely on state law.

The survey also records clan (*teip*) membership. Throughout the book, I reference scholarship that documents that clan-based explanations of Chechen politics have limited value.[17] However, because many of my interlocutors emphasized the importance of this factor, I included it in the analysis. I distinguished belonging to the *Benoi* clan, which is the clan of Ramzan Kadyrov, and thus a rough proxy of political privilege. Approximately 4 percent of the sample belongs to this clan. I also distinguished the eleven largest clans. Belonging to a large clan is likely to increase reliance on customary law because large clans have a natural advantage in systems of collective responsibility. The sample included members of more than one hundred clans. Approximately a third of the respondents belonged to one of the eleven largest clans.[18] Customary law based on the principle of collective responsibility is likely to benefit members of large clans due to their size advantage. Thus, I expected that members of large clans would be more likely to rely on customary law.

Finally, to test the argument that ethnic and religious identities drive demand for Sharia and adat, I included measures of identity salience. To measure the relative strength of ethnic and religious identity, I asked whether the respondent would allow his or her daughter to marry a non-Chechen Muslim, for instance, an Ingush or Dagestani man.[19] More than 70% of my respondents would not allow an interethnic marriage of a female relative, which highlights a very high level of ethnocentrism among Chechens. To measure religiosity, the survey asked about frequency of reading the Koran.[20] The multivariate regression

---

[17] Sokirianskaia, *Governing fragmented societies.*

[18] *Alleroi, Benoi, Chinkhoi, Chianti, Dyshni, Gendergnoi, Kharachoi, Melkhi, Nashkhoi, Tsontoroi,* and *Varandoi.* The large clans were selected based on conversations with Chechen ethnographers.

[19] There is a powerful norm in adat that Chechen women cannot marry non-Chechen men even if they are Muslim. In contrast, in Islam, all ethnic divisions within the community of believers are seen as sinful and interethnic marriages are welcomed. Therefore, I measure response to this question as an indicator of Chechen ethnocentrism.

[20] This indicator is the most reliable measure of religiosity in the Islamic context. See Jamal, Amaney, and Mark Tessler. "Attitudes in the Arab world." *Journal of Democracy* 19, no. 1 (2008): 97–110.

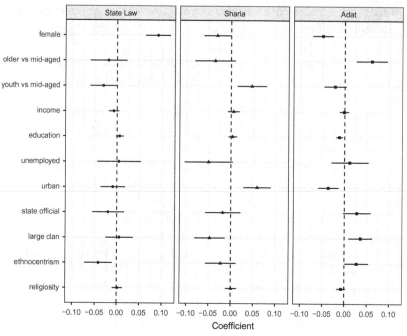

FIGURE 6.3 Factors of legal preferences. Coefficient plots for the OLS regression of the predictors of legal preferences. N = 1,213

analysis shows that individual attributes do have significant predictive power. I present the results in Figure 6.3.

First, in line with my expectations, the analysis shows that women were much more likely to choose state law than men. The likelihood of choosing state law among women is approximately eight percentage points higher than among men. Moreover, women were more likely to choose state law than men in all ten disputes, both in gendered disputes and in conflicts unrelated to gender such as car accidents or murder.[21]

Second, I found that older people tended to support adat. In comparison to middle-aged respondents, they were more likely to choose customary law by approximately six percentage points. In turn, younger people were more likely to choose Sharia. Thus, it is the middle-aged people who were to some degree socialized during the Soviet system and the period of Gorbachev's Perestroika, that are the strongest proponents of state law in

---

[21] This result is in line with Hendley's finding that women elsewhere in the Russian Federation are more likely to embrace law-abiding attitudes than men. See Hendley, *Everyday law in Russia*.

Chechnya. Alice Szczepanikova similarly found that among Chechen refugees in Europe, this generation holds the most integrationist predisposition towards the state.[22]

Another confirmed expectation is that members of large clans were more likely to rely on customary law (by approximately three percentage points) and less likely to rely on Sharia, in which responsibility is assumed at the individual level. The same is true for *Benoi* clan. Importantly for the theory, I found that ethnocentrism is a strong predictor of support for adat, confirming the normative approach towards legal choices. However, religiosity did not perform well as a predictor of demand for Sharia. One potential explanation for this is the ceiling effect: the population of Chechnya is very religious, virtually no one will say they do not believe in God or disregard religious practices. The statistical analysis revealed that urban residents were more likely to rely on Sharia law and rural dwellers were more likely to be supporters of adat. This supports the claim of the Russian sociologist Irina Starodubrovskaya, who argued that political Islam in the North Caucasus is primarily an urban phenomenon.[23] Starodubrovskaya explained that the cleavage between traditionalist rural areas and more Islamist leaning urban centers emerged in Chechnya in the 1990s. At that time, youth from the rural areas relied on the power in numbers of their large families, while urban youth – often coming from much smaller families – relied on the emerging pan-Islamic solidarity.

I also found that education was negatively associated with preferences for adat and unemployment was negatively correlated with support for Sharia. Most surprisingly, the analysis showed that in contrast to theoretical expectations, state officials were *not* more likely to rely on the state legal systems they are supposed to represent. Instead, state officials tended to prefer customary law. One potential explanation is that state officials are concerned with their status in local communities and thus show preferences for adat to signal that they are still "good Chechens" despite working for the Russian state. Another potential explanation is who those state officials are. As I describe in Chapter 5, the mode of conflict resolution in Chechnya turned former rebels who used to hold strong ethnic and religious identities that were staunchly anti-Russian into the Russian state bureaucrats. Thus, this paradoxical finding can be attributed to

---

[22] Szczepanikova, Alice. "Chechen refugees in Europe: How three generations of women settle in exile." In Le Huerou et al. *Chechnya at war and beyond*. Routledge, 2014: 264–265.
[23] Starodubrovskaya, "Sotsialnaia transformatsia i mezhpokolencheskiy konflikt."

either the strategic self-positioning of the state officials or the structural legacy of the conflict and its resolution.

The survey evidence allowed me to draw the picture of legal consciousness in contemporary Chechnya and probe factors that explain variation in legal preferences for state law and non-state legal forums. However, there is a question as to whether beliefs translate into actual legal actions. As I have mentioned above, there is no systematic evidence on the use of customary law and Sharia. However, the functioning of Russian state law is systematically recorded, which allows us to look at the variation in state penetration within Chechnya with behavioral data.

POLITICAL TOPOGRAPHY AND SOCIAL ORDER

In order to explore legal behavior, I use records of cases heard in the Justice-of-the-Peace (JP) Courts. The JP Courts are at the lowest level of the state judiciary, the local institutions that hear more than 90 percent of all cases initiated in the Russian Federation. Kathryn Hendley called these courts "the workhorse" and "the unsung heroes" of the Russian judicial system.[24] They deal with the vast majority of civil and administrative disputes and petty criminal offenses. Their jurisdiction includes most family matters, for instance, divorces where there is no conflict over children, property disputes for values not exceeding 500 days' minimal wage, and disputes over land. The courts also deal with, for instance, claims made by tax authorities against private citizens and the recovery of overdue utilities payments. Thus, the parties of the disputes include physical persons, legal entities, and the state. The JP Courts usually share buildings with other administrative institutions or are even located on the ground floor of residential apartment buildings. The courts are easily accessible, have relatively low fees, and usually do not require legal assistance. JPs have limited administrative staff and as a result, the legal process is largely based on the interactions between the judges and the court users. In fact, one of the JP Courts' distinctive features is the availability of direct access to judges during pre-trial sessions, which allows claimants to assess the strength of their case.[25]

---

[24] Hendley, Kathryn. "The unsung heroes of the Russian judicial system: The Justice-of-the-Peace Courts." *Journal of Eurasian Law* 5, no. 337 (2012).

[25] Andrianova, Varvara. "The Everyday experiences of Russian citizens in Justice of the Peace Courts." In Marina Kurkchiyan and Agnieszka Kubal (eds.) *A sociology of justice in Russia*. Cambridge University Press, 2018: 68.

In Chechnya, the Justice-of-the-Peace Courts were established in 2009. From 2009 to 2016 they've heard more than 350,000 cases. This is approximately 70 percent of all cases heard in the Russian state justice system in Chechnya in this period. The majority of the cases heard in the JP Courts in Chechnya are civil disputes (approximately 60 percent). To analyze the use of the JP Courts in Chechnya, I relied on two sources of evidence. The first is the official reports on the number of criminal, civil, and administrative cases heard in the JP Courts in 2011–2014. I obtained these reports through the Department of Support of the Justice-of-the-Peace Courts in the Chechen Republic. The second source comes from records of court hearings published on the official websites of JP Courts. Using web scraping, I collected all available data on hearings in civil, criminal, and administrative cases from 2010 to 2016. The record contains information on 217,284 civil, 44,407 administrative, and 3,346 criminal case hearings. Unfortunately, most of these records did not contain judicial decisions, so I could not analyze the outcomes of the cases. According to two clerks who worked at the Justice Department of the Chechen Republic (*Upravleniye Sudebnogo Departamenta*), the records published on the court websites were comprehensive. However, close examination of the data and comparisons with the official reports suggested that in reality these records were incomplete.[26] Nonetheless, with this massive dataset, it is possible to analyze more granular details than just the number of cases; for instance, I study the gender of the plaintiff in Chapter 8.

Here I used the complete data from the official reports on the number of court cases to look at the political topography of Chechnya,[27] i.e., uneven reliance on state law across regional social and political cleavages. At first blush, social order seems uniform across Chechnya. If you travel from one settlement to another, you will notice little difference. First you see the giant portraits of Ramzan Kadyrov, his father Akhmat-haji, and

---

[26] For a systematic investigation of the problem of incomplete data in digitized judicial records, see Liebman, Benjamin, Margaret Roberts, Rachel Stern, and Alice Wang. "Mass digitization of Chinese court decisions: How to use text as data in the field of Chinese law." *Journal of Law and Courts* 8, no. 2 (2020): 177–201.

[27] I build on Boone's notion of political topography as geographically uneven patterns of state-building and Cammett's spatial analysis of state and non-state institutions. See Boone, Catherine. *Political topographies of the African state: Territorial authority and institutional choice.* Cambridge University Press, 2003; Cammett, Melani. *Compassionate communalism: Welfare and sectarianism in Lebanon.* Cornell University Press, 2014.

Vladimir Putin. State presence seems ubiquitous. The number of courts and court personnel are proportional to the district population. Yet, the data reveal that the topography of social order in Chechnya is highly uneven. I found that while one court district might have nearly zero cases heard in state court, the neighboring district might have hundreds of cases annually. Similarly, when I visited one village, people were easily able to identify respected elders, while in another village people had a hard time agreeing on who "the proper elders" were.

In order to explore the patterns of state penetration, I analyzed the data on the number of cases brought to the JP Courts at the district level annually for the period between 2011 and 2014 and normalized it per thousand people. Cases initiated by the state reflect state supply of law, while civil cases initiated by individuals reflect the use of state law by the population. I then explored whether variation in the number of court cases maps onto the cleavages in the political topography of Chechnya. In particular, I investigated four cleavages that I came across repeatedly during my fieldwork: urban vs. rural, the divide between the Russified Northern districts and the rest of Chechnya, between the mountainous districts in the south and elsewhere on the plainland, and the political divide between the East of Chechnya, which constitutes the core of the regime, and the West that is perceived to be less controlled by the government. Figure 6.4 presents the map of the political topography of Chechnya. Investigation of legal behavior across these cleavages is also theoretically fruitful, because community characteristics, including their political alignment, are important for the story of lawfare that this book tells. The results of the comparisons are presented in Table 6.2.

First, I investigated the urban–rural divide. It is plausible to assume that state penetration is stronger in the urban areas. Chechnya has five urban centers: Grozny, Gudermes, Shali, Urus-Martan, and Argun. Grozny is the main city; officially, its population is around 270,000 people. The center of the city now has skyscrapers (by provincial Russian standards), beautiful mosques, and shopping malls. But large parts of the city are still peri-urban, and residents live in large multi-family compounds of several houses described in Chapter 2. Therefore, Grozny can be seen as a constellation of communities. The same can be said about other Chechen towns. However, there is a large gap in legal behavior between urban and rural areas. I found that urban residents were almost twice more likely to go to state courts than rural residents in Chechnya. The gap, however, is driven by civil and administrative cases; in the domain of criminal cases, there is no statistically significant difference.

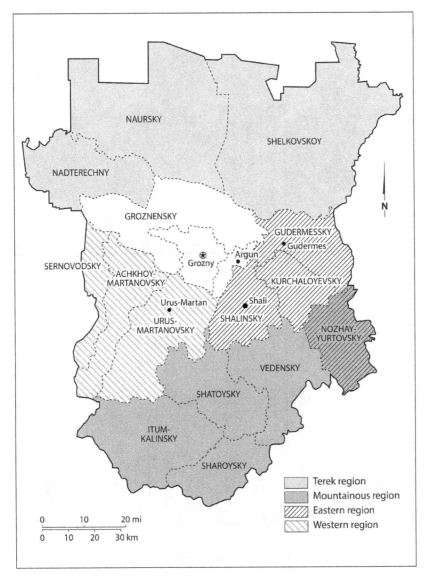

FIGURE 6.4 Map of political topography of Chechnya

Second, I explored the particularities of the North and the South of Chechnya. The North of Chechnya, also known as the Terek region, is considered to be more Russified and Sovietized, and less rebellious. The South, or the highlands, is described as "the heartland of Chechnya," and "the cradle of Chechen nation." The mountaineers – *lamro* – are believed

TABLE 6.2 *Average number of court cases across social cleavages*

	Urban Vs. Rural		Russified North vs. Elsewhere		Mountainous Districts vs. Elsewhere		West vs. East	
	Urban (N = 28)	Rural (N = 38)	Terek (N = 9)	Non-Terek (N = 57)	Mountainous (N = 7)	Non-Mountainous (N = 59)	West (N = 11)	East (N = 16)
All cases	**46.1**	26.4	41.1	33.8	27.9	35.6	**28.5**	**18.5**
Criminal	0.75	0.66	1.1	**0.64**	0.77	0.69	0.59	0.50
Administrative	17.6	10.3	15.4	13.1	10.6	13.7	5.03	3.7
Civil	27.7	16.9	24.6	21.1	24.3	21.2	17.1	10.5

Note: Bold font denotes that the difference-in-means is statistically significant (t-test p-value <0.1)

to be more authentic, less Russified, more rebellious, traditionalist, and stricter adherents of adat. This narrative is reproduced by many in Chechnya. It is also used to think about Chechnya within Russia. For example, during the Second Chechen War, the prominent liberal politician Boris Nemtsov proposed a conflict resolution plan that was based on the idea of dividing Chechnya into the pro-Russian northern lowlands and the secessionist rebel-held mountainous South.

The Terek region consisting of the three municipal districts Shelkovskoy, Nadterechny, and Naursky is indeed better integrated into the Russian state. The population there is mixed between Chechens and a sizable minority of Russians. The region was heavily overrepresented in the Soviet nomenklatura, especially during the short reign of Doku Zavgayev, the only ethnic Chechen to head the republic during Soviet times. In the post-Soviet period, the Terek region was the base of the anti-Dudayev opposition and was only nominally controlled by the secessionist Ichkeria authorities. Not surprisingly, the Terek region is characterized by a high level of Russian state law use. The number of cases in these three northern regions is higher than elsewhere in Chechnya, even if the comparisons of means do not produce statistically significant results due to the small number of observations.

The southern mountainous region consists of the Vedensky, Nozhay-Yurtovsky, Shatoysky, Sharoysky, and Itum-Kalinsky municipal districts. The population that lives in the mountains is rather small because of the harsh conditions and the deliberate Soviet and Russian state strategy to depopulate these areas. On average, the mountainous districts have a lower number of court cases per capita than elsewhere in Chechnya, but the difference – contrary to expectations – is not that dramatic and is not statistically significant.

In the previous chapter, I outlined that politically the division between the West and the East of Chechnya is perhaps even more important than the conventional divide between the North and the South. The eastern regions of Chechnya are the bastion of Kadyrov's rule, while the western regions are considered to be less pro-regime. I found that the western districts of Achkhoy-Martanovsky, Sernovodsky, and Urus-Martanovsky have significantly more court cases compared to the eastern districts of Kurchaloyevsky, Gudermessky, Shalinsky, and Nozhay-Yurtovsky. What is driving this marked difference? In the previous chapter, I described how the government is using state law as an instrument of repression and extortion against communities in the West. However, I found no difference in the number of criminal cases between two regions. The difference is driven by civil cases, and it is especially pronounced in civil cases where the plaintiff is a physical person – meaning brought to courts by the individuals. This is puzzling given that collective state violence was particularly widespread and brutal in the western part of Chechnya and relatively rare in the eastern part. In the next chapter, I will explore how wartime collective violence shaped the demand for and the use of state law.

* * *

Scholars of legal pluralism often describe it as a set of ambiguous and negotiated relationships characterized by an inherent complexity.[28] This chapter showed that this is true in Chechnya as well: alternative legal systems evolved into a hybrid legal order, one characterized by judges in state courts sometimes implementing customary and religious norms, while imams and elders participate in state court hearings as witnesses or experts. The focus on judicial authorities in state and non-state legal systems – actors in the trenches of state-building lawfare, to use Migdal's term[29] – highlighted the state-building process from within. The jurisdictional conflicts and accommodations revealed that state-building lawfare is not just an imposition from above.

The chapter also took the next step toward exploring how individuals approach the pluralistic legal order and participate in lawfare from below. The chapter documented a wide variation in preferences for alternative legal systems. The results give support to both normative and instrumental logics of legal choices. The normative perspective is illustrated by the presence of ideological camps of supporters of Sharia and adat, some of whom rely on their preferred legal systems irrespective of context. In turn, the narratives of forum-shopping and the survey results highlighted the alignment of legal preferences with group interests according to gender, age, and clan size, lending support to the instrumental understanding of bottom-up lawfare. In the next two chapters, I will explore how warfare affected bottom-up lawfare and uneven state penetration across Chechnya.

---

[28] For recent examples, see, Sharafi, Mitra. *Law and identity in colonial South Asia: Parsi legal culture, 1772–1947*. Cambridge University Press, 2014; Yahaya, Nurfadzilah. *Fluid Jurisdictions: Colonial Law and Arabs in Southeast Asia*. Cornell University Press, 2020.
[29] Migdal, *State in society*.

7

"People Need Law"

Demand for Social Order after Conflict

Malika Yunusova was a nurse in the village of Makhkety. When the journalist Anna Politkovskaya met her during the Second Chechen War, she was a young woman, but her hair was already gray. On the night of February 11, 2000, a bomb hit her house and totally destroyed it. All her cows, her family's only source of livelihood, were killed. Their neighbors gave them one of their cows in an act of solidarity. The Yunusovs built a new shed. On December 15 of the same year, there was another heavy bombing of the village. The Yunusovs were hiding in their neighbors' basement. But when a shell hit their shed and started a fire, Malika's husband Said Ali ran out to save their cow. He was showered with shell fragments. After he was denied medical treatment in the Russian hospital because the family did not have any money, he quickly died from the wounds. Malika was left to look after her three children without any food or clothes. She tried to file a claim to the Military Prosecutor of the Vedeno district, but he refused her claim. This gross wartime injustice made Malika plead: "I don't care which law I live under – Chechen, Russian, Korean, or Japanese – as long as there is some kind of law."[1]

The wars forced many Chechen families to leave their motherland, and now the Chechen language can be heard on the streets of Strasbourg, Istanbul, Vienna, Oslo, and Warsaw. Still, some Chechens, driven by political repressions and economic hardships, have been trying to get refugee status in Europe years after the conflict officially ended in 2009. One of them, Shamil, a young Chechen man, stated in an interview with the

---

[1] Politkovskaya, Anna, *A small corner of hell: Dispatches from Chechnya.* University of Chicago Press, 2007: 59.

journalist Ilya Azar in 2016: "People need law. Any law – be that Russian law, be that Sharia, even some African law. But it should work and defend human rights, so that we are able to go to court and be protected."[2] The similarity of the pleas for the rule of law in Chechnya from the wartime to almost a decade after the end of the conflict is striking. During my field-work, I've also heard numerous pleas for the rule of law, indeed "any kind of law." This calls for an investigation of this desire or demand for law and its relations with the conflict experiences.

In this chapter, I explore whether variations among people and communities in the preferences for alternative legal systems can be attributed to differences in their experiences of conflict. I organize the analysis at multiple levels. First, I explore how individual and family victimization has shifted legal choices. Second, I study the effects of community victimization, i.e., I compare communities within Chechnya that were more and less affected by wartime violence. In my analysis, I distinguish the effects of the First and the Second Chechen Wars. Finally, I analyze the macro-level effects of conflict by comparing Chechnya with Ingushetia. I start with a brief description of civilian experiences of conflict.

EXPERIENCES OF CONFLICT

Although estimates vary dramatically, conservatively the two Chechen wars resulted in approximately 70,000 dead or missing civilians.[3] More than 200,000 people became refugees or were internally displaced. The First War (1994–1996) was defined by prolonged urban warfare for control of Grozny and to a lesser extent the other urban settlements of Argun, Shali, and Gudermes.[4] There were also major battles in the rural areas. For instance, a battle for the village of Bamut that started in March 1995 took more than a year for the separatist forces to overcome the numerous assault attempts by the Russian army. The village was ultim-ately left in ruins. Many other settlements were also nearly destroyed. For example, the tiny mountainous village of Kharsenoy was wiped out by air bombing on June 1, 1995.

[2] Azar, Ilya. "Kogda vy vernetes', my vas ub'yem" [When you come back, we'll kill you]. *Meduza*, December 6, 2016.

[3] Human Rights Center "Memorial" estimate. See Cherkasov, Aleksandr. "Kniga chisel. Kniga utrat. Kniga Strashnogo Suda." [Book of numbers. Book of losses. Doomsday Book.] Polit.ru, February 19, 2004.

[4] Oliker, Olga. *Russia's Chechen wars 1994–2000: Lessons from urban combat.* Rand Corporation, 2001.

Perhaps the most well-known episode of violence against civilians during the First War is the Samashki massacre which happened in April 1995. Samashki is a big village in the western part of Chechnya. The village hosted a group of rebels and was consequently blockaded by the Russian army. The elders of the village pressured the rebels to leave in order to save the village, and most of them left. However, a small group of local fighters remained in the village and fought the Russians when they entered the village. Russian forces experienced up to sixteen casualties. In response, the Russians shelled the village. Then, the militarized police forces blockaded the village and searched for rebels and weapons in all households. This operation was accompanied by the indiscriminate killing of civilians and burning of houses. According to human rights group reports, Russian police officers threw grenades in the basements of houses where villagers were hiding.[5] The Human Rights Center "Memorial" estimates that at least 114 civilians were killed; the village elders claimed that more than 300 civilians perished. In Chechnya, Samashki became a symbol of victimhood and national suffering. The famous Chechen rebel-singer Timur Mutsuraev wrote the song "Samashki" about the massacre. The lyrics include the following passage: "Let our hearts cry, but we won't forget, Samashki, Samashki, we will get revenge for everything." According to one of my respondents, the villagers commemorate their killed relatives and neighbors every April by organizing religious ceremonies and village gatherings. After the war ended in 1996 and the Chechen rebels restored their authority, Samashki was celebrated as a symbol of national resistance.

The Second War and the counterinsurgency that followed (1999–2009) were characterized by even more severe and systematic violence against civilians. My interlocutors unequivocally agreed that the Second War was much crueler in terms of treatment of civilians. According to Emma Gilligan's assessment, "the excessive violence directed at the civilian population of Chechnya was, in fact, collective punishment."[6] During the counterinsurgency stage of the war (2001–2009), the Russian army and the pro-Kremlin government of Chechnya extensively used selective violence against the alleged supporters of the insurgency in the form of killings and forced disappearances.

---

[5] Evangelista. *The Chechen wars*: 146.
[6] Gilligan, Emma. *Terror in Chechnya: Russia and the tragedy of civilians in war*. Princeton University Press, 2009: 5.

Local administrative officials and communal leaders also ended up as targets of this selective violence.

During both wars, the Russian military was the major but not the only actor behind civilian victimization. During the course of the Second War, a large number of the rebels switched sides and joined the Kremlin in its counterinsurgency campaign against former brothers in arms, causing inter-Chechen violence.[7] The rebels in turn targeted civilians whom they suspected as having collaborated with Russians. For example, according to Dukuvakha Abdurakhmanov, the Speaker of the Chechen Parliament in the postwar period, rebels killed more than one hundred village heads, more than one hundred local police officers, and more than eighty imams.[8] In my analysis, I focus primarily on collective violence perpetrated by the Russian state because it is especially likely to shape identities and social structures.[9]

Collective violence against the civilian population in Chechnya took two major forms or techniques.[10] The first was indiscriminate air and artillery bombardment of the communities. This form of victimization characterized the early stage of the Second Chechen War (1999–2000). It was also used subsequently during the counterinsurgency phase, but to a lesser extent. According to Gilligan, the breadth of the strikes across Chechnya in the early stages of war made it nearly impossible for civilians to stay in their homes, especially in urban areas.[11] This tactic can be interpreted as a manifestation of the depopulation strategy.[12] Anna Politkovskaya characterized the change in the form of collective state

---

[7] Lyall, Jason. "Are coethnics more effective counterinsurgents? Evidence from the second Chechen war." *American Political Science Review* 104, no. 1 (2010): 1–20; Ratelle, Jean-François, and Emil Aslan Souleimanov. "A perfect counterinsurgency? Making sense of Moscow's policy of Chechenisation." *Europe-Asia Studies* 68, no. 8 (2016): 1287–1314.

[8] "Chechniya na sviazi s Ichkeriyey" [Chechnya on line with Ichkeria]. *Dosh. Kavkazskiy Nezavisimyi Jurnal* 3, no. 25 (2019): 25. Chechen social scientist Abbaz Osmaev presented somewhat different numbers. He documented that between 1999 and 2002, 230 local police officers and nine imams were killed and there were 53 assassination attempts on local administrators and their families. Cited in Klyachkina, *Reconfiguration of sub-national governance*: 222.

[9] As I wrote in the theory chapter, I define collective violence as a form of violence that involves targeting civilians based on group identity (e.g., ethnicity X) or community (e.g., village or neighborhood Y).

[10] Gutiérrez-Sanín, Francisco, and Elisabeth Jean Wood. "What should we mean by 'pattern of political violence'? Repertoire, targeting, frequency, and technique." *Perspectives on Politics* 15, no. 1 (2017): 20–41.

[11] Gilligan, *Terror in Chechnya*.

[12] Lichtenheld, Adam. "Explaining population displacement strategies in civil wars: a cross-national analysis." *International Organization* 74, no. 2 (2020): 253–294.

violence during the Second Chechen War in the following way: "the tactic of carpet bombing at the beginning of the war has been replaced with a strategy of conveyer belt destruction of people" – through the practice of *zachistka* – operations similar to the massacre in Samashki.

Zachistka literally means "the sweep" or "cleansing operation" in Russian. It denotes a special military operation that aims at rooting out separatist forces and establishing control in population centers.[13] In Chechnya, it usually included sealing a village or a town district with armored personnel carriers and ground troops and then conducting house-to-house searches for rebels, weapons, and ammunition. *Zachistka* operations ranged in duration, coverage, and form. They were notorious for civilian abuses: detention, torture, kidnapping for ransom, extrajudicial murders, ransacking, and pillaging. Gilligan wrote that "The practice of the *zachistka* fostered fear in Chechen civilians precisely because of its potentially arbitrary and undisciplined execution."[14] Anna Politkovskaya reports the words of a mother of a kidnapped boy during a *zachistka*:

Most of all now, we want to know the rules of the game. We want to understand which of us you don't like. And why? What should we be tortured for? What are the reasons you've been commanded to kill? To kidnap? Right now we don't understand anything, and everyone is being destroyed in turn – those who were with the Wahhabis and those who were against them. And most of all, those in the middle, who weren't with anyone.

Zachistka embodied more than a military practice. According to Gilligan, "it was a mindset."[15] The discourse of *zachistka* or cleansing was a crucial part of the Russian military and media representation of violence during the Second Chechen War and was used to justify and normalize it. *Zachistka* operations were used primarily in the period from 2000 to 2003. Collective violence during this period was used to humiliate and subjugate the civilian population. Gilligan concluded that "Destroying the cohesion of the local communities was central to the larger objective of weakening resistance and the will of the people."[16]

---

[13] Lyall, "Are coethnics more effective counterinsurgents?"

[14] Gilligan, Emma. "Propaganda and the question of criminal intent; the semantics of the Zachistka." *Europe-Asia Studies* 68, no. 6 (2016): 1036.

[15] Gilligan, *Terror in Chechnya*: 51.

[16] Ibid.: 16. On the media framing of the Second Chechen War see also Wilhelmsen, Julie. *Russia's securitization of Chechnya: How war became acceptable*. Taylor & Francis, 2016.

Violence during the Chechen wars was unevenly distributed across territory. As Valery Tishkov highlighted: "The direct violence (terror, fighting, and bombing, etc.) did not cover the whole territory, and there were villages and areas that did not suffer destruction – a great surprise for those watching from the moonscape to which central Groznyy had been reduced."[17] To a certain degree, violence followed the strategic logic of confrontation between the Russian army and Chechen rebels. The principal goal of the army in both wars was to establish control over Grozny, Chechnya's capital and the main city; the biggest battles, therefore, were over the city. Rebels utilized the difficult mountainous terrain, and, as a result, a lot of fighting happened in the mountainous areas in southern Chechnya and on the roads that lead to these regions too. Thus, geography and the strategic interaction between the two sides largely determined the exposure of different communities to violence.

There were also some haphazard factors: for example, a community was much more likely to be targeted by the Russian army if a famous rebel commander was from there.[18] Another factor in community victimization during the Second War was related to the approach of the generals in charge of the two major Russian armies that carried out military interventions in Chechnya. The invasion of Chechnya from the west (the Ingushetian border) was carried out by General Vladimir Shamanov, who was known for his cruelty against Chechen civilians. On its way to Grozny during the Second War, Shamanov's army bombed and almost completely destroyed many villages. I was told by two interlocutors from the region that Shamanov's approach had nothing to do with hate, however. He simply destroyed villages that refused to pay him when his army advanced. The villages that paid were left unscathed. The invasion from the east (the Dagestani border) was carried out by General Gennadiy Troshev. Troshev grew up in the North Caucasus and knew the local culture and social norms. Instead of fighting, he negotiated the surrender of the communities that were along his route to Grozny. As a result, communities in eastern Chechnya were significantly less affected by violence.

---

[17] Tishkov, *Chechnya*: 146.

[18] For example, the Russian army severely victimized the village Roshni-Chu because it was associated with Dzhokhar Dudayev; the settlement Dyshne-Vedeno, which was the native village of the famous warlord Shamil Basayev; and the village of Starye Atagi, which was home to Zelimkhan Yandarbiyev.

The conflict in Chechnya profoundly changed its society in many ways. For instance, the Soviet industrial economy was completely destroyed. The postwar Chechen economy thus relies heavily on federal subsidies and local petty trade and services. Moreover, a whole generation of Chechen youth were not able to receive education. The conflict also had a substantial negative effect on the health of the population: wartime stress, injuries, and the terrible ecological situation that resulted from the bombings of oil refineries have led to severe health consequences.[19] In Part II of this book, I analyzed the political legacies of the conflict. Here I focus on the war's social legacies and their implications for legal consciousness and legal behavior.

INDIVIDUAL VICTIMIZATION AND LEGAL PREFERENCES

For the first step of my analysis, I explore the relationship between an individual's history of victimization and preferences for alternative legal systems as recorded through my survey. This approach is prevalent in recent scholarship on the effects of exposure to violence.[20] To measure individual victimization during the conflict, my survey recorded indicators of a family member being killed, being wounded, the family being displaced during the conflict for a prolonged period of time, and property being damaged or destroyed. Descriptive statistics shows that there is considerable variation in individual victimization in my sample. Approximately 50% of my sample reported a family member being killed, and the same percentage reported a family member being wounded. Similarly, 53% of the sample reported some form of property damage. About one-third of the sample reported being displaced for more than a year.

Analysis at the individual level aims to test the alienation hypothesis which suggests that individuals victimized during the conflict should be less inclined to rely on state law. The results of my regression analysis displayed in Figure 7.1, show that among indicators of victimization, only the experience of prolonged displacement is a statistically significant

---

[19] Comprehensive documentation of the effects of war on the everyday life can be found in Osmaev, *Obschestvenno-politicheskaia i povsednevnaia zhizn' Chechenskoy Respubliki v 1996–2005*.

[20] For a review, see Bauer, Michal, Christopher Blattman, Julie Chytilová, Joseph Henrich, Edward Miguel, and Tamar Mitts. "Can war foster cooperation?" *Journal of Economic Perspectives* 30, no. 3 (2016): 249–274.

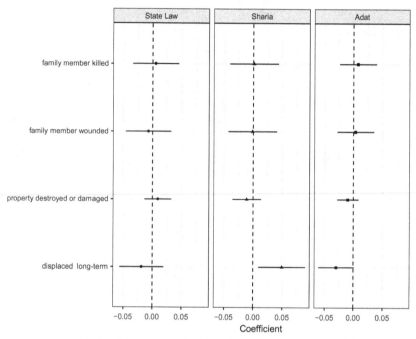

FIGURE 7.1 Relationship between individual-level victimization and legal preferences. Coefficient Plot for the OLS regression analysis. Analysis includes individual-level characteristics as control variables. N = 1,213

predictor of legal attitudes.[21] According to my data, the experience of displacement is associated with a higher demand for Sharia and a lower preference for state law and adat. My interviews with people who spent a long time in the refugee camps and with members of NGOs who worked with Chechen refugees suggest that this effect might be driven by the fact that displacement disrupted traditional social networks because families were intermixed in the camps. Degi, a man in his late twenties, told me about his family displacement experience in the following way:

The camp was big. It was built on the landfill, so there was a terrible unsanitary situation. We were cramped ... Everything became intermixed. The institutions of *aul* [village] became destroyed and nothing emerged to replace them. There were very few respected elders. The only traditions that we preserved were related to weddings and funerals ... There were many quarrels and disputes. Mostly within families. Though there were also conflicts because of theft. Women often fought about money.

[21] The details of statistical analysis are described in Lazarev, "Laws in conflict."

According to Zoya, a woman in her sixties and the head of a prominent local NGO,

> The traditional order collapsed in refugee camps. Many traditions were simply abandoned. For example, when I walked across the camps, many young men did not even stand up to show their respect – you could not have imagined that before the war. The state was present only minimally – they gave birth and death certificates, that was it ... Disputes were very common. Probably because of very harsh living conditions. There were many divorces – it was hard to live with multiple generations... The disputes were resolved by the imams. Every camp had their own imam, usually they were elected by the people. They were the only available authority for dispute resolution.

Therefore, the finding on the role displacement plays in legal preferences might not only reflect psychological effects, but also induced social habits.

In contrast, indicators of family members being killed, family members being wounded, and property damage have no predictive power – the regression coefficients for these variables are not distinguishable from zero. This is puzzling and goes against the alienation hypothesis. Why is this the case? First, the indicators of victimization lack information about the identity of the perpetrator of the violence. Specifying this information within a survey is sensitive in contemporary Chechnya. Even though the vast majority of civilian victimizations during the Chechen conflict were perpetrated by the Russian army, other actors in the conflict also inflicted violence. As highlighted above, the rebels victimized civilians whom they suspected of collaboration with the Russians or the Russian-imposed administration. Also, since 2003, most of the violence was perpetrated by Kadyrov's counterinsurgency forces, not directly by the Russian army.

Relatedly, the survey does not contain information about whether the respondents blame the Russian state for their victimization even though they were victimized by the Russian army. This question also would have been too sensitive to ask. During my fieldwork, on many occasions I encountered people who spoke about their personal or family history of victimization by the Russian army, and then blamed some external actors for what happened. For example, one young man told me during an informal conversation:

> There was little fighting here, but the army was present. One day they came to our house, took my brother and me away. Then one officer let me free – I was just 13. But they shot my older brother in front of us [the family]. I don't know why – he was not a *boyevik*, he had never fought. I really hate America and the Jews for inflaming the war here.

I interpret this and similar sentiments as a coping strategy that victimized individuals adopt to justify the fact that they have to live in the state that perpetrated violence against them and their families. Their coping strategy is to divert the blame from Russia to some other factors. Consequently, conspiracy theories proliferate in postwar Chechnya.[22]

Finally, the responses to the questions regarding family victimization might suffer from biases: even without identifying the side responsible for violence, questions about the war are sensitive in Kadyrov's Chechnya, where all mentions of war are strictly regulated. As a result, 20% of the sample avoided responding to the battery of questions on individual victimization. In the subsequent sections, I conduct the analysis at the community and the regional levels. Even though these analyses are conducted at the higher level of aggregation, they paradoxically might be more precise than individual-level analysis in light of the problems I highlighted above.

COMMUNITY LEGACIES OF COLLECTIVE VIOLENCE

As I outlined in the theory chapter, victimization at the community level is not just an aggregation of victimization at the individual level. To identify victimized communities, I rely on manual coding of the reports of violent events during the insurgency and counterinsurgency that followed the Second War (2000–2006), and that were compiled by the Human Rights Center "Memorial".[23] A community is characterized as victimized if it experienced at least one event of collective targeting of the civilian population. The most common types of civilian victimization were bombings and *zachistka* operations, as I described above. For example, in the village of Elistanzhi, which was bombed at the very beginning of the Second War in October 1999, more than one hundred civilians were killed or wounded. Because of its categorical nature, my indicator does not capture variation in the intensity of violence, but it serves as a good proxy for capturing qualitative differences in wartime collective violence in Chechnya.

[22] See also Tishkov, *Chechnya*.
[23] Baysaev, Usam, and Dmitriy Grushkin. *Zdes' zhivut liudi. Chechniya: Khronika nasiliia* [People live here. Chechnya: The chronicles of violence]. Parts 1–5. Moscow, Russia: Memorial Publishing Program, 2003–2010; Orlov, Oleg, and Alexander Cherkasov. *Rossiia-Chechnia: Tsep' oshibok i prestupleniy* [Russia-Chechnya: The chain of mistakes and crimes]. Moscow, Russia: Zveniya, 1998. See coding details in Lazarev, "Laws in conflict."

Survey Evidence

Based on my measure of community victimization, I identified communities in my survey sample that were collectively targeted by the state and communities that were not. The spatial distribution of the data is shown in Figure 7.2. Because of the drastically different nature of warfare, intensity of civilian victimization, and political contexts between the two Chechen wars, I created two distinct variables for victimization during the First and the Second Chechen Wars.

The analysis also includes a set of relevant community characteristics. To adjust for remoteness, I calculated the distance by road from Grozny, the capital of Chechnya. I also included a measure for altitude, because legal practices might differ between the mountainous part of Chechnya and the lowland part. As I described in the previous chapter, the mountainous part is widely considered to be the center of Chechen traditionalism and adat. To control for the possibility that informal dispute resolution is stronger in smaller communities, I also measured community size. Because legal practices might be influenced by cultural contact, I added a measure for the share of the non-Chechen (Russian) population in each location according to the 1989 census. Russians lived primarily in the cities and in northern Chechnya, near the Terek River, which borders the Stavropol region of Russia proper. As a result of prolonged contact with Russians, Chechens of the Terek region are considered to be more Russified.

For the first stage of the analysis, I regressed the main dependent variable of my analysis –aggregated preferences for the alternative legal systems – on the indicator of community victimization as well as individual and community covariates. The results of the analysis, presented in Figure 7.3, show that community experiences of collective violence are associated with an increase in preferences for state law and decrease in preferences for Sharia and customary law. These associations do not reach the conventional level of statistical significance of 95 percent confidence interval (potentially due to the small number of community clusters), but the direction of the effects is suggestive as well as surprising. This evidence goes against the alienation hypothesis. It suggests that the conflict might have shifted the social order toward the state rather than away from it. This is truly puzzling given that the state was behind the collective violence.

For the next step, I conducted an analysis to distinguish the legacies of the First and the Second Wars. The results presented in Figure 7.4 show

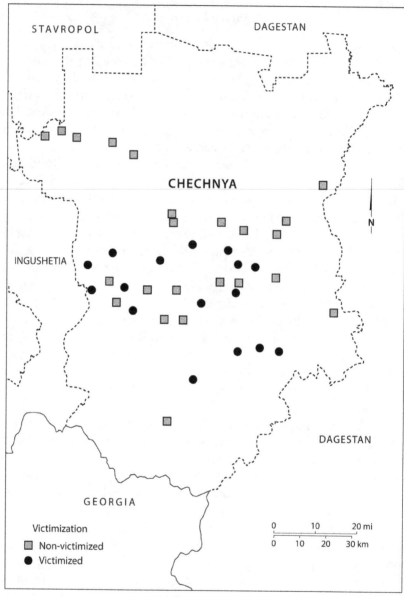

FIGURE 7.2 Map of victimization among sampled communities

that the two wars had opposite effects on preferences for alternative legal systems. Collective victimization during the First War is associated with a 13 percentage points decrease in the likelihood of choosing Russian state

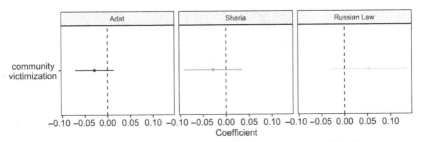

FIGURE 7.3 Relationship between community victimization and legal preferences. Coefficient plot for the OLS regression analysis. The analysis includes individual-level and community-level characteristics as control variables. Standard errors are clustered at the community level. N = 1,213

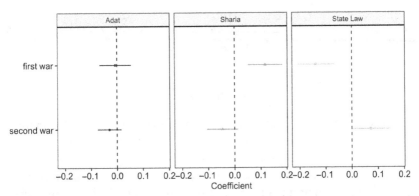

FIGURE 7.4 Relationship between community victimization during the First and the Second Chechen Wars and legal preferences. Coefficient plot for the OLS regression analysis. The analysis includes individual-level and community-level characteristics as control variables. Standard errors are clustered at the community level. N = 1,213

law and a similar increase in the likelihood of choosing Sharia. In contrast, collective victimization during the Second War is associated with a 7 percentage points increase in the likelihood of choosing state law and a similar decrease in the likelihood of choosing Sharia. This analysis has serious limitations because of the layered nature of violence: communities that were victimized during the First War were again victimized in the Second War. However, these statistical patterns correspond well with the evidence from my interviews and case studies across Chechnya. Below, I use this evidence to explore the nature of this differential effect of community victimization on social order across the two conflicts. But first I address the issue of whether attitudinal patterns gleaned from a survey

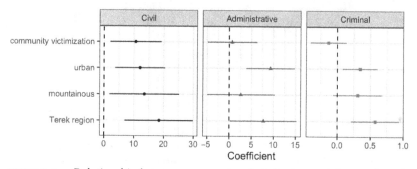

FIGURE 7.5 Relationship between community victimization and the number of cases heard annually in the Justice-of-the-Peace Courts. Coefficient plot for the OLS regression analysis. N = 66

translate into actual legal behavior. In other words, do experiences of collective violence affect the use of state courts?

Evidence from the Courts

In order to explore whether the patterns established through my analysis of the survey responses correspond to behavioral patterns, I analyzed the data from the Justice-of-the-Peace Courts introduced in the previous chapter. I again use the number of criminal, administrative, and civil cases per 1,000 people brought to the JP Courts at the district level annually as an indicator of the prevalence of the use of state courts in Chechnya. To measure exposure to conflict, I relied on the same indicators of community-level victimization used in the previous section.[24]

I ran a regression analysis with the number of cases as the dependent variable. The community-level victimization is the main independent variable and district characteristics (i.e., Terek region which proxies for the cultural contact with Russian population, mountainous terrain, and urban/rural status) are used as control variables. The results, presented in Figure 7.5, show that districts that experienced collective victimization have a higher number of civil cases. The effect is quite large substantially: districts that experienced community victimization have approximately

---

[24] I identify thirty-nine districts (seventeen settlements) as subjected to collective violence and another twenty-seven districts as less victimized. Grozny, the capital of Chechnya, and other large settlements such as Gudermes, Argun, Urus-Martan, and Shali, have multiple court districts. The results hold if the Grozny's districts are excluded from the analysis.

10.6 additional civil cases compared to those with no experience of community victimization. The average annual number of cases in a district is approximately 21.6. Using data from court hearings, I find that collective violence is associated with an increase in the number of civil cases that are actually brought by individual plaintiffs (as opposed to the state or firms). I find no association between collective violence and the number of criminal and administrative cases. That means that the use of state law in victimized communities is not just imposed from above. The analysis also confirms the previous findings that state penetration is higher in the urban areas and the northern Russified Terek districts. I also find, surprisingly, that mountainous districts have more civil cases.

The analysis has several limitations. First, the analysis does not control for the prewar state penetration across Chechnya. Unfortunately, such data do not exist. The state archive of Chechnya completely burned down during the First Chechen War in 1995. Furthermore, JP Courts did not exist in Chechnya prior to 2009, so prewar data on state penetration would likely be aggregated differently. My interviews suggest that physical state penetration across the Checheno-Ingush SSR (as elsewhere in the Soviet Union) was rather even, and therefore, measures of the numbers of state officials per district, which are often employed as a proxy for state capacity, would probably show no variation even if they existed. Another problem is that variables are aggregated at the court district level, which is not the most socially meaningful unit. As a result, some communities that were severely victimized are grouped with others that did not suffer as much. Finally, and most importantly, analysis of variation in state law penetration does not reveal anything about the use of the alternative legal systems across Chechnya.

However, despite these limitations, the fact that the results of the analysis of court cases and survey data converged is indicative. Both types of evidence suggest a surprising association between community victimization, in particular during the Second Chechen War, and an increase in the demand for state law within Chechnya. In the next section, I rely on case studies of three rural communities that exemplify different histories of violence, to further explore the link between collective violence and demand for alternative legal systems (see the location of these communities in Figure 7.6). These communities differ along many dimensions, but because the histories of violence (or the notable absence of violence) were so pronounced in each of these cases, I treat them as good candidates for differentiating the impacts of the First and the Second wars and exploring the mechanisms that relate experiences of collective violence with post-conflict legal attitudes and behavior.

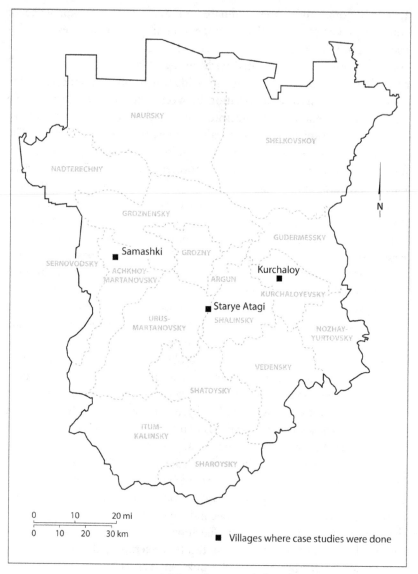

FIGURE 7.6 Map of case study locations

A TALE OF THREE VILLAGES

Samashki: The First War and Alienation

In the beginning of this chapter, I described the tragic history of state violence in the village of Samashki. Samashki truly stands out among the victimized communities. It is now a village of 12,000 people situated in the western Achkhoy-Martan district. As a result of the collective trauma, the community has become very cohesive. It did not receive any material aid from the state and instead, after both wars, the villagers organized collective efforts to rebuild the houses and village infrastructure. Even though this is a large community, everyone seems to know each other. People say that everyone goes to one another's weddings and funerals. People trust each other but are wary of outsiders.[25] Another direct legacy of the violence during the First War was the strengthening of religious identity. According to Israpil, a man in his forties, there was a proliferation of religious schools in the village during the interwar period: "Foreign teachers from Tajikistan and Uzbekistan came to Samashki. Radical Islam quickly spread in the village."

In the post-conflict period, the village shows strong signs of social cohesion and adherence to Islamic governance. For example, Ekaterina Sokirianskaia quotes one of the Samashki elders: "Now we have an imam, everybody listens to him ... Many of the community problems are solved after Friday prayers in mosques."[26] The results of my research echo this sentiment. My interviewees highlighted that the majority of disputes are solved through an imam. The villagers have a strong religious identity based on a shared history of victimization. The population is antagonistic to Russian rule and avoids dealing with Russian state justice. However, the social order of Samashki is an exception rather than the norm among the victimized communities. Unlike in Samashki, the neighboring villages that were severely victimized during the Second War exhibit a high number of cases brought to state courts.

Starye Atagi: The Second War and the Destruction of Hierarchies

The village of Starye Atagi illustrates the surprising pattern of high use of state courts in the communities that experienced collective violence during the Second Chechen War. Starye ("old" in Russian) Atagi is a big village with an approximate population of 17,000.[27] All my respondents from the village emphasized that the literary Chechen language originated from

---

[25] Characteristically, among the four interview request declines I had in Chechnya, two were in Samashki.

[26] Sokirianskaia, *Governing fragmented societies*: 144.

[27] Osmaev, *Obschestvenno-politicheskaia i povsednevnaia zhizn' Chechenskoy Respubliki v 1996–2005*: 365.

their village. Another common theme was that Starye Atagi is the home of many members of the Chechen intelligentsia. High levels of education distinguished the village during the Imperial and Soviet periods. The village was also quite well-off. As Mansur, a man in his fifties who works in the local government, noted, "Our village was rich in the Soviet period. We had a successful state-owned farm, poultry factory, sawmill, some other smaller industries. We were very famous because of the scholars and artists."

The Chechen National Revolution of 1991 polarized the village. "We had all shades of opposition here," Tamerlan, a former state official in his fifties, told me. "Some were for Dudayev, others against him." One of the most prominent leaders of the Chechen national independence movement, Zelimkhan Yandarbiyev, arguably also one of the best Chechen poets, was a native of Starye Atagi. When the war started, many among Atagi's youth mobilized to fight. During the First War, the outskirts of the village were regularly shelled by the Russian army. Yet the villagers did not experience victimization anywhere close to the Samashki massacre. Because the village was relatively safe, Chechens from Grozny and some other victimized villages found refuge in Starye Atagi during the First War.

After Dzhokhar Dudayev was killed in 1996, his vice president Zelimhan Yandarbiyev became the interim head of the Chechen state. Around the same time, a Salafi religious movement, associated with Yandarbiyev, gained ground in Atagi. This led to an internal split within the community. Mansur recounted:

Dudayev's rule and the First War divided us by *teips* (clans). But a much deeper divide happened when the Wahhabis came to our village. We, the supporters of the traditional Islam that our ancestors practiced for ages, did not accept their stupid rules. They were very arrogant and they had money. But they were a minority.

Some of my respondents explicitly blamed Yandarbiyev for the split within the village. Other villagers treated Yandarbiyev as a hero. Sulim, a man in his late twenties, showed me Yandarbiyev's modest house in the village and told me that "Yandarbiyev, our president, was a true *k'onakh!* [noble hero in Chechen]."

During the Second War, Starye Atagi experienced large-scale collective victimization in the course of the counterinsurgency.[28] The victimization

---

[28] During the First War, 114 people from Starye Atagi were killed and 14 went missing. During the Second War, 180 people were killed and 40 became victims of forced disappearances. Osmaev, *Obschestvenno-politicheskaia i povsednevnaia zhizn' Chechenskoy Respubliki v 1996–2005*: 369.

of Atagi can be attributed to two factors. First, the village is situated on a strategic road from Grozny to the mountainous areas; therefore, territorial control over the village was a major goal for both the Russian army and the rebels. Second, the village was victimized because it was home to Zelimkhan Yandarbiyev. As I mentioned before, the Russian military forces often took the origins of famous rebel field commanders as a cue of village disloyalty and used indiscriminate violence against such settlements.

During the Second Chechen War, Starye Atagi endured thirty-seven *zachistka* operations, more than any other settlement in Chechnya. These operations were accompanied by robberies, beatings, killings, and kidnappings that usually ended with torture and death. An abandoned poultry factory was used as a "filtration camp," an illegal prison where the security forces tortured detained civilians. On many occasions, all male residents of the village were detained.[29]

For example, according to the Memorial report, the Russian army conducted a "search for rebels and weapons" operation in the village in January 2000. In one of the houses, the soldiers found a newspaper with the face of separatist President Maskhadov. The soldiers arrested the owner of the house, thirty-four-year-old Khasmagomed Elzhurkaev, a man with a disability. This man's female relatives tried to prevent his detention and started arguing with the soldiers. In response, the soldiers shot at the women. One of the women died and the other six women were seriously wounded. During another *zachistka* operation in 2002, Russian soldiers detained a group of young local men. According to the Memorial reports, on February 13 the soldiers threw the corpses of these men – with multiple bullet and knife wounds – over the fence of the poultry factory.

Despite the constant *zachistka* operations, the radical Islamist rebels managed to control the village for years. By day, the village was under the control of the Russian administration; by night, it was controlled by the "Wahhabi patrols." The civilians suffered tremendously from this fragmented territorial control. The rebels also used violence against civilians. According to a prominent local scholar Abbaz Osmaev, killings of traditional authorities, bureaucrats, and police officers became "regular events" in the village during the early 2000s.[30]

---

[29] See, Politkovskaya, *A small corner of hell*: 96–107.
[30] Osmaev, *Obschestvenno-politicheskaia i povsednevnaia zhizn' Chechenskoy Respubliki v 1996–2005*: 370.

As a result of the prolonged victimization, Starye Atagi became a polarized community. Even though all the people from Atagi with whom I spoke embraced their identity as members of the "intelligentsia village," many of them acknowledged that the village is divided, especially across religious lines. Sulim told me, "We are Sunnis. We don't like these dancing Sufis – they are loyal to the government and dance for money." The Salafi-leaning part of the village community are strong proponents of Sharia law. In turn, many Sufi-leaning villagers despise the Salafi adherents. They also blame the Islamists for the suffering of the village community. Tamerlan told me: "These bearded men are to be blamed for what happened with us." As a result, a large share of the village population is skeptical of Sharia law, which is associated with the rule of the Islamists.

When I asked about the use of alternative legal systems in Starye Atagi, I was told that all three systems of law are used extensively. As one elder explained: "Disputes within families are solved by adat, disputes between clans are adjudicated by our imam. But many people also go to courts." The most influential elders in the post-Soviet period in Atagi were the leaders of the Sufi brotherhoods and one of the former heads of the village. One influential elder, Musa Abubakarov, whose authority extended far beyond Atagi, "an elder in the full sense of the word" according to one of my interlocutors, was killed by the rebels in 2000. During my interviews in Atagi, many respondents complained that the war destroyed customary order and that many young men do not respect the authority of elders enough.[31] Mansur said that the constant military sweeps left almost no elders in the village: "So many of our elders died as a result of these wars. I don't know how we [can] forgive the Russians for that." In addition, several of my interviewees in Atagi highlighted the fact that many families left the village altogether because of the repeated experiences of collective violence. This factor also plausibly contributed to the disruption of prewar networks in the village.

Said-Akhmed, the imam of the village, has been in office for almost twenty years. The imam wields considerable authority among the villagers who adhere to traditionalist religious views, but he rarely resolves

---

[31] According to survey research, the adherence to the value of veneration of elders in Chechnya decreased dramatically from 1990 to 1995. See Bersanova, Zalpa. "Sistema tsennostei sovremennykh Chechentsev" [The system of values of contemporary Chechen society]. In Dmitry Furman (ed.) *Chechnia i Rossiia: Obschchestva i gosudarstva* [*Chechnya and Russia: Societies and states*]. Moscow: The Andrey Sakharov Fund, 1999.

legal disputes, preferring to redirect conflicting parties to the Muftiat. The imam says that "If one of the parties to a dispute is unhappy with the decision, they then go to the state court. We don't have bailiffs, we don't have documents and seals, what can you do?"

The state in Atagi has long been personified in Vadgi Gadaev, a former traffic policeman who was elected village head during the First war. He held his position for over fifteen years. During the war period, Vadgi was in constant negotiations with both the Russian military and the rebels, trying to solve the problems of the residents. Many internal conflicts outside of the family domain were resolved primarily through him. After Vadgi left the office due to illness, the heads of the village often changed, but it is possible to speculate that the work of the village administration during the wartime and its aftermath helped to maintain allegiance to the state among some of the village residents.

Kurchaloy: Retraditionalization of Social Order

The village of Kurchaloy is an illustration of the social order that emerged in the relative absence of collective violence. Kurchaloy is a big village of 25,000 people situated in eastern Chechnya. It largely avoided victimization during both wars. The community is a power base of Kadyrov's loyalists and rebel-bureaucrats introduced in Chapter 5. Yet even this could not save the village from victimization entirely. For instance, on June 16, 2001, 120 men from the village were detained and beaten up. Russian soldiers looted the houses. Several of those who were detained during the targeted arrests were subsequently tortured and killed. But in contrast to other Chechen communities, the intensity of victimization in Kurchaloy was much lower. Residents of the village whom I interviewed, including the prominent human rights defender Oyub Titiev, agreed that their community suffered much less than other communities of Chechnya. For example, Adlan, a man in his fifties, said "We were lucky. The village was barely affected by the war."

The presence of state law in Kurchaloy is quite limited. I found that the number of court cases per capita in the Kurchaloy district is one of the lowest in Chechnya.[32] These numbers are echoed in my interviews. Mikail, a state official in his thirties, told me the following:

---

[32] The number of court cases per capita heard in Justice-of-the-Peace Courts from 2011 to 2014 in Kurchaloy court district is 13.7, the average is 34.8.

It was very hard to implement the policy of standardized high school exams in Kurchaloy. They have a weird attitude towards the law because of their special relations with the authorities. They just did not understand why they weren't allowed to cheat during the exam.

Another respondent, Denilbek, a former police officer turned business-man, emphasized that many disputes are solved through extended fam-ilies. He explained a dispute he had with another businessman. He did not want to go to court, so he instead met with his counterpart and asked him: "Do you think I was raised on the water?" As he explained: "That proverb means: do you think I have no relatives? My whole *teip*, thou-sands of people are behind me." In my interviews, the residents of Kurchaloy also emphasized that the elders retained significant authority in the village. As Said, one of my young male interlocutors, put it in a group discussion:

There are two types of Chechens. Real Chechens, and Chechens-light, like Coca-Cola. The latter do not follow our traditions to a full extent. For example, a girl goes out after dark. Or sons do not listen to their father. In our village, everyone is a real Chechen.

In another interview, Tabarik, a female government official in her forties said, "Almost every second marriage in the village was a result of bride kidnapping. Kidnappings increased the prestige of a woman." My respondents also said that divorces in Kurchaloy are quite rare, which presents a stark contrast with other parts of Chechnya, especially places that suffered the most from violence.

Social order based on the fusion of custom and Sharia in Kurchaloy in the postwar period was established by the rebel-bureaucrats. The village has one of the highest concentrations of *kadyrovtsy* – Russian law enforcement officials who serve in different parts of Chechnya. These Russian state officials are the main force behind undermining of the Russian state law and maintenance of the imagined "traditional order."

Comparative Lessons

The comparison of the cases illuminates the paths that linked the history of conflict and post-conflict constellations of legal systems. People of Samashki, victimized during the First War, developed strong religious identities during the interwar period based on their common trauma. The political conditions of the *de facto* independent Chechen state of Ichkeria were favorable to this collective identity formation: the separatist government made the village one of the symbols of the national liberation movement. The collective trauma made the community very cohesive and alienated it from the Russian state, which people blamed for the violence. As a result, social order in postwar Samashki rests primarily on Sharia. Religious leaders enjoy almost unquestionable authority in the village.

The case of Starye Atagi suggests several potential explanations for the association between violence during the Second War and postwar high levels of state law usage. First, the political context and the nature of violence in the Second War were different from the First War. The political conditions of the counterinsurgency in the aftermath of the Second Chechen War and Kadyrov's dictatorship prevented the development of strong group identities based on collective trauma. Furthermore, violence was much more prolonged and became "Chechenized" over time. Inter-Chechen violence polarized the community and split it along extended family and religious divides. Interpersonal trust and networks also diminished, resulting in the community becoming more fragmented, rather than cohesive. Cohesion in severely-victimized communities was also undermined by interfamily feuds. According to Tamara, a woman in her forties, who lived in a village in the western part of Chechnya:

There were many denunciations. People wrote these denunciations to the Russians to settle scores with their blood enemies or just wanted to advance themselves or make money. The federals [Russian security services] did not investigate – they just came at night and killed a man. The relatives of those killed then bribed the Russians to find out about who wrote the denunciation and took revenge. As a result, there are feuding families – they don't go to each other's weddings and funerals.[33]

Finally, the violence killed and displaced many of the communal leaders, both customary elders and religious authorities. Together these social forces weakened the customary dispute resolution system in the village and increased the demand for Russian state law. Importantly, people did not embrace Russian law because of their normative or ideological preferences. Rather, like the people quoted in the beginning of the chapter, they simply needed "any law." This is in sharp contrast to Kurchaloy, which to a large extent avoided large-scale victimization during both wars, and where "traditional" social order was established

---

[33] This dynamic of local vendettas and denunciations is analyzed in Kalyvas, *The Logic of Violence in Civil War*. Anthony Marra described it well in his novel *A Constellations of Vital Phenomena* based on the documentary evidence from the Chechen wars.

by rebels-turned-bureaucrats. Today it exhibits a very low penetration of Russian state law.

As I mentioned before, the communities included in my analysis differ along many dimensions, and the differences between them cannot be attributed solely to the legacy of violence. For example, many people in Chechnya with whom I spoke expressed a prejudice that people from Kurchaloy are "uncultured" and even told me "don't go there, it is like Oklahoma in the U.S." Some claimed that this explains the absence of state law there. However, I met at least two people from Kurchaloy who can be considered prominent examples of the Chechen intelligentsia, and they debunked this stereotype. Overall, the impact of collective violence was so deep that I believe it might have overshadowed the preexisting differences between the communities.

To summarize, the analysis of the political topography of postwar Chechnya highlighted two principal mechanisms behind divergent post-conflict social orders: (1) collective identity formation, which was most prominent in the aftermath of violence during the First War and (2) community fragmentation and disruption of traditional hierarchies, which were common results of the violence of the Second War. Differences in community histories of collective violence were shown to have lasting legacies in the post-conflict social order. However, the war in Chechnya affected the entire society. Therefore, in the next section I supplement this analysis of variation within Chechnya with a comparative analysis of legal preferences in Chechnya and neighboring Ingushetia. This investigation aims to estimate the structural impact of war on legal pluralism in Chechnya.

THE MACRO-LEVEL: COMPARING CHECHNYA AND INGUSHETIA

The Republic of Ingushetia serves as an almost perfect reference point for analyzing the impact of the Chechen conflict on the social order at the macro-level. In order to compare the two regions, I conducted an original face-to-face survey of a sample of Ingushetia's population (N = 400), similar to the one I conducted in Chechnya. Most importantly, descriptive statistics show that the social order in Ingushetia, like in Chechnya, is based on pervasive legal pluralism: 12% reported experience with dispute resolution through the state courts or police, 16% though religious authorities, and 15% through traditional elders.

The main outcome variables were measured using the same set of vignettes as in Chechnya. The only thing I changed in the vignettes were

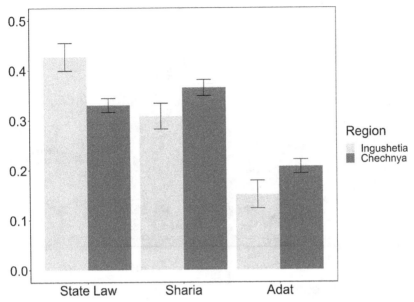

FIGURE 7.7 Aggregated preferences for alternative legal systems in Chechnya (N = 1,213) and Ingushetia (N = 400)

the names of the characters to reflect local naming patterns. The survey results show that in Ingushetia, there is a wide variation in preferences for alternative legal systems, similar to the variation observed in Chechnya. A comparison of the aggregated preferences for alternative legal systems between the two regions is presented in Figure 7.7. The comparison shows that the role of state law in Ingushetia is significantly higher than in Chechnya: the likelihood of choosing state law in Ingushetia was 42%, versus 35% in Chechnya, and support is higher in Chechnya for both Sharia (31% vs. 36%) and adat (15% vs. 21%).

These numbers correspond well with the narratives from my interviews in Ingushetia. For example, Ilyas, who works as a federal judge in Ingushetia, said that "People often sue firms and the state. Interpersonal disputes are much rarer but have been growing over time." Jabrail, a man in his forties who works as a government official, told me that

In the old times, we were laughing at people in Moscow, who after a car accident were waiting for the road safety police. We always solved everything on the spot based on shared understandings, moral norms you can say. But now, when we have insurance, we are also waiting for the road safety police. Now people are less reluctant to go to courts as well.

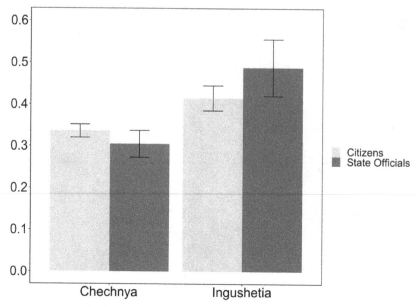

FIGURE 7.8 Differences in the aggregated preferences for state law between citizens and state officials in Chechnya (N = 1,213) and Ingushetia (N = 400)

Azamat, a man in his thirties who works as a high-level university administrator, said that "Ingushetia is much better incorporated into the Russian state than Chechnya. Ingush people are more law-abiding." Even Issa Kodzoev, a famous Ingush writer, dissident, and one of the most respected traditionalists in all of Ingushetia, said that "We are for the Russian Constitution. We want the rule of law [*verkhovenstvo zakona*]!"

My analysis of the survey evidence from Ingushetia reveals other interesting patterns too. Perhaps most crucially, I found that state officials in Ingushetia are more likely than the average citizen to rely on state law. In itself this finding looks trivial, but in comparison to Chechnya – where state officials are typically less supportive of state law than average citizens – this result is important. It highlights the prevalence of anti-state state officials in Chechnya as one of the key political legacies of the conflict. Figure 7.8 depicts the stark contrast between state officials' preferences for state law in the two regions.

My observations in the field in Ingushetia complements this survey evidence. State officials whom I observed and with whom I talked can be categorized as strong proponents of Russian state law. In addition, in Ingushetia the state legal system is much more clearly separated from adat and Sharia, which function as autonomous informal systems. Magomed, a human rights activist put it this way: "In Chechnya there is a vertical of power that blends secular and religious authorities. In Ingushetia there is no such thing. The two spheres are largely autonomous." Here Magomed succinctly illustrated one of the main claims of this book that the state-building strategy of Ramzan Kadyrov entails a fusion of custom, religion, and state power. Magomed implicitly refers to Kadyrov with the phrase "vertical of power." Introduced originally by Vladimir Putin, the phrase has come to signify authoritarian rule in the system of "nested sover-eignty" that lies at the heart of this study.

Sharia arbitration in Ingushetia is more decentralized than in Chechnya, and in fact there are several parallel Sharia forums. According to Isa Tsechoev, one of the most respected religious figures in Ingushetia:

The Muftiat have been trying to centralize Islamic dispute resolution, but in reality, there are multiple independent Islamic forums. People go to the *alims* whom they trust and respect. Salafis would never go to the Muftiat, for example.

At the same time, the Ingush population appears to be more tradition-alist than the Chechen population. According to Marem, a woman in her forties who works in an NGO, "By default everything is decided according to adat. Many disputes just never reach Sharia or state arbitra-tion." Several of my respondents acknowledged that adat is extensively used in the domain of inheritance. Isa Tsechoev said that "Usually all real estate goes to the youngest son. Daughters get nothing." He also claimed that adat survives because it is beneficial to some groups. For example, "the custom of bride kidnapping is beneficial for those who have financial troubles." He continued: "Those who are for adat would never say that they are against Sharia. They just don't know the difference." Thus, like in Chechnya, Ingushetia is characterized by profoundly high interlegality and low legal knowledge across forums.

According to my interviews, families and *teips* (clans) in Ingushetia are much more politically and socially powerful than they are in Chechnya. One small but telling detail that characterizes the strength of traditional-ism in Ingushetia is that during the interviews and conversations with family patriarchs, younger family members, usually the sons, were silently standing in the corner and came closer only to bring tea or food. This is a traditional sign of respect to the father and his guest, which I encountered in Chechnya only in the most "traditionalist" families.

One possible conclusion from the macro-level comparison between the two regions is that Russian law is more prevalent in Ingushetia because the population was not alienated from it during the war and because Ingushetia preserved the state law infrastructure including judicial and law enforcement personnel. In Chechnya, on the other hand, the legal infrastructure was almost completely destroyed. At the same time, the war in Chechnya also destroyed traditional social hierarchies, while in Ingushetia they have remained much stronger.

* * *

This chapter illuminated the profound impact of armed conflict on legal pluralism in Chechnya. The analysis provided only partial and incoherent support for the alienation hypothesis. The indicators of individual-level victimization that have been used in numerous recent studies on the consequences of conflict were found to be poor predictors of legal choices in Chechnya. I also found that community victimization perpetrated by the Russian state during the Second Chechen War increased popular demand for state law. The alienation hypothesis would predict the opposite. This increase in the role of state law in social ordering was found in both attitudinal and behavioral measures. As the qualitative analysis suggests, the increase in the role of state law in the victimized communities can be attributed to community fragmentation and the disruption of traditional social hierarchies.

Differentiation of the effects of the First and the Second Chechen Wars helped to clarify the role of the conflicts' legacies in bottom-up legal politics. Community victimization during the First Chechen War was found to be associated with a significant decrease in the role of state law and an increase in demand for adat and Sharia. This is likely because victimization during the First War led to the strengthening of ethnic and religious identities in the victimized communities and, as a result, the rejection of state law. In contrast, community victimization during the Second War resulted in an increase in the demand for Russian state law and the use of state legal institutions. I attributed this effect to the destruction of traditional social hierarchies. The Second War was more brutal, longer, and characterized by massive inter-Chechen violence. As a result, it diminished the role of elders and extended families, led to mass migration, and weakened the legitimacy of Sharia justice, which was associated with the Islamist rebels. All these factors facilitated the penetration of state law into Chechen society.

The divergence of effects between the First and the Second Chechen Wars also highlighted how the political context of the conflict moderated the effect of victimization. The First Chechen War was *de facto* won by the rebels. The secessionist government actively facilitated the formation of collective martyr identities in victimized communities. The Second War ended with a military victory by the Kremlin. The postwar Chechen government, which was imposed by the Kremlin, suppressed all public commemorations of the victimized communities. Thus, the political context can explain why victimization led to collective blame attribution after the First War but did not after the Second War. In addition, while the First War was a clear conflict between Chechen secessionists and the Russian federal center, the Second War was "Chechenized" by the Kremlin. As a result, competing factions of Chechen militias fought each other. It was therefore much harder to attribute blame for victimization, and many individuals blamed the Islamist rebels. Thus, my study highlights the role that blame attribution plays in understanding the social and political consequences of civilian victimization in conflict.

It is important to emphasize that even though the conflict increased the role of state law among some Chechens, overall it had a negative effect on the state's regulatory capacity in Chechnya. In comparison to neighboring Ingushetia, Chechnya has substantially less demand for state law *vis-à-vis* its alternatives. The weaker penetration of state law in Chechen society can at least partially be attributed to the strengthening of ethnic and religious identities and the blaming of the Russian state for the atrocities it committed against the Chechen population. At the same time, other factors were also at play. For example, the weaker presence of state law in Chechnya can be explained by the destruction of the state judicial infrastructure, disintegration of the state nomenklatura and intelligentsia, and last but not least, the deliberate policies of the Chechen government to undermine state law, which I described in Chapter 5. Thus, my study highlighted the need to study the legacies of violence on multiple levels[34] and emphasized that scholars of conflict should look beyond the psychological effects of violence and also analyze its structural impacts. In the next chapter, I will analyze the impact of war on gender hierarchies, which is one of the most significant structural effects the conflicts had on social order in Chechnya.

---

[34] Balcells, Laia, and Patricia Justino. "Bridging micro and macro approaches on civil wars and political violence issues, challenges, and the way forward." *Journal of Conflict Resolution* 58, no. 8 (2014): 1343–1359.

8

Chechen Women Go to Court

War and Women's Lawfare

News from Chechnya regularly appears on the front pages of Russian and Western media. For a long time, the news usually has been about security issues like terrorist attacks. In contrast, in May 2015 many media outlets extensively covered a wedding that took place in Chechnya. The story started when the independent Moscow-based liberal newspaper *Novaya Gazeta* claimed that Nazhud Guchigov, a fifty-seven-year-old man who served as a local police chief in one of the districts of Chechnya, tried to force Louisa Goylabieva, a sixteen-year-old schoolgirl, to marry him against her will.[1] When the story became public, Guchigov denied all accusations and said that he did not know Goylabieva, did not plan to marry anybody, and was happy with his first and only wife. However, a week later, Ramzan Kadyrov intervened in the case and announced that the marriage was going to happen and that his associates had ensured him that Louisa and her relatives all agreed to the marriage. This "wedding of the millennium" was broadcast on Chechen television and Kadyrov himself participated in the ceremony. The story of Louisa Goylabieva was widely interpreted as evidence of the abrogation of Russian state law in favor of customary practices (child marriage) and religious norms (polygamy), as well as the overall severe subjugation of women in Chechnya. The tragic story of Madina Umaeva outlined in Chapter 5 also fits this narrative. It is true that Chechnya is a conservative patriarchal society. Yet, this chapter will show that this "subjugation of women" narrative is

---

[1] Milashina, Elena. "Glava Chechenskogo ROVD zakhotel zhenitsya. Trebuyetsa pomosch" [The Head of the Chechen Police district wants to get married. Help is needed]. *Novaya Gazeta*, April 30, 2015.

simplistic and misleading. In contrast, this chapter will draw the complex picture of gender relations in postwar Chechnya and document how Chechen conflicts of the 1990s and 2000s disrupted traditional gender hierarchies and spurred women's use of state law. In this light, the story of the "wedding of the millennium" can be interpreted as an expression of the local government's backlash against women's legal empowerment.

GENDERED LAWFARE/WARFARE

A Woman's Place?

"Chechen women were oppressed, lacked any property rights, and completely subordinated to men – first fathers and brothers, subsequently their husbands."[2] This was the conclusion of Fedor Leontovich, a nineteenth-century scholar who attempted to systematize the customary laws of the different peoples of the North Caucasus. More recently, scholars have presented a more nuanced picture. For example, Magomet Mamakaev, a Chechen intellectual of the Soviet period, highlighted that Chechen women were excluded from public life, yet were the principal decision-makers in the household economy.[3] Historically, moreover, Chechen women enjoyed more freedom than in other societies of the North Caucasus.[4] According to the prominent Chechen ethnographer Said-Magomed Khasiev, Chechen women had a right to choose their future husbands themselves. They also had a right to initiate divorce from their husbands.

Women were also free from blood revenge; in turn, the killing of a woman was punished by the killing of two men from the family of the murderer.[5] Another famous provision of customary law is that women were able to stop a fight by throwing their headscarf between the two conflicting sides. Leontovich himself even highlighted that Chechen men were not allowed to kill or beat their wives. This was true even if a man

---

[2] Leontovich, Fedor. *Adaty Kavkazskikh gortsev [The customs of the Caucasian mountaineers]* Vol. 2. Odessa, 1882.

[3] Mamakaev, Magomet. *Chechenskiy teip.*

[4] Akhmadov, *Chechenskaya traditsionnaya kultura i etika*; Khasiev, *Chehentsev drevniaia zemlya*; Nanaeva, *Traditsionnoye obschestvo chechentsev.*

[5] Bersanova, Zalpa. "Obychai krovnoy mesti i praktika primireniya v sovremennoy Chechne" [The Custom of blood revenge and the practice of reconciliation in contemporary Chechnya]. *Vestnik Vosstanovitelnoy Yustitsii* 8 (2011): 50–53.

discovered that his wife had committed adultery. In such cases, a husband was simply supposed to bring his wife back to her paternal home. If the husband killed his wife for whatever reason, her relatives were supposed to avenge her death through a blood feud. Furthermore, Chechen women were not supposed to hide in their houses and did not cover their faces in the presence of men. There were also many etiquette provisions that were supposed to show respect for women: for instance, a man who was passing a woman on his horse had to dismount.

At the same time, Chechen customary law, like many customary institutions in other societies of agnatic kinship, treats men and women differently. Women remain part of their father's family even after marriage. They thus have no property rights and no rights to their children beyond their marriage. As a result – and here an example from the adat customary law is illustrative – children must stay with their father in case of divorce, and divorcees and widows do not inherit any of their former husband's property. Bride kidnapping, an infamous Chechen custom, also puts women in a precarious position.

The social status of Chechen women rises dramatically over their lifetime.[6] Most household duties are performed by the young wives of the sons of the household head. In turn, the wife of the household head supervises the work and social behavior of all other women in the house. A woman's social status increases when she gives birth to a son. The more sons, the better. Later in her life, the sons will take care of their mother and assure that she is in charge of the younger women in her household. The power of mothers-in-law in Chechen society is tremendous. This power often leads to the abuse of young wives by their mothers-in-law.[7]

Gender relations in Chechnya have also been profoundly shaped by the imposition of Sharia law in the nineteenth century during the anti-colonial war of the mountain peoples of Chechnya and Dagestan against Russian colonial conquest. Imam Shamil actively implemented Sharia law in the territory under his control. As discussed in Chapter 3, prior to this period the Chechens rarely used Sharia law to regulate daily life. Under Shamil,

---

[6] Chesnov Jan. "Zhenschina i etika zhizni v mentalitete chechentsev" [Woman and ethics of life in Chechen mentality]. *Ethnographicheskoye obozreniye*, no. 5 (1994): 109–110; Karpov, Yuri. *Zhenskoe prostrantsvo v kulture narodov Kavkaza*. [Women's space in the culture of the peoples of the Caucasus]. St. Petersburg, 2001.

[7] Szczepanikova, Alice. 2015. "Chechen women in war and exile: changing gender roles in the context of violence." *Nationalities Papers* 43, no. 5 (2015): 753–770. These patterns fit the general framework of the "patriarchal bargain." See Kandiyoti, Deniz. "Bargaining with patriarchy." *Gender & society* 2, no. 3 (1988): 274–290.

however, Chechen women were obliged to cover their faces. Shamil also banned traditional Chechen dating practices and actively encouraged polygamy, which had been absent in Chechnya before that. According to Said-Magomed Khasiev, Chechen customary law prohibits polygamy, except for in exceptional cases, such as a woman's infertility.[8] The imposition of Sharia also deprived women of their customary right to initiate divorce, which is much harder for women to obtain under Sharia. Yet the most dramatic effect of the anti-colonial struggle and its aftermath was the death of a large share of the male population. In response, polygamy became much more common in Chechnya, mostly among rich Chechens who were employed by the Shamil Imamate or subsequently the Russian imperial administration. The majority of Chechens remained poor and preserved monogamous marriages due to the lack of material resources.

Upon the consolidation of Soviet rule in Chechnya, the government tried to impose gender equality and "liberate" Chechen women in accordance with socialist egalitarian principles. The government introduced universal mass education and employed many Chechen women outside their households in collective farms and other economic sectors. The government actively combated such "vestiges of the past" as bride kidnappings, bride prices, and polygamy. Polygamy was almost entirely abolished. The government also banned the wearing of headscarves.

However, the forced deportation of Chechens and Ingush to Central Asia in 1944 undermined the effects of Soviet egalitarian policies. Communities of exiles made special efforts to police women's behavior. The famous Soviet dissident writer Aleksandr Solzhenitsyn remembered that during the deportation, Chechens did not allow girls to attend school and did not send women to work in the collective farms. Women were also not allowed to visit libraries, theatres, clubs or other social places, or to socialize with youth of other nationalities at work. Those who resisted this policing were punished. For example, "in a Karaganda shoe factory, three young Chechen women worked for a long time; then, they were suddenly 'stolen' into marriage, and forced to quit work by their new husbands."[9]

Nevertheless, the Soviet authorities still tried to mobilize Chechen women and youth to fight against "the rudiments of the past." Soviet reports stress the need to "tear [North Caucasian women] out from under

---

[8] At the same time, even though the ethnographers and "traditionalists" whom I interviewed agreed on this point, many "Islamists" disagreed. See chapter 4.
[9] Westren, *Nations in exile*: 301.

the influence of feudal-clan habits and religious superstitions," while "raising them in the spirit of consciousness towards their own political and civic equality."[10] This goal was supposed to be achieved through women's councils, parents' committees at schools and the Komsomol, and through increasing women's education. In addition, local law enforcement agencies were instructed to "strictly observe Soviet law, especially on family and marriage, and on mandatory school enrollment."[11] State organs were expected to combat polygamy and blood revenge killings with extra vigor. However, state efforts to penetrate Chechen communities and regulate gender relations during the exile period largely failed.

The subsequent marginalization of Chechens upon their return to the North Caucasus also perpetuated the conservation of gender roles. Abdulla Bugaev, a historian of the Soviet period and one of the leaders of the pro-Russian government of Chechnya in the 1990s, told me that "Chechens were poorly integrated in the Soviet society, except for party nomenklatura. Emancipation of women existed only on paper. Women received basic education, but very few worked." The majority of Chechens were not allowed to live in Grozny, which remained a largely Russian city. In contrast, rural areas of Chechnya preserved the traditional division of gender roles. According to Georgi Derluguian, in the mid-1980s "close to 60 percent of adult [Chechen] women had no formal employment at all."[12] The majority of employed women worked in collective farms, sales, and services.

Many Chechen girls did not receive a higher education either. The gender gap in education in the Checheno-Ingush Soviet Republic was significantly higher among Chechens than among Russians, and also higher than among the Ingush people.[13] Raisa, a woman in her forties in 2015, remembered that in her village, only two or three girls would stay in high school after the ninth grade, while the others married and stayed home. Indeed, Chechen women married much earlier than their Russian neighbors, sometimes as young as fifteen or sixteen. There were of course exceptions. Some Chechen women became party cadres, engineers, and professors. But these exceptions do not disprove the general pattern. The Soviet egalitarian agenda in gender relations did not succeed

---

[10] Ibid.: 180.   [11] Ibid.: 184.

[12] Derluguian, *Bourdieu's secret admirer in the Caucasus*: 245.

[13] *Checheno-Ingush ASSR 1917–1977. Collection of statistics.* Grozny: Chechen-Ingush Publishing house, 1977. As cited in Sokirianskaia, *Governing fragmented societies*: 91.

in Chechnya. Overall, Chechen culture remained highly conservative and patriarchal. Women's primary roles remained those of mother and house-wife. According to the 1989 census, in Checheno-Ingushetia 46 percent of all families had five or more children, while only 3 percent did in greater Russia. Furthermore, the divorce rate was very low.[14]

Chechen culture is a culture of honor. Women's honor in particular has always been protected especially diligently and women's behavior has always been strictly regulated. For example, during the Soviet period, according to my interviews, Chechen women were not allowed by their families to wear pants or to ride bicycles because these behaviors were considered "shameful." Women also did not drive. Young women had to be home by dusk. Chechen women were not allowed to date or marry non-Chechens. Women were strictly prohibited from drinking alcohol and smoking, habits that were quite widespread among Chechen men during the Soviet period. While families policed the behavior of women, the norms of "decent behavior" were highly internalized, and almost all my interviewees accepted them as legitimate. The conservative gender norms that persisted despite decades of Soviet rule were, however, pro-foundly challenged by the armed conflicts in the 1990s and 2000s.

Chechen Women at War

Laura Sjoberg forcefully argued that any account of the Chechen conflict that does not mention women, does not mention men, does not mention gender, and does not talk about "gendered dynamics of war and conflict, gendered wartime political economies, or gendered postwar reconstruc-tion efforts" is bound to be incomplete.[15] Indeed, several authors have shown that a notable feature of the Chechen conflict was its gendered nature.[16] When the conflict broke out in 1994, many women protested and tried to block the military convoys and tanks. These attempts were futile. During the First War, women were crucial in sustaining the insur-gency: they provided food, shelter, and intelligence to the rebels.[17] During the Second War, insurgents also used female suicide bombers, known as

---

[14] Tishkov, *Chechnya*: 151–152.
[15] Sjoberg, Laura. *Gender, war, and conflict*. John Wiley & Sons, 2014: 13.
[16] Evangelista, Matthew. *Gender, nationalism, and war: Conflict on the movie screen.* Cambridge University Press, 2011; Kurbanova, *Problemy i protsessy gendernoy samoi-dentifikatsii chechentsev*; Szczepanikova, "Chechen women in war and exile"; Zaurbekova, "Gendernyi aspect voiny v Chechne."
[17] See Parkinson, "Organizing rebellion" on the role of women in networks of rebellion.

"black widows," for terrorist attacks.[18] Furthermore, during the Second War there was a widespread myth about Chechen female snipers among Russian soldiers.[19]

Women also played a momentous role in the mobilization efforts of both wars. Some mothers prohibited their sons from taking up arms, while others actively encouraged their sons to fight. I interviewed two former Chechen rebels who resettled in Europe after the war and who independently told me similar stories about the roles of their mothers in their mobilization to fight. Adam, a man in his fifties, told me the following:

> I came to Chechnya from Moscow in the very beginning of the war to evacuate my family. But my mother said that she won't leave. Moreover, she told me "And you won't leave either – you will have to stay and defend our motherland." I was not able to refuse this call even though I wasn't even a supporter of the independence idea.

The vast majority of Chechen women during both conflicts acted as civilians and tried to maintain the basic livelihood of their families. Several of my female respondents emphasized that during the war, while men were fighting in the mountains or hiding in the basements and bomb shelters, women earned a living by trading basic goods and food in local markets. Women often sold provisions to Russian soldiers. Alice Szczepanikova presents the narrative of one of her interviewees, a woman called Zarema, who described how her older sister supported their family through trade with Russian soldiers. Zarema said:

> There were many contract soldiers (*naiomniki*). And they bought lots of vodka and food. And, well, people were selling; most people traded with the Russians. There was no other way. People did not want to sell to Russians, to enemies, what they wanted to eat and drink, but they had no other way out.[20]

In his ethnographic description of the interwar Chechnya, Derluguian writes that "except for a few male-dominated areas, like operating wildcat oil wells, maintaining satellite phones, selling videos, driving cars, or slaughtering animals at the butcher's stand, women seemed to be in charge of whatever economic activity remained in Chechnya."[21] Similarly, Kheda, one of Valery Tishkov's interlocutors, stated that

[18] Nivat, Anne. "The black widows: Chechen women join the fight for independence – and Allah." *Studies in Conflict & Terrorism* 28, no. 5 (2005): 413–419.
[19] Murphy, Paul. *Allah's angels: Chechen women in war.* Naval Institute Press, 2011.
[20] Szczepanikova, "Chechen women in war and exile": 760.
[21] Derluguian, *Bourdieu's secret admirer in the Caucasus*: 46.

"Actually, it is women alone who work in Chechnya now, while all the men hang about with automatic guns or sit at home jobless."[22] Quite often women's economic activity demanded very intense manual labor. For instance, Petra Procházková wrote the story of a woman who collected aluminum in the ruins of Grozny.[23]

Women also became the principal mediators between families, communities, and military actors. For Chechen men, any contact with the Russian army presented a very high risk of being arrested, tortured, and killed. Consequently, it was the women who crossed military checkpoints and went to the Russians to bargain for ransom for their kidnapped relatives. Women were also actively involved in collective political action: they organized mass protests and pickets against the Russian army's and its local allies' indiscriminate killings, kidnappings, and torture during the war and counterinsurgency. For example, Khasan Baiev, a Chechen doctor who became widely known for saving the lives of civilians, Chechen rebels, and Russian soldiers during both wars, narrated in his autobiography *The Oath* how women saved him from potentially deadly detainment by the Russian army during one of the *zachistka* of his native village Alkhan-Kala. Emma Gilligan has provided narratives of the resistance of women during *zachistka* operations all across Chechnya:

In Chiri-Iurt, women lay on the ground in front of an APC, demanding the release of the detained. Other women formed a circle around a group of men detained in a field on the outskirts of Tsotsin-Iurt, which led to their eventual release. After being constantly harassed during 2001, several hundred women in the town of Argun dragged, crushed and abandoned a car chassis onto the road, blocked the bridge crossing the Argun River, and demanded the release of a local schoolteacher detained on May 3 that year.[24]

Chechen refugee Tamara Abuzaidova concluded that "During a war women can often do more with their voices and their desperation than men with trench mortars."[25] As a result, attitudes toward the role of women in public life changed. Chechen scholar Zalpa Bersanova provided survey evidence confirming that the view that "women should not participate in public life" decreased dramatically between the prewar and

[22] Tishkov, *Chechnya*: 163.
[23] Procházková, Petra. *The aluminum queen: The Russian-Chechen war through the eyes of women*. Prague, Czech Republic: NLN, 2002.
[24] Gilligan, *Terror in Chechnya*: 163.   [25] Procházková, *The aluminum queen*: 145.

the wartime period. This was true among both men and women, especially among more senior generations.[26]

Many women actively participated in human rights advocacy. The most prominent human rights defender in Chechnya was Natalia Estemirova. Originally a schoolteacher, she became involved in documenting extrajudicial killings, disappearances, torture, and other crimes committed by the Russian army and later pro-Russian Chechen security agencies. Estemirova became one of the leaders of the most prominent local NGO – the Chechen branch of the Human Rights Center "Memorial." Estemirova's work amid the repressive regime in Chechnya was very dangerous. In 2009 she was abducted and murdered by unidentified gunmen.

There were also instances when women became local political leaders – for example, Malika Umazheva was elected the head of the council of elders of her native village of Alkhan-Kala in 2001. The position of elder is typically reserved exclusively for men, so Malika's elevation to this role is amazing. Subsequently, she also became the head of the municipality. Malika was an outspoken critic of the endless *zachistka* operations in her village. She was killed by unidentified armed men. Anna Politkovskaya wrote the following tribute to Umazheva in *Novaya Gazeta*:

Malika was a true heroine, a unique and marvelous one. She became the head of administration of one of the most complex Chechen villages – Alkhan-Kala (the subject of endless "sweep-up operations," executions and disfigured corpses) after the former head had been murdered. Reason would have told her: "Sit quietly. Be careful." But she did the exact opposite – she became the boldest and most committed village head in that murderous zone of military anarchy, which today is Chechnya. By herself, unarmed, she went out to meet the [Russian] tanks that were crawling into the village. Alone, she shouted to the generals who had deceived her and, on the sly, were murdering the residents of the village: "You scoundrels!" She relentlessly fought for a better fate for Alkhan-Kala. No one else permitted himself to do that in present-day Chechnya. Not a single male. She, a humble village head who had been elected by a popular assembly earned the wild hatred of the Chief of Staff of the Russian army, the much-decorated General Kvashnin. He hated her so much that he invented the vilest stories about her, using his access to the television cameras to spread them. And she? She continued along her chosen path and, in response to Kvashnin's lies, she sued him in court, knowing perfectly well that almost everyone is afraid of him.

More than 4,000 people gathered for the funeral of Malika Umazheva in her native village.

---

[26] Bersanova, "Sistema tsennostei sovremennykh chechentsev."

Even though men were more often targeted with violence – extrajudi-cial executions, abduction, torture, detention during *zachistka* oper-ations – many women were also killed and injured by air and artillery shelling of their communities. There were also instances of rape. The most well-known episode is the kidnapping, rape, and murder of Elza Kungayeva, a seventeen-year-old Chechen teenager, by a colonel of the Russian Army Yuri Budanov in 2000. In a rare case of war crime prosecution, Budanov was tried and convicted for kidnapping and murder (but not rape) and spent eight years in prison. After he was released from prison, Budanov was assassinated in Moscow. The alleged assassin, Yusup-Haji Temirkhanov, became a hero in Chechnya. When Temirkhanov died in prison in 2018, his funeral became an all-Chechen manifestation of solidarity. Tens of thousands of Chechens went to Temirkhanov's native village to offer their condolences to his family. In general, however, cases of rape were not documented and reported. Rape is a taboo topic in Chechen society and therefore it is very hard to collect any systematic evidence on its prevalence during the conflict or trace its legacies. Procházková reports the words of one of her female interview-ees: "that's something we don't talk about here. Only a handful of cases received publicity, the rest were hushed up. There are cases of girls going out and not coming home."[27]

In addition to direct violence, Chechen women suffered from unpre-cedented stress, especially when they had to worry about their missing loved ones, starvation, and war-induced health problems. The conflict also fundamentally changed relations within families. Yet the transform-ation of gender roles cannot be simply equated with "women's empower-ment." Rather, as I show below, it was a contested and psychologically difficult process. My qualitative analysis suggests that as a result of the profound transformation of gender relations in postwar Chechnya and mobilization of conservative interpretations of custom and Sharia by men, family disputes proliferated in Chechnya. Interviews with lawyers uncovered that these disputes are often the most bitterly contested. Similarly, according to my interviews with *qadis* in three Chechen dis-tricts, family disputes constitute up to 80 percent of all the cases they adjudicate. Salah-haji Mezhiev, the Mufti of Chechnya, even said that it is easier for him to "reconcile blood enemies in feud than to reach a solution in a child custody case." In what follows, I analyze whether the wartime

---

[27] Procházková, *The aluminum queen*: 27.

disruption of gender hierarchies influenced legal choices in postwar Chechnya, drawing on a quantitative analysis of survey and court case data.

HOW CONFLICT TRANSFORMED WOMEN'S LAWFARE

Individual-Level Analysis

In this first stage of analysis, I compare men's and women's preferences for alternative legal systems using survey data. Figure 8.1 shows that women are more likely than men to choose state law and less likely to choose Sharia and customary law. The results of multivariate statistical analysis, presented in Chapter 5, show that after controlling for other individual-level factors, women are eight percentage points more likely to choose state law than men.

One might assume that the differences in preferences for alternative legal systems between men and women are driven by gendered disputes such as divorce or bride kidnappings. To further investigate the role of gender, I thus look at gender differences in responses across two legal domains: private and public. I classify six disputes (child custody,

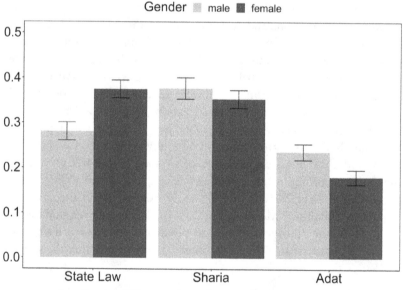

FIGURE 8.1 Gender differences in preferences for alternative legal systems

Gender ▨ male ■ female

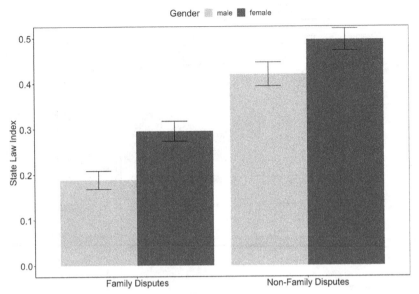

FIGURE 8.2 Gender differences in preferences for state law in family and non-family disputes

domestic violence, bride kidnapping, honor killing, polygamy, and inheritance) as family or private and four as non-family or public (property dispute, car accident, debt, and murder). The results plotted in Figure 8.2 show that even though overall support for state law is significantly higher in nongendered disputes, the gender gap in attitudes is present in both private and public domains. In other words, women are more likely than men to choose state law in both gendered disputes and in disputes unrelated to gender, such as a car accident or murder. In fact, analysis by vignette shows that a gender gap in support for state law is present in all ten dispute areas.

Even though women in Chechnya are much more likely to choose Russian state law than men, in the majority of situations (on average, in 6 disputes out of 10) they still prefer to solve disputes according to customary law and Sharia. To explore factors of support for state law among women, I analyzed predictors of support for state law in the subsample of female respondents. Along with the basic sociodemographic predictors and indicators of identity salience, I included an indicator of marital status, which often determines the utility of state law versus nonstate legal systems for women. The statistical analysis reported in Figure 8.3 provides support for the narratives on gender relations that

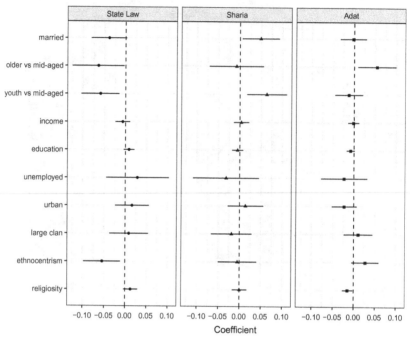

FIGURE 8.3 Factors of legal preferences among women. Coefficient plots for the OLS regression. N = 612

were present in my interviews: older women and married women are less likely to choose state law than middle-aged women and widowed, divorced, and unmarried women, respectively.[28]

This evidence can be interpreted as additional support to the instrumental logic of demand for state law: when women are protected by their status within family (through marriage, age, or having male children), they do not need state law to protect their rights. At the same time, I found that instrumental motivations are not the only ones at play: ethnocentrism among women decreases support for state law as well. Similarly, young women are less likely to choose state law and more likely to choose Sharia, which can be interpreted as a manifestation of a stronger religious identity among them. Thus, we can conclude that both instrumental and normative motivations are behind women's legal choices.

---

[28] There is a similarly large generational difference in beliefs and behaviors among Chechen female refugees in Europe. See Szczepanikova, "Chechen refugees in Europe."

The analysis above establishes large gender differences in legal preferences. This evidence supports the premise of the women's empowerment hypothesis; namely, that men and women have divergent legal preferences. In the next stages of the analysis, I test the major implication of the women's empowerment hypothesis by exploring whether the gender gaps in legal preferences can be attributed to wartime experiences of violence.

Community-Level Analysis

In order to test the hypothesis about war-induced disruption of gender hierarchies, I compare gender gaps in legal preferences in victimized and non-victimized communities within Chechnya.[29] To make sense of the results, I present them in the form of predicted values of choosing state law for men and women in victimized versus non-victimized communities. The results that followed were: men in non-victimized communities choose state law in approximately 29 percent of cases; for men in victimized communities, this value is virtually the same at 30 percent – there is no statistically significant difference. Women in non-victimized communities choose state law in approximately 35 percent of cases, which means that in non-victimized communities, the gender gap is approximately 6 percentage points. On average, women in victimized communities choose state law in 42 percent of cases. Thus, in victimized communities the gender gap is 12 percentage points, twice as large as in non-victimized communities. Figure 8.4 plots the main results. This analysis shows that the gender gap is driven by changes in women's support for state law in the victimized communities, not by men's alienation from it.

When the gendered effects of victimization are disaggregated between the two wars, it is revealed that the gender gap in preferences for state law was driven by victimization during the Second War. The interaction effect between gender and victimization during the First War is not distinguishable from zero. This is in line with the analysis in the previous chapter that highlighted that the First War led to the politicization of identities and alienation from state law, while the sustained violence of the Second War led to the disruption of societal hierarchies, which ultimately overshadowed an increase in the salience of communal anti-state identities. In

---

[29] In particular, I estimate the effect of the interaction between community collective victimization, introduced in Chapter 7, and respondents' gender on the aggregated choices for alternative legal orders. See also Lazarev, "Laws in conflict" for a detailed description of statistical analysis.

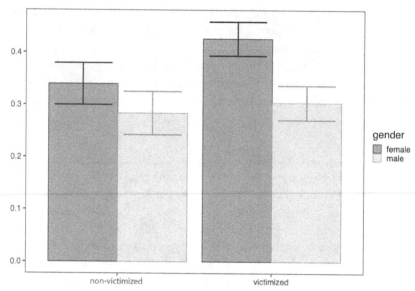

FIGURE 8.4 Relationship between community victimization, gender, and preferences for state law. Interaction plot from the regression analysis

turn, the disaggregation of the gendered effects of conflict by the type of violence shows that the gender gap in preferences for state law is associated with *zachistka* operations, not bombings of the communities. This makes sense, since as I noted above, *zachistka* operations primarily targeted men and often led to an increase in women's agency by putting them in the position of interlocutors between armed actors and the communities.

Next, I explore the correspondence of my survey results with behavioral data on civil cases heard in the Justice-of-the-Peace Courts. This analysis explores whether attitudinal patterns translate into behavioral ones. In particular, it sheds light on whether women in more victimized communities are more likely to go to state courts. Here I rely on the records of JP Court hearings from 2010 to 2016. The record has information on 217,284 court hearings on civil disputes. First, I classify plaintiffs and defendants into physical persons, firms, and state agencies. This way, I found 122,273 hearings (56%) where the plaintiff is a physical person. Second, I identify the gender of the physical person plaintiffs. In order to do that, I take advantage of the structure of last names in Russian. A last name that ends with the letter "a" signals that a plaintiff is a woman. For example, Kadyrov is male and Kadyrova is female. This rule allows me to identify female plaintiffs in Chechnya with high certainty. I find that among plaintiffs who are physical persons, women constitute 46%. I then restrict the sample to the cases where the defendant is also a physical person and classify the gender of the defendant. This leaves me with a sample of 80,612 hearings on civil disputes between individuals. With this sample, I find that women sued men in 22,785 cases (28%).

I then turn to the analysis of the relationship between collective victimization and women's use of law. Court hearings are the units of the analysis. I use an indicator of a female plaintiff as the main dependent variable. To measure exposure to conflict, I rely on the same indicator of community-level victimization used in Chapter 7. Control variables include the proxy for the presence of a Russian population (Terek region), mountainous terrain, and urban or rural status. I also include an indicator for whether the judge in a hearing is a woman. Because not all court hearings have information on the district court where it took place, the final sample is 68,827 hearings. I ran a bivariate logistic regression that aims to predict the gender of plaintiffs in these hearings. Standard errors are clustered at the district level. The results are presented in Figure 8.5.

In line with the women's empowerment hypothesis, the analysis shows that all else being equal, in more victimized communities, the likelihood of having a female plaintiff is significantly higher than in less victimized ones. Transformation of the logistic regression coefficient suggests that the difference is approximately 20 percentage points.[30] For example, in a rural non-mountainous JP Court district outside of the Terek region that was not collectively victimized, the predicted likelihood of having a female plaintiff in a civil case hearing is approximately 26%; in a victimized district with similar characteristics, the likelihood is 46%. I find similar results with an indicator of a female plaintiff against a male defendant as a dependent variable.

To address the possibility of a mechanical link between collective violence and women's legal behavior as a result of sex ratio change,

---

[30] These results should be taken with caution since the data are incomplete, as discussed in Chapter 6. Notably, the number of observations varies dramatically from year to year. Inclusion of the year fixed effects decreases the size of the positive association between community victimization and the likelihood of having a female plaintiff in a court hearing to approximately 5–7 percentage points (the result is significant at the 90 percent confidence interval). The results also hold if Grozny's districts are excluded from the analysis. In an earlier version of this analysis, I relied on a smaller sample of court hearings on family and property disputes (N = 8,495). With this sample, I found that in more victimized communities, the likelihood of having a female plaintiff is approximately 12 percentage points higher than in less victimized ones. See Lazarev, "Laws in Conflict." Subsequently, I was able to reconstruct the gender of plaintiffs in a much larger set of hearings.

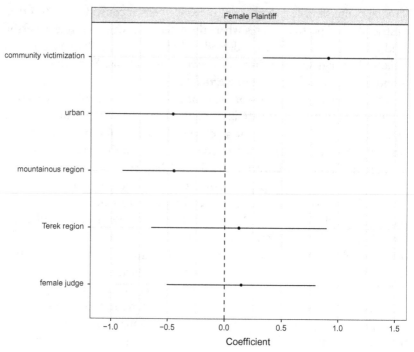

FIGURE 8.5 Predicting female plaintiff in hearings on civil disputes in the Justice-of-the-Peace Courts. Results of binary logistic regression. N = 68,827. Standard errors are clustered at the district level

I calculate the share of women in a municipal district population based on a 2010 census. I find that the inclusion of this variable does not affect the size and significance of the effect of collective victimization. In itself, the demographic variable for sex ratio is not a statistically significant predictor of having a female plaintiff. I also find that the imbalanced sex ratio is more prevalent in mountainous and rural areas and is not related to the collective victimization indicator, which can be interpreted as evidence against a simple demographic explanation of my main results. Overall, analysis of the behavioral data establishes the positive relationship between community-level victimization and subsequent use of state law among women.

Macro Effects of Conflict: Comparing Chechnya and Ingushetia

To study the legacies of conflict on gender relations and social order in Chechen society as a whole, I compared gender differences in preferences for the alternative legal systems between Chechnya and Ingushetia. The problems that women face under legal pluralism in Ingushetia are similar to those faced by women in Chechnya. Marem, a woman in her forties who works for an NGO that specializes in legal aid, told me that the most difficult problems that Ingush women have are related to divorce and child custody, inheritance, bride kidnappings, and domestic violence.

The case of Aisha Azhigova, a seven-year-old girl from Ingushetia, brought the issue of the coexistence of the Russian law, Sharia, and adat in the North Caucasus to the front pages of Russian newspapers in 2019. Aisha's parents got divorced and she was given to her father's sister's family despite her mother's pleas to keep her daughter with her. Aisha's paternal aunt terrorized the girl. Once she beat Aisha so severely that the girl ended up in the emergency room and the doctors had to amputate her arm. According to Aisha's mother's lawyer, Malika Abubakarova, who herself is from Chechnya, this case is symptomatic of the larger problem in the prevalent customary practice of giving custody over children to the father's side in cases of divorce in Ingushetia and Chechnya.

Ingushetia has also been the site of so-called honor killings and femicides. As in Chechnya, this form of violence has strong support among some segments of the population. A report on this practice quotes the words of an imam from Ingushetia:

Honor killing is justice and order. It is a law of our society. Without honor killings, there won't be any order. A woman is a mother. Her honor is the most important thing for the family, the clan. Honor is more important than wealth and status.[31]

The religious and customary authorities whom I interviewed in Ingushetia acknowledged the prevalence of gendered disputes. For example, Bashir, an Islamic arbiter in his forties who received religious education in one of the Arab countries, told me that "there are a lot of family disputes. The problem of domestic violence is quite widespread unfortunately." I was also told that a famous Ingush Islamic preacher, Khamzat Chumakov, often raises taboo topics like divorces and domestic violence in his sermons, raising awareness of so-called women's problems.

---

[31] Antonova, Yulia, and Saida Siradzhudinova. "'Ubitye spletniami': Ubiystva zhenschin po motivam 'chesti' na Severnom Kavkaze" ["Killed by the Rumors": Murder of women motivated by "honor" in the North Caucasus]. Pravovaya Initsiativa Report, 2018.

My observations in Ingushetia suggest a wider variation in women's roles within families than in Chechnya. Most tellingly, in Ingushetia one can observe groups of female friends or relatives – some in strict hijabs, and others in more European dresses and no headscarves – on the streets. In Chechnya, most women wear a traditional headscarf, while only a few wear a more strict hijab or do not wear a headscarf at all.

In order to explore the difference in legal preferences between men and women in the two regions, I turn to the survey data. I rely on the surveys in Chechnya and Ingushetia introduced previously. As with my analysis elsewhere, I treat the differences between the two regions as the manifestation of the structural impact of the conflict. In Chapter 7, I showed that support for state law is significantly higher in Ingushetia than in Chechnya, while Chechens are more likely to choose Sharia and customary law. In this section, I focus on gender gaps in the two regions.

While in Chechnya the gender gap in legal preferences is stark, I found no gender difference in legal preferences in Ingushetia. Furthermore, I found that gender differences are absent in all ten types of disputes. In the case of bride kidnapping, women in Ingushetia are even less likely than men to choose state law. This provides a notable contrast with Chechnya, where the gap is present in all disputes. Figure 8.6 compares

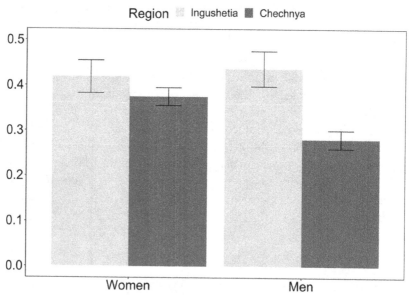

FIGURE 8.6 Gender gaps in support for state law in Chechnya and Ingushetia

the aggregated preferences of male and female respondents in the two regions for state law. The figure shows that while Chechen women are only slightly less likely than Ingush women to choose Russian state law, Chechen men are dramatically less likely than Ingush men to choose state law. This finding shows that at the macro-level, the gender gap in legal preferences is largely driven by men. Thus, this result suggests that the women's empowerment logic should be critically revisited and an explanation of the disruption of gender hierarchies and postwar women's legal mobilization should incorporate men into the analysis. In the subsequent section, I analyze the factors behind men's alienation from state law and women's legal mobilization through state law with qualitative evidence.

THE MECHANISMS BEHIND WOMEN'S LAWFARE

Why do experiences of conflict lead to differences in demand for state law among women and men? Following Marie Berry and Aili Mari Tripp, I consider several potential channels that could link exposure to conflict with women's legal mobilization, including demographic, cultural, economic, societal, and institutional changes.[32]

Demographic change is a powerful explanatory tool in the discourse of the regional authorities. Kadyrov's government often refers to the imbalanced sex ratio to justify its policies of the semiformal introduction of polygamy and stimulation of the birth rate. My interlocutors also often spoke about "the generation of widows" and "girls who had no boys to marry in our village." However, these narratives are not backed by official statistics. The aggregate results of the 2010 all-Russia census show little gender imbalance in Chechnya, which is similar to or even smaller than neighboring Ingushetia and Russia in general.[33] Of course, the reader of this book at this point knows that official government statistics in Chechnya are notoriously bad. Yet, the simple mechanical demographic explanation that links conflict with women's legal mobilization through a change in sex ratio seems problematic. First, my statistical analysis of court case data shows that the variable of sex ratio is not a statistically significant predictor of a female plaintiff in hearings on civil

---

[32] Berry, *War, women, and power;* Tripp, *Women and power in post-conflict Africa.*

[33] According to the 2010 census, the number of men in Chechnya was 622,557 and the number of women was 646,432. In Ingushetia, men numbered 184,560 and women, 227,969. Thus, the demographic gap in Chechnya was relatively smaller than in Ingushetia. In Russia overall, the gap was much larger: in 2010 there were 66 million men and 77 million women.

disputes. Second, even if demographic changes could *potentially* explain gender differences in legal *behavior*, it cannot logically explain the difference in legal *preferences* between men and women. Therefore, I leave demography aside and scrutinize the plausibility of other mechanisms relying on qualitative evidence.

Cultural Change

The rationale behind the cultural shift mechanism is that women's agency develops during wartime, which makes them more aware of their rights and pushes them toward more egalitarian views. This is a very difficult point to substantiate. Most of my female interviewees, even those whose views I would call feminist, embraced traditional Chechen culture. However, tracing changes in gender relations in the postwar period suggests a true cultural revolution.

A number of women described the war-induced gender role reversal in Chechnya to Czech journalist and human rights activist Petra Procházková. For example, Elza Duguyevova said: "Most of the husbands sit at home. I'm so frightened to let mine out in the streets on his own. When he has no choice but to go, I prefer to accompany him. I protect him, not he me."[34] Another woman, Kalimat, stated, "The war has changed the relationship between man and woman, mostly because we, the weaker sex, are more worried about our partners than they are about us."[35]

This can be seen as the cumulative effect of wartime experiences with earning money, living without men, and engaging in collective action, which increased women's sense of agency. Elza Duguyevova said that while she is at work, trying to get money to feed their five children, her husband "spends the day meditating" at home. This situation has led to profound stress and depression for the men like Elza's husband. "He finds it terribly degrading. No one ... can appreciate what a Chechen man feels like having a woman feed him. There is no greater humiliation." Elza concluded that "We [women] are a lot harder than we used to be. And our menfolk, on the contrary, are much softer."[36] Another woman, Liza Ibragimova, stated that "Quite simply an entire male generation has collapsed psychologically before our very eyes."[37] She also said that

---

[34] Procházková, *The aluminum queen*: 25. [35] Ibid.: 46. [36] Ibid.: 25.
[37] Ibid.: 111. See also Berry, *War, women, and power*: 140 on similar narratives from Bosnia.

during the war, Chechen women "discovered that we can manage without men."[38] A similar sentiment was expressed in my interviews with Chechen women. Zoya, a head of a prominent local NGO in her sixties, said that "The war led to the marginalization of men. Many were killed. Those who survived, they are suppressed. Men handle stress much worse than women." My interlocutors often noted alcoholism and drug abuse among the men who survived the war. Rosa, a member of the intelligentsia from Grozny, said that "the last real Chechen man died in the battle of Grozny in 1995. Since then the men's spirit has been lost. Women are the ones who lead in their families."

Men's humiliation and frustration also cause family fights. Elza Duguyevova recounted: "We fight like cats and dogs. As if he hated me because we've nothing to eat."[39] Furthermore, the traditional family in Chechnya received a major blow from its mass prolonged experience of displacement. According to Zoya, a prominent local human rights activist, "Families lived in refugee tents for years, some for decades. This inevitably led to family conflicts." Degi, one of my interlocutors in his late twenties, told me that this was also the case in his family.

We were in a refugee camp in Ingushetia for a long time. While my mother was working at the bazaar in the nearby town along with me and the other children, our father did not work a single day. After some time, they started fighting. They fought all the time.

Aggression became the norm in society and women often suffered from it in the form of domestic violence. Szczepanikova reports that "human rights groups have documented many cases in which fighters as well as civilian men who were subjected to torture in the hands of Russian soldiers turned violent against their wives and children."[40] Chechen director Malika Musaeva captured a related process of spillover from violent work into family life in the postwar period in her short film *Ajar Door*.[41] In one of the scenes, a wife tells her husband Ruslan, who works as a police officer: "You don't talk to me at all. Do you ever hear me? We have become alien to each other." In the next scene, Ruslan starts to strangle his wife after she has a fight with his female relative. He then

---

[38] Procházková, *The aluminum queen*: 107.   [39] Ibid.: 25.

[40] Szczepanikova, "Chechen women in war and exile." Analysis of representative surveys in Rwanda and Bosnia also show positive correlations between wartime victimization and domestic abuse. Berry, *War, women, and power*: 203, 205.

[41] Evangelista, *Gender, nationalism, and war* highlights the power of film to convey gender relations in the periods of nationalist struggle.

cools off and tells his wife: "I am crazy. Everything changed, you have to understand it. I am tired. I am tired of killing." Ruslan then leaves his wife.

Psychological stress, family fights, and domestic violence also led to a high rate of divorces, uncommon in Chechnya previously. Many men simply abandoned their wives. My interview with Umar, an official who worked in the official government registry (ZAGS), confirmed this fact. He said that

Officially, Chechnya has the lowest rate of divorces among all regions of the Russian Federation. But these are not accurate statistics. Many people never go to the registry for their marriage documents, and even less for their divorce papers. The majority do everything through the mosque.

One of the lawyers told me that according to her estimates, "there are more than 4,000 divorces per year. For a region where the real population is something like 800,000, this is a lot." Polygamy, which started to spread during the war and especially in the postwar period, is one of the leading causes of family disputes and divorces.

Furthermore, the war revived neotraditionalism in Chechen society and gave rise to militarized forms of masculinity. Zoya said that "After the war, they [the government] started to impose a cult of force and suppression of women. We never had anything like that – definitely not in the Soviet period." The conflict also transformed the treatment of women according to adat and Sharia. After the First Chechen War, won by the rebels, the secessionist government of the Chechen Republic of Ichkeria legalized polygamy and introduced strict dress codes based on references to Sharia. All the women who worked in government organizations had to wear a headscarf. However, these initiatives faced strong resistance from women. For example, Rosa, who then worked in the government, gave me the following account of her resistance:

I was a young woman. These bearded guys introduced the new rules – all women had to wear a headscarf and long skirts. As an act of disobedience to this idiotic requirement, I never wore a headscarf and had a pretty short skirt by Chechen standards.

One of the most telling descriptions of the role of women in Chechen society during the interwar period can be found in German Sadulaev's novel *Shali Raid*:

Sharia gloriously went through the Chechen land! Now they [the rebel government] prohibited Russian TV channels as they violated Sharia. The only things that they still transmitted were the news programs ... and the Argentinian soap opera *Muneca Brava* (*Wild Doll*). Chechen women loved this soap opera. Tired, exhausted, they had the weight of their households and the entire Chechen economy on their shoulders. *Muneca Brava* was women's only available drug, their window to the world of dreams and fairy tales. To ban *Muneca Brava* meant to provoke a women's riot, a riot more brutal than the war we already had. No one had the guts to do that. Everyone was afraid of women: the government, the former fighters, the Sharia proponents. Women were the major obstacle on Sharia's glorious march through Chechnya. They refused to wear Arab hijab. They said: – Don't intervene into our women's clothes! Take care of yourselves first – your corruption, alcoholism, theft. Our clothes are the last thing you should care about.

The rise of neotraditionalism was even stronger after the Second War. Zoya, the head of one of the most respected NGOs in Chechnya specializing on women's rights, told me that "After the war, adat started to be interpreted in the most draconian way. In fact, there is a variety of customs and many of them contradict each other. They brought up the most rigid ones and started to propagate them. They made women into scapegoats." In a similar vein, Petmat, a prominent female scholar in her fifties, said that "We have a male version of Islam here. The Koran is a text and all texts have multiple interpretations. Our men started to pick the harshest possible religious interpretations, the ones that are beneficial for them." Overall, as Zoya concluded: "Women of Chechnya are stuck between law, adat, and Sharia. All of these systems are supposed to protect women's rights, but men cherry-pick norms across them, they choose the most discriminatory interpretations of them, and as a result, women become completely stripped of all their rights."

Some of the activists from the women's rights NGOs told me that only mobilizing state law can help women defend their rights. They claimed that, even when customary and religious arbiters make a decision in favor of women, they often have no power to enforce it. Markha, a female lawyer in her forties, told me a story of how in one village, the qadi made a decision in favor of the woman in a child custody case, but the powerful family behind the father persuaded the qadi to change his ruling. According to Toita, another female lawyer, state agencies also shirk enforcement of pro-woman rulings in family disputes. But "if you write formal complaints, they start working."

In contrast, many other female interlocutors were strong proponents of custom and Sharia. Most notable, Satsita, my host, whose life story I narrated in Chapter 2, is a self-described supporter of adat. Fatima, a woman in her fifties with whom I spoke in the village of Starye Atagi, presented herself as a strong supporter of Sharia law. She told me that "Sharia has protected women at a time when they were treated like cattle in the West." She spoke with pride about her Islamic education and how knowledge of Islamic law is what is needed for Chechen women to advance their rights. A similar sentiment was expressed even in interviews with some female lawyers and women's rights advocates. For example, a young female lawyer, Emina, said in a group discussion that appeals to Islamic morality will be more efficient for protecting women's rights than going to Russian court in cases of domestic violence. Zoya showed me the posters on the wall of her NGO with quotes from the Koran about the strict limitations on the conditions that allow a man to beat his wife. Asya, another women's right advocate, told me that her NGO publishes a brochure with information about how Chechen adat and Sharia protect women's rights. She claims that poor knowledge of women's rights in custom and religion is what prevents Chechen women from effectively mobilizing these norms. On a few occasions I observed women trying to gain knowledge of the non-state legal norms. For example, I witnessed the meetings of a Koran reading group of five to six women in a pizzeria on the main street of Grozny. I did not have a chance to explore this phenomenon, but such groups can potentially function as hermeneutic communities that reinterpret religious and customary norms in ways favorable to women.[42]

Perhaps the most significant cultural change was that the conflict forced women to enter the public sphere. Prior to the war, despite endless Soviet attempts at change, the public sphere was largely a men's world, while women were in charge of the private sphere. Conflict reversed this. During the war and the early post-conflict period, men were excluded from the public life because of security concerns. As I highlighted above, any contact with the Russian army presented a grave threat to Chechen men, who were indiscriminately treated as enemy combatants. As a result, many men hid in the mountains, left Chechnya, or stayed at home. I personally met two men who said that they did not leave their houses for years in the early 2000s. Mothers and wives prohibited their sons and husbands from leaving home as a security measure. As a result, women were the ones who interacted with Russian military and civilian administration. Often women had to negotiate the release of their kidnapped relatives. They were the ones who had to navigate the complex

---

[42] Mahmood, *Politics of piety*; Sezgin, *Human rights under state-enforced religious family laws in Israel, Egypt and India.*

disorganized Russian bureaucracy to receive the material compensations for damages which the Russian state started to pay in 2003. They were the ones who stood in lines to receive new identification, documents for the children, documents for the deceased, and property documents. As Marie Berry wrote about similar "politics of practice" in the Bosnian case, "These mundane tasks facilitated everyday interactions with government."[43] In Chechnya, even women who remained traditionalists at heart had to learn the bureaucratic practices of the Russian state.[44] Men had, at the same time, started to forget these practices. As a result, Visait, a man in his fifties, told me that he did not know how to receive his pension or pay utilities, as his wife had been doing all this public-facing work since the war. Women also typically represented their families in interactions with NGOs in the refugee camps in Ingushetia. NGOs that distributed aid were quite bureaucratized, and thus these interactions similarly instilled Chechen women with bureaucratic knowledge. The implication is straightforward: conflict forced Chechen women to learn how to navigate the Russian state; after the war, women had the opportunity to use this knowledge to defend their rights in courts.

Economic Change

Another crucial mechanism uncovered in my interviews is economic change. Both the women and men with whom I spoke acknowledged a profound transformation in Chechen labor market roles because of war. Several respondents referred to "a husband who lies on a sofa all day and does nothing and his wife who works on several jobs and also fulfills all housewife duties" as a common family type in postwar Chechnya. An analysis of the job market supports this narrative: Chechnya is the only Russian region where women work more than men. In terms of male employment, Chechnya is at the very bottom among Russian regions. In contrast, women's employment in Chechnya is higher than in all other regions in the North Caucasus.[45]

---

[43] Berry, *War, women, and power:* 155.

[44] Chechen female refugees living in Europe, especially those who belong to the older Soviet generation, similarly serve as mediators between their families, the diaspora community, and the state and non-state institutions of the host societies. See Szczepanikova, "Chechen refugees in Europe": 263–265.

[45] According to research by FinExpertiza in 2020. See "Samymi rabotyaschami zhenschinami v Rossii okazalis' chechenki" [The most hardworking women in Russia are Chechen]. *Sekret Firmy*, December 17, 2020.

During the war, men could not work because of security concerns. In addition, the industrial sector of the Chechen economy, which was dominated by Russian speakers, but still employed some Chechen men, was completely destroyed. Prior to the war, the Chechen economy was heavily industrialized and had large oil refineries and other chemical plants and factories. During the war, all these factories were destroyed and their former workers (mostly men) were left without comparable employment opportunities.

There is also a consequential cultural element here: a Chechen man is limited in the types of jobs he can perform. For example, it is considered "shameful" for a Chechen man to work as a waiter or in most other service positions. Service jobs used to be considered "shameful" for Chechen women as well, but attitudes changed during the war, when trade and service jobs occupied by women became the sole source of income for Chechen families. After the war, women also started to work in the reestablished health sector, schools, and low-level government positions. For men, in turn, there were only two major job trajectories available: police and taxi driver. Police work remained very risky due to insurgent attacks on Chechens who worked in the Russian police. Despite the risks, police work provided substantial and regular income and as a result, postwar Chechnya has the highest number of policemen per capita among all Russian regions. It seems that the region also has the highest number of taxi drivers per capita. Women, in addition to jobs in bureaucracy, markets, schools, and hospitals, started to open small-scale businesses such as restaurants, beauty salons, and pharmacies.

Given that the majority of men remained unemployed or employed part-time in seasonal work, women's advances in the labor market changed the distribution of bargaining power within families. Women received access to material resources. These resources are incredibly important for allowing women to access state law. Navigating state law is costly due to formal fees and compensation to the lawyers, and even more so due to informal payments – bribes that are often necessary to make the system work in your favor. Thus, the fact that conflict dramatically increased women's share of the workforce is a major facilitator of women's legal mobilization through state law.

At the same time, women's advances in the labor market also caused frustration and backlash, sometimes violent, from their husbands. Throughout my interviews with women, I encountered many stories about how men negatively reacted to the economic successes of their wives.[46] For instance, Tamara, who currently works for an NGO, told me that during the war she secured a position as an interpreter at a foreign NGO. Her salary was about $100 per month, which was very good money in wartorn Chechnya. Her husband was unemployed, like most men in Chechnya. He became very envious and insecure about the fact that his wife was the breadwinner in their family. The husband started to beat Tamara and demanded that she quit her job because "I can't allow my wife to travel in a car with some foreign men. This puts shame on our family." Tamara left her husband, and their conflict over child custody ended up in state court. Similarly, Zoya, who lived for four years in a refugee camp in Ingushetia, told me that most women who lived in the camp with her worked in the markets of Ingushetia, or even opened small businesses like cafés or hair salons. Men, in contrast, mostly stayed in the camp unemployed. According to Zoya, these conditions led to many family disputes, domestic violence, and ultimately divorces, some of which subsequently led to disputes in state courts.

Societal Change

The third mechanism of change is community fragmentation and the related diminished authority of elders and extended families. The logic here is that legal choices are to a large extent determined by social pressure from families and communities, which strongly prefer dispute resolution through custom and religion and ostracize those who go to state courts. Women are especially vulnerable to social pressure not to use state courts. In the previous chapter, I emphasized the importance of community fragmentation in the relationship between victimization during the Second Chechen War and the penetration of state law within Chechnya. Here I explore whether this factor contributes to women's increased use of state law.

The effect of the disruption of gender hierarchies is indeed multiplied by the more general process of community disintegration, most notably the disruption of generational hierarchies. Extended families became substantially less powerful in victimized communities as a result of the killings of community leaders, mass migration, and intracommunal feuds. Tamara, one of my respondents from a severely victimized village in

---

[46] This again finds parallels with the experiences of Rwanda and Bosnia, in which men are especially likely to practice violence against women who are engaged in profit-making activities outside of the home. Berry, *War, women, and power*: 204–206.

Chechnya said, "There are no real elders left in our village. There are state-appointed 'elders,' but they don't have the respect of the community." In another interview, Leyla, a woman in her forties from a victimized community in the western part of Chechnya, told me that when she had a dispute with her husband over child custody, her husband sent his relatives to the elder of her extended family:

> Then they came to the elder of my clan and asked him to force me to withdraw the claim from court. But the elder told them: "I have no power over that woman." They responded, "in that case, you have to kill her if you are a real man." Our elder responded, "Are you insane? Do you want me to go to jail because of your stupid child custody dispute? No way."

This interview suggests that in victimized communities, extended families do not have absolute power over their female relatives and cannot effectively prohibit them from using state courts. In contrast, traditional institutions in less victimized communities remained more powerful and thus better able to prevent women from relying on state law.

Institutional Change

In the aftermath of some conflicts, governments, often with the encouragement and assistance of Western powers, introduce quotas for women or legislation aimed at protecting women's rights. One of the most notable cases of such institutional change is Rwanda, where in the post-conflict period more than half of parliamentary seats are occupied by women. In Chechnya, no such government-sponsored institutional changes occurred. This is not surprising, given that the West had no say in postwar political developments in Chechnya.

However, there was another channel of profound change in the institutional structure of Chechnya that was a direct product of the conflict. During the conflict, especially during the Second War, Chechnya witnessed a proliferation of NGOs.[47] Russian human rights groups such as Memorial and Citizen's Assistance, along with many foreign-based

---

[47] For parallels in other contexts see Berry, *War, women, and power*; Lake, Milli. *Strong NGOs and weak states: Pursuing gender justice in the Democratic Republic of Congo and South Africa*. Cambridge University Press, 2018; Massoud, Mark Fathi. "Work rules: How international NGOs build law in war-torn societies." *Law & Society Review* 49, no. 2 (2015): 333–364. Merry, Sally Engle. *Human rights and gender violence: Translating international law into local justice*. Chicago: University of Chicago Press, 2006.

organizations such as the Red Cross, Human Rights Watch, and the International Rescue Committee opened offices in the North Caucasus and worked in Chechnya. They documented war crimes and human rights violations, supported Chechens detained by law enforcement agencies, provided food and medical help to the population, and helped Chechen refugees in Ingushetia. Many of these organizations remained in Chechnya for more than a decade. Through working at these organizations, local cadres received unique administrative experience that helped them to develop legal consciousness.[48] Even more to the point, women were strongly overrepresented among these human rights activists in Chechnya.[49] Chechen women assisted the victims of violence and documented the atrocities committed against civilians.

In 2012, the Russian government introduced *The Foreign Agents Law*, which severely diminished the capacity of any NGO that received foreign money and worked on "politics-related" projects in Russia. This law had strong negative consequences for civil society in Russia in general, and in Chechnya in particular. Many organizations had to close. Musa, a human rights worker with a lot of experience, told me that his NGO had to close because his colleagues could not bear the shame of being called "foreign agents." Others decided to change the focus of their work. Topics of human rights protection or torture were considered "politics-related." In contrast, issues related to women's empowerment were not – at least, not always.[50] As a result, many organizations that started as broad-based human rights organizations changed their orientation and refocused on gender issues. In addition to pressure from the Russian government, another factor in such reorientation was the position of foreign donors that actively supported the agenda of women's empowerment.[51] By the time of my field research, there were sixteen NGOs operating in Chechnya that were focused on women's rights and women's empower-

---

[48] Massoud, "Work rules" shows a similar process of how local staff who worked in international NGOs acquired legal consciousness in South Sudan.

[49] Murphy, *Allah's angels*: 249–255.

[50] On the effect of legal repressions on feminist organizations in Russia, see Johnson, Janet Elise, and Aino Saarinen. "Twenty-first century feminisms under repression: Gender regime change and the women's crisis center movement in Russia." *Signs: Journal of Women in Culture and Society* 38, no. 3 (2013): 543–567.

[51] On the relationship between the global civil society and the western aid and local NGOs working on women's rights elsewhere in Russia, see Hemment, Julie. *Empowering women in Russia: Activism, aid, and NGOs*. Indiana University Press, 2007.

ment. The existence of this vibrant and professional NGO community amid a repressive dictatorship is astonishing. The NGOs in Chechnya provide, among other things, psychological help to women, programs on education, and training in different fields for young women. Most relevant for my discussion of legal mobilization, these organizations also provide legal education, legal aid, and legal representation for women free of charge. Given that navigating state law is quite complicated, access to legal representation plays a vital role for transforming women's grievances into actual legal cases. For example, Toita, who directs one of the women's rights NGOs, told me that their organization receives thousands of applications for legal aid each year. The organization has four lawyers who represent women in dozens of cases per year.

In densely connected Chechen society, access to NGO help is often facilitated by kin and other social networks. Women regularly meet their female relatives and other women in their communities at funerals and weddings. Young women are also connected though schools and universities. Subsequently, they are often connected through their children in such things like parent committees. As I mentioned earlier in this chapter, some women also participate in female Koran reading groups. Finally, digital social media platforms are very widespread and popular in Chechnya. According to my observations, almost all Chechen women have an Instagram and WhatsApp account. Women's effective use of WhatsApp can be seen in Ramzan Kadyrov's raging criticisms. On several occasions, Kadyrov urged Chechen men to prohibit "their women" from using WhatsApp. These networks allow women to easily obtain referrals to NGOs that specialize in women's rights. Overall, NGO assistance should be recognized as an indispensable factor that facilitated women's legal mobilization in Chechnya. This factor operates at the macro-level and its importance is further highlighted through a contrast with Ingushetia, which does not have such a vibrant NGO community.

The evidence points out four plausible mechanisms that link community victimization and women's mobilization of state law: (1) a cultural change through the increase of women's agency and bureaucratic knowledge and their reaction to the rise of militarized masculinity and conservative interpretations of custom and Sharia among men; (2) an increase in women's material resources due to greater access to and involvement in the labor market; (3) the fragmentation of communities and the diminished role of extended families and elders who are now less able to pressure women to abstain from using state law; and (4) the proliferation of NGOs which have provided legal aid and representation to women. These powerful social currents have nevertheless faced strong opposition from the regional government.

THE BACKLASH

My exploration so far has revealed that the recent wars in Chechnya created the conditions for women to pursue their interests through state law. At the same time, the wars and disruption of gender hierarchies bred a culture of militarized masculinity and pushed men toward conservative, rigid interpretations of custom and Sharia. Similar processes have happened in other regions of the world in which women's relative advances contributed to a reactive, but vigorous reassertion of male privilege. For instance, in Rwanda and Bosnia, Berry documented "violence against women – including physical violence, verbal assaults, accusations about sexual immorality, and so on – as a way of undermining women's ability to consolidate their postwar gains."[52]

In addition, women's legal empowerment – itself largely caused by the wars – has been met by a strong backlash from the top, as previewed by the story of Louisa Goylabiyava in the beginning of this chapter. The most notorious manifestations of the neotraditionalist policies of the Chechen government have been the semiformal introduction of polygamy, restrictions on women's dress, and encouragement of "honor killings."[53]

The backlash manifests itself primarily in the work of government agencies. For example, no police officers with whom I spoke considered domestic violence to be a crime, and none thought that a police officer had an obligation to intervene in a case of wife-beating. Other interviewees emphasized how Chechen men in charge of law enforcement shirk their responsibilities in gender-related cases if the law contradicts their beliefs. For instance, despite the presence of state court rulings in favor of the mother in child custody cases, enforcement agents often do nothing to return children to their mothers. Another telling example comes from an interview with Marha, a lawyer in her forties. She remembered the time

[52] Berry, *War, women, and power*: 203. For the cases of Algeria and the United States see Evangelista, *Gender, nationalism, and war*; Faludi, Susan. *Backlash: The undeclared war against American women*. New York: Three Rivers Press, 2006.
[53] Lokshina, "Virtue campaign for women in Chechnya under Ramzan Kadyrov."

that a male judge who was hearing a child custody case suddenly switched from speaking Russian to Chechen and asked a female plaintiff, "Why do you violate our traditions? Do you have any shame? How dare you claim your husband's child?" Most notoriously, one village head, a man in his thirties, said that in his village over the past year there had been three honor killings and that he "fully supports this."

Records of state court hearings provide additional evidence. For example, in spring 2015, Chechnya witnessed a rare court hearing on a case of an honor killing. The court heard the case of Sultan Daurbekov, who killed his thirty-eight-year-old daughter Zarema Daurbekova.[54] Sultan killed his daughter because "she put shame on his family." Allegedly, he had heard rumors that she "misbehaved," meaning had an extramarital relationship. Sultan did not deny that he killed Zarema, so in theory the case should have been very easy. But the records of the process show the complexity and high-stakes politics of legal pluralism in gender-related matters.

Ilyas Timishev, Sultan's lawyer, emphasized in court that his client had done nothing criminal, because Zarema had lived an amoral life. "Daurbekov did not kill his daughter. It is better to say that he helped her stop shaming herself, her father, and her relatives." Timishev emphasized that the case was "complicated" because it involved concerns of custom and religion. He urged the court to find "a just balance between law and context." In support of his claims, Timishev cited testimony that Zarema had refused to wear a headscarf, and when her father pointed out that this was one of Kadyrov's demands, she replied, "Let Kadyrov wear it!" Timishev further claimed that "She even drank beer, which violates not only our traditions, but also the norms of Islam!" The prosecutor pointed out that Zarema's private life had nothing to do with the criminal case. But the defense attorney disagreed: "In Chechen society there is no such thing as private life." During the hearings one of the witnesses claimed that "The Head [Ramzan Kadyrov] has said that we must cleanse the republic of this uncleanness." The prosecutor stated that "as a Chechen, he understands them," but that he was speaking as a representative of the state. In the end, Sultan Daurbekov was found guilty of murdering his daughter and was sentenced to seven years in prison.

This case shows that despite the strong influence of customary and religious norms on the functioning of state law in Chechnya and officials'

---

[54] Records of the court hearings were published by the human rights organization Memorial.

attempts to sabotage state law in gender-related cases, the state legal system still has some autonomy and can be utilized to defend women's rights. At the same time, the lawyer's appeal to Kadyrov's words illustrates the regional governmental backlash against women's rights and its major role in top-down lawfare.

The Chechen government has been actively promoting customary law and Sharia in family matters and sabotaging the enforcement of state law in gendered disputes. By promoting legal pluralism and putting forward conservative patriarchal interpretations of custom and religious norms, the government has depended on a tacit contract with men: their political loyalty in exchange for control over their families. I found some tentative support for the proposition that many men traded loyalty to the government for the reestablishment of patriarchy. For instance, Khasan, a man in his thirties who belongs to the Chechen intelligentsia, told me, "After the war ... and before Ramzan (Kadyrov took power in 2007) we had a feminist rule here. All government jobs below ministers were occupied by women. Men were simply unemployed. Now things changed. Ramzan brought back the order." Support for Kadyrov's government cannot be systematically measured due to the high political sensitivity of the issue, but my interviews suggest that many men support Kadyrov at least in part because of his reinforcement of a patriarchal social order through the promotion of Sharia and adat and implementation of gendered policies like making headscarves obligatory for women. This top-down governmental lawfare against bottom-up women's mobilization of state law illustrates how social and political orders are interconnected and how manipulations of the distribution of social control can endow peripheral rulers with political power.

* * *

This chapter showed that the conflicts in Chechnya, and in particular the Second War, created the conditions for women to mobilize state law to advance their group rights. This finding is consistent across all levels of analysis and all types of data. Data from the representative survey showed that gender was a powerful factor that explained demand for state law in Chechnya. Women chose Russian state law at a greater rate than men in all ten types of disputes presented in my survey. This held true for both gendered disputes, such as child custody and polygamy, and disputes unrelated to gender such as car accidents, debt, and murder. I interpret this as women's internalization of the fact that state law is beneficial for them in the family law domain and then expanding these preferences for state law into other domains. The large gender gap in legal behavior and attitudes in Chechnya provides an impressive contrast with the absence of such a gap in Ingushetia, which is culturally almost identical, but did *not* experience war.

At the same time, war-induced transformation of gender relations faced rising neotraditionalism from men and backlash from the regional government. The Chechen regional government started to deliberately subvert state law and promote rigid patriarchal interpretations of customary law and Sharia as a part of their legitimation strategy. In the concluding chapter, I will further discuss how the bottom-up lawfare for social order overlaps with the top-down lawfare for political control and place the findings of this chapter in comparative and historical perspectives.

Conclusion

In the summer of 2017, the government of Chechnya conducted a campaign to compel divorced individuals to reunite with their former partners. Authorities reported that in just two months, the government commission – comprising elders, religious authorities, and police officials – reunited more than 1,000 couples. Chechen state television broadcast its praise for Chechnya's ruler Ramzan Kadyrov for such a wise policy. The *New York Times* reported that "However farcical on the surface, the program, as with all social policy in Chechnya, is lethally serious. Failure to comply with demands of the regional leadership can have severe consequences, far worse than living with a despised former partner."[1]

Someone who hasn't read this book may conclude that the forced reunification of separated spouses is a result of the extravagant personality of Ramzan Kadyrov or an exotic aspect of the local culture. This study suggests a different perspective. It documents how the prolonged military conflict disrupted traditional social hierarchies in Chechnya, especially in gender relations. This, in turn, spurred the unprecedented mobilization of state law in Chechnya among women. Divorces became endemic in Chechen society, which previously had very low rates of divorce. Thus, from the vantage point of this book, the reunification policy can be seen as the local government's attempt to undermine this mobilization and reverse the disruption of hierarchies through the use of custom (elders),

---

[1] "Chechnya pushes divorced couples to reunite 'for children.'" The *New York Times*, August 26, 2017.

religion (imams), and the state (police). This highlights the importance of legal pluralism and everyday dispute resolution in Chechnya.

The story of the forced unification of former spouses illustrates two puzzles that this book has attempted to solve: why do some Chechens use Russian state law, despite the Russian state's brutal military violence against them *and* why does the government of Ramzan Kadyrov – who is a Russian bureaucrat – undermine Russian state law and advance rigid conservative interpretations of customary law and Sharia? These puzzles are interconnected. I argue that government management of the social order is used to legitimize the political order and ensure political control through coalition-formation and an increase in autonomy from the federal center. Thus, this book concurs with the perspective that state-building is about "ordering power"[2] and that dispute resolution is a very important part of this process.

The book was structured using a state-in-society approach that sees state-building through the lens of social control. In line with one of Joel Migdal's key postulates, I found that transformation in the distribution of social control between the state and society in Chechnya happened as a result of prolonged armed conflict – the Second Chechen War – which created "catastrophic conditions that rapidly and deeply undermine existing strategies of survival."[3] Massive societal dislocations, which severely weaken non-state social control, are not new in Chechen history: the Caucasian War of the nineteenth century, Stalin's deportation of the entire Chechen nation in 1944, and the First Chechen War of 1994–1996. However, these previous tragic episodes of state violence, while undermining traditional bases of social control such as clans, extended families, and territorial communities, strengthened national and religious identities and led to the periphery's alienation from the state. Here we find parallels with other cases, in which state violence alienated the population of culturally distinct peripheries, for instance, the Kurdish areas of Iraq under Saddam Hussein.[4]

During the Second Chechen War, alienation from the state was overpowered by the structural legacies of the war: the disruption of societal hierarchies. Consequently, extended families and communities that served as the loci of non-state social control became much weaker. Here I concur with Migdal. Where my analysis departs is its emphasis on the agency of individuals who mobilized state law for their personal goals after the

---

[2] Slater, *Ordering power* .   [3] Migdal, *Strong societies and weak states*: 262.
[4] Blaydes, *State of repression.*

conflict. I showed how the cultural, economic, and institutional transformations that the conflict occasioned created the conditions for these
individuals – primarily women – to employ state law. This perspective
highlights the importance of the demand for law.[5]

What was special about the Second Chechen War? What distinguished
it from the First War which happened only a few years earlier? It was
much more brutal, longer in duration, and, perhaps most importantly, it
involved massive inter-Chechen violence. These characteristics overshadowed the psychological alienation of residents from the state and
actualized disruptive effects of violence on non-state justice. At the same
time, the political resolution of the conflict – which was based on the
outsourcing of political power in Chechnya to the local Kremlin loyalists –
created a situation in which agents of the state now promote non-state
legal systems to ensure their political survival. In the discussion that
follows and concludes this book, I bring together the findings from the
different levels of analysis and various sources to draw a broader
theoretical picture.

FROM LEGAL PLURALISM TO LAWFARE

This book has shown that peripheral rulers – imperial intermediaries in
the past and governors and warlords in the present – seek to ensure their
political domination through active manipulations of state law and non-
state legal systems. The logic of political control based on management of
alternative legal systems actually dominates the Weberian logic of legal
monopolization in such cases. My findings on government subversion of
state law in Chechnya are aligned with scholarship that highlights that
rulers often have a strategic incentive to undermine state institutions or to
not enforce state law.[6]

This research further sheds light on the limitations of dominant con-
ceptualizations of state-building. It has highlighted the importance of
studying state-building through the lens of social control. If one analyzes
state-building through measures such as taxation, material infrastructure,
or number of bureaucrats per capita, Chechnya would have qualified as a

---

[5] On the demand for law elsewhere in Russia, see Hendley, *Everyday law in Russia*; Gans-
Morse, *Property rights in post-Soviet Russia*. On the similar process in China, see Wang,
Tying the autocrat's hands.
[6] Holland, Alisha. *Forbearance as redistribution: The politics of informal welfare in Latin
America*. Cambridge University Press, 2017; Massoud, *Law's fragile state*; Reno, *Warlord
politics and African states*.

great success. The Chechen government has built excellent roads and has opened administrative buildings even in remote villages. Chechnya has a higher share of police per capita than any other region in Russia. But the presence of state infrastructure does not indicate how it is used. This book showed that in cases of indirect state-building, in which the central government or an occupying force outsources state-building in the periphery to their local allies, these allies might use the state-building process against their opponents and undermine certain state-building processes in service of their strategic goals.

By revealing the strategic nature of legal pluralism promotion, my study cast doubt on explanations that assert that legal pluralism persists because of weak state capacity, ideology, or popular demand. This should not be misunderstood – all these factors have played important roles in the formation and transformations of legal pluralism in the history of Chechnya as I described in Chapter 3. During the imperial period, the Russian Empire used the classic colonial strategy of divide and rule in conditions of weak state capacity like Chechnya. The high-modernist Soviet state, in its turn, relied on strong state capacity and tried to eliminate non-state legal systems and establish legal monopoly. However, when political turmoil in the metropole freed local rulers, legal pluralism became an arena for lawfare aimed at establishing local political control.

During these times, different segments of the fragmented state – especially local rulers – strategically mobilized non-state legal systems and still do today. The argument of this book has been that local rulers promote legal pluralism to ensure their political survival. Legal pluralism allows them to borrow legitimacy from tradition and religion, increase their autonomy from the metropole, and incorporate the communal elites and the beneficiaries of the non-state legal systems into their coalition. The viability of this strategy depends on the degree of consolidation of the subnational political regime. When local rulers are unsure whether they are able to control non-state forums of justice, they are not likely to support them, fearing "the Frankenstein effect." When local rulers face political challenges, they almost inevitably rely on the legal system that is most beyond the control of their challenger. This is why some secular rulers in the North Caucasus have promoted Sharia law during confrontations with the Kremlin, and why other rulers in the North Caucasus have tried to suppress customary and religious legal systems when challenged by parties aligned with "traditionalist" and religious actors.

The remarkable parallels between the instrumental promotion of legal pluralism by the staunchly anti-Russian authorities of the secessionist Chechen Republic of Ichkeria in the 1990s (described in Chapter 4) and the similarly staunchly pro-Russian government of Ramzan Kadyrov of the 2000s (analyzed in Chapter 5) highlight the similarity of the challenges that local rulers face under nested sovereignty: building a cultural hegemony for legitimacy, ensuring autonomy from the metropole through boundary control, and accommodating the elites that are essential for social control. The coalition-formation logic is perhaps the most important one of these. In both Ichkeria and Kadyrov's Chechnya, promotion of non-state legal systems was a concession to war veterans who because of their proven capacity for violence form a real threat for those in power. However, there are also consequential differences: in Ichkeria after the First Chechen War, the political field was extremely fragmented, and the politics of legal pluralism was a tug-of-war, a game of outbidding played by the local ruler and the local challengers. In contrast, after the Second Chechen War, the political field was violently consolidated and the politics of legal pluralism was intended to keep the federal authorities at bay.

By highlighting the potential for turning legal pluralism into politicized lawfare, my book contributes to the critical perspectives on legal pluralism. While it is true that non-state legal forums based on custom and religion are more accessible, faster, less expensive, and more understandable to large shares of population in the peripheries of state power, as Boaventura de Sousa Santos states, "there is nothing inherently good, progressive, or emancipatory about legal pluralism."[7] Robert Blair has similarly pointed out that the romanticized view of non-state justice as inherently peaceful, harmonious, and adaptive is especially myopic in post-conflict environments.[8] At a fundamental level, non-state systems of justice are arenas of political power. Non-state legal authorities can be corrupt and biased. And legal pluralism can degenerate into "decentralized despotism."[9] In post-conflict conditions, vigilantes of different kinds – sometimes in traditional or religious clothes – often become unofficial police and judges. Blair thus proposed that international actors – in particular, UN peacekeepers – aid in establishing the rule of law in

---

[7] de Sousa Santos, Boaventura. *Toward a new legal common sense: Law, globalization, and emancipation.* Cambridge University Press, 2002: 114–115.

[8] Blair, *Peacekeeping, policing, and the rule of law after civil war*: 44.

[9] Mamdani, *Citizen and subject.*

post-conflict settings that are legally pluralistic. He argues that such external actors can act as a surrogate for the state as a provider of justice in the eyes of local population, and function as liaisons between state and non-state authorities in jurisdictional conflicts. My story – the story of legal pluralism in Chechnya in recent decades – does not include such external actors. The local rulers of post-Soviet Chechnya have been eager to engage in lawfare through non-state legal justice systems to undermine state law. However, at the same time, I argue, state formation can occur from the bottom-up even in the absence of external state-building interventions.

LAW AS A "WEAPON OF THE WEAK"

While politicians in the periphery and the metropole manipulate the ambiguities of legal pluralism to gain political control, individuals can also strategically maneuver across the multiple forums of justice. This study has provided support for both normative and instrumental approaches toward legal choices. On the one hand, in Chapters 2 and 6, I showed that the choices of legal forums reflect strong normative, even ideological attachments. Thus, legal choices to a significant extent can be treated as manifestations of ethnic, religious, and national identities. Previously, political scientists explored the manifestations of identities through voting or participation in violence, for example. However, the wager of this book has been that consistent preferences for resolving disputes through religious or customary authorities can also and equally be an important outcome of identity politics. This is especially true for Sharia. Much like in other parts of the Muslim world, such as Somalia, Northern Nigeria, and Malaysia, demand for Sharia in Chechnya can be understood as a reflection of a political ideology.[10]

On the other hand, my study showed that individuals in making their choices under legal pluralism follow their interests. This leads to pervasive forum shopping and a high rate of choices based on perceived outcome favorability for the groups to which an individual belongs. For example, older people are more likely to choose customary law and women are more likely to choose state law.

---

[10] Massoud, *Shari'a, Inshallah*; Hefner, *Shari'a politics*; Kendhammer, *Muslims talking politics*; Moustafa, Tamir. *Constituting religion: Islam, liberal rights, and the Malaysian state.* Cambridge University Press, 2018.

The book presented robust evidence that the wars in Chechnya created conditions for some segments of Chechen society – in particular, women – to mobilize state law to advance their group rights. Nevertheless, my results revealed that the majority of women have remained deeply embedded in traditional Chechen culture and few are willing to praise state courts. This has an obvious cause: state courts are often manifestations of red tape and corruption. However, women do mobilize state law and do go to state courts. This paradox was explained by Susan Hirsch and Mindie Lazarus-Black, who argued that both those people who actively seek inclusion in legal processes and those who "get included" involuntarily, often end up appropriating and using the procedures of law.[11]

The finding regarding women's preference for state law and their use of state courts show that state law can indeed be a "weapon of the weak." James Scott, in his original formulation of this concept, highlighted a very different set of weapons: foot dragging, sabotage, slander, jokes, gossip, gestures, and character assassination – namely, symbolic acts of confrontation occurring on the backstages of social life.[12] Yet law is a weapon of a different caliber and of a different nature. Initiating a legal dispute, and especially going to state court, is a "nuclear option" that occurs on the frontstage of social life. In contrast to Scott's original examples, law is both a legitimate and accepted political tool and unfolds in the limelight of the public arena rather than its shadows. It is much more radical and time-consuming than gossip for example, and therefore its inclusion as a "weapon of the weak" is unexpected. This is especially true given the vision of state law as an instrument of domination employed by the ruling elite. However, the Chechen women who went to court are not alone. Studies from different historical periods and different continents show that law might be a right-enhancing force mobilized by weak and marginalized groups, such as peasants, workers, immigrants, and the poor.[13]

At the same time, my study calls for a rethinking of the concepts of women's empowerment and legal mobilization. The women's empowerment perspective considered in this book is problematic for several

---

[11] Lazarus-Black, Mindie, and Susan Hirsch, eds. *Contested States: Law, hegemony and resistance.* Routledge, 1994.

[12] Scott, James C. *Weapons of the weak: Everyday forms of peasant resistance.* Yale University Press, 1985.

[13] Burbank, Jane. *Russian peasants go to court: Legal culture in the countryside, 1905–1917.* Indiana University Press, 2004; Chanock, *Law, custom, and social order;* McCann, *Rights at work;* Merry, *Colonizing Hawai'i;* Sandefur and Siddiqi, "Delivering justice to the poor."

reasons. Most notably, war-induced transformations of gender relations faced rising neotraditionalism from men and a backlash from the regional government. The Chechen regional government started to deliberately subvert state law and promote rigid patriarchal interpretations of customary law and Sharia as a part of their legitimation strategy. But even if we look only at women, there are still some problems with the application of the concept. First, the war-induced proliferation of domestic violence, divorces, and other gendered disputes undeniably had a negative effect on Chechen women's well-being. It is empowering for a woman to be able to fight oppressive relatives in a courtroom, no matter how long and exhausting the process is. However, the process of revealing and going through the traumas from domestic violence, divorce, and gender-related disputes again in a public setting is very difficult. Second, even though women are more likely to support state law than men, women still prefer either customary law or Sharia in the majority of situations. Moreover, there are vast differences in women's legal preferences related to age, marital status, whether they have sons, and other characteristics.

The classic framework of legal mobilization also does not easily fit the reality uncovered in this study. First, Russia is not a common law system and therefore strategic litigation aimed at establishing a precedent is out of the question. Second, Chechen women did not form a sustained social movement or exhibit any other form of collective action to defend their legal rights in the postwar period. The rise in the use of state courts was a consequence of largely uncoordinated individual legal efforts. However, the efforts of these individual women did present more women an opportunity to defend their rights in legal battles of crucial importance, especially in child custody disputes. In the aggregate, these efforts formed the nascent demand for the rule of (state) law in the periphery. Here we return to Scott. Paraphrasing his analysis of everyday forms of resistance, we can say that "just as millions of anthozoan polyps create, willy-nilly, a coral reef,"[14] so do thousands upon thousands of individual legal cases spur state formation from below.

Given that my analysis of the mechanisms highlighted the crucial role of NGOs, one can also draw a parallel with Diana Fu's study of disguised collective action that constitutes what she calls mobilization without the masses in China.[15] Like Fu's example of labor rights in China, collective action in the domain of family law is highly politically sensitive in

---

[14] Scott, *Weapons of the weak*: 36.
[15] Fu, Diana. *Mobilizing without the masses: Control and contention in China*. Cambridge University Press, 2018.

Chechnya. Therefore, a classic model of legal mobilization based on social movements is not viable in the face of repressive authorities. But facilitating legal cases stemming from individualized grievances might work. Other mechanisms behind women's legal mobilization uncovered by my analysis include deep structural changes in cultural, economic, and social relations occasioned by the wars. Consequently, even though the government of Chechnya managed to establish a cultural hegemony based on their interpretations of custom and religion, it cannot fully prevent women from mobilizing state law. The regional government's hostile response to women's legal mobilization is telling; it further highlights the threatening nature of this mobilization for the current political order in Chechnya.

The results of this study also show that individuals might voluntarily use the law even if it is seemingly foreign to them. This finding refutes a premise from the theory of legal transplants, which asserts that if a law violates the values of the population, it will ultimately be rejected.[16] At the same time, I show that imposed state law in Chechnya is no more a "transplant" than the supposedly indigenous customary and religious systems. In fact, adat and Sharia, as they are practiced in Chechnya today, were also imposed or invented by political actors, and their interpretations depend on the interests of powerful actors. Furthermore, seven decades of Soviet governance formed a normative horizon of stateness, even for Chechen women. True, Chechens, and especially Chechen women, were marginalized in the Soviet modernization and state-building projects, as I documented in Chapter 3. Nevertheless, generations of Chechen women participated in Soviet elections, met with Soviet local police officers, filed petitions, etc. Moreover, a small but active segment of the Chechen population embraced Soviet identity and therefore created a template for others to embrace state law after Chechnya was reincorporated into the Russian Federation in the early 2000s. Because of the particularities of the Soviet project, Chechnya had a different experience from other colonial peripheries, an experience that created a habituation of stateness.[17]

My finding regarding state law as a "weapon of the weak" is especially noteworthy given the repressive authoritarian nature of the political regime in Chechnya. To explain this paradox, I rely on the concept of

---

[16] Berkowitz, Daniel, Katharina Pistor, and Jean-Francois Richard. "The transplant effect." *The American Journal of Comparative Law* 5, no. 1 (2003): 163–203.
[17] See Mampilly, *Rebel rulers* on the concept of the habituation of stateness.

the "dual state."[18] The idea is that even under dictatorships the courts will continue to operate in a fairly normal and routine manner, *but* cases that attract the attention of those in power can be manipulated in the interests of the powerful. Thus, even in Kadyrov's Chechnya, courts enjoy some autonomy, and widespread corruption and the structural problems of the Russian judiciary notwithstanding, the courts handle mundane cases in accordance with the law, and thus allow weak and marginalized individuals to advance their rights.

A COMPARATIVE POLITICS OF STATE-BUILDING LAWFARE

No doubt, Chechnya is unique in many regards. The fact that the Chechen language is unrelated to the Indo-European language family dominant elsewhere in Eurasia highlights this uniqueness. The preservation of strong customary law despite the decades of high-modernist Soviet rule is yet another artifact of the unique Chechen path. The length and intensity of human suffering during the decade-long post-Soviet conflict also distinguish Chechnya from most other societies. One late giant of comparative politics advised me "Don't study Chechnya – it is a truly nonrepresentative case of anything you can imagine, people there went through hell." It is true that the population of Chechnya went through hell. However, I argue that we can learn a lot from these unique and tragic experiences. Exploring the politics of legal pluralism in Chechnya can teach us about peripheral state-building; nested sovereignty; subnational authoritarianism; gender regimes; religious and ethnic politics; and the legacies of conflict, colonialism, and socialism. This broad theoretical relevance can be highlighted by pointing out that some of the key findings of this study have remarkable parallels with other places and times.

Throughout this study I have compared Chechnya with Ingushetia. I claimed that Ingushetia is an almost ideal comparison for Chechnya. Like Chechnya, Ingushetia has a similar culture and similar constellations of legal systems, but no legacies of war. My research in Ingushetia helped me to see patterns that I was not able to grasp when I was doing research in Chechnya. The absence of a gender gap in legal preferences and behavior in Ingushetia was crucial in helping me understand the significance of this gap in Chechnya. Ingushetia also illustrated a "normal" situation in which state officials are the principal proponents of state law,

---

[18] Fraenkel, *The dual state*; Meierhenrich, *The remnants of the Rechtsstaat*; Hendley, *Everyday law in Russia*.

in contrast to the post-conflict situation in Chechnya in which state officials are against state law. I also compared Chechnya with Dagestan, another neighboring region. This comparison highlighted that despite popular demand, peripheral rulers can strategically suppress non-state legal systems if the authorities in charge of these non-state justice threaten local rulers' political survival.

Other Muslim-majority regions of Russia exhibit a rather limited role of non-state legal systems. During my interviews with religious authorities and state officials in the Republic of Tatarstan – a large, rich, industrial, and predominantly Muslim region situated on the Volga river – my interlocutors were rather puzzled with my questions about Sharia arbitration.[19] One imam told me that "You know, people are not very religious here. Among Tatars maybe 5 percent go to the mosque regularly. What Sharia law are we talking about?" At the same time, the authorities in Tatarstan developed a comprehensive institutional infrastructure – every district in the republic has a qadi authority in charge of Sharia. The Tatarstan regional authorities have also been actively developing institutions of Islamic banking and have invested heavily in building spectacular mosques all across the region. Given the relatively low religiosity of the population and the near absence of demand for religious justice, these measures can also be interpreted as evidence of boundary control implemented by the ambitious local rulers, who seek to further consolidate local sources of power and increase their autonomy from the center.

The political logic of legal development also finds parallels with regions of Russia that have neither a Muslim majority nor customary law. For example, Alexei Trochev has argued that Russian governors established subnational constitutional courts in order to increase autonomy vis-à-vis the federal center in the 1990s.[20] Trochev showed that subnational courts were paradoxically established only in those regions where power was consolidated in the hands of the ruler. Thus, the establishment of constitutional courts in the Russian regions in the 1990s and the promotion of customary law and Sharia in Kadyrov's Chechnya have a similar political logic of boundary control – i.e., the parochialization of power under the conditions of a locally consolidated regime.

---

[19] Tatarstan is also often compared with Chechnya, see for examples, Evangelista, *The Chechen wars*; Hughes, *Chechnya*; Sharafutdinova, Gulnaz. "Chechnya versus Tatarstan: Understanding ethnopolitics in post-communist Russia." *Problems of Post-Communism* 47, no. 2 (2000): 13–22.

[20] Trochev, Alexei. *Judging Russia: The role of the constitutional court in Russian politics 1990–2006.* Cambridge University Press, 2008.

The shared history of Russian colonialism relates the North Caucasus to Central Asia. Recent studies have explored legal pluralism in Central Asia both in historical and contemporary perspectives.[21] For example, Regine Spector's study of social ordering in the bazaars of Bishkek, Kyrgyzstan, showed the importance of the "customary" institution of elders, even if the custom was "invented" or "imagined." Generalizing the state-building experience of post-Soviet Central Asian states, Pauline Jones concluded that the main struggles in the region were not between state and society, but within the state. Local strongmen in Central Asia, similarly to Kadyrov in Chechnya, "developed within, not outside, the state apparatus; they are a core part of the state rather than representatives of the autonomous societal organizations."[22] Post-Soviet Central Asian states do not exhibit traits of institutionalized nested sovereignty in the form of federalism, like in Russia; however, the legacies of the Soviet planned economy allowed regional leaders to similarly engage in the boundary control work – these leaders undermined the central state in order to parochialize their power.

One can also find parallels in the relationship between violence and state-building in the Caucasus and Central Asia. Sarah Cameron has highlighted how the exceptional state violence during the Great Famine of 1931–1933 forged a new identity in Kazakhstan and ultimately facilitated the integration of the Kazakhs into the Soviet political project.[23] Similarly, this study showed that the major episodes of violence in Chechnya – i.e., the Caucasian war, Stalin's deportation of Chechens of 1944, and the Chechen wars of the post-Soviet period – fundamentally shaped social relations in Chechnya and paradoxically increased the role of the state in Chechen society.

The link among nested sovereignty, popular legal consciousness, and legal pluralism finds parallels in historical research too. Most importantly, Lauren Benton has described how the loopholes in the colonial judicial system allowed colonized subjects to pursue redress and accommodate their visions of justice. By shopping between forums, colonized subjects reified the notions of legal differences. Accordingly, the colonized

---

[21] Beyer, Judith. *The force of custom: Law and the ordering of everyday life in Kyrgyzstan.* University of Pittsburgh Press, 2016; Sartori, *Visions of justice*; Spector, Regine. *Order at the bazaar: Power and trade in Central Asia.* Cornell University Press, 2017.

[22] Jones Luong, Pauline, ed. *The transformation of Central Asia: States and societies from Soviet rule to independence.* Cornell University Press, 2004: 277.

[23] Cameron, Sarah. *The hungry steppe: Famine, violence, and the making of Soviet Kazakhstan.* Cornell University Press, 2018.

subjects unwillingly contributed to the development of the jurisdictional politics of empires.[24] Likewise, by going to state courts, Chechens contributed to state formation from below.

My research also echoes several studies that have highlighted how particular configurations of state and non-state legal systems are the products of political strategies and the struggles between the government and potential challengers.[25] For instance, Catherine Boone, drawing on the experience of sub-Saharan African polities, argued that "various forms of legal pluralism must be understood, at least in part, as artifacts of state design, rather than as the products of error, delay, or failure on the part of governments that should be creating unified national property regimes."[26] These similarities of colonial experiences highlight the importance of structure and agency in the study of legal pluralism. These seemingly contradictory perspectives can be reconciled by the argument that colonialism establishes the basic configuration of legal orders, but political actors and individuals strategically employ them and thus transform these configurations to a large extent.

This book showed that transformations in state-building can be brought from the bottom-up by individual women. A legitimate question is whether women's mobilization of state law is specific to Muslim women. Does this finding then feed the narrative of "saving Muslim women?" Absolutely not. In fact, historical sociologist Karen Barkey documented the reverse story of how non-Muslim women in the Ottoman Empire found "protection and relief in the Islamic courts, which were more moderate in divorce and inheritance matters than the courts in their own communities."[27] Barkey shows how Jewish women went to Sharia courts to obtain the share of their patrimony denied them in Jewish law and Christian women preferred Muslim dowry and divorce laws. Some Christian women also went to Islamic courts to fight domestic abuse tolerated by local customary laws. For example, Eirene, a young woman in a seventeenth-century Bulgarian village, persistently appealed to the Christian community court to obtain a divorce from a husband who beat her, but her pleas were refused. Subsequently, she obtained a separation from her husband through the Islamic court.[28] In general, by

---

[24] Benton, *Law and colonial cultures*; Benton and Ross, *Legal pluralism and empires*; Sartori, *Visions of justice*.

[25] Massoud, *Law's fragile state*; Moustafa, *Constituting religion*; Sezgin, *Human rights under state-enforced religious family laws in Israel, Egypt and India*.

[26] Boone, *Property and political order in Africa*: 16.

[27] Barkey, "Aspects of legal pluralism in the Ottoman Empire": 95.   [28] Ibid.: 99.

mobilizing through Muslim courts, non-Muslim women in the Ottoman Empire obtained rights that were otherwise unavailable to them. This, of course, provoked a backlash from the non-Muslim communal authorities who wanted to preserve their role as intermediaries between the state and their communities. Barkey describes how "the rabbis threatened, and the patriarchs excommunicated their people and prohibited them burial in Christian cemeteries" for turning to Sharia courts.[29] This story from the Ottoman Empire and the story told in this book are thus about power, rather than about the particularities of culture or religious doctrine.

Likewise, the results of my study regarding the consequences of conflict on gender have parallels in many other places outside of Chechnya. Scholars have recently shown that conflicts can lead to the disruption of gender hierarchies and women's empowerment in places as diverse as Bosnia and Rwanda, post-Uganda and post-Soviet Nagorno-Karabakh.[30] Like this book, these studies discuss the potential backlash this empowerment can instigate.

There are also historical parallels regarding how disruptions in social order had implications for political ordering. For example, historian Elizabeth Thompson presented a similar argument regarding backlash as a coalition-building strategy, drawing on a study of Lebanon and Syria in the 1930s, where conflict and famine led to the empowerment of women, but this empowerment was counterbalanced by the policies of the French mandate authorities who did not extend rights to women in order to secure the support of men and traditional and religious leaders.[31] Thus, the phenomena highlighted in this study are quite widespread and have parallels in history and other parts of the world. This study brings these patterns together and theorizes them through the prism of state-building.

AVENUES FOR FUTURE RESEARCH

This book inevitably missed many significant dimensions of state-building lawfare that merit future research. One potential avenue for future research is the exploration of the role of international law in the context of post-conflict legal pluralism. International law has in fact played a major role in

---

[29] Ibid.: 101.

[30] Berry, *War, women, and power*; Tripp, *Women and power in post-conflict Africa*; Shahnazarian, Nona. V tesnykh obiatiiakh traditsii: Patriarkhat i voina. [In the tight embrace of tradition: Patriarchy and war]. Aleteyia, St. Petersburg, 2011.

[31] Thompson, Elizabeth. *Colonial citizens: Republican rights, paternal privilege, and gender in French Syria and Lebanon*. Columbia University Press, 2000.

the legal behavior and attitudes of the Chechen population after the wars. Almost all Chechens know about the "Strasbourg Court" – the European Court for Human Rights. For many Chechens, this court is the only forum in which they can obtain justice for their murdered and disappeared relatives.[32] Moreover, recently, human rights actors working in Chechnya have started to mobilize international law beyond the domain of war crimes. In *Magomadova v. Russia*, the European Court of Human Rights recognized that the Russian state did injustice to the Chechen woman Zelikha Magomadova when dealing with her child custody case – a case very similar to many of the disputes discussed in this book.

Zelikha is the mother of six children. Her husband Makhsud, who worked for the Russian state police, was killed on duty in 2006. In 2010, Makhsud's brothers evicted Zelikha from her own house and prohibited her from seeing her children by referring to adat norms. They also forced Zelikha to transfer to them the state welfare benefits to which she was entitled. With the help of a local legal aid NGO, Zelikha went to a state court and received a judgment that the children should live with their mother. However, the decision was never enforced. Ultimately, Zelikha's brothers-in-law – who also worked in law enforcement – managed to win a different court hearing to strip Zelikha of her parental authority. She appealed in Russian courts but was not able to obtain justice because of her opponents' connections. On October 8, 2019, the European Court of Human Rights recognized that the Russian authorities' decision to deprive a widow of parental authority of her children was "grossly arbitrary."[33] This decision sheds light on the complex coexistence of customary, religious, and state law in Chechnya. This decision and the shadow of international law in general might shape the subsequent mobilization strategies in Chechnya's conditions of legal pluralism.

Another potentially insightful avenue for future research concerns the legal attitudes and behavior of the Chechen diaspora community in Europe and the Middle East. Migration was one of the key social consequences of the conflicts, especially the Second Chechen War.[34] Migration

---

[32] Gilligan, *Terror in Chechnya*; van der Vet, Freek. "Seeking life, finding justice: Russian litigation and Chechen disappearances before the European Court of Human rights." *Human Rights Review* 13, no. 3 (2012): 303–325.

[33] Zelikha Magomadova v. Russia; application no. 58724/14; ECHR 339 (2019) 08.10.2019.

[34] Nichols, Johanna. "Chechen Refugees, The." *Berkeley Journal of International Law* 18 (2000): 241; Iliyasov, Marat. "Researching the Chechen diaspora in Europe." *Interdisciplinary Political Studies* 3, no. 1 (2017): 201–218.

fundamentally shaped many Chechen communities and families – today, almost all Chechen families have relatives somewhere in Europe or Turkey. How do Chechens who live in Europe choose between secular state legal systems, Sharia, and Chechen customary law? Is their access to the latter two more limited than in Chechnya? Is there a gender gap in legal attitudes and behavior there? Does migration to countries with different integration policies, for example France and Belgium, have different effects on migrants' legal attitudes and behavior? Maryam Sugaipova and Julie Wilhelmsen have recently made the first step along this line of inquiry.[35] They found continued legal pluralism within the Chechen diaspora in Norway, while also revealing a gradual adaptation to the legal framework of their host country. Given the widespread nature of these migrations, including recent large-scale refugees' resettlement from conflict-affected areas, these questions will be relevant for many communities beyond Chechnya as well.

POLITICAL LESSONS

This study looked beyond the common media and academic narratives about Chechens, which have focused predominantly on the issues of violence, insurgency, and terrorism. It showed that despite the common portrayal of Chechnya as a lawless place, a large share of the Chechen population actually demands the rule of law – either in the form of Sharia, the idealized customary system, or state law. The book also challenged the narrative of the "oppressed Chechen woman" by highlighting the substantial roles that Chechen women played during the war and in the postwar period and by documenting women's use of state law to defend their rights. As Chapters 2 and 6 documented, customary law, Sharia, and state law in Chechnya are all constructed, negotiated, and interpreted in complex and ambiguous ways. Three ostensibly separate legal systems have evolved into a hybrid legal order, in which judges in state courts sometimes implement customary and religious norms, and imams and elders enforce state directives. Most importantly, as I described in Chapter 2, many Chechens deeply care about legal pluralism and are reflexive about their Imperial and Soviet history, post-Soviet conflicts, religion, family and gender relations, and academic research. Chechen society is heterogenous in its views and behaviors and many social and

---

[35] Sugaipova, Maryam, and Julie Wilhelmsen. "The Chechen post-war diaspora in Norway and their visions of legal models." *Caucasus Survey* (2021).

political cleavages cut across each other. Even the hegemonic political order, which looks like a monolith at the first glance, is tacitly contested.

The book drew a parallel between the political situation in postwar Chechnya and other colonial situations based on indirect rule. This does not mean that Putin's Russia has become a reincarnation of the Russian Empire. However, the framework of imperialism and colonialism is important for understanding Russian law and politics in the Caucasus. Contemporary Russia is a post-imperial (or perhaps not even post) federation, a site of nested sovereignty. This study suggests that Putin's policy of indirect rule through Kadyrov's government is not the only possible way of governing Chechnya. Kadyrov's policies, such as the introduction of polygamy or collective punishment, are not manifestations of popular demand, or "the Chechen political culture," but rather elements of a strategy of informal political control pursued by the local authorities. This encroachment of the state fundamentally changes Chechen customary law and Sharia as it is practiced in the region. Furthermore, this nexus between the local political regime and the non-state legal systems can erode trust in customary and religious institutions in the long run, which may further increase the demand for state law in Chechnya.

The obvious question that remains unaddressed is why the Kremlin continues to allow Kadyrov to manipulate non-state legal systems and undermine Russian state law in Chechnya. The definitive answer will only be known when the Kremlin archives on the topic are declassified in the future. Yet, Kimberly Marten has provided the most coherent answer with the limited available information. She locates Kadyrov in the framework of warlord politics. Marten shows that unlike many other instances of state reliance on warlords, Moscow was not forced into its relationship with Ramzan Kadyrov. Instead, she argues that the Kremlin

consciously created and abetted Ramzan's control, step by step, as an experiment in resolving ethnic and civil warfare at relatively low cost. The leaders of a fully developed and otherwise functioning modern state chose to outsource a piece of domestic sovereignty, largely for the sake of convenience.[36]

Marten's analysis also highlights how the Kremlin helped Ramzan Kadyrov to consolidate his coercive control. My analysis complements Marten's argument by showing that the contemporary political order in Chechnya is based not only on coercion, but also on the strategic

[36] Marten, *Warlords*: 137.

management of state and non-state legal systems. I further argue that this political order is explicitly gendered.

My argument that the promotion of legal pluralism allows the Chechen authorities to parochialize power and thus make themselves even more indispensable to the Kremlin can perhaps be extended to the Kremlin as well. Vladimir Putin undermined Russian sovereignty in Chechnya by allowing Kadyrov to pursue the strategy of building informal political control based on legal pluralism. While this increased the indispensability of Kadyrov to Putin, it also increased the indispensability of Putin to Russia's ruling class. Putin can control Kadyrov. But it is unclear whether a Russian leader other than Putin would be able to do so. What is undoubtedly known, is that this future hypothetical leader of Russia will have to deal with polygamy, honor killings, councils of elders, and Sharia law in Chechnya and thus on Russian territory. These issues are perhaps even harder to deal with than Kadyrov's personal army. In this light, Putin's policy in Chechnya can be seen as an attempt to further consolidate the view that no one other than him can manage Kadyrov, Chechnya, and – by implication – the stability of contemporary Russia. This is just a speculation, but as elsewhere in the book, the implication is that the Weberian version of state-building is frequently sacrificed when it comes to the political survival of the rulers.

References

Abu-Lughod, Lila. "Do Muslim women really need saving? Anthropological reflections on cultural relativism and its others." *American Anthropologist* 104, no. 3 (2002): 783–790.

Abubakarov, Taimaz. "Mezhdu avtoritarnost'iu i anarkhiey. Politicheskiye dilemmy Prezidenta Dudayeva" [Between authoritarianism and anarchy: Political dilemmas of President Dudayev]. In Furman Dmitry (ed.) *Chechnia i Rossiia: Obschchestva i gosudarstva* [Chechnya and Russia: Societies and states]. The Andrey Sakharov Fund, 1999.

Ahmed, Leila. *Women and gender in Islam: historical roots of a modern debate.* Yale University Press, 1992.

Akaev, Vakhit. *Islam: Sotsiokulturnaia realnost' na Severnom Kavkaze* [Islam: socio-cultural reality in the North Caucasus]. Rostov-on-Don, 2004.

——— *Sufiyskaia kultura na Severnom Kavkaze. Teoreticheskiy i prakticheskiy aspekty* [Sufi culture in the North Caucasus: Theoretical and practical aspects]. Grozny, 2011.

Akhmadov, Musa. *Chechenskaia traditsionnaia kultura i etika* [Chechen traditional culture and ethics]. Vainakh, 2006.

Albogachieva, Makka. "Blood feud in Ingushetia: differences in adat and sharia." In Voell and Kaliszewska (eds.) *State and legal practice in the Caucasus: anthropological perspectives on law and politics.* Ashgate Publishing, 2015.

Albogachieva, Makka, and Irina Babich. "Pravovaia kultura Ingushey: Istoriia i sovremennost" [Legal culture of Ingushs]. *Istoriia gosudarstva i prava* 19 (2009): 33–39.

——— "Krovnaia mest' v sovremennoy Ingushetii" [Blood revenge in contemporary Ingushetia]. *Ethnographicheskoye Obozreniye* 6 (2010): 133–140.

Aliroyev, Ibragim. *Yazyk, istoriia i kultura Vainakhov* [Language, history and culture of Vainakh people]. *Grozny*, 1990.

Aliroyev, Ibragim, and Zulai Khasbulatova. "Gostepriimstvo i kunachestvo" [Hospitality]. In Lubov' Soloviyeva, Zulai Khasbulatova, and Valery Tishkov (eds.) *Chechentsy.* [The Chechens]. Moscow, Bukinist. 2012.

Allina-Pisano, Jessica. "How to tell an axe murderer: An essay on ethnography, truth, and lies." in Schatz, Edward, ed. *Political ethnography: What immersion contributes to the study of power* (2009): 53–73.

Andrianova, Varvara. "The everyday experiences of Russian citizens in Justice of the Peace Courts." In Marina Kurkchiyan and Agnieszka Kubal (eds.) *A sociology of justice in Russia.* Cambridge University Press, 2018: p. 68.

Antonova, Yulia, and Saida Siradzhudinova. "'Ubitye spletniami': Ubiystva zhenschin po motivam 'chesti' na Severnom Kavkaze" ["Killed by the rumors": murder of women motivated by "Honor" in the North Caucasus]. In *Pravovaya Initsiativa Report,* 2018.

Arjona, Ana. *Rebelocracy.* Cambridge University Press, 2016.

Aspinall, Edward. *Islam and nation: separatist rebellion in Aceh, Indonesia.* Stanford University Press, 2009.

Avtorkhanov, Abdurakhman. *Imperiia Kreml'ia: Sovetskiy tip kolonializma* [The Kremlin's empire: The Soviet type of colonialism]. Prometheus Verlag, 1988.

Baev, Pavel. "Instrumentalizing counterterrorism for regime consolidation in Putin's Russia." *Studies in Conflict & Terrorism* 27, no. 4 (2004): 337–352.

Bakke, Kristin. "Help wanted? The mixed record of foreign fighters in domestic insurgencies." *International Security* 38, no. 4 (2014): 150–187.

Decentralization and intrastate struggles: Chechnya, Punjab, and Québec. Cambridge University Press, 2015.

Bakke, Kristin, Andrew Linke, John O'Loughlin, and Gerard Toal. "Dynamics of state-building after war: external-internal relations in Eurasian de facto states." *Political Geography* 63 (2018): 159–173.

Balcells, Laia. "The consequences of victimization on political identities: evidence from Spain." *Politics & Society* 40, no. 3 (2012): 311–347.

Rivalry and revenge. Cambridge University Press, 2017.

Balcells, Laia, and Patricia Justino. "Bridging micro and macro approaches on civil wars and political violence issues, challenges, and the way forward." *Journal of Conflict Resolution* 58, no. 8 (2014): 1343–1359.

Baldwin, Kate. *The paradox of traditional leaders in democratic Africa.* Cambridge University Press, 2016.

Barkey, Karen. *Bandits and bureaucrats.* Cornell University Press, 1994.

"Aspects of legal pluralism in the Ottoman Empire." In Benton and Ross (eds.) *Legal pluralism and empires, 1500–1850.* New York University Press, 2013: pp. 81–108.

Bateson, Regina Anne. *Order and violence in postwar Guatemala.* PhD diss. Yale University, 2013.

Bauer, Michal, Christopher Blattman, Julie Chytilová, Joseph Henrich, Edward Miguel, and Tamar Mitts. "Can war foster cooperation?" *Journal of Economic Perspectives* 30, no. 3 (2016): 249–274.

Baysaev, Usam, and Dmitriy Grushkin. *Zdes' zhivut liudi. Chechnia: Khronika nasiliia* [People live here. Chechnya: The chronicles of violence]. Parts 1–5. Memorial Publishing Program, 2003–2010.

Beissinger, Mark, and Stephen Kotkin, eds. *Historical legacies of communism in Russia and Eastern Europe.* Cambridge University Press, 2014.

Belge, Ceren. *Whose law? Clans, honor killings and state-minority relations in Turkey and Israel.* PhD diss. University of Washington, 2008.

Belge, Ceren, and Lisa Blaydes. "Social capital and dispute resolution in informal areas of Cairo and Istanbul." *Studies in Comparative International Development* 49, no. 4 (2014): 448–476.

Benhabib, Seyla. *The claims of culture: equality and diversity in the global era.* Princeton University Press, 2002.

Benton, Lauren. *Law and colonial cultures: legal regimes in world history, 1400–1900.* Cambridge University Press, 2002.

Benton, Lauren, and Richard J. Ross, eds. *Legal pluralism and empires. 1500–1850.* New York University Press, 2013.

Bergholz, Max. *Violence as a generative force: identity, nationalism, and memory in a Balkan community.* Cornell University Press, 2016.

Berkowitz, Daniel, Katharina Pistor, and Jean-Francois Richard. "The transplant effect." *American Journal of Comparative Law* 5, no. 1 (2003): 163–203.

Berman, Harold. *Law and revolution, the formation of the western legal tradition.* Harvard University Press, 1983.

Bernstein, Lisa. "Opting out of the legal system: extralegal contractual relations in the diamond industry." *Journal of Legal Studies* 21, no. 1 (1992): 115–157.

Berry, Marie. *War, women, and power: from violence to mobilization in Rwanda and Bosnia-Herzegovina.* Cambridge University Press, 2018.

Bersanova, Zalpa. "Sistema tsennostei sovremennykh chechentsev" [The system of values of contemporary Chechen society]. In Dmitry Furman (ed.) *Chechnia i Rossiia: Obschchestva i gosudarstva* [Chechnya and Russia: Societies and states]. Moscow: The Andrey Sakharov Fund, 1999.

"Obychai krovnoy mesti i praktika primireniia v sovremennoy Chechne" [The custom of blood revenge and the practice of reconciliation in contemporary Chechnya]. *Vestnik Vosstanovitelnoy Yustitsii* 8 (2011): 50–53.

Berwick, Elissa, and Fotini Christia. "State capacity redux: Integrating classical and experimental contributions to an enduring debate." *Annual Review of Political Science* 21 (2018): 71–91.

Beyer, Judith. *The force of custom: Law and the ordering of everyday life in Kyrgyzstan.* University of Pittsburgh Press, 2016.

Black, Donald. *The behavior of law.* Emerald Group Publishing, 1976.

Blair, Robert. *Peacekeeping, policing, and the rule of law after civil war.* Cambridge University Press, 2021.

Blaydes, Lisa. *State of repression: Iraq under Saddam Hussein.* Princeton University Press, 2018.

Bobrovnikov, Vladimir. *Musulmane Severnogo Kavkaza: Obychai, pravo, nasilie* [Muslims of the North Caucasus: Custom, law and violence]. Moscow: Vostochnaia Literatura, 2002.

Boone, Catherine. *Political topographies of the African state: Territorial authority and institutional choice.* Cambridge University Press, 2003.

Property and political order in Africa: Land rights and the structure of politics. Cambridge University Press, 2014.

Boucoyannis, Deborah. *Kings as judges: Power, justice, and the origins of Parliaments.* Cambridge University Press, 2021.

Bourdieu, Pierre. *Outline of a theory of practice.* Cambridge University Press, 1977.

Bowen, John Richard. *Islam, law, and equality in Indonesia: An anthropology of public reasoning*. Cambridge University Press, 2003.

Brauer, Birgit. "Chechens and the survival of their cultural identity in exile", *Journal of Genocide Research*, 4(3), 2002:

Brulé, Rachel. *Women, power, and property: The paradox of gender equality laws in India*. Cambridge University Press, 2020.

Buehler, Michael. *The politics of Shari'a law: Islamist activists and the state in democratizing Indonesia*. Cambridge University Press, 2016.

Bugaev, Abdulla. *Sovetskaia Avtonomiia Checheno-Ingushetii* [*The Soviet autonomy of Checheno-Ingushetia*]. KEP, 2012.

Burbank, Jane, and Frederick Cooper. *Empires in world history: Power and the politics of difference*. Princeton University Press, 2010.

"Rules of Law, Politics of Empire." In *Legal pluralism and empires, 1500–1850*. New York University Press, 2013: pp. 279–294.

Burbank, Jane. *Russian peasants go to court: Legal culture in the countryside, 1905–1917*. Indiana University Press, 2004.

"An imperial rights regime: Law and citizenship in the Russian Empire." *Kritika: Explorations in Russian and Eurasian History* 7, no. 3 (2006): 397–431.

Busch, Marc. "Overlapping institutions, forum shopping, and dispute settlement in international trade." *International Organization* 61, no. 4 (2007): 735–761.

Cameron, Sarah. *The hungry steppe: Famine, violence, and the making of Soviet Kazakhstan*. Cornell University Press, 2018.

Cammett, Melani. *Compassionate communalism: Welfare and sectarianism in Lebanon*. Cornell University Press, 2014.

Carter, Christopher. *States of extraction: The emergence and effects of indigenous autonomy in the Americas*. PhD diss. University of California, 2020.

Caspersen, Nina. *Unrecognized states: The struggle for sovereignty in the modern international system*. Polity Press, 2013.

Chagnon, Napoleon. "Life histories, blood revenge, and warfare in a tribal population." *Science* 239, no. 4843 (1988): 985–992.

Chanock, Martin. *Law, custom, and social order: The colonial experience in Malawi and Zambia*. Cambridge University Press, 1985.

Charrad, Mounira. *States and women's rights: The making of postcolonial Tunisia, Algeria, and Morocco*. University of California Press, 2001.

Cheng, Christine. *Extralegal groups in post-conflict Liberia: How trade makes the state*. Oxford University Press, 2018.

Chesnov Jan. "Zhenschina i etika zhizni v mentalitete Chechentsev" [Woman and ethics of life in Chechen mentality]. *Ethnographicheskoye Obozreniye* (1994): 109–110.

Chua, Lynette, and David Engel. "Legal consciousness reconsidered." *Annual Review of Law and Social Science* 15 (2019): 335–353.

Cohen, Jean, and Cecile Laborde. *Religion, secularism, and constitutional democracy*. Columbia University Press, 2016.

Comaroff, Jean, and John Comaroff, eds. *Law and disorder in the postcolony*. University of Chicago Press, 2008.

Cooper, Jasper. *State capacity and gender inequality: Experimental evidence from Papua New Guinea*. New York: Columbia University, 2018.

Cover, Robert. *Narrative, violence, and the law: the essays of Robert Cover*. University of Michigan Press, 1992.

Cramer, Katherine. *The politics of resentment: Rural consciousness in Wisconsin and the rise of Scott Walker*. University of Chicago Press, 2016.

Crews, Robert. *For prophet and tsar*. Harvard University Press, 2009.

Cronin-Furman, Kate, and Milli Lake. "Ethics abroad: Fieldwork in fragile and violent contexts." *PS: Political Science & Politics* 51, no. 3 (2018): 607–614.

Cruise O'Brien, Donal. *The Mourides of Senegal: The political and economic organization of an Islamic brotherhood*. Oxford. Clarendon Press, 1971.

Dalgat, Bashir. *Rodovoi byt i obychnoe pravo chechentsev i ingushey* [Family life and customary law of Chechens and Ingushs]. Moscow: IMLI RAN, 2008 [1934].

Daly, Samuel Fury Childs. *A History of the Republic of Biafra: Law, crime, and the Nigerian Civil War*. Cambridge University Press, 2020.

De Juan, Alexander. "'Traditional' resolution of land conflicts: The survival of precolonial dispute settlement in Burundi." *Comparative Political Studies* 50, no. 13 (2017): 1835–1868.

De Kadt, Daniel, and Horacio A. Larreguy. "Agents of the regime? Traditional leaders and electoral politics in South Africa." *The Journal of Politics* 80, no. 2 (2018): 382–399.

De Soto, Hermine G., and Nora Dudwick, eds. *Fieldwork dilemmas: Anthropologists in postsocialist states*. University of Wisconsin Press, 2000.

de Sousa Santos, Boaventura. *Toward a new legal common sense: Law, globalization, and emancipation*. Cambridge University Press, 2002.

Derluguian, Georgi. "Introduction. Whose Truth?" In Politkovskaya (ed.) *A Small Corner of Hell*, 2003.

Bourdieu's secret admirer in the Caucasus: A world-system biography. University of Chicago Press, 2005.

"Che Guevaras in turbans." *New Left Review* (2005): 3–27.

Díaz-Cayeros, Alberto, Beatriz Magaloni, and Alexander Ruiz-Euler. "Traditional governance, citizen engagement, and local public goods: evidence from Mexico." *World Development* 53 (2014): 80–93.

Driscoll, Jesse. *Warlords and coalition politics in Post-Soviet states*. Cambridge University Press, 2015.

Doing global fieldwork. Columbia University Press, 2021.

Driscoll Jesse, and Schuster Caroline. "Spies like us." *Ethnography* 19, no. 3 (2017): 411–30.

Dunlap Jr, Charles. "Lawfare today: A perspective." *Yale Journal of International Affairs, no. 3* (2008): 146.

Dunlop, John. *Russia confronts Chechnya: Roots of a separatist conflict*. Cambridge, 1998.

Eibl, Ferdinand, Steffen Hertog, and Dan Slater. "War makes the regime: regional rebellions and political militarization worldwide." *British Journal of Political Science* 51, no. 3 (2021): 1002–1023.

Ellickson, Robert. *Order without law: How neighbors settle disputes*. Harvard, 1991.

Elster, Jon. *The cement of society: A survey of social order*. Cambridge University Press, 1989.

Erie, Matthew. *China and Islam: The prophet, the party, and law*. Cambridge University Press, 2016.

Evangelista, Matthew. *The Chechen wars: Will Russia go the way of the Soviet Union?* Brookings Institution Press, 2002.

   Gender, nationalism, and war: Conflict on the movie screen. Cambridge University Press, 2011.

Evans-Pritchard, E. E. *The Nuer*. Oxford, 1944.

Ewick, Patricia, and Susan S. Silbey. *The common place of law: Stories from everyday life*. University of Chicago Press, 1998.

Fabbe, Kristin. *Disciples of the state?: Religion and state-building in the former Ottoman world*. Cambridge University Press, 2019.

Faludi, Susan. *Backlash: The undeclared war against American women*. New York: Three Rivers Press, 2006.

Felstiner, William, Richard Abel, and Austin Sarat. "The emergence and transformation of disputes: Naming, blaming, claiming..." *Law and Society Review* 15, no. 3/4 (1980): 631–654.

Finkel, Evgeny. *Ordinary Jews: Choice and survival during the Holocaust*. Princeton University Press, 2017.

Fraenkel, Ernst. *The dual state: A contribution to the theory of dictatorship*. New York, 1969.

Franco-Vivanco, Edgar. "Justice as checks and balances: Indigenous claims in the courts of colonial Mexico." *World Politics* 73, no. 4 (2021): 712-773.

Frye, Timothy. *Brokers and bureaucrats: Building market institutions in Russia*. University of Michigan Press, 2000.

Fu, Diana. *Mobilizing without the masses: Control and contention in China*. Cambridge University Press, 2018.

Fujii, Lee Ann. *Killing neighbors: Webs of violence in Rwanda*. Cornell University Press, 2009.

   "Shades of truth and lies: Interpreting testimonies of war and violence." *Journal of Peace Research* 47, no. 2 (2010): 231–241.

Furman, Dmitry, ed. *Chechnia i Rossiia: Obschchestva i gosudarstva* [Chechnya and Russia: Societies and states]. Moscow: The Andrey Sakharov Fund, 1999.

Gakaev, Jabrail. *Ocherki politicheskoy istorii Chechni (XX vek)* [*Essays on political history of Chechnya*]. Moscow, 1997.

   "Put' k chechnskoy revolutsii" [The path to Chechen revolution]. In Dmitry Furman (ed.) *Chechnia i Rossiya: Obschchestva i gosudarstva* [Chechnya and Russia: Societies and states]. Moscow: The Andrey Sakharov Fund, 1999.

Galanter, Marc. "Justice in many rooms: Courts, private ordering, and indigenous law." *The Journal of Legal Pluralism and Unofficial Law* 13, no. 19 (1981): 1–47.

Gall, Carlotta, and Thomas De Waal. *Chechnya: Small victorious war*. Pan Original, 1997.

Gallagher, Mary. *Authoritarian legality in China: Law, workers, and the state*. Cambridge University Press, 2017.

Gambetta, Diego. *The Sicilian mafia: The business of private protection*. Harvard University Press, 1993.

Gammer, Moshe. *Muslim resistance to the Tsar: Shamil and the conquest of Chechnia and Daghestan*. Taylor & Francis, 1994.

Gans-Morse, Jordan. *Property rights in post-Soviet Russia*. Cambridge University Press, 2017.

Gapurov, Shahrudin. *Rossiia i Chechnia: posledniaia tret' XVIII–pervaia polovina XIX veka* [Russia and Chechnya: Late 18th–early 19th century]. Grozny: Academy of Sciences, 2009.

García-Ponce, Omar. "Women's Political Participation After Civil War: Evidence from Peru." Unpublished manuscript, 2017.

Geertz, Clifford. "Local knowledge: fact and law in comparative perspective." *Local Knowledge: Further Essays in Interpretive Anthropology* 175 (1983): 215–234.

Gel'man, Vladimir, and Cameron Ross, eds. *The politics of sub-national authoritarianism in Russia*. Ashgate Publishing, Ltd, 2010.

Gibson, Edward. *Boundary control: Subnational authoritarianism in federal democracies*. Cambridge University Press, 2013.

Gilligan, Emma. *Terror in Chechnya: Russia and the tragedy of civilians in war*. Princeton University Press, 2009.

"Propaganda and the question of criminal intent; the semantics of the Zachistka." *Europe-Asia Studies* 68, no. 6 (2016): 1036–1066.

"Chechen compensation cases: War crimes, domestic litigation, and moral harm in the Russian Federation." *Journal of Comparative Law* 37, no. 2 (2020): 37.

Ginsburg, Tom. "Rebel use of law and courts." *Annual Review of Law and Social Science* 15 (2019): 495–507.

Giraudy, Agustina, Eduardo Moncada, and Richard Snyder, eds. *Inside countries: Subnational research in comparative politics*. Cambridge University Press, 2019.

Giustozzi, Antonio and Adam Baczko. "The politics of the Taliban's shadow judiciary, 2003–2013." *Central Asian Affairs* 1, no. 2 (2014): 199–224.

Gluckman, Max. "The peace in the feud." *Past and Present* 8, no. 1 (1955): 1–14

Gould, Rebecca, and Shamil Shikhaliev. "Beyond the Taqlīd/Ijtihād Dichotomy: Daghestani Legal Thought under Russian Rule." *Islamic Law and Society* 24, no. 1–2 (2017): 142–169.

Gould, Rebecca. *Writers and Rebels: The literature of insurgency in the Caucasus*. Yale University Press, 2016.

Grant, Bruce. *The captive and the gift: Cultural histories of sovereignty in Russia and the Caucasus*. Cornell University Press, 2009.

Green, Linda. "Living in a state of fear." In Antonius Robben and Carolyn Nordstrom (eds.) *Fieldwork under fire: Contemporary studies of violence and survival*. Berkeley: University of California Press, 1995.

Greif, Avner. *Institutions and the path to the modern economy: Lessons from medieval trade*. Cambridge University Press, 2006.

Griffiths, John. "What is legal pluralism?" *The Journal of Legal Pluralism and Unofficial Law* 18, no. 24 (1986): 1–55.

Grzymala-Busse, Anna, and Pauline Jones Luong. "Reconceptualizing the state: lessons from post-communism." *Politics & Society* 30, no. 4 (2002): 529–554.

Gutiérrez-Sanín, Francisco, and Elisabeth Jean Wood. "What should we mean by 'pattern of political violence'? Repertoire, targeting, frequency, and technique." *Perspectives on Politics* 15, no. 1 (2017): 20–41.

Hallaq, Wael. *The impossible state: Islam, politics, and modernity's moral predicament*. Columbia University Press, 2014.

Halliday, Paul. "Laws' Histories." In Benton and Ross (eds.) *Legal pluralism and empires, 1500–1850*. New York University Press, 2013: pp. 259–278.

Hassan, Mai, Daniel Mattingly, and Elizabeth Nugent. "Political control." *Annual Review of Political Science* 25 (2022): 6.1 – 6.20.

Heathershaw, John, and Edward Schatz, eds. *Paradox of power: The logics of state weakness in Eurasia*. University of Pittsburgh Press, 2017.

Hefner, Robert W., ed. *Shari'a politics: Islamic law and society in the modern world*. Indiana University Press, 2011.

Helmke, Gretchen, and Steven Levitsky. "Informal institutions and comparative politics: A research agenda." *Perspectives on politics* 2, no. 4 (2004): 725–740.

Hemment, Julie. *Empowering women in Russia: Activism, aid, and NGOs*. Indiana University Press, 2007.

Hendley, Kathryn. "The unsung heroes of the Russian judicial system: The justice-of-the-peace courts." *Journal of Eurasian Law* 5, no. 337 (2012).

Everyday law in Russia. Cornell University Press, 2017.

Herbst, Jeffrey. *States and power in Africa: Comparative lessons in authority and control*. Princeton University Press, 2000.

Hirsch, Francine. *Empire of nations: Ethnographic knowledge and the making of the Soviet Union*. Cornell University Press, 2005.

Hirsch, Susan. *Pronouncing and persevering: Gender and the discourses of disputing in an African Islamic court*. University of Chicago Press, 1998.

Hobsbawm, Eric, and Terence Ranger, eds. *The invention of tradition*. Cambridge University Press, 1983.

Hoebel, E. Adamson. *The law of primitive man: A study in comparative legal dynamics*. Cambridge: Harvard University Press, 1954.

Holland, Alisha. *Forbearance as redistribution: The politics of informal welfare in Latin America*. Cambridge University Press, 2017.

Holzinger, Katharina, Roos Haer, Axel Bayer, Daniela M. Behr, and Clara Neupert-Wentz. "The constitutionalization of indigenous group rights, traditional political institutions, and customary law." *Comparative Political Studies* 52, no. 12 (2019): 1775–1809.

Hooker, Michael. *Legal pluralism: An introduction to colonial and neo-colonial laws*. Oxford University Press, 1975.

Htun, Mala. *Sex and the state: Abortion, divorce, and the family under Latin American dictatorships and democracies*. Cambridge University Press, 2003.

Htun, Mala, and S. Laurel Weldon. *The logics of gender justice: State action on women's rights around the world*. Cambridge University Press, 2018.

Hudson, Valerie M, Donna Lee Bowen, and P.L. Nielsen. "Clan governance and state stability: The relationship between female subordination and political order." *American Political Science Review* 109, no. 03 (2015): 535–555.

Hughes, James. *Chechnya: From nationalism to jihad*. University of Pennsylvania Press, 2007.

Hughes, Melanie "Armed conflict, international linkages, and women's parliamentary representation in developing nations." *Social Problems* 56, no. 1 (2009): 174–204.

Hussin, Iza. *The politics of Islamic law: Local elites, colonial authority, and the making of the Muslim state*. University of Chicago Press, 2016.

Iliyasov, Marat. "Researching the Chechen diaspora in Europe." *Interdisciplinary Political Studies* 3, no. 1 (2017): 201–218.

Isser, Deborah. *Customary justice and the rule of law in war-torn societies*. US Institute of Peace Press, 2011.

Jacobs, Alan et al. "The qualitative transparency deliberations: Insights and implications." *Perspectives on Politics* 19, no. 1 (2021): 171–208.

Jamal, Amaney, and Mark Tessler. "Attitudes in the Arab world." *Journal of Democracy* 19, no. 1 (2008): 97–110.

Jerolmack, Colin, and Shamus Khan. "Talk is cheap: Ethnography and the attitudinal fallacy." *Sociological Methods & Research* 43, no. 2 (2014): 178–209.

Johnson, Janet Elise, and Aino Saarinen. "Twenty-first century feminisms under repression: Gender regime change and the women's crisis center movement in Russia." *Signs: Journal of Women in Culture and Society* 38, no. 3 (2013): 543–567.

Johnson, Janet Elise. "Fast-tracked or boxed in? Informal politics, gender, and women's representation in Putin's Russia." *Perspectives on Politics* 14, no. 3 (2016): 643–659.

Jones Luong, Pauline, ed. *The transformation of Central Asia: States and societies from Soviet rule to independence*. Cornell University Press, 2004.

Kadyrov, Akhmat. *Rossiysko-chechenskiy konflikt (genezis, suschnost', puti reshenia)* [Russo-Chechen conflict: Genesis, nature, and paths to resolution]. PhD diss. Russian Academy of Sciences, 2003.

Kaliszewska, Iwona, and Maciej Falkowski. *Veiled and unveiled in Chechnya and Daghestan*. London, 2016.

Kalyvas, Stathis. *The logic of violence in civil war*. Cambridge University Press, 2006.

"Ethnic defection in civil war." *Comparative Political Studies* 41, no. 8 (2008): 1043–1068.

Kamp, Marianne. *The new woman in Uzbekistan: Islam, modernity, and unveiling under communism*. University of Washington Press, 2006.

Kandiyoti, Deniz. "Bargaining with patriarchy." *Gender & society* 2, no. 3 (1988): 274–290.

Karpov, Yuri. *Zhenskoe prostrantsvo v kulture narodov Kavkaza* [Women's space in the culture of the peoples of the Caucasus]. St. Petersburg, 2001.

Kazenin, Konstantin. "Sotsiologiia islamskogo i obychnogo prava v postkonflikt-nom uregulirovanii" [Sociology of Islamic and traditional law in post-conflict regulation]. *Mir Islama* 2 (2013): 112–136.

"Perspektivy institutsionalnogo podkhoda k yavleniiu poliyuridizma na pri-mere Severnogo Kavkaza" [Prospects for an institutional approach to the phenomenon of the polyjuridicism on the example of the North Caucasus]. *Ekonomicheskaya Politika* 3 (2014): 178–198.

"Uregulirovaniye konfliktov na Severnom Kavkaze: rol' neformalnykh pravo-vykh mekhanizmov" [Conflict management in the North Caucasus: the role of informal legal mechanisms]. *Obschestvennye Nauki i Sovremennost* 2 (2016): 144–154.

Kemper, Michael. "Adat against Shari'a: Russian approaches toward Daghestani 'customary law' in the 19th century." *Ab Imperio* 3 (2005): 147–173.

Kendhammer, Brandon. *Muslims talking politics: Framing Islam, democracy, and law in Northern Nigeria.* University of Chicago Press, 2016.

Khaikin, Sergei, and Natalia Cherenkova. "Izuchenie obschestvennogo mnenia Chechenskoy Respubliki" [Studying public opinion in the Chechen Republic]. *Mir Rossii* 12, no. 3 (2003): 3–34.

Khasbulatova, Zulai. *Vospitanie detey u Chechentsev: Obychai i traditsii (XIX–early XX)* [Child rearing among Chechens: Customs and traditions (19–20th centuries)], 2007.

Khasiev, Said-Magomed. *Chehentsev drevniaia zemlia* [The ancient land of Chechens]. *Saint-Petersburg*: Seda, 1994.

Khodarkovsky, Michael. *Bitter choices: Loyalty and betrayal in the Russian conquest of the North Caucasus.* Cornell University Press, 2011.

King, Charles. "The benefits of ethnic war: understanding Eurasia's unrecognized states." *World Politics* 53, no. 4 (2001): 524–552.

The ghost of freedom: A history of the Caucasus. Oxford University Press, 2008.

Kirmse, Stefan. *The lawful empire: Legal change and cultural diversity in late Tsarist Russia.* Cambridge University Press, 2019.

Kittrie, Orde. *Lawfare: Law as a weapon of war.* Oxford University Press, 2016.

Klyachkina, Alexandra. *Reconfiguration of sub-national governance: Responses to violence and state collapse in the North Caucasus.* PhD diss. Northwestern University, 2019.

Knott, Eleanor. "Beyond the field: ethics after fieldwork in politically dynamic contexts." *Perspectives on Politics* 17, no. 1(2019): 140–153.

Knysh, Alexander. "Contextualizing the Salafi–Sufi conflict (from the Northern Caucasus to Hadramawt)." *Middle Eastern Studies* 43, no. 4 (2007): 503–530.

Kolstø, Pål. "The sustainability and future of unrecognized quasi-states." *Journal of Peace Research* 43, no. 6 (2006): 723–740.

Kovalevsky, Maksim. *Zakon i obychai na Kavkaze* [Law and custom in the Caucasus]. *Moscow*, 1890.

Kozlov V.A. et al. *Vainakhi i imperskaia vlast: Problema Chechni i Ingushetii vo vnutrennei politike Rossii i SSSR (nachalo XIX–seredina XX veka)* [Vainakhs and imperial authority: Chechnya and Ingushtia in domestic politics of Russia and the USSR (early 19th–mid 20th century)]. Moscow: ROSSPEN, 2011.

Kramer, Mark. "The perils of counterinsurgency: Russia's war in Chechnya." *International Security* 29, no. 3 (2005): 5–63.

Krause, Peter. "Navigating born and chosen identities in fieldwork." In Krause and Szekely (eds.) *Stories from the field: A guide to navigating fieldwork in political science*. Columbia University Press, 2020.

Kurbanova, Lida. *Problemy i protsessy gendernoy samoidentifikatsii Chechentsev* [Problems and processes of gender identification among the Chechens]. Krasnodar, Russia, 2012.

Laitin, David. "The Sharia debate and the origins of Nigeria's second republic." *The Journal of Modern African Studies* 20, no. 3 (1982): 411–430.

Lake, David. *The statebuilder's dilemma: On the limits of foreign intervention.* Cornell University Press, 2016.

Lake, Milli. "Building the rule of war: Postconflict institutions and the micro-dynamics of conflict in Eastern DR Congo." *International Organization* 71, no. 2 (2017): 281–315.

Strong NGOs and weak states: Pursuing gender justice in the Democratic Republic of Congo and South Africa. Cambridge University Press, 2018.

Laruelle, Marlène. *Kadyrovism: Hardline Islam as a tool of the Kremlin?* IFRI, 2017.

Lazarev, Egor. "Laws in conflict: legacies of war, gender, and legal pluralism in Chechnya." *World Politics* 71, no. 4 (2019): 667–709.

Lazarus-Black, Mindie, and Susan Hirsch, eds. *Contested states: Law, hegemony and resistance.* Routledge, 1994.

Le Huérou, Anne, Aude Merlin, Amandine Regamey, and Elisabeth Sieca-Kozlowski. *Chechnya at war and beyond.* New York: Routledge, 2014.

Lehoucq, Emilio, and Whitney K. Taylor. "Conceptualizing legal mobilization: How should we understand the deployment of legal strategies?" *Law & Social Inquiry* 45, no. 1 (2020): 166–193.

Leontovich, Fedor. *Adaty Kavkazskikh Gortsev* [The customs of the Caucasian mountaineers], vol. 2. Odessa, 1882.

Lichtenheld, Adam. "Explaining population displacement strategies in civil wars: a cross-national analysis." *International Organization* 74, no. 2 (2020): 253–294.

Liebman, Benjamin, Margaret Roberts, Rachel Stern, and Alice Wang. "Mass digitization of Chinese court decisions: How to use text as data in the field of Chinese law." *Journal of Law and Courts* 8, no. 2 (2020): 177–201.

Lieven, Anatol. *Chechnya: Tombstone of Russian power.* Yale University Press, 1998.

Lokshina, Tanya. "Virtue campaign for women in Chechnya under Ramzan Kadyrov: Between war backlash effect and desire for total control." In Anne Le Huérou, Aude Merlin, Amandine Regamey, and Elisabeth Sieca-Kozlowski (eds.) *Chechnya at war and beyond.* New York: Routledge, 2014: pp. 236–255.

Lubkemann, Stephen, Deborah Isser, and Peter Chapman. "Neither state nor custom – just naked power: the consequences of ideals-oriented rule of law policy-making in Liberia." *The Journal of Legal Pluralism and Unofficial Law* 43, no. 63 (2001): 73–109.

Lupu, Noam, and Leonid Peisakhin. "The legacy of political violence across generations." *American Journal of Political Science* 61, no. 4 (2017): 836–851.

Lyall, Jason. "Does indiscriminate violence incite insurgent attacks? Evidence from Chechnya." *Journal of Conflict Resolution* 53, no. 3 (2009): 331–362.

———. "Are coethnics more effective counterinsurgents? Evidence from the second Chechen war." *American Political Science Review* 104, no. 1 (2010): 1–20.

Macaulay, Stewart. "Non-contractual relations in business: A preliminary study." *American Sociological Review* 28 (1963): 55–67.

McCarthy, Lauren. *Trafficking Justice: How Russian police enforce new laws, from crime to courtroom.* Cornell University Press, 2015.

Mahmood, Saba. *Politics of piety: The Islamic revival and the feminist subject.* Princeton University Press, 2011.

Makarov, Dmitri. "Enacting the Sharia Laws in a Dagestani village." *ISIM newsletter* 1, no. 19, 1998.

Malashenko, Aleksei. *Ramzan Kadyrov: rossiyiskiy politik kavkazskoy natsionalnosti* [Ramzan Kadyrov: Russian politician of Caucasian nationality]. Moscow: ROSSPEN, 2009.

Malashenko, Aleksei, and Dmitry Trenin. *Vremia yuga: Rossiia v Chechne, Chechnia v Rossii* [The time of the South: Russia in Chechnya, Chechnya in Russia]. Moscow: Gendalf, 2002.

Malejacq, Romain, and Dipali Mukhopadhyay. "The 'tribal politics' of field research: A reflection on power and partiality in 21st-century warzones." *Perspectives on Politics* 14, no. 4 (2016): 1011–1028.

Malinowski, Bronislaw. *Crime and Custom in Savage Society. Transaction Publishers,* 1926.

Mamakaev Magomet. *Chechenskiy teip (rod) v period ego razlozheniia* [Chechen clan in the period of decay]. Grozny, 1973.

Mamdani, Mahmood. *Citizen and subject: Contemporary Africa and the legacy of late colonialism.* Princeton University Press, 1996.

Mampilly, Zachariah Cherian. *Rebel rulers: Insurgent governance and civilian life during war.* Cornell University Press, 2012.

———. "The Field is Everywhere." Krause and Szekely. *Stories from the Field: A guide to navigating fieldwork in political science.* Columbia University Press: pp. 277–285.

Mann, Michael. "The autonomous power of the state: its origins, mechanisms and results." *European Journal of Sociology/Archives européennes de sociologie* 25, no. 2 (1984): 185–213.

Marks, Zoe. "Gender, social networks and conflict processes." *feminists@ law* 9, no. 1 (2019).

Marten, Kimberly. *Warlords: Strong-arm brokers in weak states.* Cornell University Press, 2012.

Martin, Terry. *The affirmative action empire: Nations and nationalism in the Soviet Union, 1923–1939.* Cornell University Press, 2001.

Massell, Gregory. *The surrogate proletariat: Moslem women and revolutionary strategies in Soviet Central Asia, 1919–1929.* Princeton University Press Princeton, NJ, 1974.

Massoud, Mark Fathi. *Law's fragile state: Colonial, authoritarian, and humanitarian legacies in Sudan.* Cambridge University Press, 2013.

"Work rules: How international NGOs build law in war-torn societies." *Law & Society Review* 49, no. 2 (2015): 333–364.

"Field research on law in conflict zones and authoritarian states." *Annual Review of Law and Social Science* 12 (2016): 85–106.

Shari'a, Inshallah: Finding God in Somali legal politics. Cambridge University Press, 2021.

Mattingly, Daniel. *The art of political control in China.* Cambridge University Press, 2020.

McCann, Michael. *Rights at work: Pay equity reform and the politics of legal mobilization.* University of Chicago Press, 1994.

Meierhenrich, Jens. *The remnants of the Rechtsstaat: An ethnography of Nazi law.* Oxford University Press, 2018.

Menkhaus, Ken. "Governance without government in Somalia: Spoilers, state building, and the politics of coping." *International Security* 31, no. 3 (2006): 74–106.

Merlin, Aude. "The Postwar Period in Chechnya: When Spoilers Jeopardize the Emerging Chechen State (1996–1999)." In N. Duclos (ed.) *War veterans in postwar situations: Chechnya, Serbia, Turkey, Peru, and Côte d'Ivoire.* Macmillan, Palgrave, 2012: pp. 219–239.

Merry, Sally Engle. "Legal pluralism." *Law and Society Review* 22 (1988): 869–896.

Getting justice and getting even: Legal consciousness among working-class Americans. University of Chicago Press, 1990.

Colonizing Hawai'i: The cultural power of law. Princeton University Press, 2000.

Human rights and gender violence: Translating international law into local justice. Chicago, IL: University of Chicago Press, 2006.

Messick, Brinkley. *The calligraphic state: Textual domination and history in a Muslim society.* University of California Press, 1996.

Shari'a scripts: A historical anthropology. Columbia University Press, 2017.

Mezhidov, Jamal, and Ibragim Aliroyev. *Chechentsy: Obychaii, traditsii, nravy: Sotsialno-filosofskiy aspekt* [Chechens: Customs, traditions, manners]. Grozny: Kniga, 1992.

Migdal, Joel. *Strong societies and weak states: State-society relations and state capabilities in the Third World.* Princeton University Press, 1988.

State in society: Studying how states and societies transform and constitute one another. Cambridge University Press, 2001.

Mir-Hosseini, Ziba. *Marriage on trial: A study of Islamic family law.* IB Tauris, 1993.

Misrokov, Zamir. *Adat i Shariat v Rossiyskoy pravovoy sisteme. Istoricheskiye sud'by yuridicheskogo pluralizma na Severnom Kavkaze* [Adat and Sharia in Russian legal system: The history of legal pluralism in the North Caucasus]. Moscow State University, 2002.

Moore, Sally Falk. "Law and social change: the semi-autonomous social field as an appropriate subject of study." *Law & Society Review* 7, no. 4 (1973): 719–746.

Social facts and fabrications. "Customary" law on Kilimanjaro, 1880–1980. Cambridge University Press, 1986.

Mosedale, Sarah. "Assessing women's empowerment: Towards a conceptual framework." *Journal of International Development* 17, no. 2 (2005): 243–257.

Moustafa, Tamir. "Law and courts in authoritarian regimes." *Annual Review of Law and Social Science* 10 (2014): 281–299.

Constituting religion: Islam, liberal rights, and the Malaysian state. Cambridge University Press, 2018.

Mukhopadhyay, Dipali. *Warlords, strongman governors, and the state in Afghanistan.* Cambridge University Press, 2014.

Murphy, Paul. *Allah's angels: Chechen women in war.* Naval Institute Press, 2011.

Murtazashvili, Jennifer Brick. *Informal order and the state in Afghanistan.* Cambridge University Press, 2016.

Mustasilta, Katariina. "Including chiefs, maintaining peace? Examining the effects of state–traditional governance interaction on civil peace in sub-Saharan Africa." *Journal of Peace Research* 56, no. 2 (2019), 203–219.

Muzaev, Timur. *Chechenskiy krisis 99: Politicheskoe protivostoianie v Ichkerii* [The Chechen crisis of 99: Political confrontation in Ichkeria]. Panorama, 1999.

Souz Gortsev. Russkaia Revolutsiia i narody Severnogo Kavkaza [The union of the mountaineers. Russian Revolution and the peoples of the North Caucasus]. Patria, 2007.

Nader, Laura, and Harry Todd. *The disputing process: Law in ten societies.* Columbia University Press, 1978.

Nair, Gautam, and Nicholas Sambanis. "Violence exposure and ethnic identification: Evidence from Kashmir." *International Organization* 73, no. 2 (2019): 329–363.

Nanaeva, Baret. *Traditsionnoye obschestvo Chechentsev: Sotciokulturnyi analiz* [Traditional society of Chechens: Socio-cultural analysis]. Moscow: *ISPI RAN*, 2012.

Nichols, Johanna. "The Chechen refugees" *Berkeley Journal of International Law* 18 (2000): 241.

Nielsen, Richard. "Recite! Interpretive fieldwork for positivists." In Krause and Szekely (eds.) *Stories from the field: A guide to navigating fieldwork in political science.* Columbia University Press: pp. 36–46.

Nivat, Anne. "The black widows: Chechen women join the fight for independence – and Allah." *Studies in Conflict & Terrorism* 28, no. 5 (2005): 413–419.

North, Douglass, John Joseph Wallis, and Barry Weingast. *Violence and social orders: A conceptual framework for interpreting recorded human history.* Cambridge University Press, 2009.

Northrop, Douglas. *Veiled empire: Gender and power in Stalinist Central Asia.* Cornell University Press, 2004.

Oliker, Olga. *Russia's Chechen wars 1994–2000: Lessons from urban combat.* Rand Corporation, 2001.

Orlov, Oleg, and Alexander Cherkasov. *Rossiia-Chechnia: Tsep' oshibok i prestupleniy* [Russia-Chechnya: The chain of mistakes and crimes]. Moscow, Russia: Zveniya, 1998.

Osanloo, Arzoo. *The politics of women's rights in Iran.* Princeton University Press, 2009.

Osmaev, Abbaz. *Obschestvenno-politicheskaia i povsednevnaia zhizn' Chechenskoy Respubliki v 1996–2005* [Society, politics, and everyday life in Chechen Republic in 1996–2005]. PhD diss. Makhachkala, 2010.

Ostrom, Elinor. *Governing the commons.* Cambridge University Press, 1990.

Oushakine, Serguei. *The patriotism of despair: Nation, war, and loss in Russia.* Cornell University Press. Ithaca, 2009.

Pankhurst, Donna. *Gendered peace: Women's struggles for post-war justice and reconciliation.* Routledge, 2012.

Parkinson, Sarah Elizabeth. *"Organizing rebellion: Rethinking high-risk mobilization and social networks in war."* American Political Science Review (2013): 418–432.

Petersen, Roger. *Resistance and rebellion: Lessons from Eastern Europe.* Cambridge University Press, 2001.

Pisani, Elizabeth, and Michael Buehler. "Why do Indonesian politicians promote shari'a laws? An analytic framework for Muslim-majority democracies." *Third World Quarterly* 38, no. 3 (2017): 734–752.

Politkovskaya, Anna, *A small corner of hell: Dispatches from Chechnya.* University of Chicago Press, 2007:
A dirty war. Russian reporter in the Caucasus. Random House, 2009.

Pop-Eleches, Grigore, and Joshua A. Tucker. *Communism's shadow: Historical legacies and contemporary political attitudes.* Princeton University Press, 2017.

Popova, Maria. *Politicized justice in emerging democracies: a study of courts in Russia and Ukraine.* Cambridge University Press, 2012.

Pospisil, Leopold. *Anthropology of law: A comparative theory.* New Haven: HRAF Press, 1974.

Procházková, Petra. *The aluminum queen: The Russian-Chechen war through the eyes of women.* Prague, Czech Republic: NLN, 2002.

Ratelle, Jean-François, and Emil Aslan Souleimanov. "A perfect counterinsurgency? Making sense of Moscow's policy of Chechenisation." *Europe-Asia Studies* 68, no. 8 (2016): 1287–1314.

Reno, William. *Warlord politics and African states.* Lynne Rienner Publishers, 1999.
"Shadow states and the political economy of civil wars." In Mats Berdal and David M. Malone (eds.) *Greed and grievance: Economic agendas in civil wars.* Boulder, CO: Lynne Rienner, 2000.

Revkin, Mara. "The legal foundations of the Islamic State." *The Brookings Project on US Relations with the Islamic World* 23, 2016.

Rosen, Lawrence. *The anthropology of justice: Law as culture in Islamic society.* Cambridge University Press, 1989.

Rozenas, Arturas, Sebastian Schutte, and Yuri Zhukov. "The political legacy of violence: The long-term impact of Stalin's repression in Ukraine." *Journal of Politics* 79, no. 4 (2017): 1147–1161.

Saidumov, Dzhambulat. *Sud, pravo i pravosudie u Chechentsev i Ingushey (XVIII–XX)* [Courts and law among Chechens and Ingushs]. PhD diss. Grozny, 2012.

Sakwa, Richard, ed. *Chechnya: From past to future*. Anthem Press, 2005.

Sandefur, Justin, and Bilal Siddiqi. "Delivering justice to the poor: theory and experimental evidence from Liberia." In *World Bank Workshop on African Political Economy*, vol. 20, *Washington, DC, May*, 2013.

Sartori, Paolo. *Visions of justice: Sharīʿa and cultural change in Russian Central Asia*. Brill, 2016.

Schatz, Edward, ed. *Political ethnography: What immersion contributes to the study of power*. University of Chicago Press, 2009.

Scheppele, Kim Lane. "Autocratic legalism." *The University of Chicago Law Review* 85, no. 2 (2018): 545–584.

Schwedler, Jillian. "The third gender: Western female researchers in the Middle East." *PS: Political Science and Politics* 39, no. 3 (2006): 425–428.

Scott, James C. *Weapons of the weak: Everyday forms of peasant resistance*. Yale University Press, 1985.

    The art of not being governed: An anarchist history of upland Southeast Asia. Yale University Press, 2009.

Semyonov, Alexander. "The ambiguity of federalism as a postimperial political vision: Editorial introduction." *Ab Imperio* 3 (2018): 23–30.

Sezgin, Yüksel, and Mirjam Künkler. "Regulation of "religion" and the "religious": The politics of judicialization and bureaucratization in India and Indonesia." *Comparative Studies in Society and History* 56, no. 2 (2014): 448–478.

Sezgin, Yüksel. *Human rights under state-enforced religious family laws in Israel, Egypt and India*. Cambridge University Press, 2013.

Shahnazarian, Nona. V tesnykh obiatiiakh traditsii: Patriarkhat i voina. [In the tight embrace of tradition: Patriarchy and war]. Aleteyia, St. Petersburg, 2011.

Sharafi, Mitra. *Law and identity in colonial South Asia: Parsi legal culture, 1772–1947*. Cambridge University Press, 2014.

Sharafutdinova, Gulnaz. "Chechnya versus Tatarstan: Understanding ethnopolitics in post-communist Russia." *Problems of Post-Communism* 47, no. 2 (2000): 13–22.

Shen-Bayh, Fiona. *Undue process. Persecution and punishment in autocratic courts*. Cambridge University Press, 2022.

Shesterinina, Anastasia. "Ethics, empathy, and fear in research on violent conflict." *Journal of Peace Research* 56, no. 2 (2019): 190–202.

    Mobilizing in uncertainty: Collective identities and war in Abkhazia. Cornell University Press, 2021.

Sjoberg, Laura. *Gender, war, and conflict*. John Wiley & Sons, 2014

Skarbek, David. *The social order of the underworld: How prison gangs govern the American penal system*. Oxford University Press, 2014.

Slater, Dan. *Ordering power: Contentious politics and authoritarian leviathans in Southeast Asia.* Cambridge University Press, 2010.

Slezkine, Yuri. "The fall of Soviet ethnography, 1928–38." *Current Anthropology* 32, no. 4 (1991): 476–484.

Smith, Nicholas Rush. *Contradictions of democracy: Vigilantism and rights in post-apartheid South Africa.* Oxford University Press, 2019.

Snyder, Francis. "Colonialism and legal form: The creation of 'customary law' in Senegal." *The Journal of Legal Pluralism and Unofficial Law* 13, no. 19 (1981): 49–90.

Snyder, Jack. *From voting to violence: Democratization and nationalist conflict.* New York, 2000.

Sokirianskaia, Ekaterina. *Governing fragmented societies: State-building and political integration in Chechnya and Ingushetia (1991–2009).* PhD diss. Central European University, 2009.

Soloviyeva, Lubov', Zulai Khasbulatova, and Valery Tishkov, eds. *Chechentsy* [The Chechens]. Moscow, Bukinist, 2012.

Souleimanov, Emil Aslan. "Building trust with ex-insurgents." In Krause and Szekely (eds.) *Stories from the field: A guide to navigating fieldwork in political science.* Columbia University Press, 2020.

Souleimanov, Emil Aslan, and Huseyn Aliyev. "Asymmetry of values, indigenous forces, and incumbent success in counterinsurgency: evidence from Chechnya." *Journal of Strategic Studies* 38, no. 5 (2015): 678–703.

"Blood revenge and violent mobilization: Evidence from the Chechen wars." *International Security* 40, no. 2 (2015): 158–180.

How socio-cultural codes shaped violent mobilization and pro-insurgent support in the Chechen wars. Springer, 2017.

Souleimanov, Emil Aslan, and David S. Siroky. "Random or retributive: Indiscriminate violence in the Chechen wars." *World Politics* 68 (2016): 677.

Spector, Regine A. *Order at the bazaar: Power and trade in Central Asia.* Cornell University Press, 2017.

Staniland, Paul. "States, insurgents, and wartime political orders." *Perspectives on Politics* 10, no. 2: 243–264.

Starodubrovskaya, Irina. "Sotsialnaia transformatsia i mezhpokolencheskiy konflikt (na primere Severnogo Kavkaza)" [Social transformation and intergenerational conflict (the case of the North Caucasus)]. *Obschestvennye Nauki i Sovremennost'* 6 (2016): 111–124.

"Krizis traditsionnoy severokavkazskoy sem'i v postsovetskiy period i ego sotsialnye posledstviia" [The crisis of traditional North Caucasian family in the post-Soviet period and its social consequences]. *Jurnal Issledovaniy Sotsialnoy Politiki* 17, no. 1 (2019).

Steele, Abbey. *Democracy and displacement in Colombia's civil war.* Cornell University Press, 2017.

Stern, Rachel. *Environmental litigation in China: A study in political ambivalence.* New York: Cambridge University Press, 2013.

Sugaipova, Maryam, and Julie Wilhelmsen. "The Chechen post-war diaspora in Norway and their visions of legal models." *Caucasus Survey* (2021): 19.

Swenson, Geoffrey. "Why US efforts to promote the rule of law in Afghanistan failed." *International Security* 42, no. 1 (2017): 114–151.

"Legal pluralism in theory and practice." *International Studies Review* 20, no. 3 (2018): 438–462.

Szczepanikova, Alice. "Chechen refugees in Europe: How three generations of women settle in exile." In Le Huerou et al. (eds.) *Chechnya and war and beyond*. Routledge, 2014.

"Chechen women in war and exile: changing gender roles in the context of violence." *Nationalities Papers* 43, no. 5 (2015): 753–770.

Tamanaha, Brian. "The folly of the 'social scientific' concept of legal pluralism." *Journal of Law and Society* 20, no. 2 (1993): 192–217.

Legal pluralism explained: History, theory, consequences. Oxford University Press, 2021.

Taylor, Brian. *State building in Putin's Russia: Policing and coercion after communism*. Cambridge University Press, 2011.

Thompson, Elizabeth. *Colonial citizens: Republican rights, paternal privilege, and gender in French Syria and Lebanon*. Columbia University Press, 2000.

Tilly, Charles. *Coercion, capital, and European states, AD 990–1992*. Blackwell, 1990.

Tishkov, Valery. *Chechnya: Life in a war-torn society*. University of California Press, 2004.

et al. "The crisis in Soviet ethnography [and comments]." *Current Anthropology* 33, no. 4 (1992): 371–394.

Toft, Monica Duffy. "Getting religion? The puzzling case of Islam and civil war." *International Security* 31, no. 4 (2007): 97–131.

Securing the peace: The durable settlement of civil wars. Princeton University Press, 2009.

Toft, Monica Duffy, and Yuri M. Zhukov. "Denial and punishment in the North Caucasus: Evaluating the effectiveness of coercive counter-insurgency." *Journal of Peace Research* 49, no. 6 (2012): 785–800.

"Islamists and nationalists: Rebel motivation and counterinsurgency in Russia's North Caucasus." *American Political Science Review* 109, no. 2 (2015): 222–238.

Tolz, Vera. *Russia's own Orient: The politics of identity and oriental studies in the late imperial and early Soviet periods*. Oxford University Press, 2011.

Treisman, Daniel. *The return: Russia's journey from Gorbachev to Medvedev*. Simon and Schuster, 2011.

Tripp, Aili Mari. *Women and power in post-conflict Africa*. Cambridge University Press, 2015.

Trochev, Alexei. *Judging Russia: The role of the constitutional court in Russian politics 1990–2006*. Cambridge University Press, 2008.

Tsai, Lily. *Accountability without democracy: Solidary groups and public goods provision in rural China*. Cambridge University Press, 2007.

Tyler, Tom. "The psychology of procedural justice: A test of the group-value model." *Journal of Personality and Social Psychology* 57, no. 5 (1989): 830.

Why people obey the law. Princeton University Press, 2006.

Ubink, Janine. *Traditional authorities in Africa: Resurgence in an era of democratisation*. Leiden University Press, 2008.

Van Cott, Donna Lee. "A political analysis of legal pluralism in Bolivia and Colombia." *Journal of Latin American Studies* 32, no. 1 (2000): 207–234.

van der Vet, Freek. "Seeking life, finding justice: Russian litigation and Chechen disappearances before the European Court of Human Rights." *Human Rights Review* 13, no. 3 (2012): 303–325.

Van der Windt, Peter, Macartan Humphreys, Lily Medina, Jeffrey F. Timmons, and Maarten Voors. "Citizen attitudes toward traditional and state authorities: Substitutes or complements?" *Comparative Political Studies* 52, no. 12 (2019): 1810–1840.

Varshaver, Evgeny, and Ekaterina Kruglova. "Koalitsionnyi klintch protiv islamskogo poriadka: Dinamika rynka razresheniia sporov v Dagestane" [Coalition clinch against Islamic order: dynamics of the market of dispute resolution institutions in Dagestan]. *Ekonomicheskaya Politika* 3 (2015): 87–112.

Vatchagaev, Mairbek. "Virdovaia structura Chechni i Ingusheti" [Sufi structures of Chechnya and Ingushetia]. *Prometey* 26 (2009).

Souz Gortsev Severnogo Kavkaza i Gorskaia Respublika. Istoriia nesostoyavshegosia gosudarstva 1917–1920 [The union of the peoples of the Northern Caucasus and the mountainous republic. The history of would to be state 1917–1920]. Litres, 2018.

Chechnya: The inside story – From Independence to War. Open Books, 2019.

Viterna, Jocelyn. *Women in war: The micro-processes of mobilization in El Salvador*, Oxford University Press, 2013.

Voell, Stéphane, and Iwona Kaliszewska, eds. *State and legal practice in the Caucasus: Anthropological perspectives on law and politics.* Ashgate Publishing, 2015.

Volkov, Vadim, Aryna Dzmitryieva, Mikhail Pozdnyakov, and Kirill Titaev. *Rossiyskiye sud'i kak professionalnaya gruppa: sotsiologicheskoe issledovanie* [Russian judges as professional group: A sociological study]. European University Press, 2012.

Volkov, Vadim. *Violent entrepreneurs: The use of force in the making of Russian capitalism.* Cornell University Press, 2002.

von Benda-Beckmann, Franz. "Who's afraid of legal pluralism?" *Journal of Legal Pluralism and Unofficial Law* 34, no. 47 (2002): 37–82.

von Benda-Beckmann, Keebet. "Forum shopping and shopping forums: Dispute processing in a Minangkabau village in West Sumatra." *Journal of Legal Pluralism and Unofficial Law* 13, no. 19 (1981): 117–159.

Walter, Barbara. *Committing to peace: The successful settlement of civil wars.* Princeton University Press, 2002.

Wang, Yuhua. *Tying the autocrat's hands: The rise of the rule of law in China.* Cambridge University Press, 2015.

Weber, Max. *Economy and society: An outline of interpretive sociology. University of California Press, 1978* (1922).

On law in economy and society. Simon and Schuster, 1954.

Wedeen, Lisa. *Ambiguities of domination: Politics, rhetoric, and symbols in contemporary Syria.* University of Chicago Press, 1999.

"Reflections on ethnographic work in political science." *Annual Review of Political Science* 13 (2010): 257.

Werner, Cynthia. "Bride abduction in post-Soviet Central Asia: marking a shift towards patriarchy through local discourses of shame and tradition." *Journal of the Royal Anthropological Institute* 15, no. 2 (2009): 314–331.

Westren, Michael Herzeg. *Nations in exile: "The punished people" in Soviet Kazakhstan, 1941–1961.* PhD dis. University of Chicago Press, 2012.

Wilhelmsen, Julie. "Between a rock and a hard place: The Islamisation of the Chechen separatist movement." *Europe-Asia Studies* 57, no. 1 (2005): 35–59.

Russia's securitization of Chechnya: How war became acceptable. Taylor & Francis, 2016.

Williams, Rina Verma. *Postcolonial politics and personal laws: Colonial legal legacies and the Indian state.* Oxford University Press, 2006.

Wood, Elisabeth Jean. *Insurgent collective action and civil war in El Salvador.* Cambridge University Press, 2003.

"The ethical challenges of field research in conflict zones." *Qualitative Sociology* 29, no. 3 (2006): 373–386.

"The social processes of civil war: The wartime transformation of social networks." *Annual Review of Political Science* 11 (2008): 539–561.

Wyrtzen, Jonathan. *Making Morocco: Colonial intervention and the politics of identity.* Cornell University Press, 2016.

Yahaya, Nurfadzilah. *Fluid Jurisdictions: Colonial Law and Arabs in Southeast Asia.* Cornell University Press, 2020.

Yandarbiyev, Zelimkha. *Checheniia: Bitva za svobodu* [Chechnya: Struggle for freedom]. Lviv, 1996.

Yarlykapov, Ahmet "Adat, Shariat i rossiyskoye pravo na sovremennom Severnom Kavkaze" [Adat, Sharia and Russian law in contemporary North Caucasus]. *Rossiya i Musulmanskiy Mir* 271 (2015).

Yashar, Deborah. *Contesting citizenship in Latin America: The rise of indigenous movements and the postliberal challenge.* Cambridge University Press, 2005.

Yemelianova, Galina. "Sufism and politics in the North Caucasus." *Nationalities Papers* 29, no. 4 (2001): 661–688.

Zaurbekova, Galina. "Gendernyi aspect voiny v Chechne" [Gender aspect of the war in Chechnya]. In *Chechenskaia Republika i Chechentsy* [Chechen Republic and Chechens]. Nauka, 2006.

Zelkina, Anna. *In quest for God and freedom: the Sufi response to the Russian advance in the North Caucasus.* New York University Press, 2000.

Zemans, Frances. "Legal mobilization: The neglected role of the law in the political system." *American Political Science Review*: 690–703.

Zürcher, Christoph. *The post-Soviet wars: Rebellion, ethnic conflict, and nationhood in the Caucasus.* New York University Press, 2007.

Index

Other Books in the Series (*continued from page ii*)

Cambridge Studies in Comparative Politics

Adam Michael Auerbach, *Demanding Development: The Politics of Public Goods Provision in India's Urban Slums*

David Austen-Smith, Jeffry A. Frieden, Miriam A. Golden, Karl Ove Moene, and Adam Przeworski, eds., *Selected Works of Michael Wallerstein: The Political Economy of Inequality, Unions, and Social Democracy*

S. Erdem Aytaç and Susan C. Stokes, *Why Bother? Rethinking Participation in Elections and Protests*

Andy Baker, *The Market and the Masses in Latin America: Policy Reform and Consumption in Liberalizing Economies*

Laia Balcells, *Rivalry and Revenge: The Politics of Violence during Civil War*

Lisa Baldez, *Why Women Protest? Women's Movements in Chile*

Kate Baldwin, *The Paradox of Traditional Chiefs in Democratic Africa*

Stefano Bartolini, *The Political Mobilization of the European Left, 1860–1980: The Class Cleavage*

Robert H. Bates, *The Political Economy of Development: A Game Theoretic Approach*

Robert H. Bates, *When Things Fell Apart: State Failure in Late-Century Africa*

Mark Beissinger, *Nationalist Mobilization and the Collapse of the Soviet State*

Pablo Beramendi, *The Political Geography of Inequality: Regions and Redistribution*

Nancy Bermeo, ed., *Unemployment in the New Europe*

Carles Boix, *Democracy and Redistribution*

Carles Boix, *Political Order and Inequality: Their Foundations and their Consequences for Human Welfare*

Carles Boix, *Political Parties, Growth, and Equality: Conservative and Social Democratic Economic Strategies in the World Economy*

Catherine Boone, *Merchant Capital and the Roots of State Power in Senegal, 1930–1985*

Catherine Boone, *Political Topographies of the African State: Territorial Authority and Institutional Change*

Catherine Boone, *Property and Political Order in Africa: Land Rights and the Structure of Politics*

Michael Bratton and Nicolas van de Walle, *Democratic Experiments in Africa: Regime Transitions in Comparative Perspective*

Michael Bratton, Robert Mattes, and E. Gyimah-Boadi, *Public Opinion, Democracy, and Market Reform in Africa*

Valerie Bunce, *Leaving Socialism and Leaving the State: The End of Yugoslavia, the Soviet Union, and Czechoslovakia*

Daniele Caramani, *The Nationalization of Politics: The Formation of National Electorates and Party Systems in Europe*

John M. Carey, *Legislative Voting and Accountability*

Kanchan Chandra, *Why Ethnic Parties Succeed: Patronage and Ethnic Headcounts in India*

Eric C. C. Chang, Mark Andreas Kayser, Drew A. Linzer, and Ronald Rogowski, *Electoral Systems and the Balance of Consumer-Producer Power*

José Antonio Cheibub, *Presidentialism, Parliamentarism, and Democracy*

Printed in the USA
CPSIA information can be obtained
at www.ICGtesting.com
LVHW051514111123
763669LV00004B/31